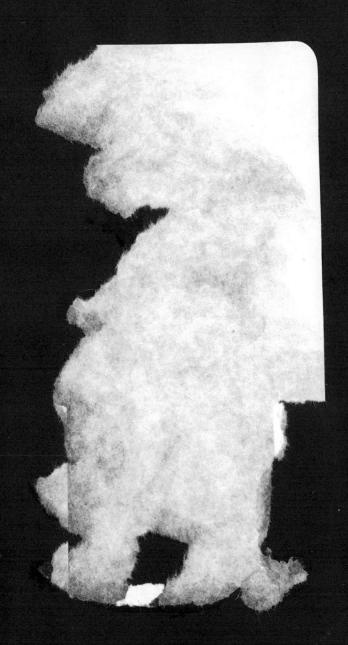

CHOPIN

CHOPIN
A New Biography

ADAM ZAMOYSKI

1980
DOUBLEDAY & COMPANY, INC.
GARDEN CITY, NEW YORK

ISBN: 0-385-13597-1
Library of Congress Catalog Card Number 79-7217

COPYRIGHT © 1979 BY ADAM ZAMOYSKI LTD.
ALL RIGHTS RESERVED
PRINTED IN THE UNITED STATES OF AMERICA
FIRST EDITION IN THE UNITED STATES OF AMERICA

CONTENTS

ACKNOWLEDGMENTS

I should like to express my thanks to all those who allowed me to make use of manuscript material in their libraries, particularly Professor Witold Stankiewicz of the National Library in Warsaw; Dr. Adam Homecki of the Czartoryski Library in Cracow; Dr. Ryszard Marciniak of the Kornik Library; Dr. Dalila Turlo of the Chopin Institute of Warsaw; Miss Dunin-Borkowska of the Bibliothèque Polonaise in Paris; Madame Hautecoeur-Millais of the Institut de France; and Sir Robin Machworth-Young, the librarian at Windsor Castle. Dr. Zdzislaw Jagodzinski and the staff of the Polish Library in London also deserve my deepest gratitude for their sustained good-will and help.

I would never have gained admittance to some of these sanctums without the kind intercession of Pawel Hertz, Vice-President of the Polish Union of Writers, Eric Jourdan and M. Julien Green of the Académie Française. Nor would I have found my way out of this labyrinth of research without the help and advice of Monsieur Georges Lubin, the eminent George Sand scholar; Mr. Marian Bizan; Mrs. Krystyna Kobylanska, the most conscientious of all Chopin scholars, and Mr. Juliusz Wiktor Gomulicki, the distinguished literary historian.

I am grateful to my editor, Philip Ziegler, for his patience, and to Peter Washington for making appropriately rude comments about my English, and I should like to dedicate this book to my mother, who has consistently refused to believe that I was capable of finishing anything.

CHOPIN

1

Childhood

Chopin's name, like Byron's, conjures up an image—that of the quintessential Romantic artist. The general impression is that of a good-looking, passionate man who wrote exciting and sentimental music and died tragically young. Yet a glance at any portrait of Chopin will reveal that he was not handsome. His life was devoid of drama and great passions. He conspicuously lacked the emotional energy, the idealism, and the exuberant confidence in his own genius that are usually associated with the Romantic artist. Temperamentally, he was closer to the spirit of the eighteenth century, from which he took his taste and his musical inspiration. His music is difficult and cerebral. It is indeed revolutionary, but not in the same way as that of most of the Romantic composers; Chopin developed the rules of the eighteenth century instead of breaking them. As for his death, it came no earlier than Mendelssohn's, and a good deal later than Mozart's or Schubert's. Yet neither of these enjoys the same aura as Chopin, and none of these obvious facts have managed to dispel it.

Chopin was reticent by nature, and when he died he left no wife or son who could provide an informed account of his private life. The majority of his papers were destroyed or scattered by several wars and one personal vendetta, with the result that biographers have on the whole worked from a series of disjointed facts, reminiscences, and anecdotes. Not surprisingly, speculation and in some cases fantasy have been used to fill the gaps. Nowhere is this more evident than in the various accounts of the composer's birth and origins, where ignorance was reinforced by nationalism, as Poles, Frenchmen, Germans, and even the Jewish minority in Poland attempted to claim him as the product of their respective cultures. It was almost a hundred years after the composer's death that someone actually went to look up parish records and discovered that his father, Nicolas Chopin, was nothing more or less remarkable than the son of a reasonably well-to-do French peasant.

He was born on April 15, 1771, in the village of Marainville in the Vosges Department of Northeastern France into a family of vine growers and wheelwrights. He was a bright and conscientious boy who somehow managed to learn to read and write, as a result of which he came to the notice of the administrator of the estate of Marainville. The château belonged to a Polish nobleman, Count Pac. The administrator was another Pole, Adam Weydlich. When in 1787 the latter decided to return to his homeland, he took the sixteen-year-old Nicolas Chopin with him, and eventually gave him a job in the tobacco factory he had set up in Warsaw.

Nicolas Chopin spent the next few years working as a clerk or bookkeeper, and he considered his prospects to be so good that he did not take advantage of the opportunity offered three years later of revisiting his family in France. Count Pac, for whom Weydlich still worked, needed some business settled in Strasbourg, and Nicolas Chopin was asked to go. But the French Revolution had broken out, and Chopin feared that he would be conscripted into the French Army if he appeared there. He preferred to follow his career and remained in Warsaw, to which he had taken a great liking.[1] The atmosphere of a state in the terminal stages of political and economic decline, which was at the same time witnessing a profound cultural and social renaissance, would have been congenial to a young foreigner who wished to better his position. Unfortunately, the decline of Poland was accomplished after Nicolas Chopin had been there for only five years, when in 1792 the neighboring states of Russia, Prussia, and Austria took over most of its territory and shared it between them.

Weydlich's business closed down and there seemed little hope of employment in Warsaw for Nicolas Chopin, who now began to think of going back to France after all. Before he could do so, he fell ill. By the time he had fully convalesced, in 1794, a national uprising had broken out in Poland. Nicolas Chopin joined the Warsaw National Guard, in which he reached the rank of lieutenant. In the following year, the Poles were defeated by the concerted might of Russia and Prussia, and Nicolas Chopin found himself wounded and once again unemployed. It was now that he had his greatest stroke of luck. In the same year he was taken on as tutor to their children by the Laczynskis, a wealthy family who lived in the country to the west of Warsaw.

Nicolas Chopin was extremely fortunate to get such a job, for Eastern and Central Europe were inundated with refugees from the French Revolution who were surviving on such posts. Minor Polish nobles thought it was quite the thing to have a *vicomte* or *abbé* hanging about the house telling stories of life at Versailles and drinking their cellars dry with impeccable manners. The fact that Nicolas Chopin managed to break in on this monopoly speaks highly of the level of education and the manners he had managed to acquire in the seven years since he had left his parents' cottage. Moreover, this new position carried with it a certain cachet of social respectability.

He spent some six years in the house of the Laczynskis

teaching the little brood, one of whom, Maria, after her marriage to Anastazy Walewski, was to become famous as Napoleon's mistress. When the children had grown up, he was passed on in the same capacity to a relative of the Laczynskis, Count Skarbek, who lived not far away on his estate of Zelazowa Wola. There he spent the next few years looking after the Count's four children, and in 1806 married Tekla Justyna Krzyzanowska, an impoverished relation of the Skarbeks who lived with them and fulfilled the functions of housekeeper.

The following year the couple had a daughter, Ludwika, and moved into one of the outbuildings of the manor, a large bungalow with a thatched roof, in which they occupied a couple of rooms. It was in one of these whitewashed rooms with its clay floor that their son was born in 1810. He was christened Fryderyk Franciszek in honor of his godfather, the young Count Fryderyk Skarbek, and Nicolas Chopin's own father, François. The register of the baptism, in the parish church of Brochow near Zelazowa Wola indicates the date of birth as February 22, but the Chopin family and the composer himself always gave the date of his birth as March 1.[2] To complicate matters still further, his age was consistently increased by a year whenever he was mentioned in the press or appeared in public as a child, giving rise to the impression, held by some of his close friends, that he had been born in 1809.[3] The parish register is not a record of birth as such, and the date mentioned would have been supplied by Nicolas Chopin or his wife. There is therefore no reason to favor either date, and one can only be thankful that the year, 1810, is certainly accurate.

Although much is made of Chopin's connection with the estate of Zelazowa Wola, the family did not stay there very long after his birth. Old Count Skarbek had been ruined and he fled to Paris in order to avoid his creditors, leaving his wife to look after the four children as best she could. Apart from the fact that they had grown up and no longer needed a tutor, there could be no question of the Countess supporting Nicolas Chopin and his little family. He himself had almost certainly been considering a move to Warsaw for some time before his son's birth.

By this stage most of central Poland had been liberated by Napoleon's campaigns and included in a new state, the Grand Duchy of Warsaw, which was organized as a satellite of France. This meant that the French language became less of a luxury and more of a necessity, which suited Nicolas Chopin perfectly. He managed to get a post as French teacher at the Warsaw Lyceum, or high school, and later another at one of the military training schools. As a result, the little family moved from Zelazowa Wola to the capital only six months after the birth of Chopin.

The Warsaw Lyceum was housed in what was commonly known as the Saxon Palace, a magnificent eighteenth-century building taking up three sides of a square with its white stucco façades. As there was no accommodation provided for pupils from the country, those teachers who wished to do so could take large apartments in one of the wings of the palace and increase their incomes by having boarders. Nicolas Chopin, who was hard-working and thrifty, naturally took this opportunity and moved into the Saxon Palace. The pattern his life fell into in Warsaw, a pattern which was not to change much over the next twenty years, suited him perfectly.

He had sometime before decided to adopt Poland as his country and to become assimilated in Polish society. In this he was not being eccentric. Most of his colleagues at the Lyceum, from the Rector Samuel Bogumil Linde down, sported names like Kolberg, Ciampi and Vogel, and were of middle-class foreign origin, but became more rabidly Polish than the Poles. For centuries Poland, which had not been a national state, had attracted great quantities of foreigners who had anxiously maintained their own ethnic traditions. Paradoxically, after the collapse of the old state and the rise of Polish nationalism, the area continued to attract foreigners, who now eagerly brandished the standard of Polish nationality. Nicolas Chopin always insisted on speaking Polish, albeit with a dubious accent, and would not tolerate the affected use of French in his home, although he himself had to write letters to his son in French.

He was, by all accounts, a rather dull man; solid and thrifty, neat and cautious, a good teacher without being in any way brilliant. He was not religious, and his philosophy of life was culled largely from the rationalism of Voltaire and the social idealism of Rousseau. He felt no reverence for the principles of monarchy and aristocracy. But Nicolas Chopin was no revolutionary, and believed firmly in acknowledging the powers that be and accepting the limits imposed by the society he lived in. His attitude to art and music was prosaic, and he was not given to being impressed by genius. He played the flute a little, until his baby son stole and broke it one day, and later tried to take up the violin, but was in no sense an artistic person. One of his pupils described him as "a rather ceremoniously grave personage with a certain elegance of manner."[4]

The only artistic influence in the household was Justyna's. She had been brought up as a noblewoman and could play the piano well and sing quite respectably. She was gentle and quiet, and her role in the family was confined to that of housekeeper and nanny. But her mouse-like presence was a considerable comfort to her son, who never succeeded in getting very close to his father. The eldest daughter, Ludwika, was intelligent and gifted and also played the piano well from an early age. Izabela, born a couple of years after Fryderyk, was a jolly girl with no intellectual or artistic pretensions, but the youngest of the brood, Emilia, was exceptionally clever and gifted, and was writing poetry by the age of eight.

The Chopin household was a paradise of middle-class orderliness, cleanliness, and morality. Without the presence of

Justyna and the remarkable characters of the children, the atmosphere might have become stifling, but it did have one great merit. The little Chopin, though not the moribund child often portrayed, was delicate and needed a well-ordered and healthy childhood if he was to survive for long, and this was exactly what he got.

The various stories which have been dredged up in order to illustrate Chopin's extraordinary sensitivity as a baby—that he would burst into tears if someone played the piano badly, or, alternatively, sit for hours under the instrument listening spellbound—can be disregarded. They are the sort of detail that someone "remembers" fifty years later, and, even if true, are largely meaningless, for there can be few babies who will not either bawl their heads off or else listen in fascination if an instrument is played in their presence. One cannot ascribe this to artistic sensitivity at the nappy stage, any more than one can believe a story coined after the composer's death to the effect that one night he waddled out of his cot, hoisted himself onto the piano stool, and began to improvise polonaises, to the astonishment of his family, who had been drawn from their beds by the sound of music.

What is certain is that by the time he was four or five, Chopin had been introduced to the piano by his mother, and that by the age of six he was creating a mild sensation by his ability to play quite difficult pieces as well as by his gift for playing around with a few notes or a motif and producing simple melodic variations. In 1816 he started taking piano lessons from an old friend of his father's, Adalbert Zywny.

Zywny was born in Bohemia in 1756, which made him sixty when he gave his first lessons to Chopin. He was a violinist who had come to Poland in the eighteenth century and held a post in a Polish aristocrat's private orchestra, later becoming a freelance music teacher in Warsaw. He was a very tall man with a huge purple nose and no teeth. He wore a lopsided, old-fashioned, and yellowed wig, a thickly quilted eighteenth-century frock coat, which along with his cravat, his waistcoat, and even his vast Hungarian boots were impregnated with snuff. He never bathed, confining himself to a rubdown with vodka on hot summer days, and his only attempt at elegance was a fine collection of fancy waistcoats. These he had had made up from a lot of breeches he had bought cheap when King Stanislaw August's wardrobe was being auctioned off after the last partition of Poland in 1795.[5] It is not clear whether this rather curious link with Poland's glorious past was intentional or not, but Zywny too had become very "Polish," not the least of the attributes which endeared him to Nicolas Chopin. There were certainly many better piano teachers in Warsaw at the time. But Chopin adored Zywny, and the latter soon became a regular member of the household, taking most of his meals with the family and often spending his evenings with them.

Zywny was a *sound* eighteenth-century musician, whose gods were Bach, Haydn, and Mozart. The only contemporary composers he acknowledged were Hummel and Moscheles, he had no time for Beethoven or Weber, and positively hated the new "Italian" music of Spontini and Rossini. His pedagogic method was much as one might expect. "Apart from his commodious half-pound snuff-box, the lid of which was decorated with a portrait of Mozart or possibly Haydn, and his large red checkered kerchief," wrote one of his pupils, "Zywny always had about him a gigantic square pencil which he used for correcting printer's mistakes in the scores, or else for rapping his less diligent pupils over the head or knuckles with."[6]

He was in many ways an unlikely person to initiate one of the nineteenth century's most revolutionary composers. But he did exert a strong and beneficial influence on the boy and his future career, and this because of his limitations rather than in spite of them. By the time Zywny had come to teach Chopin, the latter had already developed a familiarity with the keyboard which the old violinist himself probably lacked.

"The mechanism of playing took you but little time, and it was your mind rather than your fingers that strained," Nicolas Chopin later wrote to his son, adding that "where others have spent days struggling at the keyboard, you hardly ever spent a whole hour at it."⁷ Faced with this prodigy, Zywny wisely refrained from interfering. Not being a brilliant pianist himself, he could only have taught Chopin the accepted method of fingering and the traditional hand movements. In view of the boy's instinctive dexterity, he did not bother with these technicalities. Instead, he concentrated on acquainting his pupil with great music, by guiding him through all the keyboard works of Bach, Haydn, and Mozart, as well as a little Hummel, explaining the theory behind them as he went. The result of this unorthodox musical education was that from the start Chopin was allowed to develop his own method of playing, hitting the notes he wanted with the fingers he thought appropriate, and not with those specified by the textbooks. At the same time he developed a love for and an understanding of the great classical composers which he was never to lose, and which was to set him apart from most of his contemporaries.

This classical education was complemented by the music Chopin heard in homes and drawing rooms in Warsaw. Some of this was taken from the popular Italian operas of the day, but most of it was more national in character. Polish piano music was dominated by the polonaise, a musical form built on the rhythm of a court dance dating back to the sixteenth century, a slow, minuet-like dance. This rhythm had been familiar to many composers, including Bach, Telemann, and Mozart, but they had merely used it as a tempo for various pieces of their own. Thus their *polaccas* or *polonaises* cannot be considered even as pastiches of the original. Toward the end of the eighteenth century, however, Polish composers had begun to resurrect old polonaises and to write new ones of a more authentic character. The form was best understood

by Prince Michal Kleofas Oginski, a distinguished amateur
composer, and the pianist Marya Szymanowska, and by the
beginning of the nineteenth century the polonaise was a well-
defined short piece for the piano (although elements of the
form continued to be used in symphonic music by Polish and
foreign composers throughout the century). Some Polish
country dances, such as the Mazur, were subjected to an analogous development, but during Chopin's childhood it was
polonaises, usually by Oginski or Szymanowska, that ruled in
the drawing rooms of the city.

It is therefore not surprising that Chopin's own first steps
in composition should have taken this direction. By the age of
seven he was already composing short pieces which Zywny
would help him write out, as he had not mastered this skill
yet. Few of these survive. Those that do are unremarkable ad-
ditions to the great number of Oginski-inspired polonaises,
but remain impressive if the boy's age is taken into account.
It was in 1817, too, that Chopin's first printed work appeared.
It was privately produced by Canon Cybulski of St. Mary's, a
friend of the Chopin family. It was entitled, in French: "Polonaise in G minor, dedicated to Her Excellency Countess
Victoria Skarbek, composed by Frederick Chopin, a musician
aged 8." It is probable that his godfather, Count Fryderyk
Skarbek, who had just returned from studies abroad and
taken up a post at Warsaw University, had helped to pay for
this, which would account for the dedication to his sister. He
too was responsible for the long piece on Chopin which appeared in January 1818 in the *Warsaw Daily*. This hailed the
young composer as "a true musical genius" and went on to
say: "Not only can he play with great facility and perfect
taste the most difficult compositions for the piano, he is also
the composer of several dances and variations which do not
cease to amaze the connoisseurs."[8]

By 1816, Chopin had become celebrated in the academic
circles in which his family lived, but with the return to War-

saw of Count Skarbek, who was eager to promote the boy's gift, he was propelled into a wider arena. It is important to realize that this was not done on the basis of patronage in the traditional sense. The fact that Poland had never had any indigenous middle class to speak of, as well as the considerable degree to which the nobility had been leveled by the succession of national disasters, meant that there were no class barriers confronting a young man whose father was a Frenchman and whose mother a Polish noblewoman. Considerations of birth, money, and breeding played the part they always do, but in the face of the spirit of nationalism and liberalism which pervaded Polish society during this period, they counted for far less than in France or England at the same time.

This society was small and tightly knit, and it is therefore not surprising that soon after his first appearances outside the family circle he was known throughout Warsaw. One can, to a certain extent, define the type of circle in which he began to move. The first known reference to his appearance outside the family circle is to be found in the diary of a young lady who went to a soirée at Countess Grabowska's, where "young Chopin played the piano, a child in his eighth year whom the connoisseurs declare to be Mozart's successor."[9] Countess Grabowska, a cousin of the Skarbeks, was the wife of one of the governors of Warsaw University; he was later to become Minister of Education. His was one of a group of families, including the Mostowskis, the Krasinskis, the Platers, certain branches of the Potockis, the Zamoyskis, and, most important, the Czartoryskis, which could be described as making up the conservative patriotic camp. They were conservative in that they accepted the situation created by the Congress of Vienna in 1815—a Kingdom of Poland whose King was the Tsar of Russia—and tried to work within the limited autonomy this allowed.

This milieu is important, for Chopin was closely associated

with it from his earliest years and to some extent continued
to live in it during his years in Paris. It is significant that a
member of the Czartoryski family was present at his
deathbed. In Warsaw the most active salon of this circle was
that of the Blue Palace. This was the Warsaw residence of
Count Stanislaw Zamoyski, and was also inhabited by Prince
Adam Czartoryski, whose close friendship with Tsar Alexander, distinguished diplomatic career, and position as head
of what was arguably the richest and most influential family
in the kingdom, made him a key figure in Polish society and
politics. The Blue Palace was a venue for the most venerable
figures of the past and for those who were governing the kingdom now, as well as for the youngest members of the Polish
aristocracy. Countess Zamoyska and her sister, Princess Marya
Württemberg, used to organize entertainments and *thés dan-
sants* for children between the ages of eight and twelve, designed to instill good manners and patriotic values in them.
Chopin seems to have been a regular attender.[10]

The Countess was also the founder of the Warsaw Benevolent Society, and it was not long before she recognized Chopin's fund-raising potential. Julian Niemcewicz, the poet and
Nestor of Polish literature at the time, and a devotee of the
Blue Palace, describes a meeting of the society in one of his
one-act plays:

> *The Countess:* You see how poor we are; all our efforts come
> to nothing. We are begging high and low, but everyone is
> deaf to us, or rather, to the voice of the poor. There is noth-
> ing for it but to carry on with our usual methods, but with
> certain modifications. I flatter myself that Monsieur Lu-
> bienski and I have perfected our techniques. There is to be a
> concert next Tuesday in which little Chopin is to play; if we
> were to print on the bills that Chopin is only three years old,
> everyone would come running to see the prodigy. Just think
> how many people would come and how much money we
> would collect!

All: Bravo! Bravo! A wonderful idea, excellent! Let us print
on the bills that Chopin is only three years old!

Princess Sapieha: I think it would make even more of a sensation if we wrote on the bills that little Chopin will be carried
in by his nanny.

All: Bravo! Bravo! What a capital idea, princess![11]

What was probably the first of these concerts took place on
February 24, 1818. Whatever the bills may finally have said,
the press notice gave Chopin an extra year, saying that he was
nine. The event, which took place in the ballroom of a public
building often used for such things, the former Radziwill Palace, was a great success. Chopin played a concerto by the Bo-
hemian composer Gyrowetz, probably the first time he had
performed a work of this length. It was certainly his first appearance before such a large public.

After this event Chopin's fame spread throughout the capital, and it was not long before the grandest and most dreaded
carriage in Warsaw began to draw up before the Chopin
apartment in the Saxon Palace to carry the eight-year-old boy
off to the Belvedere. This was the residence of Grand Duke
Constantine Pavlovitch, the brother of Tsar Alexander and
his viceroy in the Kingdom of Poland. This schizophrenic
ogre with his extraordinary love-hate relationship with Poland
was feared and loathed throughout the country. Nicolas Chopin, however, was not one to allow sentiment to get in the
way of his son's career. It was a great honor for the little boy
to be asked to play at the Belvedere, and a great victory when
it turned out that he could soothe the Grand Duke's worst
fits of temper with his music. The Grand Duke was an obses-
sive parade-ground soldier, and Chopin won him over
when he presented him with a military march of his own
composition. It was said that when Chopin started playing it
through to him, the Grand Duke began to march up and
down the drawing room beating time, and that he was so

delighted that he had it scored for full military band and
played at parades.[12]

What was still more remarkable was that Chopin was not
fetched merely to entertain the Grand Duke and his wife, but
to play with the Grand Duke's beloved illegitimate son,
Pavel, and Alexandrine de Moriolles, the daughter of his
tutor. Nicolas Chopin could congratulate himself that his
son's future career would be all the more brilliant for such
connections. On the other hand, he was eager to prevent his
head being turned and his talent exploited. In this he was
helped by the fact that the whole Chopin family was accepted in and frequented slightly humbler circles; humbler
not in the sense of class but rather in style and outlook. In
the houses of Teresa Kicka or General Sowinski, a one-legged
hero of the Napoleonic Wars, a more republican and strictly
nationalistic spirit prevailed, and here Chopin was encouraged as a new "Polish" genius.

It was an extraordinary upbringing; from his sheltered
home with its staunchly middle-class atmosphere, he was introduced into some of the grandest drawing rooms in Europe,
where he performed before the greatest personages in the
country, was spoiled by their wives, and played on an equal
footing with their children. Because of the early age at which
he was introduced into society, he soon acquired the best manners and an ability to feel entirely at home in the most exalted company. At the same time, he lived in the far humbler
world of his family and their immediate entourage.

The Lyceum was moved, in 1817, from the Saxon Palace to
a less grandiose but more pleasant site. This was the Casimir
Palace, a much-rebuilt seventeenth-century royal residence
which now consisted of a great central building with a colonnaded portico flanked by two detached wings.* The Chopins

---

* Warsaw consisted of a medieval walled city and, stretching to the south,
along the banks of the Vistula, a fairly haphazard array of streets. There was
no systematically built-up area, and the main characteristic of the city was a
series of palaces, often standing in their own grounds, with humbler buildings

took a large apartment in one of the wings and were able to house up to six boarders. The palace was pleasantly situated in the middle of what had once been a botanical garden, which sloped away toward the Vistula behind the main building. The Chopin children, those of other teachers, and the boarders had the run of these gardens, which were still full of fruit trees and vegetables on which they would gorge themselves. It was now that the young Chopin began to make friends outside his own family. He became very friendly with Jan Bialoblocki, five years his senior, and Tytus Woyciechowski, also a couple of years older than he. Both were boarders of his father's and both good pianists, which accounted for much of the time they spent with him.

This early immersion in different worlds, combined with the sober influence of his father, had a profound effect on Chopin's character. He developed an ability to mix with any kind of person, became sociable and a little precocious, but not, by all accounts, conceited. There is an anecdote, probably authentic, relating to one of his first public appearances; when he returned home, his mother asked him what the audience had liked best, to which he is supposed to have replied: "My new English collar." Whether this is true or not, the fact is that to the end of his life he remained reticent and unassuming, particularly where his art was concerned. This was largely because his father was determined not to let music go to his head, and insisted on treating his son's gift as a pleasant amenity rather than the central feature of his life. This redounds to Nicolas Chopin's credit, when one considers how ruthlessly most child prodigies were, and are, exploited by their parents.

Chopin was of course shown off whenever the occasion arose in a context which might seriously improve his prospects. The mother of Tsar Alexander and Grand Duke Con-

interspersed. Many of these palaces had become public buildings, while others were often divided up into apartments and rented out in part or whole.

stantine, the Empress Maria Fyodorovna, visited Warsaw in 1818 and indulged in the usual round of visiting institutions and schools. When she visited his class of the Lyceum, the eight-year-old Chopin presented her with two polonaises. At the end of 1819, when the famous singer Angelica Catalani arrived and gave a few concerts in Warsaw, the boy was again exhibited, she being so impressed that she presented him with an inscribed gold watch. He was also a regular performer at the Benevolent Society's concerts and often played at soirées in aristocratic houses.

There was, however, no question of the boy playing for money or taking part in commercial concerts. Charity concerts were one thing, for here he would be performing alongside aristocratic amateur musicians or other children reciting poetry, but Nicolas Chopin was careful that his son should not be branded as a professional musician. He was a product of the eighteenth century, and to him the profession of musician was hardly more respectable than that of actor. Having risen so high in the world himself, he was certainly not going to allow his son to practice anything but a gentleman's career. While this guaranteed Chopin social standing, it also introduced into his life an element which was to endure—a slight aura of amateurishness which assured him an exceptional reputation in some circles, and unwarranted contempt in others. Even when he became a professional musician, people found it hard to think of him as one. How *he* saw himself by the time he had reached the age of eight is impossible to tell, but one thing is certain: he already knew music to be his most personal medium. Every year on his name day in December, Nicolas Chopin was presented with little hand-painted greetings from his son. The verse offering for 1818 opens with the words: "Dearly beloved father; it would be easier for me to express my feelings in musical phrases . . ."[13]

Although he was now being tutored by his father and attended some classes in the lower forms of the Lyceum, he went on practicing and writing a certain amount of music. He had by now learned to write it down, as can be seen from the beautifully written-out polonaise he dedicated and presented to Zywny on the latter's birthday in 1821, one of the few surviving compositions of this period. The vast majority of the pieces he wrote at this time remained in manuscript form among his own papers, with which they were destroyed by Russian troops in 1863, or were written into people's albums, most of which suffered similar fates. Judging from the one or two pieces which have survived, they were clever but insignificant, hardly distinguishable from the work of other Polish composers of piano music.

At about the same time, it became clear that Zywny's work was done and that there was little else he could do for Chopin. He stopped teaching him altogether, although he remained a close friend of the family and often brought his violin to play duets with his pupil. Luckily, however, another musician took an interest in the boy and assumed the task of guiding his musical education. He was Jozef Elsner, a Silesian German who had established himself in Poland some thirty years before and also caught the fever of assimilation (to the point that he tried to get around his foreign-sounding name by pretending that he came from a Swedish family which had purportedly come to Poland with the Wasa kings in the seventeenth century). He was an undistinguished composer whose many operas, masses, oratorios, symphonies, and chamber works have sunk into oblivion, but he was an excellent teacher, which was why he had been appointed head of the newly founded Warsaw Conservatoire. He was clearly interested in drawing Chopin into this institution at some stage, but for the time being Nicolas Chopin's views on the boy's future prevailed. Elsner therefore gave Chopin a few lessons in musical theory and presented him with a book on the rules of harmony. Chopin worked hard at his music throughout the early 1820s, but he worked on his own, and this fact was to influence his later development strongly. Being naturally reticent and of a lazy disposition, he tended to avoid areas in which he was unsure of himself. The long-term result of this was an uneven musical education and a limited range of output.

2

School Years

The review of a charity concert in which Chopin had taken part in February 1823 concluded with the following observation:

> The latest number of the Leipzig musical gazette reports, in an article from Vienna, that an equally young amateur by the name of List [sic] astonished everyone there by the exactness, the self-assurance, and the strength of tone with which he executed a concerto by Hummel. After this musical evening, we shall certainly not envy Vienna their Mr. List, as our capital possesses one equal to him, and perhaps even superior, in the shape of young Mr. Chopin . . .[1]

While Liszt, a year younger than Chopin, was being steered into the career of performing musician, his Polish counterpart was being discouraged from such a course. In the same year, he was entered into the fourth form of the Warsaw Lyceum as a full-time pupil. As he had no clear idea of what he wanted to do, he did not object to this development and soon began to enjoy school.

In his class he found two boys he knew well already, as former boarders of his father's. One was the older Tytus Woy-

ciechowski, the other Dominik Dziewanowski. He soon acquired another friend in the class, by the name of Jan
Matuszynski. Chopin had no difficulty in making friends and
holding his own, for while he was by no means robust and
remained under the constant care of doctors, he was not
timid. In fact he was among the liveliest members of his class,
and one of its principal sources of amusement. He had a
highly developed sense of humor, or rather of the ridiculous,
an irreverent wit, and above all an eye for caricature and imitation which soon became famous. The few caricatures of his
that survive show an instinct for catching the grotesque, while
his written imitations of Poles speaking French or foreigners,
particularly Polish Jews, speaking Polish are hilarious. He was
also very good at fooling about on the piano, "telling" funny
stories or making musical jokes. But it was above all his gift
for mimicry that astonished people. He could transform his
appearance and expression and was hardly recognizable when
he was imitating one of the Lyceum masters or some public
figure. Many years later, the famous French actor Bocage was
to say that Chopin had wasted his talents by becoming a musician.

He enjoyed his first year at school but did not neglect his
work, and in July 1824 he and Jan Matuszynski collected the
fourth form prize. This was lucky, as it meant that he could
relax during the summer holidays and take up an invitation to
go and stay in the country with his classmate Dominik Dziewanowski.

Apart from the occasional short visit the Chopin family
had made to the Skarbeks at Zelazowa Wola, this was Chopin's first real taste of the country. The Dziewanowski estate,
Szafarnia, lay in the same area of Poland as Zelazowa Wola,
the flat and rather poor Mazovian plain, west and slightly
north of Warsaw. This was the only part of the Polish countryside with which Chopin was ever to become well acquainted. The estates in that area were not rich, and the

country houses not particularly substantial. The house at Szafarnia has not survived, but it almost certainly conformed to the usual pattern of timber or rendered brick manor houses; long and low, classical in style, with a colonnaded portico. These houses tended to be elegant, sometimes even aiming for the grandiose, but the execution and detail were usually simple and rustic. The accent was on comfort and informality; there was a good piano in a fine drawing room, and geese and ducks wandering about the porch.

Part of the reason behind the Szafarnia holiday was indubitably Chopin's health. He was still weak, and it was felt that a month or so in the country would help to build him up. Health was also the main reason for his younger and sickly sister Emilia accompanying him there. Chopin himself was armed with pills and had quite a diet to adhere to; six or seven cups of acorn coffee per day, various tisanes, plenty of food, but only a little sweet wine, very ripe fruit, and no coarse country bread, which dismayed him, as it looked and smelled so good. But none of this managed to mar his enjoyment, and his letters home were full of the excitement caused by the novelty of his experiences. The books he had brought from Warsaw were hardly opened, and although he played the piano a great deal, he wrote little during his stay. Most of his time was spent out of doors, running about with his friend Dominik, going for drives through the surrounding countryside, visiting his other friend Jan Bialoblocki, whose estate lay not far away, and even riding. "Don't ask whether I ride well or not," he wrote to a friend in Warsaw, "but I do ride; that is to say the horse goes slowly where it wants, and I sit on it in terror, like an ape on the back of a bear; I haven't fallen off yet, because the horse hasn't bothered to throw me."[2] Hardly surprising, since it was being led about on a rein by Miss Ludwika Dziewanowska, Dominik's aunt.

Chopin and his sister wrote most of their letters home in the form and under the heading of the *Szafarnia Courier*, a

pastiche on the *Warsaw Courier*, using the same layout of
Home News, Foreign News, and Social Information. The cus-
tomary censor's stamp was in this case applied by Miss Ludwika. It is fairly naïve schoolboy wit, but illustrates Chopin's
wry, hyperbolic way of describing things, as well as his tendency to ridicule himself, the Pichon of these entries:

> On 15 Inst. We learned an important piece of news, namely
> that one of the Turkeys unexpectedly gave birth behind the
> larder. This significant event has not only precipitated an in-
> crease in the Turkey population, but has also increased the
> Treasury Revenues, and guaranteed their future growth. Yes-
> terday, in the night, the cat stole into a cupboard and broke a
> bottle of fruit juice; but although on the one hand he de-
> serves punishment on the gallows, on the other he should be
> commended, for he chose the smallest one. On 14 Inst. one
> of the hens went lame, and a drake lost his leg in a duel with
> a goose . . ."[3]

> On 26th Inst. Monsieur Pichon visited the village of Golub.
> Among other sights and wonders of this exotic place, he saw
> a pig (imported) which for some time totally absorbed the at-
> tention of this distinguished *voyageur*.[4]

> Monsieur Pichon is suffering great discomfort on account of
> the mosquitoes, of which he had encountered fabulous quan-
> tities at Szafarnia. They bit him all over, except, mercifully,
> on the nose, which would otherwise become even bigger than
> it is.[5]

> On 1st Inst. Monsieur Pichon was just playing "the Jew" [a
> newly composed mazurka on a Jewish dance theme], when
> Monsieur Dziewanowski, who had business with one of
> his Jewish tenants, asked the latter to pronounce judgment
> on the young Jewish virtuoso's playing. Moses came up to the
> window, inserted his exalted aquiline nose into the room and
> listened, after which he declared that if Mons. Pichon were
> to go and play at a Jewish wedding, he would earn at least
> ten thalers. Such a declaration encouraged Mons. Pichon to

study this kind of music with diligence, and who knows
whether one day he may not give himself over entirely to this
branch of the arts.[6]

Chopin found everything about the country interesting,
whether it was the servants fighting, the animals misbehaving,
or the peasants and Jews, of whom there were great numbers
in this part of the country, going about their daily business.
What fascinated him more than anything else was the, to
him, totally new world of folk music. Until now the only popular music he had heard was Warsaw street musicians' ver-
sions of folk songs and dances, which were very different from
the original article. Now he listened to peasant girls singing
their songs of love or sorrow, to the old women chanting in
the fields, and to the drinking songs issuing from the village
inns. At the end of August, when the whole house party
drove over to a neighboring estate for the harvest festival, he
saw Mazovian dances being performed late into the night.
When he returned to Warsaw in September, his head was
full of his new harmony.

Chopin did not immediately know how to master the elements of this kind of music, or indeed what to do with it.
Throughout the next year, while he worked through the fifth
form at the Lyceum, he carried on musically along former
lines. He had by now achieved such mastery of the keyboard
that the little polonaises he turned out were far superior from
the technical point of view to their Oginski models. They were
also more melodic, probably as a result of Chopin's exposure
to the Italian music of Spontini and Rossini, which had
reached heights of popularity in Warsaw and was being played
at every opportunity by the fervent "Rossinist," the conductor
Kurpinski.

Chopin was nevertheless moving further afield in his search
for musical forms and was growing more adventurous. In his
fourteenth year he began writing waltzes and mazurkas (the
Frenchified name of the Mazur, the principal dance of the

peasants of Mazovia) as well as polonaises, often for more than one instrument. Lack of documentary evidence precludes any serious analysis of what he was writing. The principal source of information on the compositions of this period is the album of Countess Izabela Grabowski, which was fortunately described and examined by a musicologist before it was lost. She was a cousin of Fryderyk Skarbek's and an enthusiastic violinist, and as she lived a stone's throw from the Chopin apartment, the young composer spent a good deal of time with her. Most of the music in the album was written, possibly in collaboration with the Countess, around 1823. The book contained a great number of compositions for the piano alone, but also quite a few for piano and violin. The musicologist who examined it thought many of these unremarkable and deeply imitative of Hummel's work, and noticed lack of experience and untidiness in the way the harmony was worked out. But he was also astonished by the number of passages which were original and seemed to announce Chopin's mature work.[7]

Lack of firsthand information prevents one from reconstructing Chopin's life in Warsaw at this time with any precision, and it is impossible to tell how often he played in public. But his reputation continued to grow, which could only have been the result of fairly frequent appearances of one sort or another. In April 1824 the capital livened up for a long official visit by Tsar Alexander, and it was Chopin who was singled out by a couple of Warsaw instrument makers to show off their latest invention at a public concert. It was a sort of miniature organ, and Chopin played on it part of a Moscheles piano concerto and an improvisation of his own at a grand instrumental and vocal concert at the Conservatoire on May 27. Both the instrument and the boy's playing caused such a stir that the Tsar came to hear of it, as the makers had hoped, with the result that a special recital was organized for him. This command performance took place in the Warsaw

Evangelical Church, with Chopin dressed in full Lyceum uniform, of blue tail-coat, breeches, and stockings, pumps with
silver buckles, and white gloves. The Tsar was so delighted
with Chopin's playing that he presented him and the maker
of the instrument with diamond rings.[8]

This recognition coincided with the first commercial publication of one of Chopin's works. It was the Rondo in C
minor, opus 1, published by Brzezina & Company on June 2,
1825. The Benevolent Society, too, lost no time and managed
to persuade all the artists who had taken part in the May concert to repeat their performance for charity on June 10. On
this occasion Chopin played his newly published Rondo on
the strange instrument, and then launched into a long improvisation, which earned him his first mention in the press
outside Poland. The *Allgemeine Muzikalische Zeitung* of
Leipzig wrote, among other things, that "young Chopin distinguished himself in his improvisation by a wealth of musical
ideas, and under his hands this instrument, of which he is a
great master, made a deep impression."[9]

International acclaim was one thing, but the laws of the
Chopin family were rigid, and by the time this little spate of
activity had dried up, the boy only had a month left before
his end-of-year exams. He was a lazy person who found it
difficult to get around to doing things, and the diligence with
which he now set to work suggests that he was keen to keep
his father's approval. As he wrote to his friend Bialoblocki,
who had now settled in the country, "I must sit and sit, sit,
still sit, and perhaps sit up all night," for he was behind with
his work and believed that he would at best scrape through
the exams.[10] In fact, he again carried off the form prize, along
with his classmate Julian Fontana. Next day he rushed out
to buy himself a new pair of corduroy breeches and then
climbed into a carriage with Miss Dziewanowska, who had
come to take him and Dominik to Szafarnia.

The summer of 1825 was so fine that Chopin did not open

any of his books and hardly even played any music. He spent his days out of doors with his friend, walking, riding, shooting, and occasionally going off on longer excursions with the whole house party. They visited various neighboring estates, dropped in on Jan Bialoblocki, who was ill with tuberculosis, and on one outing got as far as the city of Torun. Chopin spent the day there admiring the fine Gothic churches, which he thought terribly "ancient," and between mouthfuls of the celebrated Torun gingerbread managed to find time to visit the house in which Copernicus was born. The condition of the house appalled him, and he was incensed because the room in which the great man was born was now inhabited by "some German who stuffs himself with potatoes and then probably passes foul winds."[11]

The climax of the summer was again the harvest festival, which Chopin described in a letter to his parents:

> We were sitting at dinner, just finishing the last course. We suddenly heard in the distance a chorus of falsetto voices; old peasant women whining through their noses and girls squealing mercilessly half a tone higher, to the accompaniment of a single violin, and that only a three-string one, whose alto voice could be heard repeating each phrase after it had been sung through.[12]

The two boys got up from dinner and went out to watch the column of peasants approaching, led by four girls carrying the traditional wreaths and swathes of harvested crops. When they had come up to the house, the harvesters sang a long piece in which there was a verse addressed to each of the people staying at the manor. When Chopin's turn came, they teased him for his weedy looks and his interest in one of the peasant girls.

The girls bearing the wreaths then carried them into the house, and were drenched by the stable boys, who had hidden in the hall with buckets of water. Barrels of vodka were then rolled out, candles brought onto the porch, and the violinist struck up a hearty mazurka. Chopin opened the dancing with a young cousin of the Dziewanowskis, and carried on with other girls, through all the various country dances. One of the peasants brought a double bass with only one string left, and Chopin seized this and started to accompany the flagging violinist with gusto. The warm, starry night was well advanced before Chopin and Dominik were called in to bed and the peasants moved to the village to continue their drinking and dancing. The whole evening made a vivid impression on Chopin, but it left him a little wistful. He had a vague feeling that he would not be spending many more carefree holidays in the Polish countryside, for he was bent on a musical career, and this would inevitably entail travel and long periods abroad.

When he returned to Warsaw in September, he had to face his final year at the Lyceum. Although his father wanted him to enter the University after that, Chopin had firmly made up his own mind concerning the future, and was hoping to start on his travels the moment he had finished with the Lyceum. Warsaw was something of a musical backwater, and he felt a need to go to some capital where he could hear a great deal of music well performed. Also, his own position in Poland, as a gifted amateur whom everyone extolled, irritated him a little. He longed for a more professional evaluation of his own talent.

As a result, he worked harder than ever at his own musical education during his year in the sixth form. His father had at last given him a room of his own which was immediately dwarfed by his piano and swamped by music, piled on shelves, chairs, and cupboards. The composers most in evidence were Hummel, Kalkbrenner, and Ries. (Johann Nepomuk Hummel (1778–1837), pupil of Mozart and Haydn, was widely considered to be Mozart's heir. Friedrich Wilhelm Kalkbrenner (1785–1849) was a renowned pianist who composed mainly for that instrument, while Ferdinand Ries (1784–1838), pupil of Beethoven, wrote principally for the piano.) Chopin also took every opportunity of playing before an audience. He took over from the organist of the Visitandine Church every Sunday, for the Lyceum and University mass, and was often to be heard playing in drawing rooms all over Warsaw. A contemporary diary gives the first accurate account of him playing, at a soirée at Teresa Kicka's. It describes how, after playing several works, he launched into an improvisation which he drew out for a very long time. This exercise visibly drained him as he played, and he began to look so pale and exhausted after a time that the poet Niemcewicz went up to him and literally pulled his hands away from the keyboard.[13]

Chopin was much too energetic for his constitution, which continued weak. It was unwise of him to go out as much as he did. During the Christmas season, for instance, he was often at the opera, at a concert, or at a party, with the result that he was rarely in bed before two o'clock in the morning. He was incapable of taking things easy and always had to join in with whatever was going on. He described one particular evening, in a witty verse rendition of which only fragments survive, which gives a good idea of some of his evenings. He spent half of the evening playing jolly dances on the piano for the other guests, and then started dancing himself, not quiet polonaises or quadrilles, but energetic country Mazurs and Obertasses, during one of which he slipped and crashed to the floor, twisting his ankle.[14]

At the beginning of 1826 he fell ill, the main problem being apparently his throat and tonsils. He retired to bed for a time with a bonnet on his head and leeches at his throat, but was not long in recovering enough to go back to work at school. His studies do not seem to have suffered from the active life he was leading or from the now impressive volume of music he was writing. At the end of his final year, in July

1826, he once more managed to get through his exams, this time winning an honorable mention, along with Tytus Woyciechowski and Jan Matuszynski.

Chopin's hard work earned him a treat on the day after the exams; he went to the opera to see the new production of Rossini's *Gazza ladra,* but his dreams of foreign travel were not materializing quite as he had hoped. He did in fact go away that summer, but it was not the sort of journey he had in mind. His younger sister Emilia's tuberculosis had reached a critical stage, and it was necessary to try the last resort of a spa cure. The choice had fallen on Bad Reinerz in Silesia, whither Justyna Chopin traveled at the end of July with her daughter and her son, who was taken along on the principle that it could only do him good too.

Bad Reinerz was not one of the elegant spas, and it held few attractions for Chopin, apart from the mountains in which it was cradled. There was a strict routine at these watering places, and Chopin had to be at the spring along with the others by six in the morning for the first glass of mineral water. This was later complemented by draughts of whey, which were held to be good for the chest, and more glasses of mineral water at intervals during the day. An excruciatingly bad orchestra played while the clientele queued up for their glasses to be filled or walked up and down drinking it. In spite of the fact that there were several Warsaw acquaintances also spending the summer at Reinerz, Chopin was bored there. The only attraction of the place was the beautiful scenery. Chopin had never seen anything more exciting than the flat and rather monotonous Mazovian plain, and he was therefore predictably impressed by the mountains. He went for endless walks and enthused about the breathtaking views, but was depressed because he could not translate his sensations into his own medium. "There is something I lack here; something which all the beauties of Reinerz cannot make up for," he wrote to Elsner in Warsaw. "Imagine that there is not a single decent piano in the whole place."[15]

Nevertheless, when a couple of children were suddenly orphaned by the death of their father, who had come to take the waters, Chopin offered his services to those who wanted to help the poor creatures. A piano was found, and Chopin gave a small concert in the *Kurhaus* for their benefit.[16] It was so warmly received by the bored visitors to Reinerz that Chopin was persuaded to give another, which was also a great success. Humble as it was, this acclaim from an audience who had no idea of who he was provided another small encouragement to the boy. It was also a weapon to be used in the battle against his father's wish that he should enter the University rather than the Conservatoire. Both Zywny and Elsner must have been persuasive champions of the latter course, and by the time Chopin returned to Warsaw, a decision had been reached on his future. It was a compromise: he was to enter the Conservatoire for a course in harmony and composition, and at the same time to attend lectures on certain subjects at the University.

3

The Warsaw Conservatoire

The Warsaw Conservatoire had been founded in 1821, after several unsuccessful attempts to provide the capital with a musical academy. There were various courses open to entrants, but the one Chopin chose consisted of three years of study of musical theory and counterpoint. The third year was to be devoted to practical work, which, according to the curriculum, should include the writing of masses and oratorios to Polish and Latin texts, vocal compositions of various types, works for orchestra, and chamber music.

Chopin, however, seems to have evaded the rigors of this curriculum from the start. When he joined the Conservatoire in September 1826, he took only six lessons in counterpoint per week from Elsner and spent the rest of the time working on his own. Elsner was an enlightened leader who saw his role as that of adviser. As he explained: "When teaching composition, one should never provide recipes, particularly with pupils of obvious ability; if they wish to rise above themselves, they must find their own, so that they may have the means of discovering that which has not been discovered yet."[1] But Chopin found even this relaxed discipline very taxing, never having been subject to any pressure before. His health was still poor, and he was under the constant surveillance of the most eminent doctor in Warsaw. "I go to bed at nine; all tea parties, soirées and balls have gone by the board," he wrote to Bialoblocki that autumn. "I drink emetic water on Dr. Malcz's orders and stuff myself with oat gruel like a horse."[2]

According to the plan worked out by his father, Chopin was also attending lectures at the University. Although the original idea had been that he should try to follow the courses on general subjects such as history and literature, he soon narrowed this down to those closest to his heart. The only course of lectures he seems to have followed seriously was that on Polish literature given by a minor poet called Brodzinski, who collected and lectured on folk music.[3] Chopin's interests were becoming strictly limited to subjects connected with music, which explains why he was hardly aware of and played no part in the intellectual life of the Polish capital during the late 1820s, which was dominated by the new Romantic literature.

He was continually rubbing shoulders with the most exciting generation in Polish literary history, but remained unaffected by this contact. First editions of the poems by Adam Mickiewicz, greatest of the Polish Romantic poets, poems which were causing such a furor among Chopin's contemporaries, did pass through his hands, and he wrote songs to some of them as early as 1826. But his lack of fundamental interest or discrimination is amply demonstrated by the fact that he also wrote songs to poems by Stefan Witwicki. The latter, whom Chopin knew well, was greatly inferior to Mickiewicz, and his work from this period in particular was but a poor reflection of the other's genius. But Chopin was far too pedestrian in his approach to life to catch the spirit of the Romantic movement, or indeed to be able to take it seriously. As a result, he looked only for prettiness in poetry, and Mickiewicz's grandeur largely evaded him. Chopin saw himself as a craftsman and never managed to take himself seriously enough to pose as an artist with a spiritual message. It is therefore hardly surprising that he could not bring himself to take others seriously either.

The atmosphere during this first year of real musical study was also not particularly conducive to intellectual or emotional exuberance. Chopin's health was poor throughout, his lessons with Elsner brought home to him how much he still had to learn from the technical point of view, and he suffered two emotional shocks during the spring of 1827. One was caused by the rumor, which later turned out to be false, of Jan Bialoblocki's death; the other was the only too real anguish of watching his fourteen-year-old sister Emilia literally cough herself to death in April.

That summer Chopin left Warsaw again to stay on various estates in Mazovia, in a long progress which took him as far as Danzig.[4] While he was away, his family moved to an apartment in one of the wings of the Krasinski Palace, just across the road from the gates to the Lyceum. Nicolas Chopin had saved enough to be able to do without boarders from now on, and the wish to leave the apartment in which Emilia had died seems to have been a contributing factor. The two other Chopin girls were by now growing into young ladies, and the continued presence of young boarders in the apartment created an obvious hazard. The new apartment contained an elegant drawing room with a fine view over the most handsome street in Warsaw, but, being so close to his previous abode, it did not much alter Chopin's way of life. On the other hand, it was quieter, and the family now enjoyed greater privacy.

Gloomy as it had been, Chopin's first year at the Conservatoire was beneficial, and its fruits began to show during the second. The year 1827 is a landmark as that of Beethoven's death, but it can also be seen as one in Chopin's musical development. Elsner's influence had not seriously affected Chopin's musical taste, and he continued to see Bach as the basis of music—more than a decade later, he could still sit down and play all the Preludes and Fugues from memory, adding: "That is something one never forgets!"[5] As he learned more about the theory of music, he developed a greater respect for Haydn, whom he valued for his "experience,"[6] and for Mozart, who became his god. The only quarter in which Elsner's taste did affect Chopin's was in that of contemporary music. While Chopin, along with the rest of Warsaw, adored the fashionable Italian school, Elsner disliked it and steered his pupil away from it and toward Hummel, Moscheles, and Field, whom he saw as the greatest composers of the day (Ignaz Moscheles was a pianist and organist; John Field a pianist, composer, and inventor of the nocturne form). This influence can be detected in the works that Chopin was beginning to turn out in the second half of 1827 and the beginning of 1828, particularly as he was now concentrating on longer and less familiar forms.

It was during this period that Chopin made his first attempts at writing for the orchestra. The most interesting of these are the set of Variations for Piano and Orchestra on the theme of the *La ci darem* aria from Mozart's *Don Giovanni*. It is a very brilliant work in some ways, although the orchestral score leaves much to be desired. It betrays a lack of familiarity with some of the instruments and of adventurousness in handling the orchestra as a whole, and its sketchy nature suggests that Chopin was not trying very hard. The piano part, on the other hand, is melodic, elegant, and brilliant and seems to brush aside the orchestra with its own conviction. It is so obviously Chopin's work that it lends itself to being treated as a landmark, and as the *Gazette Musicale de Paris* asserted more than seven years later, the Variations "announce the superiority of Chopin's nature with as much precision as felicity."[7]

Compared to Beethoven's magnificent interweaving of

piano and orchestra, Chopin's Variations seem pale indeed, but if they are considered in the context of Hummel's works, which he was emulating, his intentions become clearer. Like Hummel, Chopin uses the orchestra essentially as an accompaniment to the piano. At no point in Chopin's works for piano and orchestra does the latter overshadow or outshine the former. Since the orchestra is not supposed to assume a dominant role, its potential is not explored. The result is that in both Chopin's and Hummel's work it appears bland and formal, and completely lacks the richness and depth of sound that Beethoven drew from it. It is wrong to think that Chopin was incapable of writing an interesting orchestral score; he was not attempting to.

In April 1828, Hummel himself came to Warsaw and gave a couple of concerts. He was introduced to Chopin, listened to him play, and was impressed.[8] For Chopin this was the first serious mark of recognition from a great musical personage, and it was probably what prompted him to send copies of the Variations and his first piano sonata to publishers in Leipzig and Vienna. Two years were to elapse before either was printed.

Chopin again spent the summer in the Mazovian countryside, in a rather fine house belonging to friends of his family. In spite of the large house party he worked hard throughout the holidays on a new Rondo for two pianos. He was back in Warsaw at the end of September, just in time to see Rossini's latest opera, *Otello*, but the production was so dreadful that he longed to strangle the whole cast. His joy was all the greater, when a few days later, the chance of visiting Berlin presented itself.

A friend and colleague of Nicolas Chopin's, Professor Jarocki, had been invited to take part in a scientific congress in the Prussian capital, and he offered to take young Chopin along, since all the expenses of the trip were paid. The boy was delighted; he would at last see a foreign capital with an

impressive musical establishment, whose giant was the celebrated operatic composer Gasparo Spontini. Chopin had no
doubt that he would meet him and the other celebrities, for
he had one important acquaintance in Berlin. This was
Prince Antoni Radziwill, a Polish aristocrat married to one of
the Prussian crown princesses. Radziwill was the King's lieutenant in what was then the Duchy of Posen, the part of
Poland ruled by Prussia, and frequently traveled between Berlin, Posen, and Warsaw in an official capacity. He was a distinguished amateur musician and had met Chopin on one of
his visits to Warsaw.

Berlin turned out to be something of a disappointment.
After five days in a mail coach, the two travelers arrived there
in mid-September. Chopin's first impressions were unfavorable; he found the streets too formal and empty and the
women ugly. He had to take most of his meals at the hotel
with Jarocki and the other scientists, whom he found ridiculous and depressing, with the sole exception of the reverend
figure of Humboldt, who was chairing the congress. Prince
Radziwill was absent, and on the one occasion when Chopin
found himself in the same room with Spontini, Zelter, and
Mendelssohn, he was too shy to introduce himself. Since
nobody thought of doing this for him, he did not speak to
any of them. He visited the factories of the best piano makers,
but there were no instruments in stock for him to see. He had
expected to find the productions and performances at the
opera magnificent, and was slightly disappointed with both.
He saw operas by Spontini, Onslow, Cimarosa, and Weber.
But the only thing that "came close to the ideal I have of
great music" was Handel's "Ode on St. Cecilia's Day," which
he heard at the Singakademie.[9] It was the first time he had
been struck by Handel's work, and his respect for that composer was to grow steadily. Seven years later, when Mendelssohn showed him a new edition of Handel's work, Chopin experienced "a truly child-like joy."[10]

The congress ended with a great banquet during which the scientists stuffed their mouths in a way Chopin found hard to believe. They drank a good deal as well, and when Zelter and his choir intoned a ceremonial cantata—presumably the one Mendelssohn had composed for the occasion—they all joined in, clinking glasses and bawling their heads off.

On the next day, Chopin and Jarocki left Berlin for Posen, where they saw Prince Radziwill, and then returned to Warsaw. Disappointing as it had been, the trip only whetted Chopin's appetite for foreign travel, and he dreamed of going further afield as he settled down for his final year at the Conservatoire.

This was the year devoted to practical exercises, but Elsner did not demand any masses or oratorios from Chopin, who was allowed to carry on with instrumental works and chamber music. The best-known compositions from this period are the Rondo on Cracovian Themes (opus 14), nicknamed the *Krakowiak*, and the Fantasia on Polish Airs (opus 13), both for piano and orchestra. Although some years later a Parisian critic was to hail the Fantasia as a landmark in musical history,[11] it is hard to see it as one now. These pieces are interesting for a number of reasons, not least of which are the intricacy and beauty of the piano parts. More significantly, a far greater degree of daring and originality obtains in these works than in any of Chopin's previous or indeed later writing for orchestra. There are passages in which the latter assumes an active role and ceases to be merely an accompaniment for the piano, but perhaps the most interesting aspect of these and other works from the same period is the way in which Chopin handles the folk element in them.

Following his sudden exposure to real folk music in 1824, Chopin had started collecting country tunes and turning them into pieces for the piano. This was accepted practice, and many contemporary musicians transcribed folk tunes for one or more instruments or wrote variations on them. But over the next couple of years Chopin had imbibed more of this ethnic music and had come to understand the mood and the theory behind it. It was like the difference between using ready-made phrases of a foreign language and learning the language itself. By 1828 he had mastered the folk idiom so thoroughly that he could write original mazurkas, often using elements of melodies he had heard in the country, but more and more often creating his own. This process was to take him further away from the traditional use of national themes and eventually led him to create what was in effect an entirely new mode of musical expression, both for the peasant lore of Mazovia and for the historic, courtly ethos which inspired the polonaise. He was no longer writing a country dance or a court dance; he was writing poems in the musical language of Mazovia, or alternately in that of the Polish nobility.

Chopin was now almost nineteen years old, and he was finding it increasingly difficult to work in the face of worldly temptations. He had grown into a fine-looking young man, not tall or well built, it is true, but slender, with a refined countenance and manner. This, as well as his great sociability and of course his musical gift, meant that he was sought after for all social activities, and he was finding it hard to refuse. The round of tea parties and dinners, soirées and balls exhausted him, particularly as he was the sort of person who plays an active part in such gatherings. "You know how awful it is when all you want to do is to go to bed, and suddenly everyone wants you to start improvising," he complained to his friend Tytus.[12] But he always complied and, having sat down at the piano, would improvise for hours.

Luckily, Nicolas Chopin had finally given his son a study of his own, at the top of a rickety staircase leading off the apartment. This "refuge," as he called it, was soon cluttered by scores and music paper, as the boy started work on his first "serious" composition—a concerto for piano and orchestra. This piece was probably meant to fall within the category of his practical work for Elsner, but it may also have been prompted by the need to have a substantial composition to show off when he did manage to go abroad. The question of travel was now uppermost in his mind and, in April 1829, Nicolas Chopin decided to tackle the question of funds by petitioning the Minister of Education. The move was not without precedent, as a slightly older Conservatoire colleague of Chopin, the pianist Tomasz Nidecki, had been given a foreign travel grant a couple of years before. Nicolas Chopin reminded the Minister that his son had "had the honor of being heard by the late Tsar" and that His Imperial Highness the Grand Duke, Supreme Commander of the Army, "had often been most graciously pleased to allow him to give evidence of his growing talent in His most serene presence."[13]

The Minister, Count Grabowski, endorsed the petition and recommended a handsome annual grant for three years, during which the young man was to visit Germany, France, and Italy, but his superior, the Minister of the Interior, turned it down, with the observation, scrawled in the margin, that "Public funds cannot be frittered away on this kind of artist."[14] It was good that neither Nicolas Chopin nor his son ever saw this remark, as the Minister's wife, Countess Mostowska, had often "allowed" the young man to play at her house. One cannot help feeling that it was Chopin's rather special social position, with the aura of amateurishness it implied, which prevented him from getting the same grant as the honestly professional Nidecki.

The disappointment caused by the failure of this petition was soon forgotten in the excitement created by the arrival, a few weeks later, of the great violinist Paganini. Chopin went to most of the ten concerts he gave and, like Liszt and Schumann, was bowled over by the sheer virtuosity of the man's playing. Paganini was the first great musician to elevate his instrument from its traditional role within the orchestra or quartet and to make it actively "speak" to the audience. He achieved this by drawing an unprecedented degree of sound and expression from his violin, and after hearing him Liszt, and to a lesser degree Schumann, set out to do the same for the piano. Chopin had been moving in this very direction long before he heard Paganini, but the latter's achievement acted as a tonic and a confirmation of his own conviction that music was made by one instrument, and that orchestration was essentially a garnishing. Chopin needed reassurance on this point, as Elsner was much opposed to it and kept trying to persuade him that he must ultimately set his sights on the symphonic and operatic forms. Returning home after one of the concerts, Chopin composed a set of variations entitled *Souvenir de Paganini*. More important, he now set to work on the first of the Études, and during the next six months he wrote four of them (nos. 8, 9, 10, and 11 of opus 10). They were exercises which were designed to help him draw a wider range of sound and greater expression from the piano, and with time they revolutionized his use of the instrument.

Paganini's visit was not the only attraction of that season in Warsaw, although by far the greatest. It was followed by what in other circumstances would have been exciting for Chopin—a series of concerts by the violinist Karol Lipinski. The latter had at one stage been regarded as one of Paganini's greatest rivals, but his concerts only underlined the Italian's genius, and Chopin was not impressed. The same was true of the concerts given soon afterward by the German pianist Stephen Heller; his playing was good but lacked the special qualities that Chopin was beginning to look for.

A more portentous event for Chopin was a concert organized by Soliva, the singing instructor at the Conservatoire, to show off his pupils. One of these, Konstancja Gladkowska, struck the young man not only by her fine voice but also by her appearance. She was dark-haired and pretty, with a face that exuded melancholy rather than vivaciousness. Of her character, not much is known. Chopin was immediately smitten but was too shy to let this show and made no attempt to court her or draw her attention over the next few months.

Before he had had time to recover from all these impressions, Chopin had his final exams before him. It is not known what form these took, but the report was written into the register by Elsner in the following terms:

"Chopin, Fryderyk; third year student. Outstanding abilities; musical genius."[15] In his own diary, Elsner jotted down that Chopin had "opened a new era in piano music through his astonishing playing as well as through his compositions."[16]

This was the logical moment for Chopin to set off on a long foreign tour, but there seemed to be no way of financing it. The best he could do for the time being was to join a party of friends from the University who were going on a jaunt to Vienna, taking in other places on the way. They left Warsaw immediately after the exams, on July 21, and made for Cracow. Chopin visited the old city with his friends, and then went on a couple of excursions to local sights. One took them down the Wieliczka salt mines, another through the beautiful scenery of the Ojcow Valley. This latter was marred because their cart got lost and then stuck in a stream, leaving them to wander for hours in the pouring rain before they found shelter and some straw for the night. Chopin did not catch cold, as his health had improved considerably in the last year or two, and in his late teens and early twenties he became strong enough to be able to endure such exertions in a way he had not during his adolescence.

The little party reached Vienna on the last day of July 1829, and Chopin immediately took a great liking to the city. After a few days there he found that the standard of musical performance exceeded his most sanguine expectations. He saw several operas, by Boieldieu, Meyerbeer, and Méhul, went to a few concerts, and found perfection everywhere. He had to a certain extent gotten over the reticence which had hampered him in Berlin, and he immediately took steps to

get acquainted with the musical establishment. He called on
Haslinger, the publisher to whom he had sent the scores of
the *La ci darem* Variations and of the C minor Sonata; on
W. W. Würfel, the former piano teacher from the Warsaw
Conservatoire who had moved to Vienna; and on an old Polish acquaintance and music lover, Count Hussarzewski. They
in turn introduced him to others, including the venerable
Schuppanzigh, the violinist and leader of the famous quartet
which had performed all Beethoven's chamber music for him;
the two foremost piano makers, Stein and Graf; and, most
important, the director of the Karntnerthor Theater, Count
Gallenberg.

"I don't know what it is, but all these Germans are amazed
by me, and I am amazed at them being so amazed by me," he
wrote to his parents a few days after his arrival.[17] Haslinger,
who had probably put aside the score of the Variations without looking at it, never having heard Chopin's name before,
changed his attitude radically when the young man sat down
at the piano in his shop and played them through. Realizing
that the public might react as he had done, he immediately
promised to publish them in a beautiful edition if Chopin
played them in public. The project was taken up by everyone
else with enthusiasm. Würfel believed that the Viennese public was "hungry for new music,"[18] Hussarzewski predicted a
resounding success, and Count Gallenberg offered his theater
free if Chopin wished to give a concert. Chopin himself was
irresolute and worried that Elsner and his family might not
approve, but was eventually persuaded to agree.

The Karntnerthor Theater was booked for August 11, an
orchestra assembled, and on Chopin's choice a Graf piano
provided. There were problems at the rehearsal that afternoon, for the two pieces Chopin intended to play with the orchestra (the *La ci darem* Variations and the *Krakowiak*
Rondo) were written out in his usual scruffy and inaccurate
way, and the disgruntled orchestra began to mutiny. They re-

fused absolutely to play the *Krakowiak*, and it was only
thanks to the diplomatic efforts of Tomasz Nidecki, whose
travels had brought him to Vienna, that a full-scale strike did
not break out. He concentrated on correcting and smoothing
the parts of the Variations, which the orchestra finally agreed
to play.

"At seven o'clock in the evening I made my appearance on
the Imperial and Royal stage!" he wrote to his parents.[19] It
was a brilliantly successful appearance. The concert opened
with the orchestra playing the overture from Beethoven's
Creatures of Prometheus, after which Chopin appeared on
the stage to play his Variations. He was not nervous of the
Viennese audience, but a little put out to find a highly rouged
gentleman sitting down next to him, boasting that he had
turned pages for Hummel and Moscheles. Moreover, the skir-
mish with the orchestra that afternoon had ruffled him, and
he launched into the piece with "exasperation," half expecting them to play a trick on him.[20] But he need not have
worried, for they played it perfectly, while the delighted audience applauded after each variation and called him back for a
second bow at the end. After an interlude of lieder sung by a
lady from Saxony, Chopin reappeared on the stage to play a
"free fantasy" without orchestra. He started off by improvising on a theme from Boieldieu's *La Dame blanche,* which
was playing to full houses in Vienna at the time, but was subsequently asked by the director of the theater to play "something Polish," whereupon he launched into an improvisation
on a peasants' wedding song, which, in his own words, "elec-
trified" the audience. When he had finished, the orchestra itself broke into applause, and he was called back for a second
bow again. Count Dietrichstein, the Emperor's director of
music, came onto the stage and publicly congratulated Chopin, urging him to stay in Vienna a little longer.

Chopin could hardly believe his own triumph. He had of
course become used to popularity in Warsaw, but to get a re-

ception like this from an audience which was used to hearing the greatest masters was something else. His four friends had posted themselves strategically in the audience and reported its reactions to him, the worst being an old lady who enjoyed the music, but sighed: "What a pity the young man hasn't got a better *tournure!*"[21] But what really went to his head was the sincere admiration of renowned older musicians like Kreutzer, Mayseder, and old Gyrowetz (whose concerto Chopin had played at his first public concert eleven years before), for he was conscious of coming from a musical backwater. It is true that when asked how he had managed to turn into such a fine musician in Warsaw, he answered that "with Messrs. Zywny and Elsner even a half-wit would learn,"[22] but this was said more out of bravado than conviction.

The only criticism to be heard, not for the first or the last time in Chopin's life, was that his playing was a little lacking in strength and volume, or, as he himself put it, "too delicate for those accustomed to the piano bashing of the local artists." This did not worry him unduly, as he anticipated it, but he felt obliged to warn his parents not to worry about it either, writing: "I expect that criticism to be made in the papers, particularly as the editor's daughter enjoys nothing like a good thump at her piano."[23] While having dinner at the hotel after the concert, Chopin overheard unfavorable reactions from a man who had just come back from the Karntnerthor, but as he remarked philosophically, "The man who will please everyone has not been born yet."[24] It was not the first time he noticed that he pleased above all refined people.

Prince Lichnowsky, Beethoven's great friend and patron, for one, could not find words enough to praise him, a reaction shared by others with resounding names like Schwarzenberg and musical reputations like that of Czerny, a pupil of Beethoven and teacher of Liszt, whom Chopin found "warmer than any of his compositions."[25] While he was still reeling under his first success, everyone began to insist on a second concert, and he accepted without protest, excusing himself to his parents, for some unknown reason, with the observation that people in Warsaw would not believe that the first had been a success unless it was repeated.

Exactly a week later, on August 18, Chopin again appeared at the Karntnerthor. By this time, Nidecki had helped him to rewrite the part of the *Krakowiak* Rondo, so he performed it. "Everyone from Kapellmeister Lachner right down to the piano tuner was astonished by the beauty of the piece," he wrote home with pride.[26] Again he was called back for a second bow, and even a third, after which the audience called for an encore, a fairly rare occurrence in those days. Rarer still, the orchestra was prepared to join in, with the result that he played through the *La ci darem* Variations as an encore. If the success of the first concert had seemed a little unreal, there was no mistaking the reactions of the audience now. Chopin had got what he had been longing for; an appraisal at the hands of an unbiased and discerning public. As he quipped after the event, he would give up music and become a house painter if he heard any more unfavorable criticism.[27]

His first brush with the commercial side of musical life did not fail to disillusion him, for Chopin was still, at the age of nineteen, naïve and inexperienced. The tetchiness of the orchestra, most of which was the result of petty jealousy, the calculations of Haslinger over the printing of the Variations, and the gracious way in which Count Gallenberg "lent" his theater without appearing to be aware that a performing artist usually receives a fee had opened his eyes, and he felt "cleverer and more experienced by four years."[28] But this was nothing in the face of his reception and of the reviews which began to appear as he was preparing to leave the Austrian capital.

These were as favorable as he could have longed for in his wildest fancies. "Chopin surprised people, because they discovered in him not only a fine, but a very eminent talent,"

one of them explained, going on to say that "on account of
the originality of his playing and compositions, one might almost attribute to him already some genius, at least as far as
unconventional forms and pronounced individuality are concerned." It went on to point out "a certain modesty which
seems to indicate that to shine is not the aim of this young
man," and summed up accurately Chopin's whole attitude
when playing before an audience: "He emphasized but little,
like one conversing in the company of clever people, not with
the rhetorical aplomb which is considered by virtuosos as indispensable." The reviews were full of compliments, hailing
him as a "true artist" and pointing out that Chopin's improvisation had delighted a public "in whose eyes few improvisers,
with the exception of Beethoven and Hummel, have as yet
found favor."[29] Another paper showered him with compliments, calling him a "master of the first rank," declaring that
his compositions bore "the stamp of great genius" and comparing his appearance in the musical world to that of "the
most brilliant meteors."[30] It must be said that the praise was
not only copious but also sensible. One of the reviews, which
was less free with superlatives, must have pleased Chopin
more than all the others when it stated:

> He is a young man who goes his own way, and knows how
> to please in this way, although his style of playing and writ-
> ing differs greatly from that of other vituosos, and indeed
> chiefly in this: that the desire to make good music predomi-
> nates noticeably in his case over the desire to please.[31]

Not surprisingly, Chopin left Vienna in very high spirits,
with his friends, who were bound for Prague. The group
spent three days in the city, sightseeing and calling on some
of the local musicians, after which they traveled on toward
Dresden, pausing at Teplitz, whence they went on an excursion to Wallenstein's castle at Dux. While in Teplitz,
Chopin bumped into a Warsaw acquaintance who was a dis-

tant relative of Prince Clary, whose seat the town was, and accompanied him to an evening at the castle. Chopin's pleasure at being in such company is obvious from his description:

> We went in; the company was small but select—some Austrian prince, a general whose name I forget, an English sea captain, several young dandies, apparently Austrian princes too, and a Saxon general called Leiser, covered in medals, with a scar on his face. After tea, before which I talked a good deal with Prince Clary himself, his mother asked me whether I would "deign" to sit down at the piano (good piano —Graf's). I did "deign," but asked the company to "deign" to give me a theme to improvise on. Thereupon the table at which the fair sex were knitting, embroidering and crocheting came to life with cries of *Un thème!*" Three princesses consulted together and finally sought the advice of Mr. Fritsche (young Clary's tutor, I think), and he, with everyone's agreement, gave me a theme from Rossini's *Moses* . . .[32]

The Clarys invited Chopin to spend another day in Teplitz, but he wanted to press on to Dresden, where he arrived with his friends on August 25. He visited the famous art gallery, went to the theater to see Goethe's *Faust*, called on some of the city's musicians, and then left for Warsaw, where he arrived at the beginning of September, feeling like a homecoming hero.

4

Frustrations

Chopin had an unpleasant surprise when he returned to Warsaw on September 12. The *Warsaw Courier* had somehow
managed to mistranslate the reviews of his concerts from the
Viennese papers, and published what amounted to an unfavorable account of his great success.[1] He was of course able
to show his friends the original versions, but it was too late to
scotch the general impression of failure which had attached
itself to his trip.

After Vienna, Warsaw seemed unexciting and empty, an
impression which was heightened because he was rather
bored. For one thing, most of his friends had disappeared.
Bialoblocki had died, Tytus Woyciechowski had retired to
the country to look after his estate, others had gone abroad
or, like Matuszynski and Fontana, were working hard at their
university studies. He on the other hand had nothing to do,
for he had finished his studies and was intending to begin his
travels in earnest at the earliest opportunity. The main obstacle was lack of money. While he had been in Vienna, the rest
of his family had paid a visit to Prince Antoni Radziwill at his
summer estate of Antonin, and the result of this was an invi-

tation for Chopin to spend the season in Berlin with the Prince. Although this at least provided an opportunity of staying in the Prussian capital free and of meeting all the people who had anything to offer musically, Chopin was not keen on the idea. Berlin had seemed to him scarcely less provincial than Warsaw, and he longed for Vienna, Italy, and Paris. He must have also considered the possibility of visiting England, for he was now, along with Julian Fontana, taking English lessons (from an Irishman called Macartney, who was perpetually drunk and was always trying to borrow cash off the two boys).[2]

Chopin filled his time as best he could, mainly with work. He struggled on with his F minor concerto (opus 21, usually referred to as No. 2, although it was the first he wrote), and with the first set of Études, but above all he was trying to perfect his musical education. He went to every possible performance at the opera and to every concert, however uninspiring, and spent much time at Brzezina's music store. Like all similar establishments, this was a cross between a store and a drawing room, with something of the atmosphere of a coffeehouse thrown in. People interested in music would drop in, see what had arrived from abroad, browse, play pieces through on the piano, and generally discuss the musical scene.

The lack of good concerts in Warsaw was made up for by Chopin and various other musicians, who used to meet on given days at the rooms of Joseph Kessler, formerly pianist to Count Potocki at Lancut and now music teacher in Warsaw. What they played depended on who turned up with what instruments. This way they managed to work through many chamber works that autumn, including pieces by Spohr and Hummel, and a Trio by Beethoven, of which Chopin wrote to Tytus Woyciechowski: "I have not heard anything quite so great for a long time—in this piece Beethoven makes fools of us all."[3]

Now that Chopin had time on his hands, he entered into

the life of the city to a greater extent and frequented the coffeehouses and haunts of the young intelligentsia, which was in a state of political ferment by 1829. The death of Alexander I in 1825 and the accession of Nicholas I to the tsardom had changed the whole political climate in Poland. While all but the radicals had been prepared to co-operate to some extent with the Russian tutelage under Alexander, this was becoming extremely difficult in view of the increasingly autocratic behavior of his successor. Chopin's generation grew restive as it watched universities being closed down, books being censored, and manifestations of nationalism suppressed, and by the end of 1829 there was a spirit of rebellion and conspiracy abroad in Warsaw. Coffeehouses like Brzezinska's, which Chopin frequented for coffee in the daytime and punch in the evenings, were the scene of fervent discussions and conspiratorial activity. But although he was with his generation in spirit, Chopin was not interested in politics, and this drove an imperceptible wedge between him and many who would otherwise have been friends. Those he did get close to were not revolutionaries but poets. Many of these, like Chopin's friends Witwicki and Zaleski, were also caught up in the nationalist movement, but the one he liked best, Dominik Magnuszewski, was an erratic dilettante poet and amateur musician with a melancholy bent and a sense of alienation from his contemporaries.

From Chopin's letters to Tytus it is clear that none of these people ever became intimate enough with him to dispel the loneliness he felt. "You cannot imagine how much I lack something in Warsaw now," he wrote. "—I haven't got anyone I can say two words to, anyone I could confide in."[4] He had a great deal he wished to confide, as he was still nurturing a desperate love for Konstancja Gladkowska. He had by now got a little closer to her, but was apparently too shy, or perhaps unwilling, to let his feelings show.

Chopin's childhood and teens had been characterized by a

forthright and effortless approach to life. He had never found the process of composition particularly laborious, and he had always been relaxed in his relations with others. Now, at the age of nineteen, he was finding it difficult to fulfill himself either artistically or emotionally, and the sense of frustration deriving from this pervades his letters. This makes it more difficult to assess Chopin's feelings toward Konstancja, as when he talks of them to Tytus, they are inextricably bound up with his general sense of frustration. She certainly had no idea of what was going through the composer's mind, and carried on flirting with a couple of officers who were less bashful than Chopin and often came to sing duets with her. Chopin's reaction to this was to withdraw into himself and wallow in self-pity, and the only person patient enough to read the resulting letters was Tytus.

In October, Chopin's somber thoughts were dispelled by a pleasant distraction. He had been asked down to the country by his godmother, Mrs. Wiesiolowska, née Skarbek, whose estate lay close to Prince Radziwill's Antonin, and although Chopin was originally unenthusiastic about the idea, he did later go and stay at Antonin. He had a delightful stay in this "paradise" with its two "Eves," the young princesses, who managed to chase all thoughts of Konstancja from his head. The Prince was charming to him and showed him his own music, among which was an accompaniment to Goethe's *Faust* which Chopin, and later Liszt, found surprisingly good.[5] As well as talking music, they made music, for the Prince was a good 'cellist. Chopin wrote a Polonaise for piano and 'cello especially for him and his daughter to play, as he explained to Tytus:

> It is nothing but glitter, for the drawing room, for the ladies. I wanted Princess Wanda to learn to play it; I'm vaguely supposed to be giving her some lessons while I'm here. She's young (seventeen), pretty, and it's a real joy placing her little fingers on the keys.[6]

"I could have stayed there until I was thrown out," he later wrote,[7] but he soon returned to Warsaw, having promised to join the Radziwills in Berlin in May 1830, which he hoped would give him time for another visit to Vienna first.

Nothing was to come of these plans, and, try as he might, he still could not get his F minor concerto finished. Depression soon closed in on him again, in spite of his activity and a couple of rewarding performances. On December 6, his father's name day, he arranged a concert in the Chopin apartment, with Zywny and Elsner taking part, and on December 19 he took part in a grand concert at the Merchants' Resource, at which he improvised so brilliantly that he was hailed in the press as never before. Having been largely ignored by the Polish press until now, he was suddenly noticed, particularly by the radical sections, which seem to have at last realized the importance of this national poet of the keyboard. The *Warsaw Courier* ended by writing:

> Mr. Chopin's works bear unquestionably the stamp of genius; among them is said to be a concerto in F minor, and it is hoped that he will not delay any longer in confirming our conviction that Poland too can produce great talent.[8]

Chopin had to delay this great moment whether he liked it or not, for the F minor concerto was still unfinished, and it was not until March 3, 1830, that he was able to perform it. On that day he made up a small orchestra in the Chopin drawing room and played the concerto, with Kurpinski conducting. On the next day, the newspapers reviewed the concert as though it had been a public event, for there had been a select audience present. The *Warsaw Courier* described Chopin as the "Paganini of the piano,"[9] while the *Universal Daily* carried a very long review, stating, among other things:

> The creative spirit of the young composer has taken the path of genius . . . I felt that in the originality of his thought I could glimpse the profoundness of Beethoven, and in their

execution the art and pleasantness of Hummel . . . All the
listeners were moved by these works, and those more closely
associated with the artist were deeply shaken. His old piano
teacher was virtually in tears. Elsner could not conceal his joy
as he moved about, hearing only praise of his pupil and his
compositions. Kurpinski conducted the orchestra himself for
the young artist. This is a real talent, a true talent. Mr. Chopin must not hide it and must let himself be heard publicly;
but he must also be prepared to hear voices of envy, which
usually only spare mediocrity.[10]

Egged on from all sides, Chopin agreed to perform, and on
March 12 the *Warsaw Courier* announced that he would be
giving a concert in the National Theater. Two days later the
same paper announced that all the tickets had been sold out,
although there were still three days to go before the concert.

On the morning of March 17, Chopin rehearsed the concerto with full orchestra, under Kurpinski, and on the same
evening played it through before his largest audience to date:
eight hundred people. He also played his Fantasia on Polish
Airs, sandwiched between overtures by Elsner and Kurpinski
and some songs by Paër. In his meticulously kept diary, Kurpinski noted that, although the theater had been packed with
an enthusiastic audience, the piano used had been too soft-
toned and that much of the effect had been lost.[11] Chopin
himself was not at all pleased with the performance. He realized that some people could not hear properly, and felt that
the music had not gotten through to the audience, whose enthusiastic applause, he insisted, was simply "to show that they
hadn't been bored."[12]

He could not have been more wrong, for, although playing
on his own quiet piano had clearly been a mistake, the reception he met with was tremendous. The Warsaw newspapers
were dominated by reviews of the performance, which in
some cases took up a good third of the whole issue. The critics could not make up their minds as to whether it was his

playing or his compositions which were the more remarkable, and comparisons with Mozart and Hummel were bandied about liberally. Hardly had the sound of his playing died away when a persistent chant for a second appearance was set up. This was quickly arranged for March 22, and a Russian general kindly lent Chopin a strong Viennese instrument for the occasion. The concert opened with a symphony by Nowakowski, an older Conservatoire friend, after which Chopin played his concerto, the *Krakowiak* Rondo, and an improvisation on a peasant song, again interspersed with other pieces.

This time the music got through to everyone, and there was wild enthusiasm in the theater. People shouted for a third concert, while a French pianist on his way to Moscow, who had dropped in out of boredom, rushed out to buy a bottle of champagne and insisted on toasting the young Pole he had never heard of before.

Chopin's playing had by all accounts been at its best. As one review put it: "It was as though his manner of playing was saying: 'It's not me—it's music!' "[13] Another explained that "Chopin does not play like others; with him we have the impression that every note passes through the eyes to the soul, and that the soul pours it into the fingers . . ."[14] Yet another, by a musical amateur called Grzymala, compared his playing to "a beautiful declamation, which seems to be the natural medium of his compositions."[15] Perhaps the most interesting note, summing up as it did the whole of Chopin's career as a performing artist as well as his attitude to life as a musician, was struck by a society lady, whose diary entry for the evening of the concert was printed in the *Polish Courier*, and after heaping praise on him, noted:

> Chopin's playing is like, if I may express myself in such manner, the social *ton* of an important and substantial person who lacks any pretentiousness, because he knows he has a natural right to everything; it is like a young innocent beauty, whose mind has not been tainted by the idea that she could

increase her charms through dress. You could be accused of
the same innocence, you interesting artist! The stage requires
brilliance, excellence, and even something of the terrible, for
while the really beautiful and gentle tones are understood by
the few, they make only a weak effect on others, and none at
all on the many. But even this reproach is a compliment to
you . . .[16]

The reproach was certainly justified, for now that he had
been reviewed and praised more than Paganini and Hummel
during their visits, now that the whole of Warsaw had finally
understood his playing and his compositions, he did not give
the third concert everyone was clamoring for, though the
money meant freedom to travel, his greatest dream. He explained his reticence to Tytus by saying that he had nearly
finished his second piano concerto (the one in E minor, usually called No. 1, although it was written second), and that,
wishing to have something new for the next appearance, he
would wait until after Easter, by which time this piece would
be ready.

The real reasons for his refusal lay elsewhere. He found the
preparations for the concerts nervously exhausting, as he had
to select musicians and decide whose music would be chosen
for the program, which, in a small place like Warsaw, was a
delicate operation. Then there was the problem of "friends,"
who were offended that he had not reserved boxes for them or
personally invited them to the event. "You wouldn't believe
what torture the three days before the concert are," he wrote
to Tytus after the first one,[17] but he was soon to discover
that the period afterward could be equally agonizing.

Chopin's great success in these, his first major commercial
concerts, inevitably aroused jealousy and resentment in certain quarters. He was not aware of this to begin with, for he
was busy fending off what he considered to be the exaggerated praise and sycophancy that accompanied his appearance.
He received verse offerings from hacks; his old friend Alex-

andrine de Moriolles sent him a crown of laurels; Antoni
Orlowski, a colleague from the Conservatoire, was writing
waltzes and mazurkas to themes from Chopin's concerto; and
the music publisher Brzezina wanted to print a lithograph
portrait of him. At the same time the newspapers carried a
number of articles discussing the nature of Chopin's genius
and its position in the world of music. One rather long and il-
logical article ended up by thanking heaven and Elsner that
the young composer had not been allowed to fall into the
hands of "some Rossinist," which was an ill-concealed jibe at
Kurpinski.[18] At this point the resentment which had been boil-
ing up exploded, and a fierce battle started between those
who were for Elsner and German music and those who supported Kurpinski and Italian music. Chopin was horrified to
find himself at the center of this fracas, and tried in vain to
smooth ruffled sensibilities and to keep the publicity to a min-
imum. He begged Antoni Orlowski not to print his compositions and refused to allow Brzezina or anyone else to publish
a portrait. Finally he retreated in horror from the scene. "I
don't want to read or listen to what anyone writes or says
anymore," he wrote petulantly to Tytus, for whose presence
he longed more than ever.[19]

The quarrel had, of course, nothing whatsoever to do with
Chopin himself, and he need not have felt in any way impli-
cated in its unpleasantness. Yet the hitherto highly sociable
and uninhibited Chopin was beginning to develop alarmingly
sensitive spots in his character. He had always been self-con-
scious enough to see the ridiculous in his own behavior, and
had in the past drawn great pleasure from describing it in letters to friends as well as in the *Szafarnia Courier*. It may be
that this emanated from a deeper fear of being ridiculed by
others; both his extreme modesty about his work and the arch
tone with which he often referred to himself would suggest a
bashful pride at the bottom of his character. As he reached
the end of his teens and began to take himself a little more

seriously—seriously enough to nurture a great passion—he shrank from making any move that might lead him into a position in which he would be exposed to the criticism or judgment of a society or a public. His first major appearances as a professional performing musician had made him into a public figure, which embarrassed him, and had provoked a squabble which disgusted and frightened him. This episode only strengthened his conviction that any sort of public activity was bound, in one way or another, to expose him to ugliness and possibly ridicule.

This was accompanied by an analogous development in his relations with other people. He still found it easy to make friends and was outwardly very sociable, but grew more and more suspicious and wary of allowing them to approach too close. This is why the absent Tytus was not replaced by any other as Chopin's confidant, and why their intimacy grew instead of waned. It also explains a great deal about Chopin's behavior with regard to Konstancja Gladkowska.

Warsaw was not a large city, and it would have been impossible for Chopin not to have seen her quite often, either socially or at musical evenings. After his triumphal concerts she must have been more than ever aware of his existence. And yet it would appear that he continued to pine from afar, without attempting to let her know his feelings. Romantic adolescents are often more interested in nurturing a feeling within themselves than in achieving intimacy with the object of that feeling, but in Chopin's case the fear of putting himself in an embarrassing or ridiculous position is almost certainly what paralyzed any move toward intimacy. It was less risky to keep pining and at the same time to channel the frustrated feeling and the self-pity toward Tytus, who remained the only real presence in Chopin's heart. After the fuss over Brzezina's attempt to print his portrait, Chopin wrote to Tytus: "Nobody apart from you shall have a portrait of me—

one other person could, but never before you, for you are dearer to me."[20]

This intimacy went beyond the purely emotional, for it embraced the subject of music. Tytus was a good pianist and wrote a little, and Chopin trusted his taste. Once he even wrote that Tytus had taught him how to "feel" music.[21] Chopin was always sending him his "rubbish" or "labored bits of dreariness," as he liked to refer to his works, particularly during the spring of 1830. "When I write something new, I'd like to know how you would like it," he wrote, "and I feel that my new concerto in E minor will hold no value for me until you have heard it."[22] Chopin had never been known to seek advice or approval for his compositions before, and was certainly not to do so after 1830. The need to do so now was the indirect result of his infatuation with Konstancja; for the first and last time in his life he was overtaken by the Romantic urge to program his music both sentimentally and thematically. "I say to my piano what I would like to be saying to you," he wrote to Tytus, and what he would like to be saying to Konstancja, he might have added.[23] The *Adagio* of the new concerto he was writing, which was secretly dedicated to her, is the only piece of his whose meaning Chopin ever tried to explain:

> The *Adagio* of the new concerto is in E minor. It is not supposed to be strong, but romantic, calm, melancholy; it should give the impression of gazing at a spot which brings back a thousand cherished memories. It should be like dreaming in beautiful springtime—by moonlight.[24]

Other pieces written during the same period are also tinged with sentimentality, like the Nocturnes opus 9, the E major Étude of opus 10, and some of the songs he wrote to Witwicki's poems, such as "The Wish" and "Where Does She Love?" (opus 74). Even Elsner noticed that some of the music from this period was inspired by "beautiful eyes."[25]

During the rest of March and April, Chopin let himself go
to pieces. He had intended to finish his second concerto
within a few weeks in order to be able to perform it publicly
at the end of April or the beginning of May, as he had to forward his career and earn more money however much it cost
him in ruffled sensibilities. He was still vaguely aiming to set
out for Berlin in May and thence go wherever seemed appropriate. But May came and went, and Chopin had neither
finished his new concerto nor arranged another appearance.
While he was heaving sighs in Warsaw, Tsar Nicholas arrived
for the state opening of the Polish parliament, and, as usual
on such occasions, various artists converged on the city from
abroad. These included the King of Prussia's pianist, Woerlitzer; Miss Belleville, a very fine pianist who had recently
played Chopin's *La ci darem* Variations at a concert in
Vienna; and, above all, the singer Henriette Sontag. The last
was an extremely beautiful woman with a magnificent voice
for whom Weber had composed the title role of *Euryanthe*
six years before. She had retired from the operatic stage after
her marriage to Count Rossi and now sang only in concerts.

She gave eight concerts in Warsaw, to most of which Chopin went. He was in ecstasy over her voice, whose elegance
and control seemed to echo his own touch on the piano. "She
seems to breathe into the stalls with the scent of the freshest
flowers, and she caresses, soothes deliciously, but rarely moves
to tears," he wrote to Tytus.[26] His interest in her grew considerably after Prince Radziwill, who had also arrived in Warsaw
for the official events, introduced them. They immediately
took a liking to each other, and since she was besieged all day
long by admiring dignitaries and aristocrats, she asked him to
come and call on her in the mornings at her hotel. At this
time of day he would find her in her *déshabillé*, and he soon
became totally infatuated with her. "You cannot imagine
how much pleasure I have had from a closer acquaintance—in
her room, on the sofa—with this 'envoy of heaven,' as some of

the local hotheads call her," he wrote to his friend, all thoughts of Konstancja banished from his head.[27]

Chopin was pleased by the opportunity to hear the visiting artists, but something went wrong with his own plans. He had intended to give a concert himself during the Tsar's visit, but for reasons which remain mysterious, no such event took place. While Miss Sontag sang to the various Imperial Majesties and Woerlitzer and Belleville played to them, people in Warsaw wondered why Chopin did not.

With the end of June, the parliament dissolved and people began to leave the city. At the beginning of July the Haslinger edition of the *La ci darem* Variations arrived in the Warsaw stores, and Chopin agreed to play them at a concert given on July 8 by a singer who had taken part in his earlier appearances. The audience was small, the public tired out by all the activity of the previous weeks, and although the reviews were favorable, the event failed to make any impact.

Chopin himself was feeling a little lost, for Romuald Hube, one of his companions on the previous year's trip to Vienna, with whom he had been intending to travel to Paris that summer, had left, while he was stranded in Warsaw with no plans at all. Since Tytus had not come to Warsaw as he had intended, and as Chopin had nothing better to do, he went to stay with him in the country, apparently intending to spend some time there. But after he had been there only two weeks, he read in the papers that Soliva, the singing instructor at the Conservatoire, had organized a concert in which Konstancja was to make her stage debut, and he rushed back to Warsaw, much to the annoyance of Tytus.

The event was obviously emotionally rewarding for Chopin, as Konstancja's performance was a great success, but when it was over he was once more at loose ends, harking back to his stay with Tytus. "Your fields have left me with a dull longing," he wrote, "that birch tree before your windows will not leave my thoughts,"[28] and in an attempt to dispel these he went to join the rest of his family who were staying with the Skarbeks at Zelazowa Wola. He spent a couple of weeks there, adding the finishing touches to his E minor concerto and relaxing with his family and friends. Some fifty years later an old peasant remembered how, as a boy during the last summer before the insurrection, he used to steal into the park on the warm August nights and listen as the young man from Warsaw played for hours on a piano which had been wheeled out onto the terrace.[29]

In the middle of August he returned to Warsaw. Although he was restless and bored, he wrote to Tytus:

> Nothing draws me abroad. Believe me that when I leave next week it will only be out of deference to my calling and common sense (which must be very small, since it cannot banish everything else from my mind).[30]

But while plans for a departure "next week for certain" were announced in one letter, this was followed by another a couple of weeks later in which he informed his friend that "I'm still here; I don't have enough will to decide on the day . . ."[31] The delays must have had something to do with Nicolas Chopin's fear of his son's getting caught up in the revolution which had broken out or that seemed imminent all over Europe, but a lot more to do with Chopin's own state of mind.

By the end of the summer, he had reached new heights of emotional turmoil, ostensibly on account of Konstancja. Having met her well over a year before and immediately recognized her as his "ideal" (the very word is redolent of schoolboy ritual), he had still not declared himself to her. "I could go on hiding my pathetic and ungainly passions for another couple of years," he wrote to Tytus, at the same time stressing their depths and force.[32] Strong his feelings may have been, but they were certainly not exclusive. The sudden blazing infatuations for the Radziwill girls or Henriette Sontag are only some of the manifestations of an acute susceptibility to women which his letters amply reveal. At one soirée in August he saw a girl (who of course reminded him of Konstancja) whom he could not take his eyes off, and who had set his heart on fire by the end of the evening. Another day, in church, he caught the eye of "a certain person," as a result of which he staggered out in a state of sensuous inebriation and nearly got himself run over by a passing carriage.

These and similar stories are recounted to Tytus, in tones of mawkish self-pity, alongside assurances that he, Tytus, is in fact the most important person in Chopin's life. While reaffirming his constant and undying love for the girl, he would write to his friend that he thought constantly of *him*, that *he* was uppermost in his thoughts: "I do not forget you, I am with you, and it shall be so till death."[33] It was Tytus who would have a portrait of Chopin before Konstancja, and it was Tytus who was the recipient of what would have been love letters to Konstancja, had Chopin dared write to her. These letters, sometimes friendly, sometimes petulant, sometimes verging on the passionate, are freely strewn with declarations of love and affinity, and contain passages of extraordinary sensuality.

This has prompted some to conclude that the two young men were, or had been, or wanted to be, lovers. On the face of it, the equivocal references to passions, secrets, and torment combine with the extremely concrete terms of endearment to make this appear plausible. In fact, the endless kisses demanded by Chopin, and the expressions like the one which can only be translated as: "Give me your lips!" were, and to some extent still are, common currency in Poland. They carry no greater implication than the "love" people send their mother, brother, or friend in this country.

Nothing is, of course, impossible, but it remains highly unlikely that the two were ever lovers. Had the slightly sentimental relationship between the older, stronger boy and his gentler, more emotional classmate really developed into a sexual rapport, it would almost certainly, knowing Chopin's malleable and undecided nature, have become an exclusive and long-lasting passion. In such a case there would have been no reason for Chopin to sit about getting bored in Warsaw while the bucolic seclusion of Tytus's estate beckoned him.

Tytus's role in Chopin's life was nevertheless a very important one. When Chopin wrote, somewhat dramatically, to his friend: "I swear that only you have power over me, you and . . . no one else!" he was not exaggerating.[34] Chopin's upbringing had marked his character in definite ways. The strong paternal authority to which he had been subjected had rendered him almost incapable of making a decision on his own. His loving mother and admiring sisters had spoiled him and led him to demand a great deal of affection from people. The sheltered and regular life of the Chopin household only served to make the outside world and its cares seem more problematic and frightening, while his early exposure to a wide social acquaintance had developed in him a gift for easy sociability, and also, apparently, a certain fear of giving himself. All this made Chopin dependent, now that he was beginning to live outside his family, on the support of friends. Since he was finding it increasingly difficult to get close to people, he clung more and more to his old friend Tytus. He kept trying to abdicate responsibility, and begged Tytus for advice and direction, but Tytus apparently evaded the functions of mentor and pressed Chopin to take more of a hold on himself. At the same time Tytus became the recipient of much of Chopin's repressed or frustrated feelings, which is why some of the letters he received from the young composer read almost like love letters.

In Warsaw, Chopin's only close friends were Jan Matuszynski, who was pursuing medical studies, and Julian Fontana, who had now, after finishing the Conservatoire, taken up law at the University. Along with Witwicki, they formed a small group which often met at the house of the young poet Dominik Magnuszewski. The latter lived in the center of Warsaw in the house of his grandfather, an old judge who, along with a couple of other gentlemen, seemed to embody the old prepartition Poland, still dressing in the traditional costume, sabers and all. Chopin and his friends loved to listen to these old men talking about that past which now seemed very distant. The atmosphere of the old state had been superseded by the more modern and secular spirit of the 1820s. Chopin was strongly drawn to what was heroic and elegant about the old state, and it was this he was attempting to capture and distill into the essence of the more sophisticated polonaises he was beginning to write.

He was often at Magnuszewski's, sometimes just playing to his friend or the old men, sometimes for an evening's amusement. As Magnuszewski's sister records in her diary:

> Chopin would usually sit down at the piano first . . . everyone always wanted him to improvise. He never tried to wriggle out of this, but first he would ask my sister Klara, who had a beautiful voice, to sing something, and it was only afterward that he would start. We would sit in silence for hours, listening to that music which fired our young souls, and afterward we would usually start dancing. At that point the dreamy improviser would turn into a lusty player and start thundering out mazurkas, waltzes and polkas until, tired of playing and eager to join in the dancing himself, he would cede the keyboard to a humbler replacement, Fontana, who played fluently and beautifully.[35]

By mid-September, Chopin was trying out various movements of his new E minor concerto in quartet or other forms, and on the twenty-second he arranged a full performance of the work in the Chopin apartment, again with a select audience of music lovers, among whom were Count Skarbek, Grzymala, and Witwicki. It was they who reviewed the event in the press and prompted a public clamor for Chopin to make himself heard. The latter's plans for leaving had again been put off by the outbreak of more disturbances in Europe and the consequent refusal of the Russian authorities to issue passports for travel to various countries. He therefore agreed to give a concert and, what is more, invited Konstancja and her fellow-pupil to take part in it. This entailed obtaining permission from the Minister of the Interior, which was not difficult, and also getting Kurpinski, who had a natural right to be the conductor, to cede his place to Soliva for the evening, which was a more delicate operation. This activity woke him from his lethargy, and he was now seriously arranging his departure as well. "A week after the concert at the latest I shall have left Warsaw," he wrote to Tytus, who had decided he might accompany him.[36] Chopin was for once decided: he had bought a trunk and clothes and was writing out the scores he would need on his travels.

The date of the concert was October 11. It was his last public appearance in his native country, and it went off perfectly. He played his E minor concerto and the Fantasia on Polish Airs. The concerto benefited from the conducting of Soliva, who took it slowly and did not let the overexcited Chopin get carried away. The result was that "I was not the slightest bit nervous, and I played as I play when I'm alone," as he wrote to Tytus. Konstancja sang an aria as she had never sung anything before and looked seductive, the other performances were good, and the Fantasia, which he played at the end, delighted him and the audience:

> This time I understood what *I* was doing, the orchestra understood what *they* were doing, and the pit understood as well. For once, the final mazurka called forth terrific applause . . . It seemed to me that I had never been so much at ease when playing with an orchestra.[37]

Chopin was delighted with every aspect of the evening, but it is worth noting that the hall, with only seven hundred peo-

ple in the audience, was not quite full, and that notwithstanding the tremendous applause there was only one review
of the concert, and that only a short one. It is difficult to explain the coolness of this reception; one can only assume that
Chopin's talent for avoiding publicity was helped by the
growing political tension which absorbed the thoughts of the
inhabitants of Warsaw.

Chopin was convinced that the theater had been full, and
was probably relieved by the silence in the press. He was by
now busy with the preparations for his departure, and had to
pay a great many farewell calls on friends and acquaintances,
many of whom gave him letters of introduction to friends and
relatives in Vienna.

On October 25 he called on Konstancja in order to take his
leave. She wrote a little verse into his album, which ended
with the lines:

> *Others may value and reward you more*
> *But they can never love you more than we do.* * [38]

At some stage during the previous weeks, Chopin had at last
given her some intimation of his feelings. This had apparently
met with a good reception, although it is impossible to tell
how serious or superficial were the feelings expressed on either side. Rings were exchanged and Chopin was allowed to
write to her, through the discreet agency of Jan Matuszynski.

On the evening of November 1 a group of friends organized a farewell dinner attended by Nicolas Chopin, Zywny,
Magnuszewski, Fontana, and others. They sang, danced, and
played late into the night, after which the whole group
walked Chopin back to his house. The next morning he made
his last farewells while Ludwika finished copying some of the
scores he was taking, and in the afternoon the family accompanied him to the coaching station. It must have been a moving scene, for neither the frightened young man nor his

---

* At some later date Chopin wrote in in pencil: "Oh yes they can!"

worried family knew how long he would be away or how he would fare alone in the world.

The coach trundled away through the dingy western suburb of Wola, but was stopped just after passing the city gates. It was surrounded by a group of men, who turned out to be Elsner with a small male choir. They proceeded to intone, to the accompaniment of a guitar, a cantata which the old man had composed for the occasion. It exhorted Chopin to remember his land, and to keep its harmonies in his soul wherever he might find himself. There was something prophetic both in the words and in the emotion with which Elsner embraced his pupil, as though he never expected to see him again. After the last tearful embrace, Chopin climbed back into the coach, which rolled away, bearing him off from his native land forever.

5

Vienna

Chopin did not remain on his own for long. At Kalisz, the first halt in his journey, he met Tytus, with whom he traveled on to Breslau. In this company, Chopin forgot the sorrows of leave-taking and his spirits rose; they spent a pleasant four days in the city. One afternoon they wandered idly into the Merchants' Hall to find a rehearsal of the evening's concert in progress. During a break, Chopin sat down at the piano and started showing off. A local pianist who was billed to play at the concert heard this and immediately renounced his role in terror, with the result that the unsuspecting and somewhat baffled public were that evening treated not to the Moscheles concerto advertised, but to Chopin playing two movements of his E minor concerto as a solo.

From Breslau they traveled to Dresden, which Chopin knew already. He revisited the famous art gallery, its main attraction for him. "There are pictures there at the sight of which I hear music," he wrote to his parents.[1] Chopin liked the beautiful eighteenth-century city, which had a large Polish colony surviving from the days when Poland and Saxony had been united under one crown, but he was less keen on the traditional form of transport, the sedan chair, which made him feel very foolish as he was carried to a dinner or soirée.

Chopin called on the principal musical figures of Dresden. Some of these suggested that he give a concert before moving on, but he refused. A concert in Dresden would have earned him some money and would certainly not have done his reputation any harm, but he was eager to hurry on to Vienna. He was in such a sanguine frame of mind that he thought it a waste of time to start giving concerts in what he regarded as slightly provincial towns. He felt that he knew Vienna, and that Vienna already knew and valued him, and it was in a mood of exhilaration and self-confidence that he arrived there on November 22. "How happy I am to have reached Vienna, where I shall make so many interesting and useful acquaintances, and where I may even fall in love!" he wrote to Matuszynski the moment he and Tytus had settled into their rooms at the Stadt London Hotel.[2] That evening they went off to the opera to see Rossini's *Otello*, eying the girls in the street on the way (although Chopin did not fail to insert a pious reference to Konstancja into his letter to the go-between Matuszynski).

On the morning after his arrival, he was paid the greatest possible compliment; Hummel hurried over to the hotel to call on him. Such a mark of respect from the most eminent composer left in what was still the capital of music could not have failed to confirm Chopin's greatest expectations. But these were a little clouded later that morning by the publisher Haslinger, whom Chopin hastened to call on. Haslinger had probably lost money on the *La ci darem* Variations, and had therefore not published the C minor sonata (opus 4) or the variations that Chopin had left with him on his previous visit. He declared that he had no intention of giving Chopin any money for the two concertos he had brought him. He did intimate that he would consider publishing one of them if

Chopin let him have the copyright for nothing, but Chopin was determined not to let himself be exploited, and, as he put it: "From now on it's: 'Pay up, Animal!' "[3] He was growing wary of the "crooks and Jews" who stood between him and making money, and decided to be intransigent on this point, something he felt he could afford to do with his reputation and contacts in Vienna.

After a few days Chopin and Tytus moved to a cheaper hotel while they waited for the lodgings they had found to become vacant. These were occupied by an English admiral "with great whiskers and a bony face," but as Chopin wrote to his parents: "An Admiral! Yes, but I shall be held in admiration, so the lodgings will lose nothing in the change!"[4]

The three spacious rooms were "beautifully, luxuriously and elegantly furnished," the rent was low, and the landlady, a pretty young widow who professed a love of Poles and contempt for Austrians and Germans, had been to Warsaw and heard of Chopin. But it was the location of the apartment, on the third floor of a house in Kohlmarkt Street, which delighted the two young men. As Chopin pointed out to his parents, it was "right in the centre of town, with a wonderful promenade below, Artaria on the left, Mechetti and Haslinger* on the right, and the opera just behind—what else could one possibly need?"[5] This was important to him; he felt that this would be the base from which he could plan his stay in Vienna. Graf, the piano maker to whose shop he had been going every afternoon in order to "loosen [his] fingers after the journey,"[6] had promised to move an instrument into the lodgings free of charge, and this would enable Chopin to invite people to come and listen to him.

Chopin's principal preoccupation was to arrange a concert. After calling on Haslinger, his first visits were to musicians and people who might help him in this purpose. He looked up Nidecki, who had decided to settle in Vienna perma-

* All three were musical publishers.

nently, and the composer Czerny, who was in a tremendously
good mood, having just finished writing out "an overture for
eight pianos and sixteen players."[7] Old Würfel, who was now
bedridden with tuberculosis, was extremely cordial and immediately started talking of a concert, of where it should be held
and which of the two concertos Chopin should play. Würfel
was categorical that Chopin should under no circumstances
perform free on this visit, advice which was seconded by
Count Hussarzewski and others who promised to help arrange the event.

One of the most prominent among the latter was a new acquaintance, Dr. Malfatti, the imperial physician and formerly
Beethoven's great friend, who held a somewhat unusual position both at court and in Viennese society. Chopin had arrived with a letter of introduction to the doctor's wife, a Polish countess, and was greeted and embraced "like a member
of the family."[8] The doctor promised to introduce him to the
most important musical personages and to arrange a concert
for him at court, which was not immediately possible since it
was in mourning at the recent death of the King of Naples.

"I shall be giving a concert, but where, when and how, I
still cannot say,"[9] Chopin wrote home at the end of his first
week, which "flew by" amid the pleasures of Vienna. The future augured well, and he was able to enjoy the luxury of living in his own rooms, of eating out in the restaurants Mozart
and Beethoven had frequented, of spending his days entirely
as he wished, and above all of going to the opera almost every
evening. This was one drain on his pocket he certainly did
not regret, and during the first week he went five times, three
of them to operas he did not know—Mozart's *Clemenza di
Tito*, Auber's *Fra Diavolo*, and Rossini's *Wilhelm Tell*. He
found the standard of singing just as high as in the previous
year, and what was most welcome to him was the continual
change of program, which meant that he could rapidly improve his education in this field.

Chopin was suffering from a cold, or "swollen nose," as he put it, which is why he did not immediately visit the grander ladies to whom he had introductions. As soon as the ailment had subsided, however, he began to make up for lost time, and called on Countess Rzewuska, where he expected to meet "the cream of Viennese society" and several other Polish ladies married to Austrians. He also delivered his most important letter of introduction: from Grand Duke Constantin to Countess Tatischeff, the wife of the Russian Ambassador. It was while he was awaiting her pleasure to receive him that, on December 5, news arrived from Warsaw which radically altered Chopin's and Tytus's position.

On November 29 revolution had broken out in the Polish capital. The Grand Duke had narrowly escaped being assassinated in his bed, while the Russian troops in the city were disarmed or ejected. Although the reports were far from clear, both Chopin and Tytus were well aware of what lay behind them and of what lay ahead, namely armed conflict with Russia. After emotional deliberations lasting all night, Tytus prepared to return to Warsaw and Chopin was prevailed upon to remain in Vienna.[10] The idyllic way of life came to an end. "After Tytus left, too much suddenly fell on my shoulders," he complained.[11]

It was not just the absence of Tytus and the anxiety he felt for his family that turned Chopin's stay in Vienna rather sour; he found himself coming into conflict with Viennese society as a result of his growing emotional involvement with the Polish cause. As far as Vienna was concerned, from Metternich down, this was a revolution against the established system, and it was feared and disapproved of as much as the French Revolution had been, in spite of the fact that after a few weeks it was headed by Prince Adam Czartoryski and all the most respectable aristocrats in Poland. Even in the cheap Trattoria where he sometimes had dinner, Chopin overheard remarks such as "God made a mistake in creating the Poles" and "Nothing worthwhile has ever come out of Poland,"[12] which he took as a personal as well as a national insult.

For him there was no question of choice. Malfatti tried to persuade him that the artist should be cosmopolitan and ignore national or political issues, but Chopin merely replied that in that case he must be a very poor artist. He had never taken any serious interest in either issue before, but now that everyone he knew and respected in Warsaw was engaged in a fight for survival, in which defeat would entail annihilation of the world he had grown up in, he felt personally involved.

As a result, he never went near the Russian Embassy, wrote to his parents telling them to sell the diamond ring he had been given by Tsar Alexander, acquired shirt studs with Polish eagles on them, and brandished handkerchiefs embroidered with Polish motifs. More to the point, he spent much of his time with other nationalist Poles in Vienna, who were either on various diplomatic or fund-raising missions from Warsaw or else returning from foreign travel to join the Polish ranks. Most of these were unable to enter Poland, since the Austrian authorities had closed the border, and they formed a rowdy element in Vienna, demonstrating and taking particular pleasure in jeering at other Poles who were lying low in the city to keep out of trouble.

The Austrian police and the Russian agents kept a close watch on the comings and goings of the Poles in Vienna, and their activities and sympathies were no secret. The result of all this was that Chopin never met "the cream of Viennese Society" at Countess Rzewuska's or anywhere else (her mother having been guillotined in 1793, her sympathies were firmly ranged on the side of law and order). In fact, during his eight-month sojourn in Vienna, Chopin did not once play in an aristocratic gathering; all the Lichnowskys and Schwarzenbergs who were so kind to him on his previous visit do not figure in his life at all during this one. No more is heard, either, of Malfatti's promises to arrange an appearance at court.

Chopin's own statements on the subject do not survive, since the original letters have been destroyed, while the known extracts were published in Poland at a time when Russian censorship was as strict as ever. It is therefore impossible to tell how far this situation was intentionally provoked by himself and to what extent he was simply a victim of general ill-will.

After the departure of Tytus, Chopin could no longer afford to keep up the spacious apartment on his own, so he sublet it to an English family, thereby making a sizable profit, and moved up one floor in the same building. Here he was unexpectedly joined by his friend Romuald Hube, who had returned from Italy (the trip on which Chopin had hoped to accompany him) and was stuck in Vienna, having tried and failed to cross the Polish frontier. Although his presence must have been of some comfort, Hube was not a close friend like Tytus, and the two led fairly independent lives, he studying and arranging the notes he had made on his tour, Chopin "always practicing on the piano, usually reworking phrases, and sometimes improvising."[13]

The new apartment was no garret, as Chopin hastened to assure his parents; his room was large and handsome, with three windows and plenty of mirrors. It contained only a bed, a large table, and the piano. It was also quiet and suited his more subdued mood perfectly. "How happy I am in this room!" he wrote to them. "Before me I see a roof, beneath me I see pygmies whom I tower above. I am at my happiest when, having played long on Graf's wonderful piano, I go to bed clutching your letters, and then dream only of you . . ."[14]

His way of life was pleasant, if a little uneventful. He was wakened every morning by "an insufferably stupid servant,"[15] with the morning coffee, which was often drunk cold, since his first action on getting out of bed was to sit down at the piano and play, sometimes for an hour or more. At nine o'clock his German teacher would call, and when the lesson was over other visitors would turn up. Nidecki used to drop in almost every morning to see what Chopin had written or to practice a little with him, and Hummel's son, who was an artist, used to come and draw him. At midday Chopin would at last leave his dressing gown and get dressed to go out. After a walk on the Glacis (once part of the city fortifications, then an elegant promenade) with one or other of his friends, he would either go out to lunch at someone's house or accompany some of his friends to one of the eating houses frequented by students, and thence to one of the more fashionable *Kaffeehäuser*. The afternoon, or what was left of it, was spent paying calls and having tea at someone's house, and at dusk Chopin would come home to dress for the evening. There was usually a dinner, soirée, or concert of some description for him to attend, but he was always back at his lodgings not later than midnight to "play, weep, read, ponder, laugh, go to bed, put out the candle, and dream of home."[16]

Christmas brought with it a greater sense of loneliness as well as the unpleasant realization that after a whole month in Vienna he had achieved precisely nothing and had lost his impetus. Musical success seemed much further away now than it had immediately after his arrival, and his letters home are listless and depressed. His letters to Jan Matuszynski, the only others which survive from this period, are heavy with introspection and self-pity. The passage describing his visit to St. Stephen's Cathedral on Christmas Eve is typical:

> I went in. There was still nobody about . . . I stood at the foot of a gothic pillar, in the darkest corner. I cannot describe the magnificence, the sheer dimensions of those great vaults. It was quiet—only now and again the steps of a sacristan lighting lamps somewhere in the depths of this temple would break into my reverie. Graves behind me, graves beneath me . . . I only needed a grave over my head . . . A gloomy harmony haunted me . . . I felt more vividly than ever my complete isolation . . .[17]

The letter meanders on, evoking deliciously romantic vi-

sions of Chopin walking alone through the busy streets of
Vienna, wrapped in his cloak and his loneliness, or returning
home to "weep out an adagio" on his piano, and dwells on his
general dissatisfaction with everything:

> Were it not for my father, to whom I should be a burden, I
> would return [to Warsaw] immediately. I curse the day I left
> . . . I am bored to death by all the dinners, soirées, balls and
> concerts which fill my life; it is so melancholy, vacant and
> dreary . . . I cannot do what I please, but instead have to
> dress up, pull on my stockings and brush my hair; in the
> drawing rooms I have to affect serenity, but when I come
> home I thunder away on my piano.[18]

Such passages have helped to create the image of misery
which hangs over Chopin's whole stay in Vienna, but it is ridiculous to take them at face value. The moments of self-pity,
in which the theme of suicide crops up more than once, are
followed by humorous anecdotes. The gloomy description of
the cathedral makes way for the story of the newly established
French sausage maker whose trays of offal produce a shudder
of dread in the Viennese, who suspect they are looking at the
remains of French aristocrats guillotined during the July Revolution. Even in his fits of depression, Chopin cannot resist
boasting of all the "balls and soirées" he "has to go to." He
was clearly anxious about events in Poland, lonely without his
family around him, and frustrated by his lack of success and
direction, so it is hardly surprising that he felt sorry for himself. Since he was twenty years old, he naturally called on images of love, death, and alienation to explain his predicament.

Another reason for these somber outpourings was that Jan
Matuszynski, his messenger to Konstancja, was supposed to
read to her passages from Chopin's letters as well as pass on
notes for her. This certainly accounts for much of the lyricism
and lines such as: "while I still have life in me . . . until my
very death . . . nay, even after my death, my ashes will strew
themselves at her feet . . ."[19] and exclamations like, "I have

not enjoyed a single moment since I arrived in Vienna!"[20] which was patently not true.

Tytus's role as protector and adviser was soon filled by "wonderful Doctor Malfatti," who took an avuncular interest in the young pianist. He looked after Chopin's health and even managed to "fatten him up," which was quite an achievement. His door was always open to the young man, and he would even have Polish dishes served at dinner, in an attempt to make him feel at home. Various other Polish households in the city vied with each other to care for Chopin, who now affected great contempt for "damned Prussians" (which was supposed to denote all Germanic people). His hankering after things Polish was not free of mawkish self-pity, nor indeed of affectation:

> Everything makes me sigh and long for home, for those delicious moments I failed to value fully . . . The people here are nothing to me; they are kind, but not out of kindness, only out of habit; everything they do is flat, mediocre, too ordered. And that dismays me . . .[21]

Chopin's disenchantment with Vienna was not limited to the social or emotional aspects. He had come as a pilgrim to the city of Mozart, Haydn, and Beethoven, only to find musical stagnation and vulgarity. Old musicians like Hummel shook their heads and told him Vienna was no longer what it had been, and he could not help but agree. The giants of the moment were Johann Strauss the elder, Lanner, and Czerny, and their success obscured all other music. "Here they call waltzes *works*, and Strauss and Lanner who play dance-music are called *Kapellmeisters!*" Chopin wrote to Elsner indignantly.[22] To the disciple of Bach and Mozart, the musical scene presented a dismal appearance:

> Among the many amusements in Vienna, the favorite is the soirée at certain inns where Strauss or Lanner play waltzes during dinner. They are frantically applauded after each

waltz, and if they play a potpourri of airs from opera, dances
and songs, the audience gets completely carried away. Which
all goes to show how the taste of the Viennese public has
declined.[23]

To this bad taste can be ascribed some of the responsibility
for Chopin's lack of success, for although Haslinger appreciated his talent and Mechetti thought his work brilliant, neither could afford to publish works which would not sell.
Chopin's would not, for they were too difficult and too cerebral for the Viennese ladies to play, while his lack of patronage and publicity did not encourage other musicians to play
them. Chopin's success on his previous visit had not made
any great impact, since his concerts had taken place during
the off season, and the new manager of the Karntnerthor was
not interested. To make matters worse, Chopin, with his reticent manner and quiet playing, was completely outshone by a
new star who had appeared on the scene—Sigismund Thalberg.

Thalberg did enjoy high patronage, being the illegitimate
son of Count Dietrichstein, the Emperor's director of music.
More important, he had a strong, controlled, and monumen-
tal style of playing. It was said of him that if he were dragged
from his bed in the middle of the night and ordered to play,
there would not be a single note out of place, so impeccable
was his style. He rapidly achieved fame and was generally considered to be the finest pianist in Europe until Liszt robbed
him of that title. Chopin liked neither Thalberg nor his playing, nor, to be just, his competition, judging by the bitterness
lurking behind his words:

> He plays remarkably, but not to my taste. He's younger than
> me, and the ladies like him. He plays potpourris of airs from
> the Mute [Auber's opera *The Mute of Portici*], gives *pianos*
> with the pedal and not the hand, takes tenths like I take oc-
> taves, wears diamond shirt-studs . . .[24]

The Viennese public had become sated with pianists, great numbers of whom had visited the city in the last months, and, having discovered Thalberg, was prepared to dismiss the rest out of hand. In this situation the little-known Chopin would have needed a great deal of help to launch himself. As this was not forthcoming, he did not stand a chance. By the time Christmas came, he realized that he was not going to be able to give a concert in the near future, but he did not despair and hoped that at some stage during the spring he would have his opportunity. He was right, although the occasion could hardly be called a success.

On April 4 he took part in a concert given by the singer Madame Garcia-Vestris, and appeared at the bottom of the list of performers simply as "Herr Chopin—pianist." He played his E minor concerto arranged as a piano solo and passed completely unnoticed. His only other public appearance in Vienna took place on June 11, when he played the same piece. At least this time he was mentioned in the press, which called him a "sincere worshipper of true art" and made a polite remark about his new concerto.[25] Chopin was not really disappointed, for he had long before this shed his sanguine hopes of a couple of triumphal months in Vienna. As he wrote in his diary before the second concert: "I feel so indifferent about it that I would not care if it never took place . . ."[26]

Uncertainty as to the future course of events in Poland clearly played its part in keeping Chopin in Vienna for eight months instead of the intended two, as did the rumors of revolution and disturbances in other European countries. But it was principally Chopin's innate inability to make up his mind on his own which kept him hanging about in the Austrian capital. When it became clear that his original plan of a successful two months there had come to nothing, he wrote to his parents, asking: "Shall I go to Italy immediately, or wait a little longer? Please write and tell me what I should do."[27]

Nicolas Chopin refused to make up his son's mind for him, with the result that after a few weeks the latter was writing to Matuszynski:

> But should I leave? My parents tell me to make up my own mind, but I am afraid to. Should I go to Paris? The people here advise me to wait a little longer. Should I come back? Should I stay here? Should I kill myself? Should I stop writing letters to you? *You* tell me what to do![28]

As nobody told him what to do, Chopin hung on in Vienna aimlessly but not entirely fruitlessly. He availed himself of every opportunity to hear a new work or a new musician, and went to the opera every time the program changed. He was as happy as any young Romantic when, for instance, Rossini's new production, *The Siege of Corinth*, came on in Vienna, particularly as the standard of singing was very high. As for the other musicians in the city, his contact with them was not as close as it might have been, particularly in the case of the older ones.

Czerny, like some of the other established Viennese musicians, had cooled markedly toward Chopin when he discovered that the latter wished to break in on the musical scene. It had been easy enough in the previous year to pat the young amateur on the head, but now that he wanted to play at the professional musician in their preserve, they were no longer disposed to be helpful. This was not so with some of the younger musicians whom Chopin met. Even Thalberg was cordial, although there was an obvious rivalry between them. But there were two musicians whose acquaintance Chopin found particularly rewarding. One was Joseph Merk, the first cellist in the Imperial Orchestra, and teacher at the Vienna Conservatoire, with whom Chopin spent much time playing duets. Chopin had a particular affection for the cello, the only instrument aside from the piano for which he wrote some memorable music, and with Merk's help he composed an Introduction to the Polonaise for Cello and Piano he had written at Antonin in 1829. They were published together later that year by Mechetti as opus 3, dedicated to Merk.

The other friend Chopin made at this time was the brilliant young violinist Josef Slavik, four years Chopin's senior and already a great virtuoso. "Apart from Paganini, I have never heard anything like it," wrote Chopin "—ninety-six staccato notes with one stroke of the bow; incredible!"[29] Chopin's high opinion of his new friend was shared by Paganini himself, and had Slavik not died two years later, he would have made a great name for himself. Chopin and Slavik spent many afternoons playing together, and finally decided to write a set of variations for piano and violin, and chose a theme from Beethoven. Chopin is known to have been working on the *Adagio* at one moment, but no trace of such a work survives, and the passages he did write were probably incorporated into later works.

As a whole, Chopin's output during the Vienna period is insubstantial and somewhat erratic. This was largely due to his lack of conviction as to what he should be writing. On the one hand he tried to pander to the Viennese taste by writing the *Valse Brillante* (opus 18), the Five Mazurkas (opus 7), and other pieces which are pretty, easy to play, and were supposed to be danced to. They did not in fact elicit any enthusiasm from the publishers and were not printed until much later. On the other hand, he struggled on with several works in the grand style; his third piano concerto, a concerto for two pianos and orchestra, the variations for piano and violin, and the *Grande Polonaise Brillante* (opus 22), the last piece he ever wrote for the orchestra. But he was finding the work on these, particularly on the concertos, increasingly taxing and unrewarding. While his early works for piano and orchestra, like the *La ci darem* Variations or the *Krakowiak* Rondo, reveal that Chopin was at least interested in the part the orchestra could play, and not averse to trying out some of its

possibilities, the two piano concertos, written in 1829 and
1830 respectively, tell a different story. In these, Hummel's
influence is more evident than ever, and the role of the orchestra is very limited. It is used with less originality than in
the earlier works, and rarely intrudes on the attention of the
listener, which is naturally concentrated on the piano part.
The orchestra in these concertos is little more than a vehicle
used to carry the piano. How inessential this vehicle was can
be gauged from the fact that Chopin usually played the concertos as piano solos. This was accepted practice, and made
sense with his concertos, as it did for those of Hummel or
Kalkbrenner. But it makes a good deal less sense with Beethoven's, Liszt's or Schumann's, in which the orchestra is an in-
tegral part of the whole.

Chopin was losing interest in writing for the orchestra, not
so much because he could not do so successfully, as because
he felt it was a useless garnishing which tended to impinge on
the piano part. This growing feeling coincided with a greater
concentration on the instrument itself. While he struggled
unsuccessfully to compose his third concerto, he was also
working on his first set of Études, and on two works which
belong among his greatest; the Scherzo in B minor (opus 20)
and the Ballade in G minor (opus 23), the Ballade being the
first piece he wrote in this form, his own invention. Both of
these announce Chopin's ultimate aim; to achieve depth of
sound and feeling with a single and self-sufficient instrument.
But although he never got beyond the first movement of his
third concerto, this did not correspond to any major decision
on his part, and he still saw himself as having to follow the
accepted tradition of composing grand works.

This was also being demanded of him from another quarter. Now that most of his friends, such as Matuszynski,
Tytus, and Fontana, had taken the field with the Polish army,
Chopin felt more cut off than ever, and longed to unite himself with them at least in spirit. "Oh, why can I not be with

you, why can I not at least be your drummer-boy!!!" he wrote
to Matuszynski after Christmas.[30] On another occasion, he
spoke of trying "somehow to grasp and capture those songs
whose shattered echoes still drift here and there on the banks
of the Danube—the songs that John's army sang."[31] (A reference to John Sobieski's relief of Vienna in 1683.) He did not
quite know how to realize this on the appropriate scale, and
ended up by setting more of Witwicki's poems to music.
Some of his earlier songs had achieved enormous popularity,
and were sung everywhere, including the battlefield. In a letter expressing his gratitude, Witwicki suggested that Chopin
write a national opera, explaining:

> The mountains, forests, waters and meadows have their own
> inner voice, though not every soul can hear it. I am con-
> vinced that a Slav opera, conceived by a true talent, by a
> composer who thinks and feels, will one day rise in the musi-
> cal world like a brilliant new sun.[32]

Witwicki was not the only one to have had this idea. The
nationalists could see the propaganda value of an opera based
on some theme from Polish history being staged in European
capitals, for opera at that time attracted a larger and broader
audience than any other form of entertainment. On the other
hand, there were those, like Elsner, who believed that, opera
being regarded as the most complete musical form, Chopin
could never achieve the renown he deserved until he had written one. Chopin himself saw the justice of this view and had
almost certainly assumed, during his last years in Poland, that
he would eventually write one. He was not averse to discussing the idea, and his godfather, Count Skarbek, had written a
couple of rough librettos for him to think about.

The reality of this idea began to recede along with Chopin's loss of interest in orchestration, but was not completely
killed until a little later. To begin with, it was principally
Chopin's indolence and horror at the magnitude of the un-

dertaking that kept him from writing something that would almost certainly have been damaging to his reputation. As it was, he did exactly what Witwicki advised, but with the piano as sole medium. As he drew further away from his native land, he strove more and more to recapture its essence and that of his people in his work.

By mid-May, Chopin had finally decided to continue his tour. Italy being still troubled by revolutions, Paris seemed the obvious next stop. The situation in Poland was encouraging, as the Poles had won the first round of large-scale military operations, and he no longer needed to be anxious about his family. Having made a firm decision to leave Vienna, however, he found himself beset by a multitude of difficulties. Unable to cope with the prospect of a journey on his own, Chopin had found himself a traveling companion, a young man called Kumelski, but the latter promptly fell ill and the departure was delayed by several weeks. When Kumelski had recovered, Chopin was informed by the Vienna police that his passport had been mislaid and that he must obtain a new one from the Russian Embassy (he was still technically a Russian subject, and passports, both internal and external, were already obligatory in that state). After a few more weeks, the police found his original passport, but the Russian Embassy would not endorse it for travel to Paris, which was considered a hotbed of revolutionary activity. His friends advised him to pretend that he was in fact on his way to London, and only aimed to pass through Paris, and this inclined the Russians to allow him to go. Having successfully negotiated the Russian bureaucracy, the two friends now came up against the Austrian, for there was a cholera epidemic in Vienna, and health certificates were required in order to leave the capital.

Chopin took advantage of these delays to see the remaining sights and attractions of Vienna. With Nidecki and Kumelski he went to the pleasure gardens, where, although he himself enjoyed rushing down a terrifying slope in a toboggan, he was appalled to see how "healthy and refined people amuse themselves and kill serious thought within themselves."[33] He also went on a pilgrimage to the Kahlenberg Heights, where King John Sobieski had pitched camp and served at mass before riding down to do battle with the Turks in 1683. In a charmingly *époque* gesture, he plucked a leaf from the spot and sent it to his sister Izabela for her album.

On another occasion, Chopin went to see the famous collection of musical manuscripts in the Imperial Library, where he had a pleasant surprise:

> Imagine my amazement when among the newer manuscripts I saw a box labeled CHOPIN. It was beautifully bound and looked quite thick. I could not remember ever having heard of another Chopin, but there was a Champin, so I assumed they had just misspelled his name. I pulled it out and looked; it was my handwriting all right—Haslinger had apparently donated the manuscript of my Variations to the Imperial Library. I thought to myself: "What a lot of rubbish you do keep here."[34]

The delays in leaving Vienna, and the attendant inactivity, accentuated his sense of aimlessness and impotence. Inactivity was, throughout his life, Chopin's worst enemy, and his nervous disposition would make up for it by an almost feverish changeability of mood. This can be detected from entries in his diary, and he explains it in a letter to his parents:

> I don't lack anything—except perhaps a little more life, more spirit; I feel weary, and then sometimes I feel as merry as I used to at home. When I feel sad I usually go to Mrs. Szaszek's, where I always find several Polish ladies whose sincere and comforting words inevitably cheer me up so much that I then start mimicking Austrian generals—this is my new act. You haven't seen it yet, but those who do always fall about laughing. But then again there are days when you cannot get through to me or squeeze a word out of me. On those days I

spend 30 *Kreuzers* on going to Heitzing or some such place in
order to distract myself. I have grown side-whiskers on the
right, and they're nice and bushy. You don't need them on
the left, as you always have the audience on your right.[35]

The memory of Konstancja kept cropping up in his
thoughts too, even on occasions like Malfatti's party, in his
beautiful summer residence in the hills overlooking the city,
when Chopin and others played and sang in the huge mir-
rored drawing room with its french windows open onto the
terrace and the smell of orange blossoms in the warm night
air. "Her image is continually before my eyes," he wrote in
his diary, adding that "sometimes I think I no longer love
her, but at the same time I cannot get her out of my head."[36]
The ideal loomed just as large at a distance, even though he
clearly found it difficult to love the person, and it was now
being invested with the aura of things past. Chopin was still
a child in many ways, and showed great reluctance to grow
up; he turned his twentieth birthday into a dramatic moment
and harked back to all the things which he felt he had lost ir-
retrievably.

On July 20, Chopin and Kumelski finally left Vienna, traveling through Linz to Salzburg, where they of course visited
Mozart's birthplace with the utmost piety. In Munich, their
next stop, Chopin found that the money his father had promised to forward had not arrived, and as a result he was obliged
to break his journey for a month. He soon made the acquaintance of the musicians in the city, who persuaded him
to give a concert. He was no longer in the euphoric mood
that had caused him to refuse in Dresden, and he willingly
agreed. The event took place in the Philharmonic Society
Hall on August 28, Chopin playing his E minor concerto and
the ever-popular Fantasia on Polish Airs. Both were well received. The review of the concert which appeared in the local
musical gazette was effusive on the subject of his "excellent

Justyna and Nicolas Chopin. A drawing after A. Miroszewski.

Ludwika Chopin by A. Miroszewski.

Left, Izabela Chopin.

Below, Emilia Chopin.

Fryderyk Chopin, painted by A. Miroszewski in 1829.

Jozef Elsner.

Adalbert Zywny, Chopin's first piano teacher, by A. Miroszewski.

Caricatures drawn by the young Chopin.

The Warsaw Lyceum in 1824. The Chopin family lived in the building on the left from 1817 to 1827. Chopin himself would have worn a uniform similar to that seen on the boys in the picture.

Left,
Konstancja Gladkowska.
A portrait painted some ten
years after the time Chopin
was infatuated
with her.

Below,
Tytus Woyciechowski.
A photograph taken
in the 1870s.

This painting by Michal Stachowicz depicts a harvest festival in front of a typical Polish manor house in 1821. The house at Szafarnia would have been very similar.

Above,
Friedrich Kalkbrenner.
Lithograph by Vigneron.
Courtesy Radio Times
Hulton Picture Library.

Right,
Franz Liszt.
Daguerreotype of 1841.
Courtesy Radio Times
Hulton Picture Library.

virtuosity," his "developed technique" and "charming delicacy of execution," and praised the works themselves highly.[37]

Chopin's next stop was Stuttgart, where he spent a couple
of weeks, alone, since Kumelski had stayed in Munich. He
was in a state of morbid depression, as the very long entries in
his diary reveal:

> Strange! This bed I am about to lie on has probably served
> more than one dying person, and yet that does not worry me.
> Perhaps more than one corpse has lain on it—and for many
> days? But what makes me any better than a corpse? Like a
> corpse, I have no news of my father, mother, sisters, of Tytus!
> Nor do corpses have lovers! Corpses are pale like me, cold
> like my feelings. A corpse has ceased living, and I have lived
> enough . . . Why does one go on living this miserable
> life? . . .[38]

Chopin reviews his whole life, pointing to its worthlessness
and to the fact that, cut off from everything dear to him, it
made no sense. There is less affectation here than in some of
his letters from Vienna, and the feelings expressed have a genuine ring to them. The twenty-year-old composer felt lost and
anxious over his future, which must have seemed more uncer-
tain than ever. He was now completely alone and further
from home than he had ever been. Not the least of his wor-
ries was the fact that, while philandering in the company of
Kumelski, he had caught a venereal disease.[39] To the young
man who still wanted to dream of his "ideal" this must have
been a source of great humiliation. If he had invested his
twentieth birthday with such significance, he can hardly have
seen this new development as anything but a watershed in his
existence.

But he did not have much time to indulge his own mis-
eries, as only a couple of days later he received news which
was to change his whole life—the Polish army had been completely defeated and Warsaw had fallen to General Pashkie-

vitch, a notoriously brutal character. In his diary Chopin wrote:

> I wrote the preceding pages without knowing that the enemy had already broken in—the suburbs are destroyed, burned down—Oh, Jas! Wilus probably died on the ramparts! I can see Marceli in chains! Sowinski, that kind old man, in the hands of those monsters!* Oh God! You exist! You exist and yet You do not punish! Have You not seen enough Russian crimes? Or perhaps—maybe You are a Russian Yourself! My poor father! My dearest! Perhaps he has nothing left to buy my mother bread with! Perhaps my sisters have succumbed to the fury of the Russian rabble! Pashkievitch, that dog from Mohilev, has stormed the capital of the first monarchs of Europe! The Russian is master of the world!? Oh, father, so this is your reward in old age! Mother, suffering, gentle mother, you watched your daughter die, and now the Russian marches in over her bones to come and oppress you! . . . Did they spare her grave? They trampled it and covered it with a thousand fresh corpses! They have burned the city! Oh, why could I not have killed at least one Russian! Oh, Tytus, Tytus! . . . What is happening to *her*, where is she?—unfortunate creature!—Perhaps she is in Russian hands? The Russians are pressing her, stifling, murdering, killing her! Oh my love, I am alone here, come to me,—I shall wipe away the tears and heal the wounds of the present with memories of the past . . . when there were no Russians . . . Perhaps I have no mother anymore, perhaps the Russians have killed her, murdered her . . . my sisters unconscious, yes, or struggling; my father in despair, helpless—no one left to pick up my dead mother. I am inactive, I sit here empty-handed, just groaning, suffering on the piano, in despair . . . and what next? God, God! Move the earth—may it swallow up the people of this century. May the cruelest tortures fall on the heads of the French, who would not come to our aid! . . .[40]

* Jas Matuszynski; Wilus (Wilhelm) Kolberg; Marceli Woyciechowski; General Sowinski, in whose house Chopin wrote the Fantasia on Polish Airs.

Having cursed the French, Chopin set off for Paris a few days later. He was to make a new home there which suited him better than Warsaw would have done, but the sense of loss sustained on that night in Stuttgart never left him. It came to embrace everything—home, country, family, friends, love and youth—and remained the fundamental inspiration for his music. As he had promised Konstancja, he would "heal the wounds of the present with memories of the past."

6

Paris

The Paris that Chopin saw for the first time in September 1831 was a formidable place. It was the largest and most modern city he had ever seen: its magnificent monuments, its elegant new streets and boulevards, and the gas lighting to be seen here and there made Vienna look like a market town in comparison. Paris was also striking by its diversity and animation. "Here you have the greatest luxury, the greatest squalor, the greatest virtue and the greatest vice—everywhere you look there are notices about ven. disease—you simply cannot imagine the shouting, the commotion, the bustle and the dirt; one could positively lose oneself in this anthill, and the nice thing is that nobody cares what anyone else does," Chopin wrote to Kumelski after a few days in the city.[1]

The revolution which in the previous year had swept the Bourbon Charles X off the throne and replaced him with the Orléanist Louis Philippe had been incomplete. Unrest continued to disturb the streets, fueled largely by the arrival of defeated revolutionaries from countries like Italy and Poland. Unlike Vienna, the Polish cause was ultrafashionable in Paris, and from the start Chopin met with good-will at every level.

Unlike Vienna, too, the city exuded a permissive atmosphere which shocked and delighted him. Apart from the bright lights, what struck him most were the whores who pursued him in the street, the chorus girls who were so keen on "duets" as he coyly put it, and the lady upstairs who suggested they share a fire on cold days. But, as he pointed out to Kumelski, he was prevented by his ailment from "tasting the forbidden fruit."[2]

The intellectual life of the French capital was as partisan as its politics, and as exotic as its manners. The progress of the Romantic revolution against the literary establishment was marked by violent battles, as the supporters of Victor Hugo and his opponents resorted to every physical as well as literary weapon at their disposal. As a result, the city drew people like a magnet from all over Europe, from Russian princesses bored by St. Petersburg and their husbands to left-wing intellectuals and artists in search of a congenial environment.

Chopin had taken rooms on the fourth floor of a house in the Boulevard Poissonière, a newly built-up area of the city. He soon got used to this part of Paris, and as with most things he got used to, he never strayed far from it over the next seventeen years. "You wouldn't believe what a nice apartment I have," he wrote to Kumelski; "a small room beautifully furnished in mahogany, a little balcony overlooking the boulevards, with a view stretching from Montmartre to the Panthéon and embracing this whole beautiful world."[3]

Although Chopin had brought with him only two letters of introduction, and those to musicians, he found French society far easier to penetrate than its Viennese counterpart. Strong links had always existed between Poland and France, and there had been many Poles living in Paris before 1830. Some, such as Countess Kissielev, a Potocka separated from her Russian husband, were well-known figures and kept salons frequented by some of the most interesting people in Paris. Others, such as the Komar family, with their three beautiful daughters, had left Poland just before the insurrection and had settled in Paris. Chopin had met them in Dresden, where he had been particularly struck by the beauty of one of the daughters, Delfina. She was married to Countess Kissielev's brother, Mieczyslaw Potocki, but lived away from him, and on her arrival in Paris began to lead a very independent life, receiving a great deal. Other Poles that Chopin found settled in Paris were those who, like Count Ludwik Plater and his family, had been sent on diplomatic missions by the insurgent government. They too received, and Chopin soon became a regular guest.

From September on, a stream of disbanded soldiers from the defeated Polish armies began to trickle steadily into the French capital, bringing welcome news that none of his family and few of his friends had suffered from the war. Chopin found himself reunited with such school friends as Kazimierz Wodzinski, and Conservatoire colleagues Antoni Orlowski and Julian Fontana. The latter soon left for London, where he hoped to make a living, but was to reappear in Paris a few years later and become one of Chopin's closest friends. The presence of these combined with the good-will and hospitality of the Parisians to make Chopin feel at home, and the sense of not belonging which had spoiled his stay in Vienna did not trouble him here.

But the greatest joy of being in Paris was musical. "I'm delighted with what I have found here," he wrote to Kumelski. "I have the best musicians and the best opera in the world."[4] It was true. Beethoven, Weber, and Schubert were dead, while the next great generation had as yet made no significant impact (Mendelssohn was twenty-two, Schumann and Chopin twenty-one, Liszt twenty, Verdi and Wagner seventeen), so the musical establishment of Paris, consisting as it did of a handful of eighty-year-old venerables like Cherubini (director of the Conservatoire), Paër, and Lesueur; such renowned opera composers as Auber and Herold; and above all, the two lions of the moment, Rossini and Meyerbeer, was indeed the most renowned in the world.

Paris also boasted the finest collection of performing musicians, and the three orchestras, of the Conservatoire, the Academy (Opera) and the Italian Opera, were magnificent by any standards. The singers at the two opera houses included such legendary names as La Pasta and La Malibran, and when he went to performances of Rossini operas under the baton of the composer himself, Chopin felt that he was hearing a different work from that he had heard in Vienna or Warsaw. The grandeur of the productions overcame his critical faculty, and when he saw the incredibly elaborate first production of Meyerbeer's *Robert le Diable*, with its cast of hundreds, its pyrotechnics and stage machinery, Chopin termed it a "masterpiece of the new school," and declared that "Meyerbeer has immortalized himself,"[5] strong words from someone as reserved in his praise as Chopin.

In the concert halls he heard the pianists Herz, Liszt, Osborne, and Hiller. The last made a particular impression on him. "A boy with immense talent, a pupil of Hummel's," he wrote to Tytus, "—something in the manner of Beethoven, but a man full of poetry, fire and soul."[6]

When he arrived in Paris, Chopin had only a letter from Elsner to Lesueur and one from Malfatti to Paër, the master of the royal music, but the musical world of the city was so tightly knit that within a couple of weeks he had met all the most prominent musicians, including Cherubini and Rossini, and the eminent pianist Kalkbrenner, whose works he had so often played in Warsaw. Chopin could not get over the impression that the pianist's playing made on him, as he wrote to Tytus: "You won't believe how anxious I was to hear Herz, Liszt, Hiller, etc., but they're all zeros next to Kalkbrenner. If Paganini is perfection itself, so is Kalkbrenner, but in a totally different way. It is difficult to describe his composure, his enchanting touch—unbelievable evenness and mastery are evident in every note of his—He is a giant who tramples underfoot all the Herzes and Czernys, and, by the same token, myself."[7]

Kalkbrenner listened while Chopin played through his E minor concerto, and he was impressed. He complimented him by saying that he played like Cramer with Field's touch, but declared that he "lacked method" and would never be able to play or compose properly until he had acquired this. He also put a red pencil through the manuscript of the *Adagio*, arguing that it was too long and repetitive. In spite of this, and of reservations on the part of others (the forty-five-year-old Kalkbrenner, who was dubbed "the mummy" by Heine, was very unpopular with most of the younger musicians in Paris), Chopin liked him, and persisted in thinking him "the first pianist in Europe—the only one whose shoelaces I am not worthy of untying."[8] Kalkbrenner himself was anxious to turn Chopin into his own idea of a superior pianist and agreed to teach him, suggesting a course of three years. Chopin was of half a mind to agree, although the length of time and the expense worried him, and he informed his parents of the plan. The Chopins were a touch puzzled by the idea that "little Frycek" still needed to learn to play, and Elsner, who was also informed, exploded. "I can say with pride and self-congratulation that I was able to give you a few lessons in harmony and composition," he wrote, but the idea that anyone thought they could *teach* Chopin to play the piano was to him preposterous. He saw in it a trick of Kalkbrenner's to eliminate competition. Elsner also took the opportunity to say that Chopin was too obsessed with the idea of being a pianist, which he considered to be only the first step in a musical career. He argued that Beethoven's and Mozart's piano concertos had been forgotten, while their operas lived on, and that Chopin should seek immortality through the operatic form and take his place between Mozart and Rossini.[9]

Chopin retorted that he could not possibly compete with anyone except as a pianist, and that he felt he still had much to learn. The sudden exposure to the musical magnificence and grandeur of Paris had terrified him and persuaded him to leave alone musical forms with which he was not familiar. He not only gave up all notion of writing an opera, but also stopped work on his third piano concerto, and instead concentrated on the Études and other works whose purpose was to explore the possibilities of the piano. Nevertheless, he decided against becoming Kalkbrenner's pupil. Far from taking this amiss, the latter volunteered to help Chopin get started on his own in Paris.

The question of a concert was made simpler by the fact that Kalkbrenner was a partner in the firm of Camille Pleyel, the son of a German composer, who had established himself as a piano maker in Paris and owned a small concert hall. Through Kalkbrenner's good offices the hall was booked for Christmas Day, and Chopin set about finding other musicians to take part in his debut. Kalkbrenner himself offered his services and those of one of his pupils, Osborne. Hiller, too, agreed to take part, while Norblin, the Polish cellist settled in Paris, managed to collect a quartet which included the famous violinist Baillot. Chopin also had to invite Sowinski, a Polish pianist of dubious worth living in Paris, out of politeness. But the real problem was the question of singers, because most of the better ones were on contract to one or other of the opera houses, and their managers were loath to let them sing in private concerts. Even with Rossini's intercession there was nothing to be done, and the concert had to be put off until January 15, 1832.

Although Christmas, the second he had spent away from home, brought with it a fit of depression, this was not the result of loneliness or frustration. His career was not exactly flourishing, but he was doing as well as could be expected in the circumstances. The continuing political disturbances and a cholera epidemic were keeping a large proportion of the aristocracy away from Paris, so there was not enough teaching work available for the plethora of pianists trying to survive in the capital. Chopin had played a couple of times at the British Embassy, and he already had a few pupils, mainly from the richer Polish families, such as the Komars, Platers, and Wolowskis, and from the English colony in Paris. The musical publisher Schlesinger had already asked him to write some variations on a theme from *Robert le Diable,* and Chopin had every reason to be confident that the concert would be a success. He had already made up his mind to spend at least three years in Paris and consequently asked Paër to obtain a permit for him (the French government was trying to resettle impecunious Polish refugees in distant and less inflammable areas of the country). As he wrote to Tytus: "One breathes sweetly here."[10]

What might have but had not depressed Chopin was the news of Konstancja's marriage. He remarked in a letter to Tytus: "It doesn't preclude a platonic love,"[11] which suggests that the thought of her had grown distant amid all the excitement of the last months. Nevertheless, the advent of Christmas brought on the usual access of self-pity and the old sense of alienation. To Tytus he wrote:

> I wish you were here—you cannot imagine how much I suffer from not being able to pour out my heart to anyone. You know how easily I make friends, how easily I can talk to anyone about blue mushrooms—well, I'm up to my ears in that sort of acquaintance, but I have nobody I can sigh with—when it comes to my feelings, I'm always in syncopation with others.[12]

Much of this might appear affected, but it is true that Chopin's apparent ease with people hid a great reserve and a fear of letting anyone approach too close. This had become noticeable during his last years in Warsaw, but when he left

Poland and found himself surrounded by foreigners (and the closest English word to the one he uses is "aliens"), he withdrew more and more into himself and became increasingly suspicious of any intimacy. Everyone was struck by this reserve, some seriously put off by it, and Liszt echoes the general feeling when he writes that "he was prepared to give anything, but never gave himself."[13] Liszt also notes that Chopin could hide his feelings under a cloak of composure and serenity: "Good-natured, affable, easy in all his relationships, even and pleasant-tempered, he hardly allowed one to suspect the secret convulsions which agitated him."[14]

Now that Tytus was no more than a distant correspondent, his role in Chopin's life as the sole confidant was being gradually usurped by another. This was the German pianist and composer Ferdinand Hiller, one year younger than Chopin but more experienced and stronger-willed. A sort of *amité amoureuse* sprang up between them. Hiller was fascinated by the figure of Chopin, "as supple as a snake and full of charm in his movements," as well as by his inimitable touch on the piano.[15]

He proved a useful acquaintance, for he helped Chopin to find his bearings in Paris, and it was he who introduced him to Felix Mendelssohn, who arrived in December on his way to England. Chopin and Mendelssohn liked each other, and the latter agreed to take part in the concert on January 15. The programs were already printed and everything ready when Kalkbrenner suddenly fell ill. The event was put off once again, but even while Chopin was waiting in exasperation for his Parisian debut, the first great mark of recognition as a composer was bestowed on him.

In July 1831, Robert Schumann, some three months Chopin's junior, had picked up the score of the *La ci darem* Variations in a Leipzig music store, intrigued by the unfamiliar composer's name. He spent two perplexing months trying to play the Variations and found them very difficult, but as he labored at it, his conviction grew that here was a work of extraordinary importance, both musically and, for lack of a better word, politically. This opus 2 by an unknown composer struck him as being not only brilliant but also exactly what modern music should be aiming at. He saw it as a piece of program music illustrating and dramatizing scenes from Mozart's opera, and he was so excited by his discovery that he wrote a review of the work for the *Allgemeine Muzikalische Zeitung* and sent another, longer version to the *Revue Musicale* in Paris. Chopin was shown the manuscript, which struck him as being utterly ridiculous:

> He says that in the second Variation Don Juan is running about with Leporello, that in the third he is embracing Zerlina while Mazetto is getting angry (the left hand)—and as for the fifth bar of the Adagio, he sees Don Juan kissing Zerlina on the D flat! Plater was wondering yesterday just what part of her anatomy her D flat might be, etc.! One can but marvel at the German's imagination . . .[16]

He begged Hiller to use his influence in order to prevent publication of the piece in the *Revue Musicale*. But the other version did appear in the December issue of the *Allgemeine Muzikalische Zeitung,* and whatever Chopin thought of it, it constituted an impressive accolade, with its famous verdict of: "Hats off, gentlemen—a genius!" One can of course understand Chopin's embarrassment at the rather pompous style of the piece, but it was a lot better than the review by a critic named Rellstab. Writing in a musical journal called *Iris,* the latter pointed to the "vandalism perpetrated on Mozart's melody" as typical of a work originating in "the primitive roots of the Slav nations."[17]

Chopin's Parisian debut finally took place on February 26 in the Salle Pleyel, with a brilliant program including Beethoven's quintet opus 29, played by some of the best musicians in the city, headed by the violinist Baillot; a couple of arias, not, it is true, by the best singers; Chopin played his F minor concerto as a solo and his *La ci darem* Variations; and ending up with a monstrous Polonaise for six pianos specially composed by Kalkbrenner and played by himself, Chopin, Hiller, Sowinski, Osborne, and Stamaty. Mendelssohn having dropped out at the last moment.

Opinions on the success of the event vary. Osborne claims that few Parisians turned up, but his evidence is not reliable,[18] and other sources provide a different picture. There were of course many Poles present, as well as a whole bevy of musicians; the two Herz brothers, Pixis, Mendelssohn, and the young Liszt, who applauded furiously. Chopin's friend Antoni Orlowski wrote home to his family: "Our dear Fryc has given a concert, which brought him a great reputation and some money. He has wiped the floor with all the pianists here; all Paris is stupefied."[19] Whether the whole of Paris was stupefied or not, the performance was well reviewed. Fétis wrote in the *Revue Musicale:*

> Here is a young man who, surrendering himself to his natural impressions and taking no model, has found, if not a complete renewal of piano music, at least a part of that which we have long sought in vain, namely an abundance of original ideas of a kind to be found nowhere else . . . I find in M. Chopin's inspirations the signs of a renewal of forms which may henceforth exercise a considerable influence upon this branch of the art.[20]

Chopin tried to follow up his success. In March he petitioned the Société des Concerts to allow him to give a concert in the Conservatoire Hall, where he would have the benefit of the excellent orchestra of that institution, but this was not a privilege easily granted, and Paris was full of more distinguished musicians than himself. As he put it to a Polish colleague who was thinking of trying his luck there, there were too many "virtuosos, charlatans, politics and cholera" in Paris.[21]

In May, Chopin took part in a charity concert in the Conservatoire Hall, but apart from the obvious fact that he did not get any money out of it, the joy of being able to perform the first movement of his F minor concerto with the best orchestra in Europe was diminished by the fact that his soft playing was drowned by it. The *Revue Musicale*'s critic could not hear the piano part and thought the orchestration poor. Depressing as this must have been to Chopin, it could not have been unexpected. He was by now well aware that his manner of playing was not suited to large halls; as he once told Liszt: "I am not fit to give concerts; the crowd intimidates me and I feel asphyxiated by its eager breath, paralyzed by its inquisitive stare, silenced by its alien faces; but you, you are made for it, for when you cannot captivate your audience, you at least have the power to stun it."[22] (The French word *assomer*, which was used here, has the secondary meaning of "bore them to death.")

This is the moment at which, according to the great majority of his biographers, the penniless and starving Chopin was preparing to leave for America, where he hoped to fare better. He was saved from such a drastic expedient by a dramatic chance encounter with Prince Walenty Radziwill, who allegedly took him to dinner at the house of an unspecified Rothschild, where the hungry composer was first allowed to eat his fill and then to play before the assembled company, which represented, of course, the cream of the French aristocracy. The effect of his playing was such, the story goes, that not only did Chopin go home with hundreds of bookings for lessons, but became overnight the darling of *le tout Paris*.

This is, of course, rubbish. Apart from the fact that Chopin's three closest friends in Paris at the time had no inkling of any plan to go to America or anywhere else and denied the Rothschild episode energetically,[23] it is easy to ascertain that he was not particularly hard up. During his first three months in Paris, he was subsisting on money received from his father, supplemented by the odd lesson or paid soirée. Then, in February, he made some money from the concert; with the hall free and the tickets at ten francs each, he would have made a handsome sum even if it had only been half full. On the morning after the concert, he was visited by a publisher who offered to buy everything Chopin had in his portfolio. He paid him cash down for the two concertos, the G minor Trio, the Grand Rondo, and the Fantasia on Polish Airs, and the down payment for so many works of that size could not have been less than substantial.[24]

It is possible, indeed likely, that at some stage in 1832 Chopin was asked to give lessons to the wife of Nathaniel de Rothschild, to whom he later dedicated one of his ballades. But where introductions to the world of the French aristocracy were concerned, Chopin was well provided for through his Polish connections. French society was made up of the old legitimist Bourbon aristocracy inhabiting the Faubourg St. Germain; the Napoleonic aristocracy; and the Orléanist world, made up partly of elements of the other two and partly of a new middle-class meritocracy. Though such families as the Potockis and Czartoryskis had links with the first of these groups dating back to the time of the *ancien régime*, many of the French émigrés, including Louis XVIII himself, spent most of their exile during the French Revolution and Empire in Poland. On the other hand, tens of thousands of Poles had fought in the Napoleonic armies. Dominik Dziewanowski, for instance, gave Chopin an introduction to the Duke of Montebello, who was the son of Marshal Lannes, with whom his uncle had served for many years. The present Orléanist establishment was still easier to penetrate, besides which one of Chopin's first pupils was having an affair with the heir to the throne, who was a frequent guest at her informal soirées, to which Chopin also went. Before he had been a year in Paris he was being invited on all sides, and not merely as a pianist, but as a guest. Berlioz recounts one anecdote illustrating how Chopin reacted to being treated as a tradesman:

> I remember how he let fly one evening at the master of a house where he had dined. Scarcely had the company taken coffee than the host, approaching Chopin, told him that the other guests who had never heard him hoped he would be so good as to sit down at the piano and play them some little trifle. Chopin excused himself from the first in a way which left not the slightest doubt as to his inclination. But when the other insisted in an almost offensive manner, like a man who knows the price and the purpose of the dinner he has just given, the artist cut the conversation short by saying with a weak and broken voice and a fit of coughing; "Ah, sir! . . . But I have only eaten very little!"[25]

It would be wrong, however, to think of Chopin as spending most or even a large proportion of his time with the French aristocracy. He was just as often to be found at the house of humbler music lovers, such as Thomas Albrecht, the Saxon Consul in Paris, or the banker Auguste Leo, whom he had met through Hiller. Much of his time, too, was spent with his compatriots.

By the first months of 1832 a great many Poles had settled down in Paris. The Czartoryskis—Prince Adam, who was the figurehead of Poland in exile; his wife Princess Anna, and his mother-in-law, Princess Sapieha (the one who had suggested the nanny for Chopin's first concert)—had set up house on the Rue du Roule just in time to give Chopin and his compatriots the traditional Polish Easter lunch. The Platers, whose daughter Paulina was a favorite pupil of Chopin; the Komars; and Delfina Potocka also kept open house, and soon a new Polish capital had been founded in Paris, peopled by the most interesting debris of Warsaw society. The intellectual elite was well represented by people like Adam Mickiewicz and Chopin's friend Witwicki, who turned up in the middle of 1832. This had its depressing aspects, typified by an evening at the Platers', where, according to the poet Slowacki, "we sat around from ten in the evening till two in the morning getting frightfully bored, but thank God toward the end Chopin got drunk and started improvising beautiful things on the piano."[26] But the émigré colony in Paris was no ghetto; Chopin's French friends often accompanied him to Polish evenings, and vice versa. "At the house of the charming Countess Plater we used to play while the Polish émigrés danced, and we came to know a mazurka so physical and full-blooded that we might have been in its native land," Hiller later reminisced to Liszt.[27]

After Chopin's first concert in Paris in February, Liszt, who had been living in the French capital for a couple of years, conceived a great enthusiasm for him. The two were diametrically opposed in character; Liszt, the great extrovert, a sort of musical athlete, fiery, enthusiastic, and elemental, had little in common with the reserved, delicate, and fastidious Chopin. But Liszt valued Chopin for his refinement, for his musical polish, and for his individuality. Liszt had been mercilessly exploited for his performing ability at the expense of all else, and he was in many respects too crude a character for Chopin's taste, but Chopin was impressed by his virtuosity, his ability to draw sound out of the piano like no one else, and his gift for playing faultlessly a piece he had never seen before straight from the score (the second time around could be disastrous, as by then Liszt would be bored and would as often as not start introducing his own embellishments).[28] Chopin was, during this period in his life in particular, eager to study all the possibilities of the piano—hence his enthusiasm for people like Kalkbrenner or Liszt, who had some particular skill which he himself lacked.

Liszt introduced Chopin to another musician, the twenty-year-old cellist Auguste Franchomme. After their first meeting at dinner with Liszt, Franchomme accompanied Chopin back to his lodgings, listened to him play for a while, and

"immediately understood" him (a typically Romantic notion
—could one conceive of Vivaldi listening to Bach and "understanding him"?). Chopin was partial to cellists and warmed
to the quiet, gentle, unassuming artisan that Franchomme
was, and the two became close friends.

Through Liszt, too, Chopin met Heinrich Heine, the German poet in voluntary exile in Paris, and, at the end of 1832,
Hector Berlioz, just back from his Italian stay. Chopin now
found himself in the kitchen of the Romantic movement.
They would meet for dinner in a restaurant; for an evening of
music at Chopin's, where the light of one candle cast great
shadows in which, Liszt declares, some of the greatest names
of the next decade listened in silence;[29] a picnic lunch at
Berlioz's; or at Liszt's, for "hours of smoky discussions, with
[his] long pipes and Turkish tobacco."[30]

These discussions must have left Chopin a little bewildered
and isolated. Liszt had no close acquaintance with Bach's
work,[31] Berlioz disliked it cordially, yet Chopin thought it
the essence of music. Liszt and Berlioz, like most Romantics,
had no time for Mozart or Haydn, Chopin's favorite composers, and they saw Beethoven as the great one, the man
who had started the Romantic revolution and liberated music
from its shackles. Chopin had reservations about him for that
very reason, for, as he once told a friend, "Whenever [Beeth-
oven] is obscure and seems to lack coherence, this is not the
result of the slightly savage originality with which he is cred-
ited; it is because he turns his back on eternal principles—
Mozart never."[32] According to Franchomme, Chopin felt
that in Beethoven "passion too often approaches cata-
clysm,"[33] and for this reason he preferred Hummel. He realized that Hummel was not as great a composer as Beethoven,
but valued his restraint, which always prevented him from falling prey to vulgarity.

They could hardly have agreed on anything. Chopin did
not really like any of the more modern composers; he was

lukewarm toward Weber, never seems to have digested Schubert at all, thought little of Mendelssohn's music, and less still of Schumann's. Admire as he might the clever pianist in Liszt, he could not bring himself to like or approve of his compositions, and between Chopin and Berlioz there was mutual incomprehension. Berlioz found his Polish friend's music soporific and uninteresting, but above all lacking in rhythm and cadence. The story of Chopin illustrating Berlioz's method of composition, by dipping a pen in ink, bending it back and then flicking it at a piece of lined paper is almost certainly apocryphal,[34] but a more reliable source records Chopin's statement that "Berlioz puts down a lot of chords and then fills in the intervals as best he can."[35]

The differences of opinion went deeper than liking or disliking each other's music, and had more to do with how these young men saw themselves and their careers. In simple terms, the Romantic movement in music was a revolution against the eighteenth-century role of music as an amenity and of the musician as an artisan. The movement which began with Beethoven was to make a new position for music at the apex of the arts and for the musician as the quintessential artist. Chopin was to benefit from this; only half a century after Mozart was laid in the common grave, Chopin was to have a funeral worthy of a great statesman. But he did not fit easily into the Romantic movement, because at heart he saw himself more as an amateur craftsman than an artist in the modern sense.

The Romantic movement insisted on functions. In order to be great, music, too, had to have a function, the only argument being as to whether that function was to be cathartic, spiritual, or political. And if art had a function, then the artist had a mission. Chopin could never take himself seriously enough to see himself as having a mission, and he was neither insecure nor educated enough to start formulating theories about his work. Had he done so, he would have certainly ad-

mitted that he practiced it entirely for its own sake. As in the
case of Bach, music for him was an exercise in which form
and development were the all-important factors, and while it
was indeed a form of self-expression, it remained a personal
and reticent one. As he once told Hiller, he would like to be
considered a lyric poet, "something like your Uhland."[36] Liszt
and Berlioz, on the other hand, would probably have chosen
Lamartine or Victor Hugo, for they were more grandiloquent
and rhetorical and wanted to reach out to large numbers of
people. In a sense, the end result varied only in style and degree, for, as a critic wrote in the *Gazette Musicale de Paris*,
"with [Chopin] thought, style, concept, everything, even the
fingering, everything is individual, but it is an individualism
which is communicative, expansive, and its magnetic influence can be ignored only by very superficial people."[37]

These differences were not so apparent to begin with, and
Chopin was quite happy to be part of the group, for he liked
Liszt and particularly Berlioz. The latter's ebullient wit and
child-like qualities endeared him to Chopin, who, as one acquaintance wrote, "died at forty, still adolescent."[38] There are
letters from the timorous Nicolas Chopin rebuking his son
for referring to various musical eminences as "cowshit." One
suspects that Berlioz's iconoclastic influence lurked behind
Chopin's bravado.

The winter season of 1832–33, Chopin's second in Paris, was
brilliant from the musical point of view. Berlioz marked his
return to France by giving a performance of his *Symphonie
fantastique* at the Conservatoire. But in the symphonic genre
Chopin was more excited by the performance by the same orchestra with full choirs of Beethoven's Ninth Symphony,
which neither he nor Paris had heard before. Chopin's erstwhile idol John Field, the inventor of the nocturne form, also
gave three concerts, but Chopin had already heard him play

during the summer and had been terribly disappointed by the
crudeness and lack of fluency of his style. After the new year,
which he saw in at a party at the Austrian Embassy, where he
played along with Rossini, Liszt, and Kalkbrenner, Chopin
gave a concert himself. Although he did not make much
money out of it, he was delighted with his own performance
and the reception.[39] At the beginning of April he played a
duet with Liszt at the concert given by Berlioz to raise money
for Harriet Smithson, the English actress he was in love with,
after she had broken her ankle, and a few days later joined
Liszt in another concert.

That Chopin was enjoying life in his new environment can
be seen from a letter he wrote to Dominik Dziewanowski in
the spring of 1833, which also shows how little he had
changed with the years:

Darling Domus!

If I had a friend (a friend with a big, crooked nose, because that's the one I mean) who several years ago had
played with me in Szafarnia, who had always loved me with
conviction, and my father and aunt with gratitude, and if he,
having left the country, had not written a word to me, I
should think the worst of him, and however much he begged
and sniveled, I should never forgive him—and yet I, Fryc, still
have the nerve actually to try to excuse my negligence, and I
write, after a long time of sitting tight like a beetle which
only raises its head above the water when nobody has asked it
to. But I shall not try to make excuses, I prefer to own up to
my guilt, which may loom larger from afar than it does here,
for I have been torn apart by people in all directions. I have
made an entry into the highest society, I sit next to ambassa-
dors, ministers, princes; and I don't really know how it happened, because I didn't push myself. At the moment this is
very important to me, because that is apparently where good
taste is dictated; you immediately have great talent if you
have been heard in the English or Austrian embassy, you play
better if the Princesse de Vaudemont patronized you—I can-

not write *patronizes*, since the woman died a week ago . . .
(she had a multitude of black and white dogs, canaries, par-
rots, and was the owner of the most amusing monkey in
Paris, which used to bite other countesses at her soirées).
Among artists I have friendship and respect; I wouldn't write
this to you if I hadn't been here over a year, but their respect
is proved by the fact that people with a great reputation dedicate their works to me before I have similarly honored them;
Pixis dedicated his new Variations with a Military Band to
me, and they also compose variations on my themes; Kalkbrenner has written variations on one of my mazurkas. Pupils
of the Conservatoire, pupils of Moscheles, Herz, Kalkbrenner, in a word, accomplished artists, take lessons from
me, place my name under Field's—in fact, if I were even
more stupid than I am, I would think that I had reached the
peak of my career; but I can see how much I still have before
me, I can see it all the more clearly as I live very close to the
first artists, and I can see their shortcomings. But I'm
ashamed of writing all this rubbish; I have been boasting like
a child; I would cross it all out, but I haven't got time to
write another letter, and anyway, perhaps you still haven't
forgotten my character, and if you do remember it you'll see
that I haven't changed much, with the exception that I have
one side-whisker—the other won't, simply won't grow—Today
I have to give five lessons; you may think I'll make a fortune,
but a cabriolet and white gloves cost more, and without them
you wouldn't have *ton*.—I love the Carlists, hate the
Philippists, and I'm a revolutionary myself, so I don't take
any notice of money, only of friendship, for which I beg you.
FFC.[40]

The tone of this letter betrays a degree of euphoria which,
given Chopin's character, could only mean that he was sure
of himself and his future. He had in fact achieved a rather
special reputation without any apparent struggle, and by the
beginning of 1833 was considered as one of the brightest stars
of the Parisian firmament. The reason for his success in carv-
ing out a place for himself among so many better-known art-

ists lay in the fact that he had something unique to offer and offered it in the right way, taking care not to challenge or threaten any of the other musicians.

His piano playing had developed greatly over the last couple of years, and it was now quite unlike any other's. Those who heard him play in the right circumstances were immediately captivated. Charles Hallé, a German pianist, was "fascinated beyond expression" when he first heard Chopin:

> I sat entranced, filled with wonderment, and if the room had suddenly been peopled with fairies I should not have been astonished. The marvelous charm, the poetry and originality, the perfect freedom and absolute lucidity of Chopin's playing at that time cannot be described. It was perfection in every sense . . . I could have dropped to my knees to worship him.[41]

The first thing that struck people about Chopin's playing was the elegance and control displayed. There was no apparent exertion, no difficulty, no exaggerated movement, his fingers moving quite effortlessly over the keys. "His delicate and slender hands cover wide stretches and skip with fabulous lightness," observed another pianist.[42] This agility was largely the result of having been allowed to teach himself in his youth, for his fingering was highly unorthodox; he would play black keys with his thumb and think nothing of passing a longer finger over a shorter one, thereby achieving a unique fluency. He could play rapid trills or *legato* like nobody else, producing the effect of strings of pearls or, as Hiller put it, the flight of a swallow.

Perhaps Chopin's most distinctive characteristic was his touch; he could play the same note in various ways, producing a whole range of nuances. This was why he was so fond of Pleyel's pianos, which were by far the most sensitive. He heightened these nuances with his revolutionary use of the sustaining pedal, but above all with his application of *tempo rubato*. This has been greatly exaggerated and misinterpreted, but with Chopin it meant that while his left hand played in strict time, his right would just hint at the anticipation of a phrase or else reluctance to begin it. "Let your left hand be your conductor and keep strict time," he would tell his pupils,[43] and as a result, according to Hiller, "rhythmic precision in his case was linked with a freedom in his leading of a melody, which gave the impression of improvisation."[44]

Combined with the expression of harmonious concentration on his face—no knitted brows or passion, just an expression of deep thought—this always gave the impression that it was spontaneous creation, whether it was indeed an improvisation or a written work he was playing. "The whole man seemed to vibrate, while under his fingers the piano came to life with its own intensity," wrote another pianist. "It was so magnificent that it caused shivers of delight."[45] The idea of spontaneity fascinated the Romantics and Chopin's strongly developed gift for improvisation, sitting down at the piano and creating music for an hour or two, held people spellbound, not merely by its own beauty, but also by the consciousness of something great taking place. "He made a single instrument speak the language of the infinite," wrote one novelist,[46] while a French poet, Henri de la Touche, always spoke with reverence of "that pallid Pole who holds the Heavens open," as he improvised.[47]

Chopin's person was in complete harmony with the way he played. The frail, thin body itself suggested something ephemeral, while the rather more commanding head, with its abundant and fine dark blond hair, its pronounced nose, its tender and intelligent eyes and slightly fussy mouth, seemed to suggest superiority with an element of mocking irony. His movements and deportment were graceful, and his whole figure emanated a sense of harmony and elegance. "His bearing had so much distinction," according to Liszt, "and his manners such a *cachet* of good breeding that one naturally treated him as a prince."[48] After his first meeting with Chopin, Legouvé thought that "he looked like the natural son Weber might have had with a duchess."[49]

This naturally gave Chopin an enormous advantage in Parisian society. Before the July Revolution of 1830, musicians, even if they were Liszt or Rossini, were let in by the back door, listened to and then sent back and paid at the back door by the butler. After 1830 their position became better established. The musician would be invited to the soirée almost like a normal guest, politely asked to play, and a gift or money would be discreetly forwarded to his address the next day. Chopin, who had learned to sit at table at the Blue Palace and the Belvedere, and had been on easy terms with the most exalted from an early age, was both more welcome and more at ease. As a result, he was invited on all sides, and the invitation would often contain some such proviso as: "It is, of course, understood that you may leave your fingers at home."[50] Another result was that he had no shortage of pupils who could pay a high fee for lessons, and he soon became the most sought-after teacher in Paris. There are letters in which aristocratic ladies beg him in the most deferential terms to take on their daughters; another in which a marquess interceding on behalf of the daughter of the Count Maréchal de Castellane concludes: "Liszt desperately wants to give lessons to Madame de Contades, and she to take them from you."[51] His popularity, moreover, did not merely embrace the aristocracy; Chopin was also giving lessons to Conservatoire students and professional musicians. As the demand for his lessons grew, he was able to become selective, and only took on genuinely talented pupils.

By the beginning of 1833 he was giving up to five lessons a day at twenty francs a lesson, which meant that he could earn six hundred francs a week from this source alone. When one considers that a cab fare was one franc, the best seats at the opera about ten, and that the most expensive tailor would

make a frock coat for under 150, one realizes that Chopin was
doing extremely well financially. On top of this there was the
sporadic but substantial income from the publication of his
music, which was beginning to come out regularly in France
and Germany.

In December 1831 the publisher Schlesinger had commissioned Chopin to write something on a theme from the then
popular opera by Meyerbeer, *Robert le Diable*. With the help
of Franchomme, Chopin had produced a Grand Duo Concer-
tante for Piano and Cello, which appeared in print early in
1833. Following Chopin's Paris debut in February 1832, Farrenc, a publisher of no great standing, bought the rights to all
Chopin's larger works, paying a cash deposit while the scores
were being copied for the printers. But Chopin, "out of indolence and a complete lack of interest in his affairs," as Farrenc
put it, failed to produce any fair copies as the months went
by.[52]

Chopin had taken the money from Farrenc because he
needed it, but he was aware that there were better publishers
about, in particular Schlesinger in Paris and Probst in Leipzig, who had already written to him in Vienna asking about
rights.[53] While living off Farrenc's advance, Chopin negotiated with them, and by the autumn of 1832 had reached a
long-term agreement with Schlesinger. In November, Farrenc, exasperated with the "lazy and utterly eccentric" Chopin, who had still produced no clean copies, lost his temper
and tore up the contract.[54] One can only speculate as to
whether Farrenc got back his advance; knowing Chopin, this
is by no means certain.

For all his apparent insouciance and his lackadaisical approach to questions of money, Chopin had grown very canny
and deeply suspicious of all entrepreneurs. He had rightly
assessed Farrenc as a poor businessman, for the latter was proposing to publish a whole series of grand works for piano and
orchestra by someone who was still an unknown composer.

Schlesinger, on the other hand, bought the rights to all the large works Farrenc had wanted, but also acquired those on three nocturnes, eight mazurkas, and twelve études. These were what he intended to publish first, knowing that they would sell quickly and easily. He also farmed out the German rights to Probst in Leipzig. By March 1833, Nicolas Chopin wrote to his son that the Leipzig edition of the nocturnes and mazurkas had reached the music stores in Warsaw and been sold out in a matter of days.

As Chopin's financial situation improved, his father's letters began to dwell more persistently on the subject of putting aside some money, but in spite of his ever dutiful answers, Chopin did nothing of the sort. He moved into an elegant little apartment on the Rue de la Chaussée d'Antin, more central, though not far from his previous home. Although the higher rent was mitigated by the fact that he took a lodger, a young Polish acquaintance, Dr. Hoffmann, he indulged every conceivable temptation to spend money. He began to dress at the best tailors, bought expensive furniture, and drove everywhere in a hired cabriolet rather than a normal cab. He was continually buying presents for people and unnecessary luxuries for himself, and he spent a great deal of money on flowers to fill his rooms with. He was always lending money to impecunious Poles and even seems to have lent Berlioz's fiancée, Harriet Smithson, a generous sum when she broke her ankle.[55] He was busy, carefree, and seldom alone for long enough to worry about anything. As his friend Orlowski wrote:

> Chopin is well and strong. He is turning the heads of all the ladies and making all the husbands jealous. He is in fashion. Soon we shall all be wearing gloves à la Chopin. Only sometimes he suffers from homesickness.[56]

Who these ladies may have been, and what grounds for jealousy their husbands may have had, is impossible to tell in the absence of any firsthand evidence. Many biographers, distressed to find a sexual blank in Chopin's first six years in Paris, have seized on the figure of one of his pupils in order to fill it. Chopin could certainly not have made this husband jealous. Having been married off at an early age to a brutal man, Countess Delfina Potocka subsequently left him, ostensibly to live with her parents, the Komars. When they reached Paris, she set up house on her own and began to enjoy life on the princely allowance her husband sent her. During the early 1830s she had a series of affairs, some of which, like that with the Duke d'Orléans or with Talleyrand's natural son, the Count de Flahault, became notorious.

"The Great Sinner," as she was dubbed by Adam Mickiewicz, was three years Chopin's senior. She had no trouble in indulging her epic sexual appetite, as her great beauty was enhanced by a seductive manner and one of the finest singing voices in Europe. It is more than likely that Chopin, who saw her often during his first years in Paris, and who valued highly both her talent for the piano and her voice, was under her spell. Many biographers have gone on to assume the existence of an affair, and some to describe what they believe to have been its deeply carnal nature. Nothing, of course, is impossible, but evidence, to say the least, is scarce.

There are only two pieces of what might be termed evidence to support the existence of such a liaison. One is a letter from a Pole in Paris to his sister, in which he censures Countess Delfina's conduct and lists Chopin as one of her many lovers. It was, however, written after the composer's death by someone who did not know him, and was, at best, a good specimen of the contemporary gossips.[57] The other is the information given to an early biographer by the widow of the Dr. Hoffmann who shared Chopin's apartment for a few months in 1833. According to her, her husband had stated that Countess Delfina often came to the apartment late at night in order to play, sing, and sleep with Chopin, and that he occasionally returned the courtesy at her house. But Mrs. Hoffmann's evidence is not as reliable as it might appear. She only married some ten years after the putative events, and related them fifty years after that to a man who was determined to prove the existence of an affair, and almost certainly prompted her memory. She is also unreliable on points of detail, stating, for instance, that her husband had lived with Chopin for many years. She would even have us believe that the worthy doctor had helped Chopin with his compositions, suggesting alternative harmonies which the latter eagerly seized on.[58]

The moribund theory of a liaison between Chopin and Countess Delfina was given a new lease of life by the appearance of what purported to be copies of his letters to her. These were produced in 1945 by a lady who suggested various provenances but could not be pinned down to a single version of where the originals were and where she had seen them. In the muddled conditions of postwar Poland, nobody paid much attention to such inconsistencies, and the texts were accepted by many as being authentic. The style of the letters seems Chopinesque enough—too much so, on closer examination—but the texts reveal an entirely new Chopin. The reticent man who never made significant statements about music, who recoiled from making judgments on other musicians, and who rarely mentioned his own compositions, is seen here expatiating on the theory of music, making crude and merciless criticisms of Liszt and Schumann, and explaining the meaning of his own works. Moreover, the collection of texts includes two love letters full of extraordinarily earthy eroticism, which accords ill with what is known of Chopin's character, style of conduct, and tastes. The texts have since been subjected to thorough examination and dismissed as forgeries (for a more detailed discussion of the texts and their history, see Appendix B). One must therefore conclude that, possible, likely, or probable as the affair might seem, there is not one shred of real evidence to prove its existence.

All available information of a reliable nature points in a different direction. Konstancja's marriage had not significantly altered Chopin's passion for her. She had been little more than a piece of romantic furniture in his heart, and although its position had shifted somewhat, it was still there. As can be seen from Chopin's letter to Tytus and to his sister Ludwika, he still regarded Konstancja as the now unworthy object of his affections, and her image remained a conveniently disembodied focus for surplus emotion and effusions of sentimentality. This did not, of course, prevent him from being aware of other women, as his letters to Tytus bear out, but both the degree of his interest and his reluctance can be gauged from an episode which he recounted in one of them. The pianist Pixis, whom Chopin had met in Stuttgart, arrived in Paris accompanied by a fifteen-year-old "pupil," whom he kept securely locked away, with the intention of marrying her in due course. Chopin went to call on Pixis one day and, finding him absent, was just explaining the object of his visit to the young lady when her aging beau came panting up the stairs. Pixis was convulsed with suspicious jealousy, much to the amusement of Chopin, who was astonished that "anyone could think me *capable* of such a thing!" which suggests that he did not see himself as being capable of it. "Me—a seducer!" he could not get over the drollness of the idea.[59]

The turning of ladies' heads seems to have remained on a fairly innocent level, as indeed Orlowski's remark suggests. Chopin had had physical relations with at least one girl before reaching Paris, and may well have availed himself of the opportunities afforded by the chorus girls and the whores he mentions, but five years later, when he found himself on the point of consummating his love with a woman of his own world, he recoiled at the thought of transposing his emotions

onto the physical plane.[60] This is the reaction of someone
who associates the act with whores and shame. It strongly
suggests that Chopin had never, up to that point, taken his
affection for a woman to its physical conclusion. This was not
particularly surprising in his case, as his natural reticence was
reinforced by his code of behavior, which in turn was dictated
by his position and career. Chopin was invited to sit with exalted company and to teach young ladies from the most aristocratic families precisely because he was discreet and knew
his place. Had the slightest smell of scandal regarding a pupil
attached itself to his person, his carefully nurtured reputation
would have suffered immeasurably. His own inclination was
to avoid all unseemliness, and he was rapidly becoming fastidious in everything. As Liszt points out, he always wore an air
of chastity, and winced as much at a crude thought or word as
he did at a muddy shoe or a speck of dust on his frock coat.[61]
He loved the company of women, but he liked them well
bred, well dressed, and unattainable, and the resulting flirta-
tions were little more than an understated game which enliv-
ened his lessons and his social life.

Fond as he was of this kind of company, Chopin did not
take up the invitation from Liszt's mistress, the Countess
d'Agoult, to spend the summer on her estate. Instead, he
spent it with Franchomme's family near Tours. He was just
as happy being looked after and fattened up by his friend's
very humble family, and when he returned to Paris wrote that
"when I look back on it all, it seems such a charming dream
that I wish I could be still dreaming it."[62]

The cellist Franchomme had become a close friend of Chopin, and hardly a day passed without his calling on him, often
accompanied by Liszt. A typical afternoon is evoked by a letter Chopin was trying to write to Hiller, who was on holiday
in Frankfurt. "I am writing without knowing what my pen is
scribbling, because Liszt is playing my Études and banishing
all other thoughts from my head," he wrote, and added wist-

fully, "I wish I could rob him of the way he plays my Études."
This provoked a few lines of modesty from Liszt, and a few
words from Franchomme. Liszt wrote that the Études were
"magnificent," which was followed by more modesty from
Chopin, and tuttings from Liszt, interspersed with comments
like "by the way, I bumped into Heine yesterday, who told me
to hug you cordially" and "Berlioz sends his love."[63] The latter was less in evidence since he had married Harriet Smithson. They had moved to the country village of Montmartre,
but even there they would sometimes organize picnics for
friends like Liszt, Hiller, Chopin, and the poet Vigny. Berlioz
was as keen as ever to prattle on about "art, poetry, thought,
music, drama; in a word, everything that makes up life."[64]

On the whole, Chopin preferred Hiller's company. "I think
I can say that Chopin loved me, but I was in love with him,"
explained Hiller.[65] It was he who introduced Chopin to Vincenzo Bellini, who came to Paris in the autumn of 1833.
Chopin felt a greater affinity with these two than with Liszt
or Berlioz, and they all used to congregate in the small apartment on the Boulevard St. Germain of the singer Lina
Freppa. There, according to Hiller:

> We used to chatter about music, sing and play; chatter, sing
> and play. Chopin and Madame Freppa would take turns at
> the piano—I would also do my best to play a part—and Bel-
> lini would make observations, accompanying himself in one
> of his cantilenas, rather to illustrate what he was saying, than
> to show off to his listeners.[66]

It was largely thanks to friendships such as these that Chopin's yearning for family and home began to recede. By the
end of 1833 he had weaned himself from it and had decided
to remain in Paris for a very long time. The Tsar, eager to iso-
late the real exiles, had offered an amnesty to those who had
not played an important part in the insurrection. Chopin
could easily have availed himself of this, which would have

allowed him to return to Poland whenever he wanted, but he did not do so and thereby burned his boats. In his case being a refugee did not present serious problems, as his French parentage and his contacts saved him from the more irritating inconveniences such as having to register with the police, not being allowed to live where one wanted, or needing permission before moving about France or leaving it.

But in spite of the pleasure he found in French society and in the international world of the musicians, he could not suppress certain manifestations of homesickness and insecurity, such as his need to speak Polish from time to time in order to relax. This need could now be satisfied in Paris as well as anywhere else. There were households, such as the Czartoryskis' and the Platers', where he could go whenever he wanted either for a meal or just to sit quietly if depressed. There was the Polish Club, around the corner from him on the Rue Godot de Mauroy, with its collection of old generals and scruffy young poets, where he could have a cheap dinner or play billiards. Above all, he now had a few Polish friends settled in Paris, such as his Conservatoire colleague Fontana, who had failed to make a living in England and returned to Paris, and Albert Grzymala. The latter, a remarkable man in many respects, had led an eventful life which on two occasions led him into Russian jails, once in 1812 as a prisoner of war, once in 1826 for his connections with the Decembrist movement. He had held high office in the Polish Treasury and during the insurrection had been sent to London to negotiate a loan. After staying there for a couple of years he had come to Paris, where he made a living off the stock exchange. His magnificent looks and zest for life involved him in a succession of affairs, and he soon became a well-known, even notorious, figure in Parisian society. He was a cultivated man with a wide range of artistic and musical interests, and had known and encouraged Chopin in Warsaw. Moreover, the forty-year-old Grzymala exuded strength and resilience, and gradually began to fulfill the role of big brother in Chopin's life, becoming confidant and adviser in all matters.

Finally, at the beginning of 1834, Jan Matuszynski, whose medical studies had been interrupted by the insurrection and had been obliged to finish them in Germany, turned up in Paris to take a teaching post at the École de Médecine. "My first thought was to call on Chopin," he wrote to his parents. "I cannot tell you what joy it was to meet again after five years of separation. He has grown tall and strong, and I hardly recognized him."[67] Chopin was so delighted to see his friend again that he persuaded him to come and share his lodgings (Dr. Hoffmann's addiction to his pipe had irritated Chopin so much that he had gotten rid of him). According to Hiller, "even when Chopin stayed in of an evening playing the piano, he had to have at least one friend with him."[68] Now he had all the friends he could wish for.

Considering how he had settled down in Paris, it may appear strange that during the 1833–34 season Chopin did not, as far as is known, give a single concert. He appeared in public once, on December 15, at Hiller's concert, when he played a Bach *Adagio* with Liszt and Hiller "with an understanding of its character and perfect delicacy," according to the *Revue Musicale*.[69] This apparent obscurity was self-imposed, for he could now afford to subsist from other earnings and no longer needed to perform for his living. He did not mind taking some small part in a friend's program, for this did not involve any great responsibility, but from now on he avoided giving concerts himself, as he could not stand the strain of putting together a program, selecting other musicians, and taking care of all the organizational aspects. As a rule he only played in events taking place in a small venue, such as the Salle Pleyel or the Salle Érard.

With the publication of many of his works, Chopin's reputation as a composer began to grow. It is of course difficult to gauge this solely from the reviews, as a partisan spirit prevailed in many quarters. In France, the *Gazette Musicale*, founded by Chopin's publisher, Schlesinger, was consistently favorable, while its rival, *La France Musicale*, tried to pass the first works over in silence. This does not mean, however, that the opinions expressed were insincere. The *Gazette* indeed consistently pointed to his importance as a composer but admitted that to many, even his most fervent admirers, he was an "inexplicable phenomenon" in the sense that he did not seem to belong to any tradition.[70]

In Germany, Schumann was Chopin's greatest champion, reviewing every work as it came out in more or less ecstatic terms in his own paper, the *Neue Zeitschrift für Musik*. While most other critics in Germany were also generous in their praise, Rellstab simply could not bring himself to regard Chopin with anything but horror. Having accused the *La ci darem* Variations of being Slavonic vandalism, he attacked the nocturnes no less vehemently, stating that if one were to hold Field's "charming romances" (his nocturnes) up to a concave distorting mirror, one would see Chopin's coarse new works reflected. When reviewing the Études opus 10, he strongly advised anyone attempting to play them to have a surgeon in attendance, as permanent finger damage was unavoidable.[71]

Whatever the critics wrote, the works sold and were played. The nocturnes, waltzes, and mazurkas were ideally suited to the home or small gathering, and these fields were by now dominated by the piano, thanks to the rapid technical development of the instrument and the rise of a large middle class with musical aspirations. By the 1830s there was a piano in every home, particularly in countries like Germany, and where there was a piano there were scores of Chopin's music.

When, in the spring of 1834, Hiller suggested that Chopin accompany him to the Lower Rhine Music Festival, organized by Mendelssohn at Aachen, he agreed. It must have been in a spirit tinged with triumph that he set off to revisit Germany, which he had passed through only three years before as an unknown pianist.

On their arrival in Aachen, Chopin and Hiller called on Mendelssohn, who was overjoyed to see them and offered them his box for the concerts. The rest of the time was spent showing off to each other on the piano. As Mendelssohn wrote to his family:

> They have both developed their technique, and Chopin is now as a pianist one of the very best—he astonishes one with novelties, like Paganini on the violin, and introduces wonderful things which one would have thought impossible. But they both suffer a little from the Parisian love of despair and emotional exaggeration, too often losing sight of time and sobriety and of true musical thought; I on the other hand have them in too small measure, so we complement and teach each other, which makes me look like an old schoolmaster faced by a couple of *"mirliflores"* [dandies] or *"incroyables."*[72]

After the festival Chopin and Hiller followed Mendelssohn back to Düsseldorf, where the exchange of virtuosity continued. Hiller recorded one occasion in the house of the painter Schadow:

> There we met several of the most promising young painters, and a lively conversation was struck up. Everything would have been fine but for poor old Chopin, whose reticence kept him in the corner, unnoticed. Both Mendelssohn and I knew that he would get his own back on us for this, and we waited in happy anticipation. Eventually, the piano was opened and I played for a while, followed by Mendelssohn. But when we asked Chopin to play something too, everyone looked around in surprise. He had only played a few bars when everyone, especially Schadow, began to look at him in a very different way—they had never heard anything like it before. In wild enthusiasm they begged him to play again and again.[73]

At the end of May they took a steamer down the Rhine, Mendelssohn accompanying them as far as Cologne, and

Chopin and Hiller sailing on down to Koblenz. "Today I feel like the steam from our boat," Chopin wrote to Hiller's mother, "I evaporate into the air and feel one half of me wafting off toward my country and my people, the other toward Paris and you."[74] A few days later he followed the second half back to Paris.

7

Success

"Chopin is all sadness," Liszt wrote to his mistress in September 1834. "Furniture is a little more expensive than he had thought, so now we're in for a whole month of worry and nerves."[1] It was true. At the end of the summer he had decided to move to a more elegant apartment on the same street, the Rue de la Chaussée d'Antin, not far from where the Paris Opéra now stands. The rent was high and the furnishings he selected were in keeping with his reputation as the most elegant and one of the richest musicians in Paris. His slightly precious and unconventional taste manifested itself strongly. The fashion of the times was for heavy fabrics, deep colors, and ornamental furniture, but Chopin covered his walls with pale gray paper, his chairs with plain, dove-colored material, and all his windows and his bed were curtained in voluminous swathes of white muslin and silk. There was not much furniture, but what there was tended to be fussy, and while there were few pictures, there was a collection of exquisite objects and bibelots of one sort or another distributed around the rooms. "He lived like a woman, almost like a cocotte," in the words of one of his pupils.[2]

The rent was shared by Matuszynski, who had moved with him, but its size shows that Chopin was by now earning a great deal of money, mainly from teaching. Part of his reputation as a teacher rested on the fact that he actually enjoyed giving lessons and therefore gave them well. He found the routine relaxing and therapeutic for his nerves, and since by now he could afford to teach only genuinely talented people and people he liked, he enjoyed the social and professional aspects as well. "Liszt cannot equal Chopin as a teacher," wrote one young pupil. "I do not mean that Liszt is not an excellent teacher; he is the best possible until one has had the good fortune of knowing Chopin, who is, in terms of method, far ahead of all other artists."[3]

This method was highly idiosyncratic. He insisted on what, by the standard of most of his contemporaries, was a low seat, the elbows level with the white keys. He wanted the player to be able to reach all the notes at the extremities of the keyboard without leaning or moving his or her elbows; the complete antithesis of Liszt's way of playing, which always gave people the impression that his whole body was climbing over the keyboard.

For Chopin all suppleness and intelligence should be concentrated in the fingers themselves. Unlike his contemporaries, he believed that every finger had different attributes and that these must be developed to the full. All possible finger movements were permissible. The whole point of this method was to develop the touch, which to him was the beginning and end of piano playing. He discouraged the use of the pedal until a pupil's touch had been perfected, for he believed that tone must be created through the fingers and not by the artificial agency of the pedal, which could then be used in a more sophisticated way. When pupils did not understand what he was driving at, he used to tell them to go to the Italian Opera and listen to the Italians using their voices.[4]

Chopin's approach was on the whole a gentle one. He discouraged pupils from practicing very much, but he remained strict on questions such as time; he always used a metronome himself and told his pupils to do likewise. The music he put them through was daunting; Bach fugues; Clementi's *Gradus ad Parnassum,* preludes and exercises; and works by Cramer, Handel, Scarlatti, Hummel, and Mozart. He did sometimes set more modern works by Beethoven, Weber, Field, or Moscheles, but on the whole avoided those of Mendelssohn, Schumann, Schubert, and Liszt.

The pupils would sit at the Pleyel grand piano, while Chopin either stood or sat making remarks or corrections, sometimes going over to the upright piano in the same room to demonstrate or accompany. He was usually gentle and polite, but, particularly as he got older, could become very irritable, and then he would pace the room breaking pencils or nervously tugging at his hair. He was even known to fling scores across the room, and once broke a chair in his irritation.[5] This sort of behavior was usually limited to his professional pupils; he demanded more of them and at the same time they were more prepared to take it from him. Chopin was not lucky with his professional pupils: some of the most promising died young, others never grew into great pianists. His first, Caroline Hartmann, died in 1834, the year he took in another, Adolf Gutmann, who was to become a lifelong favorite but never struck anyone else with any brilliance. Some of the best pianists he left behind him were in fact aristocratic amateurs, and they accounted for the greater part of his income.

He was supplementing this by selling his compositions. The first batch of earlier works having been published and sold, he was now trying to collect a second, but this was difficult, because he was so busy in Paris that he had little time for composing, a laborious and lengthy business with him. He dug into his manuscripts and pulled out the Grande Polonaise for piano and orchestra and the G minor Ballade, both of which he had written in Vienna. He now wrote an

Andante Spianato to precede the first of these and sold it to
Schlesinger, and polished up the Ballade. He also sold four
mazurkas (opus 24), two polonaises (opus 26) and two nocturnes (opus 27), recently written, and was working on the
second set of études and some of the preludes.

It is surprising that he found time to write at all, for his
days were heavily booked with lessons, while his evenings, particularly with the start of the season, were taken up with social or musical events of one sort or another. On December 1
there was a private concert given by Delfina Potocka, in
which Chopin certainly took part. On December 7 he played
a movement of his E minor concerto and the new *Andante
Spianato* sandwiched in between *Harold in Italy* and the *King
Lear* Overture at Berlioz's concert at the Conservatoire. On
December 25, he joined Liszt at the Salle Pleyel to play a
Moscheles duo for four hands and a Liszt duo, being acclaimed by the critics in both performances.

More exhausting than the few public performances were
the great number of soirées Chopin attended at this time.
Usually he would hold back from playing at them, only to be
seduced into doing so very late, as Berlioz writes:

> A small circle of select auditors, whose real desire to hear him
> was beyond doubt, could alone determine him to approach
> the piano. What emotions he would then call forth! In what
> ardent and melancholy reveries he loved to pour out his soul!
> It was usually toward midnight that he gave himself up with
> the greatest abandon, when the big butterflies of the salon
> had left, when the political questions of the day had been
> discussed at length, when all the scandalmongers were at the
> end of their anecdotes, when all the snares were set, all the
> perfidies consummated, when one was thoroughly tired of
> prose, then, obedient to the mute petition of some beautiful,
> intelligent eyes, he became a poet and sang the Ossianic loves
> of the heroes of his dreams, their chivalrous joys and the
> sorrows of the absent fatherland, his dear Poland.[6]

As Legouvé records, Chopin was a good pianist until midnight, when he became sublime.[7] But he was very sensitive to atmosphere, and if there were someone vulgar or irritating in the corner of the room, he could only play little waltzes and nocturnes. He needed great concentration to start on one of his improvisations, which was what everyone wanted. Hearing such an improvisation for the first time, Charles Hallé wrote: "There is nothing to remind one that it is a human being who produces his music. It seems to descend from heaven, so pure and clear and spiritual is it."[8]

Spiritual it clearly was, but the physical strain of playing, and particularly of improvising, was immense. In spite of Matuszynski's attempts to keep him at home in the evenings that winter, Chopin managed to exhaust himself thoroughly. In March he caught the influenza which had half of Paris in bed, developed bronchitis, and by the middle of the month was coughing up particles of blood. Matuszynski was worried about Chopin's lungs and prescribed the waters and baths of Enghien, just north of Paris, followed by waters in Germany in the summer. But before he could think of his health, Chopin had to pull himself together for three end-of-season events.

One was the Herz brothers' concert at the Salle Pleyel on March 22, which he and Hiller had promised to take part in. Another was a Polish charity concert to be held on April 4. He had suggested this as a means of raising money for the Benevolent Association of the Polish Ladies in Paris, founded in the previous year by Princess Czartoryska, of which Grzymala, Matuszynski, and the Platers were active members. He now found himself lumbered with the task of organizing it. As usual when Chopin tried to organize something, everything started going wrong, particularly when it came to finding singers. As Jules Janin wrote in the *Journal des Débats*:

This concert, which had started by looking promising, ended up looking very inauspicious. First of all everyone had promised, and then nobody kept their word. We could just picture the moment when, for lack of singers, the noble president of this concert, Princess Czartoryska, would have no option but to send for the drummers of the 11th Legion and to announce to the audience, after a fine drum roll: "Gentlemen, here is the best music the grand-daughter of the Jagiellons could muster in the whole of Paris to help her destitute compatriots!"[9]

The situation was, however, not quite that desperate, and after concerted efforts by Chopin, Grzymala, and a musical friend of theirs called Jelowicki, the program at the Théâtre des Italiens on April 4 was one that many a charity could envy. Habeneck conducted while Chopin played one of his rare performances of the E minor concerto with full orchestra, which was greeted with enthusiastic applause. The famous tenor Adolphe Nourrit sang Schubert lieder and duets with Madame Falcon, who also sang a couple of Rossini arias, Hiller played a piece of his own, and the evening ended with a duo played by Liszt and Chopin on two pianos.[10] The event was a financial success too: even after Liszt and Hiller had been presented with diamond rings, Habeneck and Nourrit with snuffboxes and tiepins, and Madame Falcon with a bracelet, the profits were considerable.[11] Hardly had Chopin recovered from the exertion and nervous tension of this when he had to return his favor to Habeneck and take part in the latter's own concert at the Conservatoire on April 26. He played the *Andante Spianato* and Grande Polonaise with tremendous effect and was enthusiastically reviewed in the press.

Whether Chopin did take the waters of Enghien that summer is not known, but it is probable that he spent some time in the country, for there follows a three-month gap in the documentation. It is unlikely that he would have gone to Germany for the waters, either, had he not suddenly received a letter from his parents saying they had left for Karlsbad themselves. In one of those untypical moments of decision, he set off forthwith, and, after a few days and nights spent in the mail coach, arrived in Karlsbad on August 15.

It was late in the evening, and since cursory inquiries informed him that his parents had not arrived yet, he went to bed. At four o'clock in the morning he was wakened by Nicolas and Justyna, who had arrived before him and been told of his presence by another Pole. They fell into each others' arms and later that morning wrote a joint letter to the rest of the family in Warsaw. "Our joy is indescribable!" wrote Chopin. "We don't stop telling each other how many times we have been thinking of one another."[12]

They spent a month together in the beautiful watering place. "We drink, eat together, hug each other, reproach each other; I am at the height of my happiness!" There were plenty of other distractions as well. The little town was full of Poles, who wanted to give a celebration dinner for the composer but in the end decided that a public manifestation would do them no good when they got back to their Russian-occupied country.[13] There were other acquaintances, too, like Count Franz Thun-Hohenstein with his two sons, who had taken lessons from Chopin in the previous year. The time passed in walks through the surrounding hills, picnics, soirées and musical evenings, in which Chopin was joined by the 'cellist and composer Jozef Dessauer, also staying in Karlsbad.

The Thuns were insistent that Chopin should come and stay with them when they returned to their castle at Tetschen on the Elbe, particularly as Josephine, one of the count's daughters and also a former pupil of Chopin, was pining to see and hear him again. Since Tetschen was vaguely on the way back to Warsaw, he decided to take up the invitation and accompany his parents thus far on their homeward journey. They left Karlsbad in the second week of September and, after a few days at Tetschen, Nicolas and Justyna left for

Warsaw on the fourteenth, leaving their son to stay on in the picturesque castle. But much as Chopin enjoyed such surroundings, as well as the company of his former pupil Josephine, to whom he gave a waltz in manuscript, he was eager to get back to Paris, and on September 19 he left, accompanied by one of the young counts, who was going to Dresden.

Climbing out of the mail coach that evening in Dresden, Chopin unexpectedly met a former boarder of his father's, Feliks Wodzinski, who was staying there with his whole family. Chopin of course called on the Wodzinskis, and the pleasure of renewing an old acquaintance was heightened by the effect that the eldest daughter, Maria, made on him. He had last seen her as an eleven-year-old girl in Warsaw, and now beheld a striking young woman of sixteen with a slightly swarthy complexion, black hair, and magnificent eyes which had already set more than one heart beating fast.

Instead of hurrying back to Paris as he had intended, he spent two weeks in Dresden, mainly in the company of the Wodzinskis. Maria was musical and played the piano well, even occasionally writing pieces for it. Chopin copied a waltz into her album and gave her a little card bearing the first bars of one of his nocturnes and the inscription "*soyez heureuse*" (be happy), the only tangible signs that they were infatuated with each other. But some of the other Poles in Dresden did not fail to notice the fact.[14]

What Maria felt can only be deduced from the letter she wrote after he had left Dresden on October 3, in which she lets a certain amount of feeling slip through the bounds imposed by her age and education. Nevertheless she takes great care to keep her own feelings aligned as closely as possible with those of her family. "On Saturday, when you had left us, we all wandered about sadly, our eyes filled with tears," she wrote, and went on to describe just how sad first one brother, then the other, then her father, and finally her mother had

been, her mother who was missing her "fourth son Fryderyk."[15]

The two weeks spent in Dresden had delayed Chopin's return to Paris, and he had already promised Mendelssohn that
he would stop in Leipzig for a few days. Mendelssohn had of
course alerted Schumann, who was staying in Leipzig with his
future in-laws, the Wiecks, and they all awaited him avidly.
"Tomorrow or the day after, Chopin is arriving here from
Dresden, but he will most likely not appear in a concert, for
he is a great idler," wrote Wieck, who was deeply suspicious
of him.[16]

Chopin reached Leipzig on October 4, but "he did not
want to stay for more than a day, so we spent it together,
without parting, and made music," Mendelssohn wrote to a
friend. He was impressed by the mastery Chopin had at-
tained, and was "glad to be with a perfect musician again."
While he acknowledged that their styles were diametrically
opposed, he claimed that he could "understand Chopin perfectly":

> It was an unusual evening, that Sunday; I played my Oratorio
> at his request, while curious Leipzigers silently slipped in,
> eager to see Chopin; and when, between the first and second
> parts, he played his new Études and his new concerto in very
> quick time to the astonished Leipzigers, and I followed with
> the rest of my St. Paul, it must have sounded to them as
> though an Iroquois had met up with a Kaffir for conversa-
> tion.[17]

Mendelssohn's praise of Chopin is interesting, for his attitude to the other's compositions until now had been one of
bewilderment and slight distaste. In February that year he
had told Moscheles in London that "a new book of mazurkas
by Chopin and other new pieces of his are so mannered they
are hard to stand,"[18] and only a couple of weeks before Chopin's visit had written to the same correspondent denigrating
Chopin's playing.[19]

Having made Mendelssohn change his mind, Chopin then managed to placate the irate Wieck, who had spent the whole day at home waiting for him with Schumann. He played himself, to Schumann's and Clara Wieck's delight, and then listened to her play. Afterward he declared her to be the only woman in Germany who could play his compositions properly.

Having promised Mendelssohn that he would be back in Germany for the spring (Chopin had already made vague plans to join the Wodzinskis then), he set off on the next day for Heidelberg. But the traveling and the autumn weather, as well as the excitements and exertions of the last two months, told on his health, and upon his arrival he fell seriously ill. The severe bronchitis of that spring had been a warning he felt he could ignore, and indeed people like Matuszynski and his parents, who had not seen him since Warsaw, all found him looking much stronger and healthier than when he had left Poland. But this second attack, which was so severe it started a rumor in Germany that he had died, suggests that the exertions of the last year had undone all the previous years' success in building up his constitution.

Chopin finally limped back to Paris at the end of October. He had to look to both his health and his finances, which was not made any easier by the arrival of Maria Wodzinska's elder brother, Antoni, a scatter-brained and restless character, whom both mother and sister begged Chopin to look after. "Antoni is thoroughly good-natured, in fact too much so, for he is always being taken in by others," wrote Maria. "Besides he is careless and never gives a thought to anything, or at least very rarely . . ."[20] Mainly out of a desire to earn some credit with the Wodzinskis, Chopin acquitted himself honorably, taking Antoni from opera to theater to concert and giving him dinners in the finest restaurants.

He had only just finished playing host to Antoni Wodzinski when he found himself obliged to help the violinist

Karol Lipinski, who had come to Paris in the hope of giving a concert. He arranged a musical soirée in order to launch him, but subsequently quarreled with him because the violinist would not help him with the various Polish charity events in which Chopin was involved.[21]

These included a ball and a small concert,[22] and just before Christmas a charity bazaar, which gave Chopin a good deal of trouble. He was better placed than most to collect "jumble," as he knew half of Paris and could ask his lady pupils to give or make things for the sale. The result was a collection of books, drawings, pictures, embroidered purses, and knick-knacks, with the occasional manuscript by Chopin and Liszt thrown in. This was sold in an elegant shop lent by an oblig-ing tradesman on the Chaussée d'Antin. The stalls were held by such ladies as the Duchess d'Abrantès, Princess Belgiojoso, the Duchess Decazes, Princess Czartoryska and her little daughter Princess Iza. Chopin played for hours at a time dur-ing the three evenings of the sale. It is hardly surprising that the whole of Paris had to be there, and that the rummage sale made an enormous profit.[23]

Notwithstanding Matuszynski's protests, Chopin rarely passed up an invitation and was out every evening, and his friend's attempts to make him wear thick boots during the winter were thwarted by his dandyism. Nicolas Chopin's ad-monitions on the same subject, heavily larded with hints that if he did not look after his health and his pocket, his plans re-garding "certain persons" would come to nothing, were not heeded either, and in March, Chopin again fell ill. From now on every period of exertion, particularly during bad weather, would bring him down. A long, relaxed convalescence could have built up his strength to what it had been, but he could not find the right conditions for this, whether physical or psy-chological, and it was not to be.

The rumor of his death, occasioned by his illness in Heidel-berg, had reached Warsaw at the beginning of December

1835, and in spite of various mentions of his appearances in the Paris press, which greatly relieved his alarmed family, the story persisted to such an extent that the Warsaw papers had to publish a denial of it at the beginning of January.[24] The rumor had brought, among other things, a worried Mr. Wodzinski to pay an apparently casual call on the Chopins in Warsaw. Although nothing had been stated openly, Chopin's parents knew that their son was in love with Maria and intended to visit the Wodzinskis in Dresden that summer. What is more, he had suggested that his mother accompany him to Dresden, an obvious step in the direction of formalizing the affair. The Wodzinskis, although equally noncommittal, paid several calls on the Chopins in Warsaw and gave the impression of encouraging the familiarity.

For some reason, possibly his health, Chopin did not stick to his original plan of going to Germany in the spring. This is the more surprising in that Paris quieted down considerably with the end of the season. In March, Hiller had left in order to settle in Frankfurt, Berlioz had left earlier, and Liszt was in Switzerland with his mistress. Antoni Wodzinski had gone to fight in the Spanish Civil War, and Delfina Potocka had decided to go back to her husband in Poland.

At Easter, which came early in April, Chopin gave the traditional Polish dinner for a group of compatriots at his own apartment, and then went to stay at Enghien. Whether this was dictated by his health and with whom he was staying are questions that at present are impossible to answer. They are the more tantalizing in that there are reasons to believe that Delfina Potocka had a villa there, at which she might have stayed while she was settling her affairs in Paris. A year later, as Chopin was driving past the place, a friend recalled:

> He turned my attention to the wide lake, and, on its edge, the little villa in which he had spent the previous summer. His face became suffused with the pleasantness of the memory; it must have been a very happy period in his life.[25]

Another person who made him welcome in that part of the world was the Marquis de Custine, whom he had met at the Czartoryskis' and elsewhere during that season. Custine was the last scion of a very old family. His father and grandfather had both been guillotined in 1793, and his mother, the celebrated Delphine de Sabran, had lived on to become the mistress of Chateaubriand, father of the French Romantic movement. Custine had been brought up by her in exile, and after his return to France in 1815 had married and had a child, but the death of both wife and child had precipitated a crisis which brought to the surface his latent homosexuality. In 1824 he had been beaten up and dumped in a ditch, naked and half dead, by a group of artillerymen of the Royal Guard, with one of whose comrades he had arranged a tryst. This affair, impossible to hush up, had resulted in his banishment from the Boulevard St. Germain and had forced him to create a world of his own, based on his literary and artistic interests. The revolution of 1830 made this easier, and by the middle of the decade he had been accepted as one of the features of Parisian society. The dinners he gave at his spectacular apartment on the Rue de la Rochefoucauld were among the most exclusive in the city, and apart from such old habitués as the Duchess d'Abrantès (who wanted to marry him) or his uncle the old Count de Sabran (a wonderful *ancien régime* hangover of poetry and of whom Chopin was particularly fond), regular guests included Chateaubriand, Madame Récamier, Heine, the Victor Hugos, Meyerbeer, Lamartine, and Berlioz.

Custine's Paris apartment was only a pied-à-terre; his main residence was at St. Gratien, on the other side of the Lake of Enghien, where he had "a beautiful Florentine villa arranged in the English manner,"[26] filled with fine and exotic objects collected on his travels, and furnished in a taste rather similar to Chopin's, with white predominating. The house stood in a fine park on the lake and was one of the most relaxed residences in France, with its doors permanently open to a chosen group of intimates. "Perfect house. Delightful room," wrote Stendhal after his visit. "All that is most perfect about the country at only 1¾ hours from the Opera."[27]

Although Sainte-Beuve later wrote that Custine's "pretty house in the valley of Montmorency was a perfect Sodom and Gomorrah,"[28] this is an isolated opinion. Custine did, however, live with a younger Englishman, and had recently extended his protection to the eighteen-year-old Count Ignacy Gurowski. Custine was a large man of forty-five with a plump, somewhat womanish face. His manners were impeccable, his conversation witty and full of charm. He was an emotional person, and his affection was deep and enduring; his loyalty toward people like Gurowski, even after the latter got married, was exemplary.

Chopin quickly became the object of some of these sentiments, but there is no reason to believe that they went beyond a deep appreciation of him and his music and the same avuncular tenderness which Chopin sought and encouraged in others. "You know that you are the only person who can come whenever he likes, knowing that you will always give pleasure," Custine wrote to Chopin in March. "Once and for all then, do not ever ask whether you can come, just come when you feel like it."[29] Chopin certainly availed himself of the invitation that spring and summer. He loved the area to the north of Paris and spent many happy days on excursions through Chantilly and Ermenonville, in the park of Montmorency, just outside which lived his old friend the poet Julian Niemcewicz. The latter's diary records one occasion on which Chopin arrived for lunch with him and an old general who lived with him. They were unexpectedly joined by Adam Mickiewicz, and after lunch, during which Chopin had everyone in stitches with his impersonations and his jokes, they went off to the village of Montmorency and joined in a country festival.[30]

At the end of May, Liszt turned up in Paris, hoping to catch Thalberg, who had given a couple of concerts and been acclaimed as the greatest pianist in Europe, for he longed to measure up to his rival and defeat him. Thalberg had left, but Liszt nevertheless gave a concert in which he impressed Chopin by the progress he had made in the last year. The occasion was marked by a dinner given by Liszt, at which the guests included Meyerbeer, the tenor Adolphe Nourrit, and the painter Delacroix, whom Chopin met for the first time.[31] At the beginning of June, Liszt returned to his mistress in Switzerland and Chopin went back to Enghien-les-Bains to await news of the Wodzinskis' movements.

In the first days of July he heard that they were in Marienbad, and promptly set off himself, arriving there at the end of the month. He found Mrs. Wodzinska alone with her two daughters. He put up at the same hotel and settled down to spend the whole of August with them. He must have been deeply in love with Maria, to spend so much time in one place doing very little, considering how he hated being away from Paris for long periods and how restless he was by nature. The Wodzinskis and their Marienbad acquaintances were not the most exciting people to be with for one used to the company Chopin kept in Paris. As Custine, who turned up with Gurowski in mid-August, remarked, apart from Chopin, "There was nobody in Marienbad" except for "a few very second-rate Poles."[32]

Chopin's health was not good, for the benefits of taking the Enghien cure had been offset by the exertion of his comings and goings, and as a result there were not so many picnics and walks in the hills that year, and more sitting around with the Wodzinskis at the hotel. He taught Maria to play his new étude and composed a song for her to a poem by Witwicki, while she painted a watercolor portrait of him and sat embroidering a pair of slippers. Nothing was said, although it was obvious to all the other Poles in Marienbad that the two were in love. Before the end of the month the

Wodzinskis moved to Dresden, whence they were to make for Poland. Chopin, who was to return to Paris by way of Leipzig, followed them to Dresden, and after putting it off from day to day for two weeks, proposed to Maria at the "gray hour" of dusk on his last day in the city. Maria seems to have been delighted and her mother was immediately informed. It could have come as no surprise, for allowing her daughter to spend six weeks almost entirely in the company of a young man who was visibly in love with her was tantamount to encouraging him.

On the next morning, before his departure, Chopin talked the matter over with Mrs. Wodzinska, who was slightly absentminded and suffering from a toothache, and could therefore not "give sufficient attention to the subject of the Gray Hour," which had already become the code word for the proposal. What she did say was that, without her husband present, she could not promise anything definite; for the time being it must remain secret. She enjoined Chopin to look after his health. "Everything depends on that," she wrote, and added, after instructions about going to bed early and wearing warm socks, that "you must realize that this is a trial period."[33]

On this note, Chopin left Dresden that afternoon and arrived in Leipzig on September 12, astonishing Schumann, who had just written a letter to him and did not expect to see him walk through the door. "My joy was great," Schumann wrote to a friend, and described how Chopin presented him with a copy of his new G minor Ballade, saying that of all his own works it was the one closest to his heart. As for Chopin's playing, Schumann declared that it was "complete perfection, mastery which does not even seem to be aware of its own worth . . ."[34] His description of Chopin playing his new études, however, is extravagant:

> Imagine an aeolian harp that had all the scales, and that these were jumbled together by the hand of an artist into all sorts of fantastic ornaments, but in such a manner that a

deeper fundamental tone and a softly singing higher part were always audible, and you have an approximate idea of his playing.[35]

Schumann took all this very seriously and was conscious of undergoing an artistic experience. This annoyed Chopin as much as his review of the *La ci darem* Variations had done, for Schumann had still not understood what Chopin was trying to do in his music. On this occasion Schumann complained of Chopin's "dreadful habit of passing one finger quickly over the whizzing keyboard at the end of each piece, as though to get rid of his dream by force."[36] As he is the only person ever to have mentioned this habit, one is led to suspect that Chopin did it on purpose to annoy him and tease his ponderous enthusiasm.

The two musicians later called on Wieck—Mendelssohn was away from Leipzig—and then on Henriette Voigt, a pianist much admired by Schumann. "He moved me strangely," she wrote of Chopin. "Wonderful is the ease with which his velvet fingers glide, I might almost say fly, over the keys."[37] But Schumann was more interested in Chopin the composer, and he kept trying to understand and explain his works, without much success. In his review of the F minor concerto earlier that year, he had written that it was clear Chopin had been principally inspired by Beethoven's piano concertos, not realizing that Chopin had almost certainly never heard a Beethoven piano concerto before he left Poland, by which time he had written both of his own concertos. He claimed him as a truly Romantic composer, seeing rebellion in his work, and had recently written that "if the powerful autocrat of the North [the Tsar] knew what a dangerous enemy threatens him in the works of Chopin, in the simple melodies of those mazurkas, he would banish this music. The works of Chopin are like cannons hidden beneath flowers."[38]

On his return to Paris, Chopin found a letter from Mrs. Wodzinska confirming what she had said and reminding him of his promise to look after himself. The slippers embroidered by Maria had also arrived—one size too big, so he would have to wear thick socks inside them. Chopin settled down to observe the rules he had set himself: work in the morning, lessons all afternoon, dinner at six, then going out, but always coming home by eleven, and above all "playing of the gray hour."

Letters were now coursing regularly between Chopin and Maria and her mother. Maria told of her sadness at parting and her longing to see him again in "May or June at the latest," and although her letters are rather naïve and noncommittal, and a little too full of requests for music, novels, and for a new Pleyel that he had promised to choose and ship for her, there is no doubt that she was committed to the idea of becoming his wife.

The plan as it stood clearly included his return to Poland; one cannot help wondering how he envisaged this. In the heady atmosphere of Marienbad he would not have given it much thought, but back in Paris he could not have failed to ponder the issue. He loved Paris as a city, he loved it for the quality of his life there, he loved it for being the artistic capital of Europe. A move to Warsaw, let alone the Polish countryside, would have spelled misery for him, and it is hard to believe that he ever considered the possibility seriously. It is more likely that he did what he always did when faced with similar dilemmas: avoided thinking about the concrete aspects and transposed the question onto a theoretical plane. He probably even dwelled on the pleasant or romantic aspects of such a return to his homeland. As for his good resolutions about staying in at night and looking after himself, they were not to last long.

Liszt had spent the last year in Switzerland with his mistress, the Countess d'Agoult, a society lady who had left her husband in order to live with him. They had been leading a quiet existence, insofar as the celebrity and style of Liszt would allow, and she was hoping to steer him away from the life of virtuoso pianist toward that of the secluded composer. That summer, while Chopin was in Marienbad, they had been joined by a friend and admirer of Liszt, George Sand.

George Sand, or rather Aurore Dupin, had settled in Paris after her marriage to Baron Dudevant had broken up, and had at first led a frugal existence trying to survive by working in journalism. She had written a novel in collaboration with another journalist, Jules Sandeau, which was published under his name and scored a great success. Sandeau realized that the merit was hers and backed out of the partnership, leaving her to write her next novel alone. The result was her first novel *Indiana*, which came out under her new pseudonym of George Sand and made her famous overnight. She continued writing, and the feminist style and aggressive message of her books, combined with the masculine pen name and her habit of wearing men's clothes (originally so that she could go to the cheap seats in a theater without being molested), earned her the reputation of a scandalous and dangerous woman. In 1833, the same year she met Liszt, she had fallen in love with Alfred de Musset, the *enfant terrible* of French Romantic literature, and they proceeded to have a tempestuous and destructive affair. Its high point came with their "honeymoon" in Venice, where he fell ill and she took off with the doctor, whom she brought back to Paris. After Musset's return to Paris the affair went through several more convulsions of extraordinary violence and finally burned itself out in a blaze of sadomasochistic passion. George Sand then had to face her husband, and managed, by the beginning of 1836, to obtain a legal separation, to reclaim her dowry and her small country estate, and to get custody of her two children, with whom she now arrived in Switzerland.

The little group roamed Switzerland, behaving, with the

exception of Countess d'Agoult, like a gang of students on holiday, dressing to shock and provoking the stuffy reactions of respectable English travelers by setting up what must have looked like a gypsy encampment in their hotel rooms.* One Englishman, horrified to see himself sitting opposite a long-haired, strangely clad, gesticulating youth, asked his neighbor who that "fellow" might be, whereupon the little group hooted with laughter. Liszt and his countess were dubbed "the Fellows," while George Sand gave herself a sobriquet based on the slang word for a nose, *pif*, with a Swiss twist to it: Piffoël.

There could hardly be a greater contrast between the noisy, flamboyant, and often extremely childish behavior of the Fellows and Piffoël on their holiday and Chopin's quiet, reticent, and naïve courtship in Marienbad. While Chopin returned to Paris to work, look after his health, and dream of the Gray Hour, Liszt and particularly his lady had very different ideas on how they were going to spend their next few months. Having forfeited her place in Parisian society by running off with her pianist, Marie d'Agoult was determined to create for herself a new position, as literary lady and hostess of a salon.

When she returned to Paris in the first week of October 1836, she took an apartment with a large reception room in the Hôtel de France on the Rue Lafitte and sent Liszt out to bring in the celebrities. The coterie they mustered included Meyerbeer, Berlioz, Chopin, Adolphe Nourrit, and various other musicians; Heinrich Heine; the Abbé de Lamennais, the famous renegade Catholic priest and editor of *Le Monde*; the Baron d'Eckstein, a converted Jew who had become a militant Catholic; Albert Grzymala; the Saint-Simonian philosopher Pierre Leroux, and the Polish poet Adam Mickiewicz, as well as a host of lesser figures. This was soon swelled

* In one hotel register Liszt filled in the questionnaire as follows: Place of birth: "Parnassus," Occupation: "Musician-Philosopher," Coming from: "Doubt," Going to: "Truth" and so on.

by George Sand, who arrived in Paris on October 24 and
moved into a small room at the Hôtel de France.

Chopin did not much like Marie d'Agoult and was no
longer very friendly with Liszt, whose style, both musical and
social, irritated him, and who had finally transgressed against
Chopin's code when one day he had used his apartment to
make love to Marie Pleyel, the pianist and wife of the piano
maker.[39] The atmosphere at the Hôtel de France was also a
little on the heavy side as far as Chopin was concerned.
Music and philosophy were strongly represented, and the in-
evitable result was much talk of the social and political rele-
vance of music, the outcome of which was a woolly theory of
"humanitarian art." This involved people like Nourrit going
off to the slums of Paris and conducting choirs of hundreds of
workers while they sang hymns to words by Lamartine. Chopin did not feel that this was what music was about. Nor did
he like the atmosphere in which music was made at the Hôtel
de France, which was parodied by Musset in a piece on the
"Humanitarian Parnassus":[40]

> Inspiration descends, the eye of the God [Liszt] lights up, his
> hair shudders, his fingers arch and pound the keys with fury.
> He plays with his hands, his elbows, his chin, his nose. Every-
> thing that can strike pounds away . . . "Sublime!" they ex-
> claim. "That'll cost me twenty francs in repairs!" moans the
> Divinity of the House [Marie d'Agoult].

This was not really Chopin's style. Nor was the conversation, which Sainte-Beuve described as "a mass of affecta-
tions, vanities, pretentiousness, of bombast and uproar of
every kind," adding that it was made up of people whose
talent was "out of control."[41] Even Berlioz was later forced to
admit that "one talked too much . . . One did not listen, one
philosophized."[42]

Nevertheless, Chopin did frequent the Hôtel de France,
and it was there that he met George Sand for the first time,

probably in the last week of October. A few days later, on November 5, he entertained her, Liszt and his countess, Mickiewicz, Grzymala, and the writer and traveler Ferdinand Denis. The last-named noted that Liszt played magnificently, making a great effect on George Sand, who "really felt that powerful music" and that the host merely clowned about on the piano.[43] On November 9, Chopin went to dinner at the house of Count Marliani (an expatriate Italian who had the post of Spanish Consul in Paris), where he again spent the evening in the company of George Sand, Liszt, and his countess. The following day the three dined at Chopin's.

It is impossible to know Chopin's day-to-day movements, but it is certain that he was caught up in the life of this group at this time. On December 13, Jozef Brzowski, a composer who had arrived from Warsaw, received a card from Chopin which ran:

> Today I shall have a few guests, Madame Sand among them; Liszt will play, Nourrit will sing. If this pleases Mr. Brzowski I await him this evening.[44]

Brzowski was of course more than pleased, and he duly arrived to find a dazzling array of people. There were only two ladies present, as Brzowski writes:

> Both of them, though close in sympathy, were striking by their apparent diversity. The countess, blond, lively, attractive, with a humorous and graceful manner, dressed with exquisite taste, was a typical high-class Parisian lady. George Sand was quite the opposite, dark-haired, solemn and cold, not at all French, with regular features and a calm, rather dead physiognomy, in which one could read only intelligence, thought and pride; her dress was fantastic, and betrayed a desire to show off. Her white smock was girt by a wide crimson scarf, her little white tunic of strange cut had crimson facings and buttons. Her black hair, parted evenly in the middle, fell on either side of her face in curls and was tied with a gold band across her forehead.[45]

The two ladies were not the only contrast that struck the baffled Pole: there was the effervescent long-haired Liszt; the huge scruffy Custine with his regal manner; the plump and gentle Nourrit; the staid middle-aged legitimist deputy Berryer in impeccable white tie and tails; the seedy pianist Pixis; the splendidly mustachioed Grzymala; the playwright Eugène Sue; the republican journalist Schoelcher; Wlodzimierz Potocki, the nephew of Delfina's husband; Heinrich Heine; Jan Matuszynski; Ferdinand Denis, and Bernard Potocki, the young son of the author of the *Saragossa Manuscript*.

"While the Countess d'Agoult was entertaining the guests with her sparkling, witty and enchanting conversation, and a sweet smile lit up her face framed by blond locks *à l'Anglaise*," continues Brzowski, "George Sand had put herself on the little sofa placed diagonally before the fireplace, and, lightly puffing out clouds of smoke from her cigar, replied sparingly and solemnly to the questions of the men who sat down next to her."[46] Liszt, as often, drew attention to himself, leaping about making jokes and raising issues of philosophical import, which were promptly scuppered by some cynical observation from Chopin. Brzowski got bored by the talk and asked him to make Liszt play, so Chopin invited him to play a Moscheles sonata for four hands. The two sat down side by side, Chopin as always taking the bass part, while Pixis turned the pages, occasionally looking up to cast glances of breathless admiration in the direction of Brzowski, who had never heard anything like this.

After the sonata, Chopin served ices to his guests, followed by tea which was poured out by the Countess, while George Sand remained "nailed to her sofa and did not leave her cigar," as the diarist records. "She would occasionally cast a glance at the person talking to her, but mostly just stared into the fireplace at the dancing flames."[47] Accompanied on the piano by Liszt, Nourrit then sang several Schubert lieder, but Liszt himself, whom Brzowski so wanted to hear on his own, would not be lured to the keyboard, and instead got involved in a heated philosophical discussion with Bernard Potocki. At length the tedious talk irritated Chopin, spoiled the Countess's perfect temper, and even bored George Sand, who usually loved such discussions.

In a period of under six weeks Chopin had spent the evening in the company of George Sand at least as many times, but while he had no objection to being in the same circle as Europe's most famous woman writer, she made little impression on him. "What an unattractive person La Sand is," he commented to Hiller as they walked home from the Hôtel de France one evening, "but is she really a woman?"[48] He echoed the same sentiments in a letter to his parents, adding that there was something verging on the repellent about her.[49] It is easy to see that, quite apart from the fact that his heart was bent on Maria Wodzinska, George Sand did not answer to Chopin's ideal of womanhood. Heine thought that her body was too short and plump, her eyes rather dull, and that "her slightly hanging lower lip seems to suggest exhaustion of the senses."[50] Marie d'Agoult, who had known her better, dwelled on her eyes, which "seemed to see without looking, and although they were powerful, did not emit anything; a calm which made one anxious, something cold like one imagines the Sphinx of antiquity."[51]

George Sand was far too dazzled by some of the other people in the group to take any notice of Chopin. Musically, she was more impressed by the breathtaking acrobatics of Liszt, whose genius was more obvious, more assertive; by Meyerbeer, whose spectacular grand operas were all the rage at the time; by Berlioz with his romantic ebullience; and by Nourrit's gentleness and philanthropy. To be Polish in Paris at that time was of course glamorous in itself, but even here Chopin was outshone in her eyes by Mickiewicz, whom she thought "the first cousin of Goethe and Byron,"[52] and whose growing obsession with the interrelation of religion, culture, and politics brought him closer to her and took him further from Chopin. In Grzymala, whom she had dubbed her "dear convict" on account of his spells in jail, she had found a kindred soul in a more personal sense. So it is hardly surprising that the reticent, aristocratic Chopin, who avoided all philosophical or political discussion, who refused to compete musically with people like Liszt, and who hid his pride behind a façade of irony and jest, was somewhat eclipsed. It is worth mentioning that while Heine, Hiller, Custine, and Liszt himself considered Chopin the greater artist, the more politically minded of the group, including Mickiewicz and Grzymala, rated him as a salon musician and gave their admiration to Liszt, in whom they saw a potential political force. Mickiewicz, for instance, resented what he saw as Chopin's policy of wasting his artistry on the French aristocracy, when he could have been using it to speak to the masses and threaten the tyrants. Chopin's frivolous manner and refusal to take himself seriously, his reluctance to behave like a great Romantic artist, made it difficult for these people to treat his talent seriously.

Soon after this soirée, George Sand returned to her country estate and the Hôtel de France circle was gradually obscured in Chopin's life by the usual hectic activity of the Paris season. At the end of the month there was a joint concert given by Liszt and Berlioz, there was the annual Polish Ladies' sale, there were dinners and dances at Chopin's French and Polish friends', while Christmas Eve was spent at the house of an émigré Polish publisher. The guests included Jelowicki, Mickiewicz and old Julian Niemcewicz, who got drunk and kept them up till one o'clock with stories of Poland in the eighteenth century. Afterward Chopin played, and "everyone was so taken up by his playing and the good cheer that nobody had noticed it had dawned half an hour before."[53]

This was hardly the way to heed Mrs. Wodzinska's instructions, and she was aware of it through the gossip of other

Poles in Paris, although Chopin kept writing to her protesting of his good behavior. He wrote letters, sent presents to both the mother and the daughter, and complained: "Why is it not true about those mirrors in which one can see everything, about those magic rings which can transport one to the place in which one's thoughts would like to wander . . ."[54] He also went to see a fortune-teller, who predicted the happy fulfillment of all his dreams, but this turned out to be a poor prediction. Imperceptibly, things began to go wrong. Mrs. Wodzinska had returned to Poland in October and had had ample time to talk over the whole matter with her husband and send Chopin the formal reply he was awaiting. But Christmas came and went and no decision was forthcoming. The tone of the letters Chopin was receiving altered as time passed. In October 1836, Maria had signed off:

> Adieu, mio carissimo maestro, do not forget Dresden, or, soon, Poland. Adieu, au revoir . . . Au revoir, au revoir, au revoir! It gives one hope.[55]

By the end of January, however, the references to "May or June at the latest" had been dropped, and replaced by a forlorn "when we meet again."[56] And a couple of months later, Maria was signing off: "Adieu, I hope you will not forget us."[57]

At the same time, Mrs. Wodzinska's letters now made no mention of the Gray Hour and, although full of references to the Chopin family, whom she had seen once or twice in Warsaw, grew more impersonal. The Wodzinskis were clearly stalling.

The reason most frequently given is that the aristocratic Wodzinskis (who are graced with a title in most biographies of Chopin) thought too highly of themselves to give their daughter away to a commoner, however famous. This needs to be qualified. First of all, the Wodzinskis could by no stretch of the term be included in the ranks of the Polish aristocracy, and they had no right to any title. They were comfortably off gentry with aspirations. By birth they were less distinguished than the family of Chopin's mother, and could have no grounds for comparison with his father, a foreigner whose origins were kept scrupulously quiet. They would not have been remotely disgraced by marrying their daughter to the artist who was everywhere proclaimed as one of Poland's greatest geniuses and had the entree to the houses of people like the Czartoryskis and the Radziwills, before whom people of the Wodzinski class would have had to bow in the old Poland. Moreover, when Maria had returned to Poland that autumn, there had been a conspicuous lack of interesting suitors.

This all points to other reasons, such as Chopin's failing health, his refusal to behave as soberly as he had been asked to, the gossip reaching Poland from Paris about his contact and possible relations with "scandalous" women like the Countess d'Agoult and George Sand, the obvious conflict between his life in Paris and theirs in the Polish countryside, and a general feeling that a match with a county neighbor would be less fraught with problems of one sort or another. Mrs. Wodzinska, who had encouraged the whole project, was now in a very awkward position, particularly as she genuinely liked Chopin. She made no definite statement, probably hoping that the matter would die a natural death.

While Chopin endeavored to lead his own life in Paris, he could not entirely escape from the Hôtel de France clique. Marie d'Agoult had joined George Sand on her country estate at Nohant, but Liszt was very much in evidence, because at the beginning of 1837 Thalberg arrived in Paris. The time seemed right for a confrontation between the two most renowned pianists in Europe. Liszt opened up with a vitriolic attack on Thalberg and his facile repertoire in the *Gazette*

Musicale on January 8, and followed this up by turning up late at his rival's concert, coming in noisily while the latter was playing, and making mocking asides throughout the performance. He then announced a series of concerts he would give at Érard's in order to teach the Parisian public what real music was.

The first of these took place on January 28 with a program including Beethoven trios hitherto not heard in Paris, Schubert lieder sung by Nourrit, and Liszt himself playing some Beethoven, Chopin's new études, and some pieces of his own. The next three were equally impressive, both in the repertoire and its performance. Thalberg admitted total defeat, saying publicly that if he possessed a tenth of Liszt's talent, he would consider himself a great artist. Liszt was not satisfied and was only just dissuaded by Marie d'Agoult from writing another article rubbing the point in.

Thalberg proceeded with his program and gave a concert at the Conservatoire on March 12, the success of which annoyed Liszt so much that he himself booked the large Conservatoire Hall on a Sunday and managed to fill it at short notice for a magnificent performance. But the affair was not to rest there, for Princess Belgiojoso, an Italian expatriate and great Parisian hostess, asked Liszt, Thalberg, Pixis, Chopin, Czerny, and Herz to help her collect money for Italian nationalist refugees by playing in her salon. They were all to improvise on themes from Bellini's opera *I Puritani*. Even at the staggering price of forty francs a seat there were no empty ones on March 30 for this duel which only needed weapons to become deadly.[58]

Nobody paid much attention to Chopin or the others, and all the attention focused on the two main protagonists. Liszt's playing was by all accounts stupendous, and Heine was appalled at the effect it had on the audience, which was hypnotized by it. Princess Belgiojoso declared that Liszt was the only pianist in Europe. Liszt shook hands with his rival and invited him to dinner but with such hauteur that Thalberg left Paris the next morning.

Chopin had at first been amused and delighted by Thalberg's humiliation in the concert halls, for the memory of Vienna still rankled, but Liszt's vicious persecution of the man horrified him. According to Brzowski,[59] he did not mince his words when he reproached Liszt for it after Thalberg's departure. It was typical of everything that Chopin disliked about Liszt. Chopin had been confined to his bed several times during the last couple of months, but never seriously, and it is difficult to tell whether the plea of illness, which he invoked in order not to take part in Liszt's concert a few days later, on April 9, was genuine or not.

As Chopin cooled more and more toward Liszt, his countess, and their coterie, they grew more and more keen to draw him into their society. While he sat in Paris, "coughing with infinite grace," as Marie d'Agoult put it, and waiting for news from the Wodzinskis, great efforts were being made to drag him down to Nohant, George Sand's estate. She was living there permanently, having a stormy physical relationship with a bald left-wing lawyer from a neighboring town, and trying to help Liszt by keeping his countess there while he performed in Paris. In the interests of keeping Marie d'Agoult happy, George Sand was prepared to have anyone down to stay, though she herself hoped for Mickiewicz, whom she had promised to help with the French translation of one of his works. When, at the beginning of April, Marie d'Agoult had gone to Paris to help Liszt through his concert and then to bring him down to Nohant, George Sand wrote: "Tell Mick. (noncompromising manner of spelling Polish names) that my pen and my house are at his disposal and only too happy to be so, tell Grzzzz . . . that I adore him, Chopin that I idolize him, all whom you love that I love them, and that they will be welcome if brought by you." On the next day she added:

I want the Fellows, I want them as soon and for as long as possible. I want them madly. I also want Chopin and all the Mickiewiczes and Grzymalas on earth. I even want Sue, if you like. What else would I not want, if it was your whim? Even M. de Suzannet or Victor Schoelcher—anything, except a lover![60]

But, as Marie d'Agoult pointed out, "Chopin is irresolute; with him only his cough is dependable."[61] Although Chopin wrote to a friend that he might be going to stay at Nohant, he did not, much to the disappointment of the Countess, who seems to have conceived a plan to pair him off with George Sand. The reason for Chopin's irresolution was of course that it was now April, and "May and June at the latest" were approaching without his having heard a word from the Wodzinskis about their plans for the summer in Germany. At the beginning of May he heard that Antoni Wodzinski had been wounded in Spain, and although Chopin kept the wound a secret from Mrs. Wodzinska, hoping to be able to break the news gently when he saw her, this gave him an excuse to write again, for Antoni needed money. For the time being Chopin sent him some of his own and wrote to the Wodzinskis, dropping heavy hints about not knowing what he was going to do that summer. Mrs. Wodzinska's reply was cordial and chatty but did not mention any plans. Nor was there the usual postscript from Maria.

Chopin's illness had not been particularly severe that winter, but his constant activity prevented his getting over it fully, and the nervous agitation caused by the baffling behavior of the Wodzinskis made it worse. As Custine wrote to him that spring, "You are at the limit between the torments of the mind and sickness of the body," and strongly advised him to spend a couple of months quietly at St. Gratien, at the same time offering to lend him money for a journey to the waters in Germany that summer.[62] Chopin did avail himself of Custine's invitation to St. Gratien several times, but the visits were hardly calculated to restore his health.

Brzowski's diary describes one such excursion, on a Sunday at the beginning of June.[63] It was a fine day, and Brzowski admired the countryside as they rolled out of Paris through the Porte de Clichy in their hired cabriolet and then drove through St. Denis to St. Gratien, where they were met by Custine and a lady, as well as his two acolytes, Edward Saint-Barbe and Count Ignacy Gurowski. Having arranged to meet Gurowski for dinner at Enghien at six and then return to St. Gratien for the evening, they set off for Montmorency, a small village which was full of people come from Paris to spend the day in the beautiful adjoining park.

After a copious breakfast of bread, butter, and fresh milk, they went to hire donkeys, the accepted conveyance for visiting the countryside. Chopin was immediately accosted by two young girls who remembered him from the previous year, and the girls and their donkeys were duly taken. They set off, each mounted on his animal, with the two girls on foot leading them. Brzowski was taken up by "the May green of the trees, the delicious smell of the forest, the unexpected vistas between trees or along valleys," while Chopin was engaged in flirtatious conversation with the girl leading his donkey. At length they reached the Hermitage, where they were shown Rousseau's workroom, the desk on which he had written *Julie, ou la Nouvelle Héloïse*, and the decrepit old piano on which Grétry had composed.

On their return journey they were caught by a sudden downpour and had to hurry back, Chopin expertly trotting along on his donkey and hooting with laughter at the disconsolate Parisian ladies in their flowery dresses. Back at Montmorency, they took their leave of donkeys and girls and climbed back into their cabriolet, which made for Enghien and the inn where Gurowski should have been waiting. There was no Gurowski in sight, and Chopin wanted to while away the time at the piano which stood in the corner, but the land-lady refused to unlock it, fearing that the long-haired gentle-man from Paris might ruin it. Gurowski finally showed up, driving a fine carriage himself, and insisted that since it was such a fine evening they must go and call on a rich English-man who lived by the lake. They drove over to the place, only to find that the Englishman was out in a boat. When they had waited for him to come back to the shore, Gurowski de-cided to go boating himself, so it was some time before they got back to the inn and sat down to dinner. As they were all in high spirits and hungry, they ate well and washed the meal down with several bottles of champagne, some good hock, and fine claret. It was a completely drunk Gurowski who drove them back to St. Gratien at breakneck speed, sending other vehicles rolling off the road. Custine was annoyed at how late they were, for he had arranged a musical evening and everyone was waiting.

After a rapid change and an attempt to sober up a little, they came down and entered the fine drawing room, whose white walls decorated with large flowers were hung not with pictures but with two huge mirrors in gorgeous gilt frames. Comfortable sofas and armchairs covered in white brocade to match the curtains were scattered informally around the room, and the only touch of color was lent by the magnificent oriental vases standing on the white marble fireplace and the Pleyel grand piano. The assembled company included the Duchess d'Abrantès, Sophie Gay, the Countess Merlin, Ber-lioz and his wife Harriet, the tenor Duprez and his wife, and several others, including "an old writer" who was almost cer-tainly Chateaubriand. Victor Hugo and his wife were ex-pected but did not arrive. The whole group clustered around Chopin, who found it difficult to hide his lingering intoxi-cation, and after a while the music started.

First Duprez and his wife sang a duet from a Donizetti opera. Duprez had recently arrived from Italy and quickly supplanted Nourrit as the leading tenor in Paris, with the result that the other had to quit the capital. Duprez then sang a duet from Bellini with the Countess Merlin, a gifted amateur singer, after which Custine invited Chopin, who played a couple of new études and his second ballade. Altogether everyone begged him for a mazurka:

> Chopin immediately offered them one of his bucolic national poems, and then, like some kind of prophet inspired, started on a somewhat warlike piece. It was an improvisation. The beautiful melody and the fiery spirit in which he rendered it electrified these legitimist souls, which had sunk into a reverie under the influence of the melancholy song of the mazurka. When he had finished and risen from the piano, everyone got up and surrounded the triumphant virtuoso . . .[64]

The company then adjourned to the dining room, where they did justice to a luxurious supper, after which some of the guests left. The remainder begged the Countess Merlin to sing some Spanish songs (she was a Cuban by birth). Custine rummaged about and dug up some castanets, Chopin sat down at the piano and began to take the melody and the cues from her, and the Countess was soon dancing around the room as she sang. When this was over, Custine insisted that it was "the magician, the Sylph of St. Gratien," who must top off the evening, and Chopin once more launched into a long improvisation. It was well after midnight when the last notes died away, and in spite of being pressed by Custine to spend the night, the two Poles climbed back into their cabriolet and returned to Paris. Chopin could not have been in bed before two.

Before Brzowski left for Warsaw in June, Chopin took him and Matuszynski out to dinner, typically enough at one of the grandest restaurants in Paris, the Rocher de Cancale, on the Rue de Montorgueil, where one or two of the famous eating houses which used to throng it still survive. The dinner was meticulously recorded by Brzowski:

One climbs to the first floor, and already on the stairs leading out of the lower room, there are relays of *garçons*, one of whom counts how many there are in the party and shouts to the others to prepare a room suitable for the number. So we found ourselves in a *cabinet* for three in which we settled ourselves comfortably. On the table in the center of the room lay a book listing the dishes, a sheet of clean paper, and pen and ink. The elegant, slim but comprehensive volume, listing everything most refined that Paris can offer the gourmet, became the object of our scrutiny and discussion. Finally we gave complete freedom of choice to Chopin. He wrote out what we wished to eat and the waiting *garçon* was handed the note. We were soon served. We started with oysters—excellent! Next came soup, a cream of game—wonderful! Next they served us matelot.* This dish, equal only to nectar, by its wonderful texture and exquisite taste, seemed to be trying to proclaim with pride that we were indeed dining at the Rocher de Cancale. The next dish was asparagus—beyond all praise. Then came other savory dishes, and the whole meal was noisily accompanied by the most magical champagne . . . With cigars in our teeth we set off for coffee at Tortoni's.[65]

Chopin was certainly not behaving like someone who was looking after his health, and although he still bandied about names like Ems and Wiesbaden in a note to Mrs. Wodzinska, fishing desperately for a clue, he remained in Paris, or, rather, hopped about between Paris and Enghien. In mid-June, Custine tried to take him along when he left for Wiesbaden, while Marie d'Agoult encouraged him to "come and create a new motherland at Nohant" with Mickiewicz and Grzymala, but Chopin was intractable. Then, suddenly, he made a very different decision. His friend the piano maker Pleyel was going to London for a couple of weeks, and Chopin decided to join him.

They arrived on July 7, 1837. Fontana had told Chopin

* Probably *matelotte*—a fish stew with herbs.

that England had an "Italian sky" in the summer, but Chopin found it gray and sooty and was soon coughing a great deal. But he loved London: "The English women, the horses, the palaces, the carriages, the wealth, the luxury, the space, the trees, everything, from the soap to the razors—everything is wonderful—everything ordered, everything educated, everything well scrubbed," as he wrote to Fontana.[66] He was trying to drown his anxieties in hectic activity, and the account given by Kozmian, a friend of Fontana who acted as his guide, is revealing:

> Chopin had been here for two weeks incognito. He knows nobody and wishes to see nobody but me. I spend the whole day with him, and sometimes even the whole night, like yesterday. He is here with Pleyel, famous for his pianos and his wife's adventures . . . They have come to "do" London. They have put up at one of the best hotels, they keep a carriage; they are simply looking for ways of spending money. One day we go to Windsor, another to Blackwall, another to Richmond . . . I often go to the opera. I haven't seen *Ildegonde* yet, because Chopin does not want to listen to boring music. The concert for the Beethoven memorial was not a success. There were very few people, but the performance of his last great symphony was very good. Devrient sang *Fidelio* and Moscheles played a long concerto. Chopin says his playing is very "baroque."[67]

Chopin did not call on Moscheles, which was rude to say the least, as the latter was bound to (and did) find out that he had been in London. Luckily for Chopin, everything was put down to the state of his health, which appeared very bad indeed to those who saw him. It was probably his nervous condition and the suspense in which the Wodzinskis held him which brought on this desire to remain incognito. One evening that Pleyel spent with his English counterpart, Broadwood, Chopin accompanied him, but insisted on being introduced as Mr. Fritz. He successfully disguised his identity until late in the evening when, after everyone had played the piano a little, he could not resist the urge himself, and, sitting down at the instrument, had everyone gaping in astonishment after a few bars. The truth was soon out, and Chopin went on to improvise. As one of those present wrote, those who heard him "will never forget that memory."[68]

After almost three weeks of frenetic activity, Pleyel and Chopin left London, accompanied by Kozmian as far as Brighton, and reached Paris in the last week of July. While in London, Chopin had received a letter from Mrs. Wodzinska which informed him that they were not going to Germany or anywhere else that summer. The letter has not survived, and it is possible that it contained something more definite, for when he wrote back to her on August 14 (he now had to inform her of Antoni's wound by letter), the final paragraph suggests that he had understood:

> Your last letter reached me in London, where I whiled away the last month. I had thought that from there I might travel through Holland to Germany . . . I returned home, the season is getting on, and for me it will probably come to an end in my room—I await a less sad letter from you than the last. Perhaps my next will only be a postscript to Antoni's.[69]

The season did indeed end for Chopin in his rooms, in the middle of a deserted Paris, with Custine in Germany, the Czartoryskis in Brittany, Liszt and his countess in Italy. George Sand spent most of the summer in Paris looking after her dying mother, but then returned to Nohant in a gloomy state of mind. Looking back over the tempestuous last years, she felt horrified and spent. She decided to remain in the country and work; for her children took a tutor who was at the same time a lover for her; and settled down to "no longer count the bad days or look forward to better ones."[70]

The autumn of 1837 was a quiet time for Chopin too, even when his various acquaintances had returned to Paris. He was smarting under the cruel denouement of the Wodzinski affair and did not get over it for a long time. He made a packet of all Maria's letters and on the envelope wrote two words which can only be translated as "my tragedy." But this was not enough to bury the episode, and it would appear that he kept Maria firmly in his mind just as he had Konstancja, as an image and an object for emotional self-indulgence.

His finances too must have been in a pitiful state, for his life-style over the last year had been regal. Sometime in the previous year he had acquired a servant, he entertained often in his rooms, and he was always buying people expensive presents. The chaotic summer must have made it impossible for him to give lessons regularly, and the trip to London gave the final deathblow to his means. He now had to work hard at the lessons and also to sell a few compositions. His life during most of that year had been far too hectic to allow him the relaxation and concentration he needed in order to write. He had been steadily working at some of the preludes and had written some mazurkas and nocturnes, but it was only in the autumn that he could concentrate enough to polish up some of them for publication. Of the longer works produced that summer and autumn, the most important are the famous Funeral March, which he did not publish now but later included in a sonata, and the B flat minor Scherzo, opus 31. Both of these are highly dramatic, though restrained, pieces, and they provide a good example of the direction in which Chopin was moving.

Chopin had enjoyed his apparently effortless ascent in Parisian artistic and social life, and his position as one of the city's distinguished artists was, by 1837, unassailable. But the price had been high; his health had given way, and as he approached his twenty-eighth birthday he felt as rudderless and isolated as ever. Playing the part of the fashionable cosmopolitan artist in French society had been something of a failure. He had little in common with the Berliozes and the

Liszts, less still with their intellectual friends. As for the French aristocracy, he realized better than anyone that his relationship with it was on the most superficial level. The few exceptions, such as Custine or the Count de Perthuis (the King's director of music), could not obscure this fact. He had one or two humbler French friends, such as the journalist Legouvé or the cellist Franchomme, and a few sincere admirers including the banker Auguste Leo, the Dutch Ambassador, Baron Stockhausen, and the wine merchant and Saxon Consul, Thomas Albrecht, perhaps the closest of all Chopin's non-Polish friends, to whose daughter he had stood as godfather.

Chopin was by no means a self-sufficient person, and this collection of friends did not constitute the "family" that he needed. What is more, they could not speak Polish. This was an important factor. Chopin's French was not as good as it might have been; he spoke haltingly and with a strong accent, while his letters reveal that he could neither spell nor construct his sentences properly. He found speaking French continuously very strenuous, and he needed to resort to his mother tongue in order to relax as well as to express himself adequately. The style of his letters to friends like Grzymala or Fontana is lazy and allusive; sentences often lack an ending and thoughts are not carried through or explained. With friends like these, he obviously did not need to develop his thoughts or feelings, and that is why they got closer to him than any foreigner. For the same reasons, he found Poles in general more relaxing to be with, and it was with them that he would spend the evening when he was tired or depressed. As he explained to one French lady; "You may think it insignificant, but one's greatest solace in a foreign land is to have someone who carries one's thoughts back to the homeland every time one looks at him, talks to him or listens to his words."[71]

Chopin was not as deeply committed to the Polish cause as

many of his countrymen would have liked. Most of them were cut off not only from their country, but also from their position in society and their means of livelihood. This tended to make their patriotism more radical and uncompromising, and drove many of them, particularly the intellectuals, toward religion or mysticism of one sort or another. Chopin was cut off from home and family only through his own choice, and this did not affect his career at all. He would almost certainly have spent most of his life in Paris whether the uprising had taken place or not. This placed him in a different position from the other émigrés, many of whom felt that his patriotism was superficial. He of course gave generously to all Polish charities and never failed to offer his services for any émigré event, but at the same time he gave lessons to members of the Russian aristocracy passing through Paris, and could certainly not be accused of chauvinism in his relationships. What irked people like Adam Mickiewicz and the poet Slowacki was that he wasted his talent "caressing the nerves of the French aristocracy" instead of sowing rebellion with his music.[72]

This opinion stemmed from a total misunderstanding of Chopin's work. What they expected him to write is difficult to imagine; probably they did not know themselves. Nevertheless, there was a definite, if rarely voiced, grudge against him. This was why he spent more time with people like the Czartoryskis, Grzymala, and the Platers than with the intellectuals and the poets, for the former understood his attitude and tended to be more realistic. Chopin's patriotism and his nostalgia for Poland were theoretical, notwithstanding their strength, as theoretical as most of his passions. Although they hung about him like an aura, they did not obtrude into his way of life, and although they were the primary inspiration for most of his music, they remained on an emotional and not a political plane.

That year there was another Polish bazaar for Chopin to

help with, shortly before Christmas, and it was a busy season for him in other respects. Musical attractions included the first performance, on December 5, of Berlioz's *Requiem* at the Invalides. In the last days of February, Chopin was called to the Tuileries to play before the Royal Family. Each time he did this he was presented with a gift: a silver-gilt tea set for one performance, a pair of Sèvres vases for another, and a Sèvres dinner service for a third, all inscribed: *"Louis-Philippe, Roi des Français, à Frédéric Chopin."*

A few days later, on March 3, Chopin took part in a concert given by the young pianist Alkan. Chopin, Zimmerman, Gutmann and Alkan played Alkan's arrangement of Beethoven's Seventh Symphony for eight hands on two pianos, a typically popular concert piece. Later that month Chopin traveled down to Rouen to help his friend Antoni Orlowski, who had settled there and needed to make his mark by giving a concert. What Chopin had not anticipated was that all the Paris music critics as well would go to Rouen for the occasion. The result was that Orlowski was the Cinderella of the evening. "Here is an event which is not without importance in the musical world," wrote Legouvé in the *Gazette Musicale* of March 25. Chopin played at length before an audience of five hundred, who were "penetrated, moved, enraptured." The review concluded with the exhortation:

> Forward then, Chopin! Forward! Let this triumph decide you; do not be selfish, give your talent to all; consent to pass for what you are; put an end to the great debate which divides the artists; and when it shall be asked who is the greatest pianist in Europe, Liszt or Thalberg, let all the world reply, like those who have heard you: It is Chopin![73]

Instead of persuading him to return to the life of a performing pianist, this seems to have put Chopin off. This appearance was his last in public for a long time. Heine, who had just written an article on Chopin, understood him rather better than Legouvé:

> Chopin does not derive his satisfaction from the fact that his hands are applauded by other hands for their agile dexterity. He aspires to a greater success; his fingers are the servants of his soul, and his soul is applauded by those who do not merely listen with their ears, but also with their souls.[74]

8

George Sand

In the spring of 1838, Chopin was often to be seen at the soirées of Countess Charlotte Marliani, whom he had met a couple of years before. She was an undistinguished but affable Frenchwoman who had married the Spanish Consul in Paris. He was an exiled Italian revolutionary, and since there was mutual sympathy between the Polish and Italian exiles in Paris, his wife's salon was a meeting place for members of both groups. The regular guests included Grzymala, Mickiewicz, and the Czartoryskis, as well as notable Italian expatriates like Princess Belgiojoso. Although she was no intellectual, the Countess had also opened her doors to some of the debris of Marie d'Agoult's "humanitarian" salon of the previous year. As a result, her elegant apartment on the Rue de la Grange Batelière was cosmopolitan and artistic in its atmosphere.

It was there that George Sand decided to stay when she came to Paris on business for two weeks in the middle of April. Liszt had sometime before written to her from Italy, urging her to "see Chopin a little."[1] He need not have bothered, for the two inevitably met once again, after not having seen each other for fifteen months.

They had both changed a great deal during that period. In the autumn of 1836, the happy, frivolous Chopin, who was hoping to marry Maria Wodzinska, had turned his nose up at the Hôtel de France group, rarely played the piano, and usually clowned about or took off Liszt when he did so. George Sand had probably been put off Chopin by his apparent superficiality and snobbishness. Now Chopin was sad, lost, and more serious; George Sand weary and reflective. The surroundings in which they saw each other were more conducive to their appreciation of each other's qualities. In response to the homely atmosphere of the Marliani apartment Chopin played a great deal and played at his best. At Custine's apartment, where they both had dinner on May 8, George Sand could see him in his element. The guests, who included the Duchess d'Abrantès, Countess Merlin, the Victor Hugos, Jules Janin, Sophie Gay, Charles Nodier, and Lamartine, listened to Duprez singing Gluck arias, Franchomme playing his cello, and finally to Chopin. It was a warm evening and the scent of the garden wafted in through the open french windows of the dining room where they sat. Chopin improvised for hours in the semi-darkness, with only a "magic glow" lighting up the vast painting covering the wall behind him.[2]

George Sand fell in love with Chopin. "I must say that I was confused and amazed at the effect this little creature wrought on me," she wrote some two weeks later. "I have still not recovered from my astonishment, and if I were a proud person I should be feeling humiliated at having been carried away by my emotions at a moment in my life when I had thought that I had settled down for good."[3] She was only thirty-four years old, six years older than Chopin, but she had lived with such intensity and packed so much experience into those years that she felt played out. Balzac had described her only a month or two before:

Physically, she has developed a double chin, like a Church Canon. She hasn't a single gray hair, in spite of the terrible experiences she has been through. Her swarthy complexion has not altered; her lovely eyes are as lustrous as ever. She always looks stupid when sunk in thought, for, as I told her after studying her a while, all her expression is concentrated in the eyes.[4]

Those eyes were now devouring Chopin, who soon found himself gazing back into them and realizing that the flamboyant, cavalier, cigar-smoking panache which she sported in public was a mask behind which she hid her shyness and femininity. These sphinx-like eyes exercised an immense power of silent attraction, and it was not long before Chopin was irresistibly drawn toward George Sand. His response was by no means passive, and there can be little doubt that his feelings toward her were ardent. But he was bewildered and anxious, as this hastily scribbled note to Grzymala indicates:

My darling, I must see you urgently today, even at night, at 12 or 1. Don't fear any embarrassment for yourself, my dearest, you know I have always valued your good heart. It's a question of advice for me.[5]

Having spent the last two years dreaming of a love affair in which every move forward, every step in intimacy would be drawn out over a period of months, he was knocked off balance by this new development and the rapidity with which it was taking place. After only a couple of weeks, he was on the brink of sexual consummation, at which point he hesitated. George Sand had to return to Nohant, as her son had fallen ill, and on her last evening in Paris, May 14, she was at Grzymala's with Delacroix, listening to Chopin playing into the small hours. At the moment of parting, Chopin grew embarrassed, as he sensed that it was incumbent on him to make a physical advance. He shied away from it and made some remark about "not spoiling the memory" of the past three weeks. This suddenly revealed to her that he still thought of lovemaking as "dirty," an attitude that could not fail to jar her, who had slept with almost every man she had ever loved.

She returned to Nohant perplexed and worried. "We allowed ourselves to be swept along by a passing wind," she reasoned, but found that reasoning got her nowhere.[6] While she was wondering what to do next, Chopin was doing the same in Paris. The image of Maria suddenly loomed, presumably as a sort of counterbalance of respectable purity to the frighteningly real sexual possibilities of the situation in hand. His chronic irresolution and inability to make up his mind played its part too, and he went running to "Uncle Albert" Grzymala. The upshot of this was that Grzymala wrote to George Sand—it is not known whether Chopin knew of this or not—discussing the matter at some length and apparently warning her not to trifle with Chopin. He also told her that Chopin still cherished the memory of someone else, at the same time expressing misgivings as to whether he could ever be happy in marriage.

George Sand replied with a very long letter, in which she laid bare her thoughts and begged Grzymala to form a judgment, by which she swore to abide. The two had become intimate in the last couple of years and admired each other greatly; it is not impossible that Grzymala might have briefly enjoyed her favor as a lover. "I believe in your gospel without knowing it well and without examining it, for if it has an adept like you it must be the most sublime of gospels," she wrote, and then proceeded to analyze the main issues as she saw them:

> This person, whom he wants to or feels himself bound to love, will she make him happy? Or will she increase his sufferings and his sadness? I don't ask whether he loves, whether he is loved by her, whether it is more or less intense than with me. I know more or less what is happening inside me, and what must be happening inside him. I want to know

which of us two he must forget or abandon for his own peace
of mind, for his own happiness, for his life even, which seems
to me too fragile and tottering to be able to resist unhap-
piness.

Having said this, and having stressed that she did not wish
to play the part of a wicked angel and sniff "the incense intended for another altar," she rambled on in an incoherent
and contradictory manner. She pointed out that "there is a
being, excellent, perfect from the point of view of his heart
and his honor, whom I shall never leave," by which she
meant the playwright Mallefille. But a page or so further on
she admitted that his caresses were a good deal less welcome
since she had fallen in love with Chopin. She declared that
Mallefille was as malleable as wax, and that he would not
stand in the way of any decision she made. She had been
deeply horrified at Chopin's deficient or unhappy sexual experience, and virtually suggested that it was her duty to sort him
out. Recoiling from this, however, she put forward another
solution, which appealed to her image of herself as a reasonable, grown-up person in control of her destiny:

> I think that our love can only last in the condition in which
> it was born, that is to say only from time to time, when a
> good wind brings us together, when we can take a trip to the
> stars, after which we can part in order to walk on earth.

This essentially meant that she would keep Mallefille as
her lover, that Chopin could love as many Polish ladies as he
wished, and that she would "chastely press him in my arms
when the celestial wind deigns to snatch and waft us up into
the heavens." (It is one of the failings of Sand's prose style
that when she hits upon a convenient metaphor, she labors it
to death.) This was not humbug or hypocrisy, as some have
tried to make out; George Sand rarely planned what she was
going to write, even in her novels, and never crossed out what
she had written, and the length and rambling nature of this

letter confirm that she was simply working toward a solution. Her summing up ran as follows:

> If he is happy or will be happy through her, *let him be*. If he will be unhappy, *stop him*. If I can make him happy without spoiling his happiness with *her*, *I can arrange my life accordingly*. If he can only be happy with me by ruining his chances of happiness through her, *we must avoid each other and he must forget me*. There is no avoiding these four points.[7]

But there was a fifth "point"; she was in love with Chopin and no longer wanted Mallefille, while Chopin did not know what he wanted but was deeply attracted to her. George Sand was a curious mixture of eighteenth-century reason and Romantic impulse, and, having reasoned everything out on paper, she proceeded to act in total contradiction to her conclusions. It is not known whether Grzymala ever replied or what he would have said, but, having laid the whole matter in his lap, she now took it firmly back into her own hands and dashed off a note to him saying:

> My affairs are calling me back. I shall be in Paris on Thursday. Come to see me and try to keep it a secret from the Little One. We shall give him a surprise. Yours, dearest, G.S.—I shall, as usual, be staying with Mme. Marliani.[8]

Grzymala promptly warned Chopin of the surprise that lay in store for him, and received the following answer:

> My dearest! I cannot be surprised, because yesterday I saw Marliani, who told me she was coming. I shall be at home till five, giving lessons, rottenly (I'm just finishing my second). What will come of all this, God only knows. I feel really awful. I've been calling on you every day to give you a hug. Let's have dinner somewhere together.[9]

On June 6, George Sand arrived in Paris, and both reasoning and scruples quickly gave way before natural instinct. The affair was only slightly complicated by the arrival in Paris of

Mallefille, who still considered himself to be the official lover and accompanied George Sand much of the time. She took a little garret room not far from the Marlianis', ostensibly so that she could get on with her work, and thereby guaranteed herself some freedom. The evenings were usually spent at the Marlianis', where the deception was made easier by the fact that the small group of friends who would gather there, Delacroix, Grzymala, and Mickiewicz, were all in on the secret. The unfortunate Mallefille listened to Chopin playing—"hidden in the darkest corner of the room, I wept while following in my thoughts the desolate images conjured up"—little realizing that he had more urgent cause for tears.[10] While he sat down and wrote a gushing poem exalting Chopin and his country, the latter was sitting in Delacroix's studio on the left bank with George Sand, posing for a joint portrait. A Pleyel piano had been moved into the studio in June, and Delacroix painted Chopin playing it, with George Sand sitting just behind in an ecstatic pose.

In August, she sent Mallefille off with her son on a trip around Normandy, and was at last able to see Chopin whenever she wanted. A month of bliss followed, and George Sand wrote to Delacroix of "the delicious exhaustion of a fulfilled love." In September she was declaring:

> I am still in the state of intoxication in which you last saw me. There has not been the slightest cloud in our clear sky, not a grain of sand in our lake. I am beginning to think that there are angels disguised as men.[11]

Being George Sand, she had to explain to herself and others that her love was "neither a preconceived decision, nor a substitute, nor an illusion born of boredom and solitude, nor a caprice, nor any of those things with which one deceived oneself by deceiving others." Refuting all that she had written and decided in the past year, she exclaimed to Delacroix: "Love above all, don't you agree? Love above all when one's star is in the ascendant, art above all when the star is in decline!"[12] The heavy philosophical novel she was halfway through was put aside, and she embarked on a musical-artis-tical-philosophical drama entitled *Les Sept Cordes de la Lyre*, in which the Spirit of the Lyre, a symbolic Chopin, exclaims: "Listen to the voice that sings love and not to the voice that explains it." She could hardly have said more clearly that Chopin was in and the "humanitarians" were out.[13]

At the beginning of September, however, the "celestial wind" theory came into sharp conflict with reality, for Chopin was getting possessive and jealous, and George Sand could not face carrying on with Mallefille, who was back in Paris. As a result, the man she would "never leave" was un-ceremoniously dismissed. He proved to be a good deal less malleable than she had thought, and when he realized what lay behind his dismissal, he became wild. There are two ver-sions of what happened. One is that he posted himself out-side Chopin's apartment, on the Chaussée d'Antin, and tried to seize George Sand as she emerged, she taking advantage of a heavy goods wagon which rolled between them and leaping into a passing cab. The other alleges that, after nearly break-ing down Chopin's door one night, he attempted to strangle the unfortunate composer and was only stopped by the inter-vention of Grzymala. Whichever is closest to the truth, Mallefille was wandering around Paris uttering wild threats, and the two lovers had to be careful throughout September, during which they did not go out much together.

George Sand had for some time been planning to spend that autumn and winter in Italy on account of her delicate fifteen-year-old son Maurice, and Chopin's poor health cou-pled with Mallefille's threats made such a plan still more ex-pedient. For some reason, Italy was dropped in favor of Ma-jorca, which was presumably suggested by some of the Spaniards who frequented the Marlianis'. One of these, the Marquess of Valldemosa, though a Majorcan himself, seems to have known the place but vaguely and threw out a few optimistic remarks about the good climate. Without further ado, or a thought for the fact that Spain was still in the throes of a bloody civil war, George Sand made up her mind and started to make her preparations.

Chopin hesitated as he always did before making a decision. Grzymala expressed misgivings about the advisability of the journey, and the prospect of leaving Paris for some six months for an unknown destination did not fill Chopin with enthusiasm. On the other hand he could not resign himself to letting this woman who meant so much to him go off and leave him alone, so he borrowed money, presold the almost completed set of preludes, and arranged for Pleyel to have a piano shipped out.

On October 18, George Sand left with her two children and a maid, traveling by easy stages. Chopin was to meet them en route, and began to say his farewells in Paris. On October 20 he went to St. Gratien for the day and made a painful impression on Custine, who wrote:

He is leaving for Valencia in Spain, that is to say for the other world. You simply cannot imagine what Madame Sand has managed to do with him in the space of one summer! Consumption has taken possession of that face, making it a soul without a body. He played to us a farewell, with the expression that you know. First a polonaise, which he had just written, magnificent by its force and verve. It is a joyous riot. Then he played the Polish prayer. Then, at the end, a funeral march, which made me burst into tears in spite of myself. It was the procession taking him to his last resting place; and when I reflected that perhaps I would never see him again on this earth, my heart bled. The unfortunate creature cannot see that the woman has the love of a vampire! He is following her to Spain, whither she is preceding him. He will never leave that country. He did not dare tell me he was going; he only spoke of his need for a good climate and for rest! Rest!— with a Ghoul as traveling companion![14]

Chopin left Paris on October 25, in the company of the brother of the Spanish minister Mendizabal, traveling night and day in order to catch up with George Sand at Perpignan. They arrived there on October 30, Chopin "fresh as a rose and pink as a turnip, looking well and having borne heroically the four nights in the mail coach."[15] The next day they took the ship from Port-Vendres and reached Barcelona on November 2. They had to spend five days here, awaiting the departure of the weekly packet to Palma, during which they made the acquaintance of the French Consul, dined aboard a French brig standing in the harbor, and even went on a long excursion into the surrounding countryside. In spite of the civil war, of which they were continually reminded by bursts of distant gunfire, the city was thronged with people pretending that nothing out of the ordinary was going on, and the warm evenings were dominated by the sound of guitars and merry-making.

On the evening of November 7 the party embarked on the *Mallorquín*, the little steamer which plied between Majorca and Barcelona, and after a warm and perfectly calm night crossing, sailed into Palma harbor in the late morning under a blazing sun. While Chopin and the children remained on the quayside being stared at by the locals, George Sand set off in search of a hotel, only to return a few hours later having discovered that there was no hotel in Palma, and that such rented accommodation as there was had been taken up by refugees from the mainland. The locals kept telling her to have "*mucha calma*," advice which drove her frantic with irritation.

She eventually found a couple of squalid rooms in a noisy and poor area of the city, where they could at least camp for the time being, and on the next day set off in search of better lodgings, trusting in the introductions she had brought to people in Palma. She had letters to the Canut family, the foremost bankers in Palma, to the family of the Marquess of

Valldemosa, and to various other members of Palma society, but, while some of them were pleasant enough, most were rather guarded in their behavior, and none offered any help. As Madame de Canut points out in her memoirs, the Majorcans were taken aback by the arrival on the scene of an unattached woman who wrote books and smoked cigars, accompanied by two long-haired boys and a little girl who wore boys' clothes, none of whom went to church, and whose manner exuded a strong odor of immorality.[16] This of course excited the local rakes, and on the one evening that she went to the opera with the Canuts, she was stared out of existence with either disapproving or lecherous looks. She therefore left Majorcan society to itself and turned for help to the much more congenial French Consul in Palma, Monsieur Flury.

With his help she tracked down a Mr. Gomez, who was prepared to rent her his little villa at Establiments, a couple of miles from Palma. They moved in on November 15 and were delighted with the primitively furnished but picturesque house called S'on Vent. As Chopin wrote to Fontana on the next day:

> My dearest, I am at Palma, surrounded by palms, cedars, cactuses, olives, oranges, lemons, aloes, figs, pomegranates, etc.; everything the Jardin des Plantes has in its hothouses. The sky is like turquoise, the sea like lapis lazuli, the hills like emeralds, the air like in heaven. During the daytime it is sunny and hot, and everyone walks about in summer clothes; at night you hear guitars and singing for hours. Huge balconies overhung with vines; Moorish battlements. Everything looks out toward Africa, like the town itself. In a word, this is the most wonderful life.[17]

George Sand, too, was delighted with the place, which she described as "a green Switzerland under a Calabrian sky, with the solemnity and the silence of the Orient."[18] She declared to a friend in Paris that "we shall never leave Majorca."[19] Both Chopin and Maurice went for long walks, and their

health seemed to be thriving, but George Sand's optimism
was a little premature, for after one very long walk, during
which the weather changed suddenly, Chopin had an attack
of bronchitis. This would not have been serious had the
weather remained fine, but it now deteriorated. Torrential
rains came down, the cold set in, and the charming villa, with
its paneless windows, thin walls, and chimneyless braziers,
soon turned into a cold, damp, smoky hole. Chopin's bronchitis grew worse, and by the end of November he was coughing and spitting in a desperate way. George Sand was so
alarmed that she called in a doctor, who brought a couple of
colleagues each of whom examined Chopin:

> The first sniffed at what I had coughed up, the second tapped
> at the place I had coughed it up from, the third poked about
> and listened while I coughed. The first said that I was dead,
> the second that I was dying, the third that I was about to
> die.[20]

The doctors departed and Chopin's condition improved independently of them. This was largely thanks to the way in
which George Sand looked after him, cooking special meals
for him and at last managing to get an artisan to build her a
Lhomond stove, which meant that the room could be heated
without being fumigated. Although she was irritated by the
fact that "instead of making literature, I am making the
food," as she wrote to Grzymala,[21] she kept her spirits up and
continued to write enthusiastic letters to her friends in Paris.
Chopin, who had been "dreaming of music but could not
make any,"[22] since the Pleyel had still not arrived, managed
to rent a local piano and get down to work on the remaining
preludes, and even wrote a new mazurka (no. 1 of opus 41).
    Just as things were beginning to look up a little, the
weather deteriorated further, the walls of the house swelled
like a sponge with the moisture, and Chopin's health took another plunge. In mid-December he wrote to Fontana that

"my manuscript lies dormant, while I cannot sleep—I can only cough and, covered in poultices, lie here waiting for the spring, or something else . . ."[23] The doctors who had caused such amusement had in fact diagnosed tuberculosis, and they had done what was demanded by Spanish law in such cases: reported it to the authorities. As soon as he heard of this, Mr. Gomez told the party to decamp forthwith and to pay for the whitewashing of the house and for new furniture, as by law all effects touched by a consumptive had to be burned.

George Sand had in fact been thinking of moving anyway. On one sightseeing excursion, at the beginning of their stay, they had visited the Carthusian monastery of Valldemosa, which she thought "the most romantic spot on earth."[24] After its dissolution, the monastery had been taken over by the government, which rented out cells to anyone who wished to stay there. She had immediately rented one, thinking that she might come and write there sometimes. As the damp weather made itself felt in Palma, she began to consider moving to the higher ground of Valldemosa, but was put off by the difficulty of finding furniture for the cell. However, just as Mr. Gomez told her to vacate his house, a family which was moving out of Valldemosa offered to sell their furniture. On December 15, therefore, the little party loaded up the rented piano, the stove, and all the effects they could take and set off up the mountainside. This in itself was no easy undertaking, for there was no proper road up to the monastery. "Many times I have traveled from Palma to this place, always with the same carter, always by a different route," Chopin later wrote to Fontana. "The roads are created by streams, repaired by avalanches; today you cannot get through here because it has been plowed up, tomorrow only a mule can get through—and you should see the local carts!!!"[25]

The monastery itself nestled in the mountains and enjoyed the most magnificent view over the surrounding countryside and the sea, "one of those views which overcome one, because they leave nothing to be desired, nothing to be imagined," as George Sand wrote. "Everything the poet and the painter might have dreamed up has been created in this place by nature."[26]

The cell which they moved into comprised three large chambers reached from a passage which served the other cells as well. The furniture consisted of camp beds, rickety tables, rush chairs, and a white wood settee. The clay floor was covered with rush matting and white sheepskins. As Chopin described it:

> Valdemosa, between the mountains and the sea, a huge abandoned Carthusian monastery, where, in a cell with doors larger than any pair of gates in Paris, you can imagine me, my hair uncurled, without white gloves, pale as ever. The cell is in the shape of a tall coffin, with a great dusty vault; a small window, and, outside; oranges, palms, cypresses. Opposite the window, my bed of straps, under a moorish filigree rose. Next to my bed there is a hopeless square desk I can hardly write on, on it a leaden candlestick (a luxury here) with a candle in it, my Bach, my own scrawls, someone else's papers . . . silence . . . you can yell . . . silence still. In a word, it is a strange place I am writing from.[27]

Among the other inhabitants of the monastery were a local apothecary; the guardian of the place; an old servant of the monks; and a woman from the mainland who offered to help George Sand with the cooking and domestic work. The sense of isolation felt by the little party, which was heightened because they had still not received a single letter from Paris, was not unpleasant to them at first.

Although he had slightly recovered from the crisis of the first weeks of December, Chopin was still "very weak and feeble" at the end of the month, and every time the weather took a turn for the worse his health would follow suit. It was only after spending a couple of weeks at Valldemosa that George Sand discovered why the whole of Palma did not retire to the mountains during the winter. She explained to Charlotte Marliani:

> There are rainstorms here that you can have no idea of anywhere else. It is a terrifying deluge. The air is so damp that one feels utterly exhausted. I am a mass of rheumatic pains.[28]

But while Chopin's health was in an appalling state, and there was no possibility of his recovering effectively until the warm weather returned, George Sand's later accounts of his condition, like all her recollections, must be taken with a pinch of salt. "Death seemed to be hovering over our heads, waiting to snatch one of us," she wrote a couple of years later,[29] which was blatantly not the case at the time. Similarly, a decade later she wrote that "the poor great artist was a detestable patient . . . he was completely demoralized,"[30] which contrasts strongly with what she wrote to Charlotte Marliani from the monastery. "If you knew him how I have got to know him, you would love him even more, my dear," she then said. "He is an angel of patience, gentleness and goodness."[31]

Chopin was not remotely demoralized. Whenever he was not actually laid out by illness, he was working on the preludes, writing, as he put it to Fontana, "in the cell of an old monk, who may have had more fire in his soul than I, but stifled it, stifled and doused it, for he had it in vain."[32] While there were a thousand irritations and problems to complain about, he felt that "it all pales into insignificance next to this sky, the poetry with which everything here breathes, next to the color of these beautiful places still unfathomed by any human eye."[33]

The only thing that did afflict him seriously, as he explained to Grzymala, was to "see her continually anxious, nursing me (God forbid the local doctors), making my bed, sweeping my room, brewing tisanes, denying herself everything for my sake, with children needing her constant atten-

tion . . ."³⁴ George Sand had indeed taken on great respon-
sibilities. She had to spend part of each day looking to the
education of her children, she had to go on churning out
quantities of prose for her clamoring editor, and she had to
cater for all the practical needs of the little group. The maid
she had brought with her seems to have been of little use,
while the woman who had offered her services so generously,
and had subsequently been joined in this by another local
woman and a little girl, turned out to be taking her due (having refused any payment) by scrounging shamelessly and eating all the food. This was particularly galling in view of the
difficulty of obtaining food in the first place.

If the ladies of Palma had decided that the Chopin-Sand
party was a little unorthodox, the peasants of Valldemosa
found it deeply immoral. As the local *alcalde* told a Polish
traveler who happened to drop in on Valldemosa in January,
the foreigners never talked to anyone and never went to
church, the young boy went about sketching all day long and
the little girl was dressed as a boy. The locals had heard that
George Sand herself slept much of the day and spent the
nights writing, drinking endless cups of coffee, and smoking
cigarettes. All this added up to godlessness, and her manner
was not calculated to soothe the suspicions of the locals.
Combining financial considerations with those of principle,
they began to charge her more for food. She made the mistake of thinking that she could bargain and play one off
against the other. Their solidarity proved equal to the test,
and they raised their prices to ridiculous levels, refusing to do
business except on their own terms. Few things can irritate
the left-wing intellectual more than to come up against the
sullen contempt of a boorish peasantry, and George Sand
never forgave them for the humiliation. In the end she had to
buy her own goat in order to have a supply of milk, and
dispatched frantic messages to Flury in Palma, who would
send his cook out with provisions.

Apart from the irritation involved, she must have been deeply anxious at finding herself saddled with responsibility for a sick man and two children in an increasingly hostile place, particularly as her financial reserves were dwindling rapidly. Nothing had been cheap on this holiday, even the doctors who had been called in to see Chopin had charged more than the best in Paris. George Sand had soon spent all the money she had brought, and was drawing ever more heavily on her credit at the Canut bank. Chopin's cash too had been whittled away, and to cap it all, the Majorcan customs demanded a duty equivalent to half its value when the Pleyel piano finally arrived in Palma harbor on December 21. It took nearly three weeks to strike a bargain with the customs, who finally let it go for half the amount.

The arrival of the piano in the middle of January coincided with the sudden appearance of spring, and spirits rose immediately. George Sand and her children again went for long walks, while Chopin could sit out in the garden and breathe more easily. Above all he could now get down to work seriously. All but four of the twenty-four preludes had been more or less finished before his arrival in Palma, and he had somehow managed to write those four (nos. 2, 4, 10, 21) using the primitive local piano, but he could not polish up or revise any of them until he heard them on the Pleyel. When this arrived he did so in no time at all, and a few days later was able to send the completed manuscripts off to Fontana in Paris. He then finished the mazurka he had started at S'on Vent, wrote two new polonaises (opus 40) and the F major Ballade, opus 38, all of which he finished and sent off before two weeks had elapsed, and started on a new Scherzo (C sharp minor, opus 39). Such activity, unusual in Chopin at the best of times, is eloquent evidence of his good spirits.

Just as they were beginning to enjoy life again, and soon after George Sand had written to Charlotte Marliani saying that they had no particular urge or plans to leave, they suddenly made up their minds to go, and go as soon as possible. The reason for this sudden and unwise move remains obscure, as later accounts by George Sand are conflicting.[35] On February 11, 1839, after fifty-six days at the monastery of Valldemosa, they left for Palma, but already on this first lap of the journey its inadvisability became obvious. George Sand had tried to borrow a sprung carriage in which to take Chopin down the mountainside, but nobody wished to have to burn theirs after its use by a consumptive, with the result that he had to make the nine-mile journey in great heat in a rough cart along the dreadful road. On arrival at the lodgings of Flury, who had offered them accommodation while they waited for the *Mallorquín* to sail, Chopin was convulsed with coughing and was spitting out particles of blood. After a good night's rest, however, he seemed to improve, and waited patiently for the next lap of the journey.

George Sand now found that the Pleyel piano was liable to draconian "export duty" and decided to sell it in Palma. This was no easy matter, for nobody wished to touch an infected piano. Finally the French Madame de Canut sold her own and took in Chopin's. Having settled that, they could finally leave, and on February 13 they boarded the *Mallorquín*, only to have another nasty surprise. On the passage from Barcelona they had been able to wander about the empty deck in happy ignorance of the fact that this was reserved, on the return journeys, for the island's principal export—live pigs. Now the party was taken to their cabin and told to remain below deck throughout the voyage. It was a very warm night and the airless cabin in which Chopin gasped for breath was filled with the stench of the pigs. There was no question of sleep, as the pigs had a tendency to seasickness if allowed to remain still, and were therefore periodically chased about the deck.

By the time they sailed into Barcelona, Chopin was hemorrhaging and coughing up "bowlfuls of blood." George Sand wanted to take him ashore immediately, but the captain refused to give her one of the boats, which were needed to

Left,
Auguste Franchomme.

Below,
Hector Berlioz.
Copy of a portrait by Signol.

Countess Delfina Potocka. Drawing by Paul Delaroche.

Above,
Countess Marie d'Agoult.
From a painting by Lehmann,
c. 1835.

Right,
Maria Wodzinska.
An unfinished portrait.

Above,
Jan Matuszynski.
Watercolor by an unknown
artist painted in Paris
in the late 1830s.

Left,
Stefan Witwicki.
Oil painting by an unknown
artist painted in Paris
in the mid 1830s.

Right,
Albert Grzymala.
Lithograph by Bazin.

Below,
Julian Fontana.
Photograph taken in 1852.

Left,
Vincenzo Bellini.

Below,
Sigismund Thalberg.
Lithograph by G. F. Madeley.
Courtesy Radio Times
Hulton Picture Library.

Left,
Felix Mendelssohn.
Painted by Wilhelm von Schadow
in 1835.

Below, Robert Schumann.

Left, Astolphe, Marquis de Custine. Watercolor by Countess de Menou, 1846. Right, Adam Mickiewicz. Pencil portrait by Eugène Delacroix on a sheet of George Sand's writing paper, c. 1832.

Bohdan Zaleski. Engraving by James Hopwood, 1840.

Ignaz Moscheles.

unload the precious porcine cargo. In despair she tossed a coin and a note to a passing fisherman, begging him to row over to the French brig, the *Méléagre*, which was still at anchor in the bay. The captain of the *Méléagre* himself came over and took Chopin and the Sand party off the *Mallorquín*, over to his own ship, whose doctor immediately stopped the hemorrhaging and sedated Chopin. Before they were put ashore, the ship's doctor examined him thoroughly and diagnosed no disease and no perceptible damage to the lungs, merely stressing that Chopin had a delicate chest which should never be put to undue strain.

In Barcelona they stayed at a hotel, and it was again necessary to go through the rigmarole of paying in advance for bedding and effects which would subsequently have to be destroyed, in spite of the French doctor's clean bill of health. Chopin's condition improved markedly during the week they spent there, and on February 21 the whole party was able to board a French ship bound for Marseilles.[36] George Sand and her children shouted: "*Vive la France!*" as they climbed aboard.[37]

It was not merely the expression of a happy homecoming; a few days before, George Sand had written to Charlotte Marliani that "one would have to write ten volumes if one wanted to give some idea of the baseness, the bad faith, the egotism, the stupidity and the wickedness of this dumb, thieving and bigoted race."[38] Even taking into account the possibility that she and Chopin had been trying to keep up their morale while in Majorca, the letters they both wrote from the island tell a very different story from the ones she began writing now. The last week, during which the problems of getting away had culminated in Chopin's brush with death, had made the cup overflow, and it was through a mist of indignation and fury that she looked back on the whole holiday:

Another month in Spain and we should have perished there, Chopin and I; he of melancholy and disgust, I of fury and indignation. They wounded me in the most sensitive spot in my heart, under my very eyes they pierced a suffering person with pinpricks. I shall never forgive them, and if I ever write about them it shall be with venom.[39]

She was as good as her word. The accounts of the holiday she included in two different books[40] are violently exaggerated and lurid in their description of the Majorcans and conditions on the island. In fact, she had taken a group of people, two of them sickly, to a country in the throes of civil war, whose language she could not understand, of whose climate and manners she knew nothing, and to whose primitive society she had reacted with arrogance and scorn. She was not cast in the mold of a traveler and would have been more at home on a package tour. The holiday had not been a success, and somebody else had to be blamed, so, at different moments, the Majorcans were blamed, Chopin was blamed, and the weather was blamed.

On February 24, after a calm passage, the ship docked at Marseilles. Chopin was deposited in the competent hands of Dr. Cauvière, a friend of the Marlianis, a fine doctor whose skill and wisdom were further enhanced in George Sand's eyes by the fact that he was an ardent republican. He began with a thorough examination of the sick man but could find no "lesions," no "cavities," and no serious illness of any kind. "He is nursing him like his own child," George Sand wrote, "visits him every morning and every evening, takes him for walks, panders to him and is full of little attentions."[41]

Chopin's health improved rapidly, but Cauvière made George Sand abandon her original intention, which had been to move out of Marseilles and take a house in the country, and later to go to Italy for a couple of months. Cauvière insisted that what Chopin needed was a long rest, as his constitution had been weakened by the continuous traveling. They settled down in a hotel close to the doctor's house in order to recover, and now George Sand found that she was not well herself, for the constant strain of the last months was beginning to tell. As a result she was quite happy to sit quietly with her "little Chop."

After two weeks, the latter was writing to Grzymala that his health was better: "—vesicants, diet, pills, baths and the incomparable care of my Angel are slowly putting me back on my feet."[42] "I'm much better," he wrote to Fontana a couple of weeks later, "I'm starting to play, eat, walk and talk like everyone else."[43] While George Sand started working furiously on a new novel and on a long article comparing Mickiewicz with Goethe and Byron, Chopin got back to the C sharp minor Scherzo, and above all to sorting out his financial situation, which was in a terrible mess. The relatively complete surviving correspondence affords an insight into the petulant and frequently childish way in which he conducted his financial affairs.

Before leaving Paris, Chopin had presold the preludes to Pleyel for two thousand francs, of which he was advanced five hundred. The agreement included the shipping out of the piano, worth between twelve and fourteen hundred francs. He had also borrowed a thousand francs from his banker friend Auguste Leo, and another thousand from an unidentified person. The loan from Leo was only supposed to be a short-term one, repayable from the remaining fifteen hundred to be delivered by Pleyel on receipt of the completed preludes, which should have reached him long before Christmas. But the delays in finding suitable lodgings and the non-arrival of the piano, not to mention Chopin's illness, had ruined these plans. Leo started clamoring for his money, which elicited the following reaction from Chopin in his letter to Fontana at the end of December:

> Leo's a Jew! I cannot send you the Preludes, as they're not ready; but I'm better now and will hurry up, and I'll write the Jew a nice letter thanking him, so he feels awful (he can feel what he likes as far as I'm concerned). The crook! And I

called on him specially on the even of my departure . . .
Schlesinger is an even bigger dog, to include my Waltzes in
an album! and to sell them to Probst [for Germany] when
out of kindness I had let him have the [German rights] for
his own father in Berlin—but all these lice don't worry me
now. Let Leo rage![44]

By the end of January, Chopin had sent Fontana the completed preludes, for which the latter was to collect, after copying them neatly, the remaining fifteen hundred francs from
Pleyel. With this money he was to repay the anonymous cred-
itor and the landlord at the Chaussée d'Antin. He was then to
sell the German rights to Probst for a thousand francs, with
which he was to repay Leo. Unfortunately, Pleyel seems to
have felt that the fifteen hundred was in some measure surety
for the piano, for which Canut had not yet forwarded the
money, and he refused to pay up. This news reached Chopin
in Marseilles. "I had not expected such Jewish behavior from
Pleyel," he wrote to Fontana, and urged the latter to try to
sell the French and English rights of the new ballade to Pleyel
for a thousand francs, and the universal rights to the two
polonaises he had just finished for fifteen hundred francs. If
this could not be done, Fontana was to take the two works to
Schlesinger, and not Probst, as Fontana suggested:

If we must deal with Jews, let's at least stick to the Orthodox
ones. Probst could play some filthy German trick on me—
there's no holding him. Schlesinger has always been slippery,
but he's made enough money out of me, so he won't refuse to
make more; but be polite with him, because the Jew likes to
cut a good figure. So, if Pleyel starts making the slightest
difficulties, go to Schlesinger and tell him I'll give him the
Ballade for France and England for 800, and the Polonaises
for France, England and Germany for 1500 (and if he balks
at that, let him have them for 1400, 1300 or even 1200). If he
mentions the Preludes (I'm sure Probst will have told him
about those), tell him that I promised them to Pleyel a long

time ago, as he wanted to publish them and begged me before my departure, which was indeed the case. You see, my dearest; I could afford to break with Pleyel for Schlesinger's sake, but not for Probst's . . .[45]

Chopin was upset by Pleyel's behavior, and sensed, rightly as it happened, that the latter had heard rumors of his illness and wondered whether he would ever return to Paris. "I'll come back all right, and both he and Leo will get their thanks!" he wrote to Fontana.[46] In the meantime he pinned his hopes on Schlesinger, his usual publisher, a little optimistically. In a letter to Fontana at the end of March, when everything should have been sorted out, he wrote:

My dearest, since they're such a band of Jews—stop everything, till my return. The Preludes are sold to Pleyel (so far I've received only 500 Frs), so he can wipe the other end of his stomach with them if he chooses, but as for the Ballade and the Polonaises, don't sell them to Schlesinger or Probst.[47]

What Schlesinger had done is not known, but the fact is that the next eight major works by Chopin to appear in Paris (with the exception of the preludes) were published not by Schlesinger, but by a new publisher called Troupenas, and it was two more years before Schlesinger once again became Chopin's publisher. In the meantime, Chopin had to borrow money from Grzymala and to allow his apartment on the Chaussée d'Antin to be relet, and all he could do was rage at people who owed him money, mostly Poles like Antoni Wodzinski.

These were, however, only minor irritations, and they did not manage to cloud the happiness of the months spent in Marseilles. The tribulations George Sand and Chopin had been through had served to bring them closer together, and they were as much in love as ever. Chopin was full of admiration for his "Angel" and wrote to Grzymala: "You would love her even more if you knew her as I now know her."[48]

She, on the other hand, might easily have grown bored with the situation, for she was not used to spending much time with one man. She was also a very physical person who could not have had much satisfaction from Chopin since they had left Paris in the autumn, for both his illness and the continual presence of the children precluded any extensive intimacy. In one sense it must have been frustrating for her, as she could not really understand why Chopin was weak, but at the same time his frailty pandered to her deep-rooted instinct for devoting herself to people (or causes). She found, for the first time in years, that she could still be in love once the element of passion had largely evaporated, and she remained fascinated by this creature, so different from herself, as she explained to Charlotte Marliani:

> Chopin is an angel. His goodness, his tenderness and his patience sometimes make me anxious; I feel that he is too fine, too exquisite, too perfect to live long in this crude and heavy earthly world. In Majorca, when he was mortally ill, he made music which smelled of paradise. But I have grown so used to seeing him in heaven that I do not think life or death means anything to him. He does not really know himself which planet he is on. He has no idea of life as we think of it and as we feel it.[49]

It was almost certainly something to do with their relationship that made Chopin write in his letter to Fontana on March 7:

> I told you that in my desk, in the first drawer on the side of the door, there was a little note which you, or Jas, or Grz could open; I now ask you to take it and burn it without breaking the seal or reading it—I beg you on our friendship to do this—the note is now unnecessary.[50]

The fact that the next thought in the, as usual, rambling and chaotic letter concerns Antoni Wodzinski would seem to suggest that the note had something to do with his sister, or at least a subject linked with the thought of her. It looks very much as though Chopin were now definitely burying the past and settling for a life with his new companion.

It was a quiet life, since Chopin was still being kept in by Dr. Cauvière and was anyway not tempted by Marseilles, which he found ugly. He had to admit to Grzymala that he was a little bored. Another reason for staying at home was that their arrival was something of an event in the life of the city, and they were besieged by "enthusiasts of literature and music." Apart from a few of George Sand's friends and a Polish poet who lived nearby, they admitted nobody, but, in the words of George Sand, "luckily Chop, with his piano, dispels the boredom and brings poetry back into our lodgings."[51]

While they were still in Marseilles, news reached them that Adolphe Nourrit, who had gone to try his luck in Naples after falling from grace with the Paris public, had committed suicide there. This afflicted Chopin deeply, for apart from his friendship with Nourrit he always responded badly to news of deaths. George Sand tried to make him believe it was just a rumor, but when, a few days later, Madame Nourrit turned up in Marseilles with her husband's body, her six children and a seventh in her womb, reality could not be avoided. When arranging the service to be held in the cathedral, she asked Chopin if he would play the organ. Many people turned up, for this news had spread, and they came in the hope, as George Sand put it, of seeing herself sitting astride the coffin smoking a cigar and of hearing Chopin make the organ explode. They were disappointed, for not only was the organ in question a rather wheezy and rickety instrument, but Chopin restricted his contribution to one of the Schubert lieder the singer had done so much to popularize, "not with the exalted and glorious tone Nourrit used to lend it, but in a plaintive, soft tone, like the distant echo from another world."[52]

By the beginning of May, Chopin was quite recovered, and

as he was getting restless, Cauvière decided that an excursion to Italy was now practicable. The party consequently set off for Genoa, where they spent a couple of weeks sightseeing. Chopin felt well and energetic throughout, and even weathered "with valor" the terrible storm that caught them on the return journey.

After a couple of days at Marseilles, they set off, on May 22, for George Sand's country estate at Nohant, traveling by ferryboat up the Rhône as far as Arles, and thence by easy stages in a carriage. They arrived on June 2, and Chopin received his first impression of this place which was to play such a large part in his life from now on. "We arrived safely," he wrote to Grzymala, "lovely countryside, nightingales, larks . . ."[53] "I hope that a few months of Nohant will have good results," wrote George Sand, "and he seems to want to stay here as long as possible. But I shall take him at his word only as long as I see that this place is truly beneficial to him."[54]

9

A New Way of Life

George Sand had inherited Nohant from her father, a Napoleonic cavalry officer descended from an illegitimate daughter of the Maréchal de Saxe, himself a bastard of one of the Saxon kings of Poland. It was a comfortable eighteenth-century manor house standing on the edge of a village, with its own large garden stretching away on the other side. Not far away flowed the river Indre, and the country all around was beautiful, if a little melancholy.

Chopin was given a sunny room on the first floor with red and blue Chinese wallpaper and windows onto the garden. On one side a door led into a small book-lined room, the other side of which was George Sand's bedroom. On the other side of Chopin's bedroom was a small room into which he eventually moved an upright piano. Life at Nohant was informal and there were no hours except for the one communal meal of dinner at six o'clock. Guests could get up when they liked and have whatever breakfast they wished brought into their room, after which they were free to do anything they chose until the dinner bell called them.

George Sand used to spend the night writing, going to bed

at five or six in the morning and never getting up before eleven or noon. She would not pay any attention to her guests until dinner, after which she would sit with them until they retired and then go back to work. Chopin, on the other hand, was always up early in the morning, spent the day working, and went to bed early. "We dine out in the open," wrote George Sand, "friends come over, first one, then another, we smoke and talk, and in the evening, when they have gone, Chopin plays to me in the dusk, after which he falls asleep like a child."[1] Not surprisingly, after only a couple of weeks of this regime, she was able to write to Charlotte Marliani that "his health makes wonderful progress at Nohant. This life at least seems to be good for him."[2]

The moment they had arrived, George Sand had called one of her oldest friends, Dr. Papet, to examine Chopin thoroughly. His verdict was that there was no trace of tuberculosis, only a chronic infection of the larynx, and he was of the opinion that a steady diet, fresh air, and a regular, restful life could repair Chopin's constitution completely, echoing what the doctor of the *Méléagre* and Cauvière had said. This contradicts the diagnosis of the Majorcan doctors and the evidence available now, for it seems fairly certain that the composer did have the disease in some form. This discrepancy was not the result of their trying to keep their findings from the sick man (Papet would certainly not have kept them from George Sand), but of the existence of two different schools of thought on the subject. The southern school, which included Spain, believed, rightly as it happened, in the contagiousness of tuberculosis and diagnosed the disease on the first telling symptoms, which Chopin's condition bore already. The other school, which governed French medicine at the time, did not believe in the theory of contagion, and was not prepared to diagnose tuberculosis until definite damage to the lungs had been ascertained. Chopin's seemed to be in good condition. They did all, however, spot a weakness in the larynx, which seemed to be the main problem at this stage. Chopin's constitution was frail, but he was only twenty-nine and was still capable of great exertion if necessary. It was generally felt that if he looked after himself he could last a long time.

It is very difficult to tell how far his appearance had been affected by the previous year's experiences, for contemporaries are notoriously unreliable. Jane Stirling (who had almost certainly not known him before) stated that "after his return from Majorca, it was noticeable that he had been very ill, and he no longer mimicked his friends or seemed to enjoy life."[3] Most of this assertion can be proved wrong and was inspired by a desire to discredit George Sand. Liszt, on the other hand, claimed that the trip had been a wild success and had put his friend's health completely right. Others merely alluded to his moribund looks, but these had much to do with the build of his face, which grew thinner as he entered his thirtieth year, as well as with the expression of refinement and melancholy stamped on it.

George Sand herself, never prepared to accept anything that was not palpably plain and reasonable, did not believe in the existence of any disease, and felt that many of his relapses were brought on by mental or spiritual torment, accompanied by hypochondria. She often found herself thinking that Chopin would outlive her and most of her friends, for she believed his constitution to be enduring.

Insofar as one can state such things a century and a half later, it seems beyond doubt that Chopin did have tuberculosis, which apparently attacked his larynx more obviously than his lungs. But the disease was not particularly virulent in his case, making slow progress until the last two years of his life. He himself had learned to live with it and merely believed he was cursed with a poor constitution and a bronchial condition, but often when his health gave way he would go to pieces and become aware of the proximity of death.

It is important to keep all this in mind, for it has direct

bearing on a problem which faces the biographer at this point. A couple of weeks after the couple's return to Nohant, on June 19, 1839, George Sand took a knife and carved the date on the paneling of her bedroom. In the absence of any similar graffiti, one is led to assume that the date was a significant one from her point of view, and while it could have been something to do with her personal spiritual life, her books or even the date of planting a tree, it has usually been associated with Chopin, and often with the subject of sex. It has been pointed out quite plausibly that this could be the anniversary of the consummation of their love—the date would indeed seem to fit the bill. This is of course pure speculation, but it is the most reasonable explanation, for this was the first affair she had had which had lasted for a full year without going sour, and it looked like continuing happily for some time to come. But there is another tentative explanation often put forward: that on this day she decided to stop having sexual relations with Chopin. This is based on her assertion, first made in a letter to Grzymala at the height of her quarrel with Chopin and reiterated in *Histoire de ma vie* (much of which was written under the influence of her son, who did his utmost to eliminate the memory of Chopin from her life), that she stopped having sexual relations with Chopin on account of his bad health, and that their cohabitation over the next eight years was entirely chaste.

Neither of these sources can be treated as impartial, and both contain a good many untruths on other subjects.[4] Whether or not Chopin and George Sand did make love and when is not something one can pronounce on with any certainty. It seems most unlikely that they should have stopped so early in their relationship, and even more so that it should have been done in such a categorical way. The theory that the occasional lovemaking would kill Chopin holds no water, in view of George Sand's own assessment of his health. Still more to the point, she believed passionately in natural and simple remedies, and would have been the first to prescribe a healthy bout of sexual activity for the nervous tension and frustration which she held responsible for all his ills.

In *Histoire de ma vie* she makes light of the whole relationship. She claims that she did not really want Chopin to hang about her after the return from Majorca, and that it was against her will that he assumed the position of her common-law husband. According to her, she went along with his wishes out of fear that he would have a breakdown and die if she left him to himself. These sentiments accord ill with her treatment of Musset, whom she dumped dangerously ill in a foreign country in order to run off with his doctor, and of Mallefille, whom she would "never leave" but left a few weeks later. It seems ridiculous to argue that any woman would allow herself to remain publicly mistress as well as mother and nurse to a man she did not love for eight years, merely out of compassion, particularly if that woman were George Sand.

At Nohant, their cohabitation settled down to a routine which did not allow for much passion, as they were, after all, two creative artists who had to work. George Sand was frantically writing new books in order to patch up her finances, while Chopin quickly got down to composing. "He has already produced some beautiful things since his arrival here," George Sand wrote in mid-July, and it was true.[5] Apart from polishing up a few pieces, such as the mazurka he had written in Palma, he now composed the Scherzo and Finale of the B flat minor Sonata, opus 35 (the third movement, the famous *Marche Funèbre*, had been written in 1837), three new mazurkas (opus 41), and two nocturnes (opus 37). He was pleased with his work, and particularly the three mazurkas, "which I think are pretty, as all new children appear to their aging parents," as he put it to Fontana.[6] In the afternoons, when he had nothing better to do, he would give Solange, George Sand's eleven-year-old daughter, piano lessons, or else he would sit reading Bach's *Well-Tempered Clavier* and correcting his edition—"not just the engraver's mistakes, but also passages accepted by those who claim to understand Bach (not because I pretend to understand him better, but from a feeling that perhaps I can sometimes guess right)."[7]

In August, Chopin wrote to Fontana that he would not be returning to Paris until the weather changed, as the fresh air of the country was doing him good. But the moment he felt better, Chopin began falling prey to boredom. George Sand saw this coming and put more urgency into her invitation to Grzymala to join them. A little relief was provided by the visit of Witwicki, who was spending the summer not far away, because Chopin could at least have a good gossip in Polish, something he missed when surrounded by foreigners. This, however, only lasted a few days. Some of the neighbors who dropped in occasionally provided entertainment, particularly George Sand's half-brother, Hippolyte Chatiron, a rowdy and perpetually drunk country bumpkin whom Chopin took a great liking to, but they could in no way make up for his need of close friends and of Paris. By the middle of August, George Sand wrote to Grzymala:

> Your little one is fair to middling. I think he needs a little less of the calm, solitude and regularity which country life entails. Who knows, perhaps he needs a little outing to Paris. I am ready to make any sacrifice rather than see him consume himself with melancholy. [Are those the words of a woman who wants to get rid of her companion?] Come and take the pulse of his morale. Who will ever define the limit between physical illness and moral languor? It is not to me that he will want to admit he is bored. But I think I can guess it.[8]

Grzymala did come down for a short stay at the end of the month, and Chopin cheered up visibly, but after his departure he resumed his former state, "always a little better or a little worse, never decidedly well nor decidedly ill," as George Sand put it. This does not seem to have been such a bad state, however, for "when he feels a little stronger he becomes very jolly, and when he is feeling melancholy he goes to his piano and composes beautiful pages."⁹ The pages in question were the F sharp major Impromptu, opus 36.

In September, George Sand decided that she would have to spend that winter in Paris, since a play of hers had been accepted at the Comédie Française and she wished to supervise its production. Also she could no longer go on providing her children's education herself, and this could best be seen to in Paris. Chopin was already looking forward to getting back, because, as George Sand put it, Paris "is good for his morale, and natures like his need to be surrounded by refined civilization."¹⁰ But the return to the capital involved various problems, the first of which was the finding of a new apartment. This in fact meant mobilizing Grzymala and the unfortunate Fontana, who were issued endless instructions as to area, situation, floor, layout, and general aspect. The brunt of this task fell on Fontana, who was still engaged in various wranglings with publishers on Chopin's behalf, and with astonishing speed and efficiency he found the perfect flat, at No. 5 Rue Tronchet, just behind the Madeleine. His duties did not end there. A stream of letters flowed from Nohant, and this one, dated September 25, is fairly typical:

My Dearest,
Thank you for your kind, friendly, very un-English, very Polish soul.* Choose a wallpaper like the dove-colored one I used to have—only glossy or varnished—for both the rooms, and a not too wide dark green strip for the borders. Get something different for the hall, but make sure it's respectable. If you find something more beautiful; some newer, more fashionable paper which you like and know I would like, take that. I always prefer something smooth, clear and quiet to anything common or vulgar or grocer. That's why I prefer

* Fontana's admiration for the English and their ways earned him continual jests about his "Englishness."

pearly colors, they're quiet and not vulgar. Thank you for
fixing about the servant's room, I shall be needing that. As
for the furniture, it would be wonderful if you could take care
of that too. Believe me, I didn't dare to bother you with that
problem, but since you're so kind as to mention it, do get it
and move it in. I'll ask Grzym to give you money for the
moving; I'll write to him myself. As for the bed and the desk,
they ought to be given to some cabinetmaker to be freshened
up. Don't forget to take the papers out of the desk first—lock
them up somewhere, I don't have to tell you how to do these
things. Do whatever you want and whatever you deem necessary. Whatever you do will be fine. You have my fullest
confidence. That's one thing. Now something else; you must
write to Wessel [Chopin's London publisher] and tell him
that I have six new manuscripts, for each of which I want 300
francs (how many pounds is that?). Write to him and get an
answer. (If you think he won't give that much, write to me
first.) Write and tell me whether Probst is in Paris. Also try
to find me a servant—Perhaps some kind, decent Pole. Tell
Grzymala to look too. He'll have to look after his own meals
and don't offer him more than 80. I shall be in Paris toward
the end of October, not before, keep that to yourself. The
elastic mattress on my bed ought to be repaired, if it's not too
expensive—if it's expensive, leave it. Have the chairs and
things properly beaten and dusted. I don't know why I'm telling you all this, you know very well what to do. Give my love
to Jas [Matuszynski]. My dearest, I sometimes wonder in my
heart—Let the Lord grant him what is best, but he mustn't
let himself be taken in; although on the other hand . . . Yes,
no, I don't know—That's the greatest Truth on earth! And
while it is so, as it always will be, I shall love you for the
kind soul you have, and Jas for another. Love to you both.
Write. Soon.
Your
Ever longer-nosed
Ch.[11]

The lack of any attempt at construction and the heavy

crossings-out which litter the page make this into more of a list of chores than a letter, and it is only one of many such. The letters to Grzymala, though also taking for granted a multitude of favors, presume a little less, and Chopin assured him that "if you need someone to help you or go running about for you, use Fontana. He'll do anything for me, and in business he's as exact as an Englishman."[12] But Fontana, who was presumably paid in some way for some of his secretarial work, and who depended on Chopin for getting pupils, seems to have thought nothing of this. Throughout his life Chopin managed to make slaves of his friends, and his behavior toward them is often that of a spoiled child.

Fontana's prowess in finding an apartment for Chopin won him the desirable task of seeking accommodation for George Sand, who intended to set up house in Paris along with her son, while Solange was sent to boarding school. Again he was sent detailed instructions, including a sketch showing the layout of rooms wanted, and again he acquitted himself remarkably well. He found two small pavilions in a garden courtyard just off the Rue Pigalle, in a newly built area in what was then the northern suburb of Paris. One of the pavilions was for George Sand, while the other could accommodate Maurice, his studio (for he wished to take up painting), and the servants she would bring from Nohant.

Once the apartments had been found and the furniture moved, Fontana was sent scurrying around the tailors and hatters of the capital, for Chopin suddenly realized that, having been away for a whole year, most of his wardrobe would be out of fashion. It was only after this that the poor factotum was given his final instructions:

> And since you're so good at all these things, arrange the apartment so that I should get no somber thoughts in it, and no fits of coughing—and set it up so that I should be good—and don't forget to have them sweep out many episodes from

my past. And, if you can manage it, I would like to find the next few years' work finished and waiting for me.[13]

When he did return, on October 10, the work loomed before him. News of his arrival had spread, and within a couple of days he was besieged by would-be pupils, but at least this offered escape from some of the cobwebs which Fontana could not sweep out, and which were to prove a major irritation.

George Sand and Chopin had told few people of their plan before leaving Paris, but a good many knew anyway, and there was no particular attempt at keeping it secret. Charlotte Marliani could not resist showing around some of the letters she received from Majorca, and while the travelers spent months without any news from Paris, most of Paris was well informed of their movements. At the beginning of January, Berlioz was remarking in a letter to Liszt that "Chopin is ill in the Balearic Islands,"[14] and a couple of months later he was writing to Chopin in Marseilles to find out whether he was still alive, for at this stage rumor had taken over and declared him to be dying. The susceptible and fastidious Chopin, who might well have been anxious about all the publicity afforded to his relationship with France's most scandalous woman and the consequences this might have on his relations with Parisian society, was not worried. "I am not surprised at the various tales; you must realize that I knew I should be exposing myself to them," he wrote to Fontana, who faithfully reported everything. "Anyway, it will all pass, tongues will rot, and nothing can touch our souls."[15]

Chopin was right, for the gossip did not affect his way of life in Paris. What did was the vindictiveness of Marie d'Agoult, who had reappeared on the scene. She had last seen George Sand at Nohant in the summer of 1837, a full year before the beginning of the Sand-Chopin liaison, which she had done so much to encourage. The leave-taking between the

two ladies had been edifyingly tearful, and vows of mutual esteem and love had been exchanged as the Countess set off for
Italy with Liszt. The vows had been false on both sides.
George Sand had already given Balzac all the material he
needed for a novel which she could not afford to write herself,
and he used it in his *Beatrix*. When it came out in the spring
of 1839, the novel was recognized as a blatant vivisection of
the Liszt-d'Agoult affair. Moreover, the Countess's defects
were depicted with a venomous insight which could not have
been Balzac's. "Now I've really managed to set the two fe-
males at each other's throats!" the delighted Balzac exclaimed
to Bernard Potocki at the Opéra one night a few weeks
later.[16]

But Balzac had only added fuel to a fire that was already
smoldering. Shortly after her last meeting with George Sand,
Marie d'Agoult had started spreading gossip about her
"friend," to whom she continued to write sugary letters full
of love and devotion. One of Liszt's biographers explained
that Marie d'Agoult had "the makings of a brain." She certainly failed to use it in her choice of confidante, for she now
began to vent her spite and dislike of George Sand in her letters to Charlotte Marliani. The latter was delighted to receive
these and encouraged them, at the same time notifying
George Sand that there were "murky plots and foul betrayal"
afoot against her.[17] Eager to lend a note of morality to the intrigue, she showed the letters to the Abbé de Lamennais, who
was horrified and suggested that George Sand break off all
relations with the Countess and ignore her letters.

Meanwhile Marie d'Agoult's affair with Liszt had begun to
founder, and in the summer of 1839 (while Chopin was at
Nohant) they decided to part; he to go on a performing tour,
she to return to Paris. In order to make her life there bera-
ble, she would have to be on good terms with George Sand.
She realized that something was wrong, since George Sand

had not answered her last few letters, but decided to brazen it out, and therefore struck a righteous note in her next letter:

> I cannot really believe that you have anything to complain of in my behavior . . . I have searched my conscience and can find no shadow of guilt on my side. Franz too is wondering how it is that your close connection with a man he feels he has the right to call his friend should have had the immediate result of breaking off all communication between us . . .[18]

It was obvious that Marie d'Agoult's truculence had a great deal to do with the fact that the George Sand-Chopin ménage seemed to be flourishing while hers was not. She was the great lady who had sacrificed everything to go and live with her pianist, and now someone else seemed to be stealing the show. To make matters worse, she was disappointed in Liszt, who, instead of sitting quietly in Olympus with her, insisted on being a performing artist. George Sand's pianist, on the other hand, would have suited her perfectly.

George Sand felt inclined to ignore Marie d'Agoult's peace-making approaches, but the Countess, who was back in Paris in October, carried on her bluff, telling everyone that George Sand had wronged her and dropped her, and that this was not unconnected with Chopin's jealousy of Liszt as a pianist. As a result, George Sand realized that she would have to do something, for, as she explained to Charlotte Marliani:

> [Chopin's] pride would prevent him from offering any explanation of his own behavior, and if this were not demanded of him, which is possible (my silence being equivalent to an admission of guilt), he will have earned the bitterness of Liszt and the hatred of Madame d'Agoult. Knowing her, she would provoke embarrassments and ructions which he can do without—he so nervous, so discreet, so exquisite in all things.[19]

Meanwhile Marie d'Agoult went on complaining that she had been a victim of malevolent slanders, and wrote imploring letters to George Sand full of protestations of her inno-

cence: "George, once again, *for the last time!* You are wandering in a labyrinth of gossip, where I *shall not* follow you.
In the name of heaven . . ."[20] Her lofty tone faltered when
she discovered that the source of the "gossip" was her own
letters, which Charlotte Marliani had by now handed over to
George Sand. There was an icy moment on November 13
when the two women came face to face in the Marliani drawing room, but by now Marie d'Agoult was as eager to save her
face as George Sand to put an end to the whole intrigue. A
private interview was arranged, after which the two ladies advertised their renewed friendship.

Marie d'Agoult proceeded to take the war underground;
she kept up a sustained flow of vituperative gossip about
George Sand, and above all worked hard to drive a wedge between Chopin and Liszt. At the beginning of November, for
instance, she informed Liszt that Chopin and Berlioz disapproved of his tour of Austria and thought him ridiculous (her
own opinion was that he was behaving like a mountebank). A
few days later, she wrote that Grzymala and Chopin were
being "rude" and ostracizing her, a week or two later again
that Chopin was behaving fatuously, "like an oyster sprinkled
with sugar."[21] Since none of this was having a dramatic
enough effect, she informed Liszt that "Chopin, whom you
were naïve enough to regard as a friend," had not even had
the decency to call on her, even though the whole of Paris
knew that Liszt was ill and that only she had news of him.
She went on to say that in view of this there was only one option open to them: to collect their allies and declare open war
on the Chopin-Sand coterie as soon as Liszt returned to Paris
in the spring.

Luckily for everyone involved, Liszt had not the slightest
intention of being placed in a foolish situation by his former
mistress, and was seriously alarmed at the confrontation she
was trying to bring about between him and Chopin. He therefore humored her as much as possible, assuring her that she

was a far greater personality than George Sand, and made light of Chopin's behavior:

> I wouldn't like you to take Chopin's rudeness too seriously. I should think that by now you have punished him enough for it. You know what a deplorable influence the Piffoellic bedlam can have. One must not blame Chopin too much for his gaucherie. Sharper men than he (though he is very, and above all would like to be thought infinitely sharp) have got lost in it.[22]

Liszt managed to restrain his countess to some extent, but could not stop her from gossiping and stirring the pot at every opportunity. Far from bringing Liszt any closer to her, as she had hoped, the whole intrigue put him off and had the effect of isolating her in Parisian society. While she predicted that George Sand was about to jilt Chopin and "take her lofty sentiments elsewhere,"[23] her efforts only served to bring them closer together and to make them avoid potential battlefields.

"I never see Chopin at all," Stephen Heller, a German pianist just arrived in Paris, wrote to Schumann in January 1840. "He's up to his ears in the aristocratic swamp . . . he prefers exalted salons to lofty mountaintops."[24] This was less true than ever during this season. Chopin was working hard at his lessons, giving up to eight a day, which sometimes exhausted him, but only physically. As Friederike Müller, a new pupil, pointed out: "Feeble, pale, coughing much, he often took opium drops with sugar or drank gum-water, rubbed his forehead with eau de cologne, and nevertheless taught with a patience, perseverance and zeal which were admirable."[25]

Another distraction that season was the arrival in Paris of Moscheles, one of the musicians Chopin had deeply admired from his earliest years, and with whose music he was very familiar. Chopin's opinion had undergone some change, but he still regarded him highly. Moscheles, for his part, was a little perplexed by Chopin's music, and was keen to meet the man in order to find out what to think of it. He had been told by Mendelssohn, with whom he was in close touch, of Chopin's importance, but still kept certain reservations. In 1835, for instance, Moscheles noted in his diary apropos of the second set of études (opus 25): "I am a declared admirer of his genius; he has given to pianists everything that is most novel, most enchanting," but went on to say that, try as he might, he simply could not play the wretched things.[26] To Mendelssohn he once wrote: "On the whole I find his music too sweet, not manly enough, and hardly the work of a profound musician."[27] To this he added that there was much in Chopin that "appeared unscholarlike" to him. The idea that music must be manly and scholarly might seem novel, but it was in fact deeply rooted in the German Romantic tradition, which was frightened of things getting out of hand. Mendelssohn's opinion of Berlioz, for instance, was that "his orchestration is such a frightful muddle, such an incongruous mess, that one ought to wash one's hands after handling one of his scores."[28] Their opinions of Liszt were equally damning. Mendelssohn described his manner as "a perpetual fluctuation between scandal and apotheosis"; Moscheles considered him scruffy and inartistic; and Schumann felt that there was "too much tinsel" about his playing.[29]

These were not just personal opinions. There was a growing feeling in Germany, and to some extent England as well, that the mood in which music was being written by the Parisian composers was to be avoided and discouraged, as all too often it led to charlatanism of one sort or another. But when he finally met Chopin, at the house of Auguste Leo in mid-October, Moscheles forgot his reservations, as his diary shows:

> He played to me at my request and now for the first time I understand his music, and can also explain to myself the enthusiasm of the ladies. His *ad libitum* playing, which, with

the interpreters of his music degenerates into disregard for time, is with him only the most charming originality of execution; the dilettante-like hard modulations which strike me disagreeably when I am playing his compositions no longer shock me, for he glides lightly over them in a fairy-like way with his delicate fingers; his *piano* is so softly breathed forth that he does not need any strong *forte* in order to produce the wished-for contrasts. It is for this reason that one does not miss the orchestra-like effects which the German school demands of the pianoforte-player, but allows oneself to be carried away, as by a singer who, little concerned by the accompaniment, entirely follows his feeling. In short, he is unique in the world of pianists.[30]

The two composers saw much of each other during the next weeks, often playing together at soirées, and, as a result, it was together that they were asked to go and play to the Royal Family at St. Cloud on October 29. They were fetched by the Count de Perthuis, the director of the King's music, who drove them out to the palace, where, according to Moscheles:

We passed through many state rooms into a *salon carré* where the Royal Family were assembled *en petit comité*. At a round table sat the Queen, an elegant workbasket before her; beside her were Madame Adelaide, the Duchess d'Orléans, and ladies-in-waiting. The noble ladies were as affable as though we had been old acquaintances. Chopin played first a number of nocturnes and studies, and was admired and petted like a favorite. After I had also played some old and new studies, and had been honored with similar applause, we seated ourselves together at the instrument—he again playing the bass, which he always insists on doing. The close attention of the little circle during my E flat major Sonata was interrupted only by the exclamations: "Divine! Delicious!" After the *Andante* the Queen whispered to a lady-in-waiting: "Would it be indiscreet to ask them to play it again?" This was naturally equivalent to a command to repeat it, so we played it again with increased abandon. In the finale we gave ourselves up to musical delirium. Chopin's enthusiasm throughout the piece must, I think, have affected the listeners, who now burst forth into eulogies. Chopin again played alone with the same charm and called forth the same sympathy as before.[31]

A few days later Chopin received a handsome piece of Sèvres, while Moscheles was presented with an elegant traveling case, which, Chopin is supposed to have quipped, was a hint for him to go.

Chopin himself did not take part in any concerts that season, and does not seem to have gone to many either. He went to the Italian opera with Custine, and was present at Charles Hallé's first public concert, in which Franchomme also took part, but more often than not he would drive to the Rue Pigalle when his lessons were over and while away the evening with George Sand. Her lodgings there are described by Balzac in a letter to his Polish lady:

> She lives at No. 16 Rue Pigalle, at the end of a garden, over the carriage house and stables of a house which looks onto the street. She has a dining room furnished with carved oak, her little salon is mushroom colored, and the sitting room in which she receives is garnished with superb Chinese vases full of flowers. There is always a jardinière full of flowers; the furnishings are green; there is a dresser full of curiosities; paintings by Delacroix, her portrait by Calamatta . . . the piano is magnificent, upright, square, of rosewood. Chopin is always there . . . She only gets up at four o'clock, and at four o'clock Chopin has finished giving his lessons. One goes up to her room by a ladder staircase, steep and straight. Her bedroom is brown, her bed consists of two mattresses on the floor, Turkish style . . . There is a portrait of [Grzymala] in Polish Castellan's costume in the dining room.[32]

Grzymala was one of the habitués of the Rue Pigalle, along with Delacroix; Emmanuel Arago, a lawyer friend of George

Sand; Marie Dorval, the actress with whom she is often accused of having had sapphic relations; and Pauline Garcia-
Viardot, the famous nineteen-year-old singer whom George
Sand had "adopted" and around whose person she was con-
structing her new novel, *Consuelo.* The informal family atmosphere at the Rue Pigalle attracted Chopin more and
more, and he soon virtually moved in himself. He would use
his apartment on the Rue Tronchet for lessons and for receiving visits, and occasionally entertained there in the evenings,
but otherwise he was almost always to be found at the Rue
Pigalle, where he usually slept. This had obvious advantages
for both of them. When Chopin fell ill again in April with a
sudden pain which attacked him in the middle of the night,
George Sand was wakened up and was able to help. She did
not like the idea of Jan Matuszynski continuing to treat Chopin and called in a French doctor. Matuszynski was himself
slowly dying of consumption and was convinced, rightly as it
happened, that Chopin had the disease, but George Sand felt
he was wrong. Admittedly, the symptoms of this particular
crisis involved no coughing or spitting up blood, merely a
cramp-like pain in the chest which restricted his breathing
but did not otherwise affect him. This crisis prevented Chopin from attending the concert on April 20 given by Liszt,
who had turned up in a conciliatory mood. Chopin, who by
now decidedly disliked Liszt, wanted to keep up appearances
and was seriously annoyed at not being able to go. "With my
health one cannot do anything," he told one of his pupils on
this occasion. "It is very annoying—I don't have the time to
be ill!"[33]

The arrangement suited George Sand as well; Chopin—
"the gentlest, the most modest, the most hidden of all men
of genius"—was rarely in her way.[34] Moreover, his presence
represented a certain security and support to her. "Without
his perfect and delicate friendship I would often lose heart,"
she wrote to her half-brother Hippolyte, as the problems of

staging her play loomed before her.³⁵ Chopin also provided both the excuse and the means for her to grow out of the affectation and licentiousness which had characterized her life during the 1830s. She had already felt a need to settle down to a more constructive life before she had taken up with him, but the lack of a suitable companion had condemned her efforts to failure. At the time of their second meeting, she was still, with her philandering and her fantastic clothes, an object of scandal in many quarters. After a year or so with Chopin, she was rarely to be seen in anything but the simplest gray or black dresses, and her behavior had grown generally more dignified. People could see that Chopin, the most sensitive and refined of characters, had been neither killed nor jilted by her, and this helped to allay some of the mistrust of Parisian society. Her quiet life with Chopin over the next few years silenced the gossips and effaced her old reputation for nymphomania, and she gradually became an object of respect and even admiration.

This was not all Chopin's doing; although his influence is evident, he certainly never tried to change her character or opinions. They led their own lives, often going out independently in the evenings, but with time they pooled their friends, and Chopin soon found that people as respectable as the Czartoryskis and as fastidious as Custine accepted George Sand wholeheartedly. To begin with, however, this was of scant importance to Chopin, who was happy to bask in the family atmosphere of the Rue Pigalle and to leave Parisian society to itself. George Sand's play *Cosima* was staged at the end of the season and was a resounding flop. She lost money on the production and could therefore not afford to open her house at Nohant for the summer. Instead, she remained in Paris, only leaving for a week in the middle of August in order to accompany Pauline Viardot on a concert tour. Chopin felt even this short absence, and was clearly as lost without her as Maurice, who wrote: "Chopinet and I spend the evenings staring at each other by the light of two candle ends."[36]

Chopin got on quite well with the seventeen-year-old Maurice, a rather effete and weak-minded boy who was studying painting under Delacroix; but he preferred the twelve-year-old Solange, a difficult, turbulent girl who was not her mother's favorite and felt it, particularly now that she had been confined in a boarding school. Chopin often took her out at weekends, and he, Delacroix, and Grzymala spoiled her terribly. Chopin must have been a welcome addition to the household as far as the two children were concerned, for he was good company and was always prepared to amuse them by his acts or by teaching them Polish tongue-twisters. They would make fun of his appalling French accent and his bad grammar, and would sign their names "Solangska Sandska" or write notes in a pastiche of Polish, like "Salutxi a Grrrzzziiimallla, quilski ne courski paska les filleski."[37] (*Saluts à Grzymala, qu'il ne courre pas les filles.*)

A vignette of this family life is drawn by George Sand in a letter written that September:

> This morning we have acquired a delightful little puppy, no bigger than a fist, dark brown, with a white waistcoat, white stockings in front and white shoes on the hind legs. This gentleman followed Chopin in the street, and simply would not leave him. Then, O miracle! Chopin took the little dog *in adoration* and has spent the whole day looking after it, even though it did its "something" in the drawing room and gave us all fleas. Chopin finds this charming, mainly because the dog is all over him and cannot stand Solange. Solange is fiercely jealous. At this moment the little thing is sleeping at my feet. It has been called Mops, which is, quite simply, the Polish for Pug.[38]

The advent of the season did not disrupt the tranquillity of Chopin's existence. He did not want to give any concerts, and he felt no urge to go to other people's, convinced as he was of the worthlessness of most of the modern music to be heard. The only exception was Pauline Viardot's concert at the Conservatoire on February 7, 1841, an event he would never have missed. Adam Mickiewicz, who had just been made Professor of Slavonic Studies at the Collège de France, inaugurated his chair with a series of public lectures to which George Sand took Chopin. She was fascinated by the Polish poet and had been one of those responsible for getting him the job. The lectures were something of a social occasion, as they were attended by the entire Parisian intelligentsia, from Victor Hugo down to Custine, who was particularly interested, since at that moment he was editing the book which was to make him famous, his *Lettres de Russie*. Chopin must have felt a little out of his depth as he listened to Mickiewicz's airy expatiations on the origins of the Slavs and their literature, but George Sand lapped it all up.

Although Chopin went out far less than usual and led a more relaxed existence during the period 1840–41, he did not compose very much. In fact, his output for the whole year of 1840 seems to have consisted of no more than three waltzes, one song, and a polonaise (F sharp minor, opus 44), which compares poorly with that of other years. This was not the result of indolence or lack of inspiration. This period was a breathing space during which he, as it were, collected his thoughts before embarking on the final and greatest stage of his work as a composer.

Chopin's thoughts and attitude were, of course, affected by the quieter life he led and the company he kept. He had paid little or no attention to the vapid discussions of the "humanitarian" group, and before that had listened in wonder or amusement to those of Liszt, Berlioz, and Hiller. But the little group of intellectuals and artists that gathered around George Sand at this period was more successful in drawing him out. Although no great talker herself, she had a way of creating discussion around her. "She's a good listener," remarked Heine,[39] while Liszt explained that "she absorbed everything like a sponge . . . she made one more eloquent."[40] George Sand was interested in music and in the interrelationship of the various arts, which were well represented by the various members of the group, and the talk compulsively dwelled on these subjects. As far as Chopin was concerned, the most interesting members of the group were Pauline Viardot and Eugène Delacroix. Pauline Viardot was not yet twenty years old and came from a highly gifted family, which included the famous singer La Malibran, her elder sister. When Liszt had met her as a young girl, he had wanted to make a pianist of her, while her gift for drawing made many people regret that she had not become an artist. She was also very intelligent and well educated, and this, according to some people, enhanced her magnificent singing voice. She could give new depth to an operatic role or a song. Chopin had, from his earliest years, been fascinated by the human voice, the most perfect instrument of all, and in Pauline Viardot he found not only one of the greatest voices of the nineteenth century, but also a musician of extraordinary refinement and intelligence. He spent a great deal of time listening and talking to her, and helped her compose songs of her own. When he felt uninspired and bored, he would long for her company, as he claimed she could "restore his musical faculty."

Equally interesting as an influence on Chopin is the painter Delacroix. Chopin had met him half a dozen years before and had occasionally run across him in Paris over the next years, although the painter rarely went out into society. Delacroix was, however, a friend and admirer of George Sand, and consequently Chopin began to see a great deal of him after the beginning of his own liaison with her. Delacroix had been immediately struck by Chopin's genius, but his respect and admiration were not reciprocated by the latter. Chopin did not like the exuberance and the daring of Delacroix's work of the 1830s, and felt more at ease with the academic formality of the painter's great rival Ingres. It is more than likely that the reason the joint Chopin-Sand portrait was never finished was that Chopin did not like it. The two men did nevertheless become close friends, and they had much in common. In spite of a happy childhood, Delacroix had grown up with a slight sense of alienation and had few close friends. Like Chopin he was fastidious—the two were forever exchanging names of tailors and bootmakers, and Delacroix's collection of waistcoats was as legendary as Chopin's of gloves—and like Chopin he cultivated refinement of manners in himself and others. He was deeply interested in music and held the same unfashionable views on it as Chopin, liking Haydn, Mozart, and Bach better than Beethoven, and only acknowledging Bellini and Rossini among his contemporaries.

In 1840, Delacroix was forty-two years old and was embarking on a new stage in his career; he had recently been given a series of commissions for the large ceilings of public buildings, and this imposed on him a different approach to painting. He abandoned the spontaneity of his earlier Romantic style, studied the classical painters more closely, grew more controlled in form and more intense in his use of color. He also began to develop theories on the relationship between the artist and his instrument and that between the various forms of art. Like Heine, he saw Chopin as the quintessential artist, rather than just as a musician, and he was fascinated by the mixture of spontaneous creation and controlled purpose in Chopin's improvisations.

Chopin certainly influenced Delacroix, although indirectly; what is more difficult to assess is the influence Delacroix exerted on Chopin. There is no written word of Chopin's to point to. George Sand's accounts of conversations between them are highly fantasized, and smack much more of her own idea of the two artists than of their actual opinions. What is certain is that the two did talk a great deal about art and music, and that this exchange ushered in a new phase of work for both of them. The year of 1840, which Delacroix spent in coming to grips with his developing ideas on form and expression, was almost fallow for Chopin. But the F sharp minor Polonaise (opus 44), written toward the end of it, took Chopin firmly into the last span of his creative life. It clearly belongs to Chopin's most mature period, during which he displayed many of the same tendencies as Delacroix; his music grew more and more dramatic and intense, and at the same time more controlled and subtle in form. The next few years were to see the birth of the great polonaises, the Barcarolle, and most of his masterpieces.

10

Greatness

"A great, grrreat piece of news is that little Chip-Chip is going to give a grrrreat concert," George Sand wrote to Pauline Viardot in London on April 18, 1841.[1] On the next day Marie d'Agoult wrote to a friend; "A small malevolent coterie is trying to resuscitate Chopin, who is going to play at Pleyel's."[2]

Needless to say, the idea had not come from Chopin but from a group of friends. He only agreed to play, according to George Sand, because he was certain that the various difficulties in the way of arranging the event would finally induce them to drop the idea. Things moved quicker than he expected and in a couple of days everything had been prepared, while three quarters of the tickets had been sold before the concert had even been announced in the press. "He then awoke as from a dream," writes George Sand, "and there can be no funnier spectacle than the meticulous and irresolute Chip-Chip obliged not to change his mind anymore." He did in fact try to cancel the whole event when he realized that Pauline Viardot would not be able to return from London in time to take part in it, but was finally prevailed upon to ask

Madame Cinti-Damoreau to sing for him instead. No more than a week elapsed between the launching of the project and the concert, but it was a week fraught with anxiety for Chopin, who hated the responsibility that had been put on him, and would retire to his room and play Bach fugues in order to calm his nerves.[3] As George Sand explained:

> This Chopinesque nightmare will take place in the Salons of Pleyel on the 26th. He doesn't want any posters, he doesn't want any programmes, he doesn't want a numerous audience. He doesn't want anyone to talk about it. He is afraid of so many things that I have suggested he play without candles, without an audience on a mute piano.[4]

On April 26, Delacroix came to collect George Sand and drove with her to the Salle Pleyel, where they found an audience of about three hundred people filling the hall, most of whom were friends or acquaintances of Chopin. From the musical world there were Berlioz, Franchomme, Liszt, and dozens of others, there were Heine and Custine, and the Polish colony, including Grzymala, Witwicki, Mickiewicz, and the Czartoryskis. As Liszt described the scene in his review of the concert:

> At eight o'clock in the evening, the Salons of M. Pleyel were splendidly illuminated. At the foot of a staircase covered with carpets and perfumed with flowers, numerous carriages continuously deposited the most elegant women, the most famous artists, the richest financiers, the most illustrious aristocrats, a whole elite of society, a whole aristocracy of birth, fortune, talent and beauty. A grand piano stood open on the podium, the places closest to it were universally coveted, ears were strained in advance, people recollected themselves, telling themselves that they must not lose a single chord, a single note, a single intention, a single idea of the one who would come and seat himself there. And they were right to be so avid, so attentive, so religiously moved, for the one they awaited, the one they were going to see, hear, admire, ap-

plaud, was not just an able virtuoso, a pianist expert in the art of making notes; he was not merely an artist of great renown, he was all of that, and much more than that—he was Chopin![5]

Chopin sat down at the piano and played a selection of mazurkas and preludes, after which Madame Cinti-Damoreau sang a couple of pieces. He then played a duo with the violinist Ernst, and finished with more of his own works. The variegated program with a dozen or so heterogeneous artists taking part, which had been so fashionable in the 1820s and 1830s, had by 1840 given way to the recital. The principal artist now used a singer mainly in order to provide himself with a breathing space between his own performances.

It was the first time Chopin had played in public since the spring of 1838, and it was also the first time he had played a large selection of his own music; in all his previous appearances, he had played no more than one or two pieces of his own, and never any of the small jewels for which he is famous. The success of the event is therefore hardly surprising, and the reviews were unanimous in their praise. *Le Ménestrel* asserted that in Chopin "heart and genius alone speak, and in these respects his talent has nothing to learn."[6] *La France Musicale* acclaimed him as the creator of a school of piano playing and of a school of composition and added that he "should not and cannot be compared to anyone."[7] The curious thing about the reviews was that they all spoke more of Chopin and his position than of either his playing or his composition. Liszt, writing in the *Gazette Musicale*, virtually gave the history of his friend's career, while Heine dubbed Chopin as "the Rafael of the pianoforte."[8] It was as though Chopin had through this concert graduated into Parnassus, for, as Liszt wrote: "A complete silence of criticism had already established itself around his reputation, as though posterity had already arrived; and in the brilliant audience which came run-

ning to hear the poet too long silent, there was no reservation,
no hesitation; every mouth had only praise."[9]

This was not, strictly speaking, true; a particularly rude intrusion into the silence was to be made later that same year
by the critic of the *Musical World* of London, who wrote, in
a review of some newly published mazurkas:

> Mr Frederick Chopin has, by some means or other which we
> cannot divine, obtained an enormous reputation, a reputation
> but too often refused to composers of ten times his genius.
> Mr Chopin is by no means a putter-down of commonplaces;
> but he is, what by many would be esteemed worse, a dealer in
> the most absurd and hyperbolical extravagances. It is a
> striking satire on the capability of thought possessed by the
> musical profession that so very crude and limited a writer
> should be esteemed, as he is very generally, a profound classi-
> cal musician. Mr Chopin does not want ideas, but they never
> extend beyond eight or sixteen bars at the utmost. The works
> of the composer give us invariably the idea of an enthusiastic
> schoolboy whose parts are by no means on a par with his en-
> thusiasm, who *will* be original whether he can or not. There
> is a clumsiness about his harmonies in the midst of their
> affected strangeness, a sickliness about his melodies, despite
> their evidently *forced* unlikeness to familiar phrases, an utter
> ignorance of design everywhere apparent in his lengthened
> works . . . The entire works of Chopin present a motley sur-
> face of ranting hyperbole and excruciating cacophony.[10]

As though determined that nobody should take him
seriously, the critic went on to wonder how George Sand
could be "content to wanton away her dreamlike existence
with an artistical nonentity like Chopin." Although this review testifies to Chopin's popularity in England by combating
it so savagely, it does reflect, admittedly with some distortion,
views which were prevalent among English musicians. It
must be remembered that the extraordinary popularity of
Mendelssohn in England left little room for other composers,

and that anyway there was something about Chopin and his music which militated against his full acceptance as a serious composer. One Victorian writer on the subject declared that the nocturnes "bewitch and unman"; another assured his readers that the Polonaise-Fantaisie "on account of its pathological contents, stands outside the sphere of art." An early biographer warned the public against the B flat minor Sonata (the one which contains the famous Funeral March), stating that: "The music grows more and more passionate and in the concluding portion transcends the limits of propriety,"[11] a judgment which conjures up attractive images of Victorian misses losing control in the concert hall.

These sexual undertones did not, however, prevent the music from enjoying wide popularity in England, or from being accepted at its face value in other countries. Its popularity had not ceased to grow in Germany, where even the acrid Rellstab had announced in 1839 that either times had changed or he had changed or else Chopin's music had undergone some transformation, for he now found it all beautiful. Schumann, although deeply worried by the burning question of whether the B flat minor Sonata was music or not,[12] continued to treat Chopin as one of the greatest composers of the age, as did Mendelssohn himself.

Undoubtedly the greatest obstacle to the full acceptance of Chopin as one of the leading composers, then as now, is the fact that he did not progress through all the musical forms, and that apart from his two piano concertos, not themselves particularly brilliant examples of the form, he never wrote any grand works. The symphony and opera were considered the zenith of musical creation, and the dimensions of their works were to some extent reflected in the reputations of the composers. That very year, while reviewing the two nocturnes of opus 37, Schumann exhorted Chopin to write a grand work in order to achieve greater effect than he was doing.[13] As Elsner had pointed out to Chopin years before, a piece for piano compared to a piece for orchestra was like an engraving compared to an oil painting.[14]

The fact that Chopin did not attempt to write grand works in his maturity gave rise to the opinion that he was in some way incapable of it. Liszt explains that Chopin was unable to achieve perfection in any form that he had not himself created, which is why, he argues, his sonatas and concertos are less successful than his polonaises, mazurkas, and ballades. "If Chopin never tried his hand at symphonic music in any of its forms, it was because he did not want to," he writes. "It was not out of some extreme modesty or misplaced disdain; it was the pure and simple consequence of the form which suited his sentiment best."[15]

He could have added two other considerations which undoubtedly played their part in determining the size and nature of Chopin's work. One was the neurotic perfectionism which kept Chopin struggling for up to a week on the composition of a few bars, a labor which became more and more daunting as he grew older and assumed terrifying proportions in this final stage of his creative life. At such a rate a symphony would have taken him five years of agony to produce, and an opera ten. Another factor was his reticence and fear of complications of any sort; he had witnessed the harrowing problems that faced Berlioz each time he wanted to put on a performance of one of his orchestral works, and Meyerbeer having to wait six years to see a performance of one of his operas.

"But," according to Liszt, "that which for anyone else would have been a certain cause of total oblivion and obscurity, was exactly what assured him a reputation above the caprice of fashion, and what sheltered him from rivalry, jealousy and injustice."[16] Even Schumann, who did not condone the direction in which Chopin now began to move, wrote in 1840 that "By now Chopin does not write anything which could as well come from another; he remains faithful to him-

self, and he has good reason for this."[17] As Debussy was later
to point out, "by the very nature of his genius, Chopin eludes
all attempts at classification,"[18] and that particular genius,
one might almost say that particular and highly personal art
form that Chopin had developed, elicited a strong response
throughout Europe, and particularly in France, where the decline of the exuberant Romanticism of the 1830s had left a
slight void.

The quiet craftsmanship of Chopin, which had been outshone in the Paris of the 1830s by Meyerbeer, Rossini, Liszt,
and Berlioz, now appeared to a whole segment of the Parisian
intelligentsia as the ultimate in artistry and seemed to embody something more essential than the bombast of the previous decade. The result was that, as Liszt explains: "In those
days it was not so much the school of Chopin as the Church
of Chopin."[19] Of Liszt, Balzac now wrote: "He is the Paganini of the pianoforte, but Chopin is totally superior to
him."[20] In his novel *Ursule Mirouët* he explained that Chopin was not merely a musician in the strict sense of the word,
but rather an artist who had a heightened gift for expressing
the lyricism in his soul.[21] It was no coincidence that Custine,
in the note he sent Chopin after the 1841 concert, spoke of
"the thoughts you express in spite of your instrument, for it
is not the piano that you play, but the soul itself,"[22] or that
Delacroix described his music as "one of those nourishments
of the soul which are so rare in our age, and indeed in any
age."[23] Heine, whose position as a baptized Jew and an
émigré from Germany made him sensitive on such points,
discovered in Chopin a purer and therefore more universal
artist than any other:

> Yes, one must admit that Chopin has genius in the fullest
> sense of the word; he is not only a virtuoso, he is also a poet;
> he can embody the poetry which lives within his soul; he is a
> tone-poet, and nothing can be compared to the pleasure he
> gives when he sits down at the piano and improvises. He is

then neither a Pole, nor a Frenchman, nor a German, he reveals then a higher origin, one perceives then that he comes
from the land of Mozart, Rafael and Goethe, his true father-
land is the dream-world of poetry . . .[24]

Only in the light of such judgment can one understand the
religious enthusiasm with which the concert had been
greeted, as well as the absence of any precise criticism of his
playing or his compositions. The public knew what they were
coming for, and they got it; the press merely marked the
event with appropriate solemnity. There had been no comparable ceremony attendant on the event which took place on
the day before at the Conservatoire: Liszt's concert to raise
money for the Beethoven memorial, in which he had played
and Berlioz had conducted a performance of the Pastoral
Symphony.

The moral victory implicit in the event was accompanied
by material satisfaction, for, as George Sand wrote to her half-
brother: "Chopin has put himself in the position of being
able to loaf all summer, by giving a concert where, in a period
of two hours, with a couple of flourishes of the hand, he put
six thousand and several hundred francs in his pocket, amid
applause, encores and the flutterings of the most beautiful
women in Paris—The Scoundrel!"[25] The sentiments were
echoed by Witwicki, who wrote to another poet: "You just
try and recite your verse for a couple of hours and see if they
give you six thousand francs!"[26] There was now nothing to
stop Chopin accompanying George Sand to Nohant, where
he hoped to be able to get down to his much-neglected compositions. He had plenty of ideas and rough sketches, but
could never find the right degree of concentration and the
time to turn these into finished works, a process which he
found more and more difficult as time went on. By the 1840s
the problem had become almost insuperable; as one of his pupils explains:

The other day I heard Chopin improvise at George Sand's. It is marvelous to hear him compose in this way; his inspiration is so immediate and complete that he plays without hesitation, as though it had to be thus. But when it comes to writing it down and recapturing the original thought in all its details, he spends days of nervous strain and almost frightening desperation. He alters and retouches the same phrases incessantly and walks up and down like a madman.[27]

His difficulty made him long for the peace of Nohant. Only ten days after his arrival there at the beginning of June, he was able to send Fontana the first of the completed works, the Tarantella (opus 43). This was followed over the next month or two by a prelude, two nocturnes, and, most important, the A flat Ballade (opus 47) and the Fantaisie in F minor (opus 49). These "cobwebs and manuscriptical flies," as he called his manuscripts, which did admittedly sometimes resemble the peregrinations of a spider through a series of ink blots, were dispatched to Fontana for copying with the apology that "the weather is beautiful and my music hideous."[28]

The weather was indeed fine that summer, and Chopin's health was good as a result. "But as he is still at least ten years too young to be a really good boy," explained George Sand, "he often gets bored in this happy state and thinks he is being idle since he is not crushed by work."[29] It was not just boredom which made Chopin fear inactivity, but also a sort of nervous restlessness which manifested itself from the moment he arrived at Nohant, in the first place through a stream of finicky letters to Fontana asking him to procure hundreds of things, most of which were declared to be unnecessary in the next letters. The following missive, quoted in full, provides a typical example:

> My Dearest,
> I enclose a hundred francs for various expenses, from which you can subtract what I owe you for the *Charivari* [a French equivalent of *Punch*], pay the rent, pay the postman

for my letters, the flower woman, who wants six. At Houbigant Chardin of Faubourg St. Honoré you can buy me some benzoin soap, two pairs of Swedish gloves (take an old one from somewhere for the size), a bottle of patchouli, and a bottle of Bouquet de Chantilly. In the Palais Royal, in the gallery on the same side as the theaters, almost in the center, you will find a shop with *galanteria* (as we say in Poland); it has two windows filled with various caskets, jokes, gifts, gleaming, elegant and expensive. There you can ask if they don't have any ivory head scratchers; you must know the kind; a white curled hand set on a black stick. I think I saw one like it there—ask them. Find one and send it to me, but don't spend more than 10, 15, 20 or 30. Get Pleyel to give you a copy of my preludes, and get Schles. to give you all my études. If my little bust by Dantan is available at Suss', buy two and have them well wrapped, if not, then go to Dantan's, who lives in St. Lazare, near Alkan (give him my love if you see him), and ask where you can get them, at the same time ask him about the bronze one he was supposed to cast for me. Somewhere in the upper reaches of my cupboard you'll find a Polish tin bottle covered in flannel for placing against the chest, also an inflatable new pillow which I bought for the journey. You can throw in Kastner [*Théorie abrégée de contrepoint et de la fugue*, by J. G. Kastner] and send it all, well-packed (there's a packer opposite you), in a case of reasonable size through Lafitte et Cayard, addressed like the letters. Please hurry. Keep the rest of the money for other things I shall want sent. Don't pay Schlesinger, and don't delay the sending if he hasn't got Kastner in stock, but don't fail to send Cherubini's *traité*, I think, *de contrepoint* (I cannot remember the title). If he won't give you the Cherubini without money, pay him, as it may be that Cherubini paid for the printing himself. I shall write to Troupenas in a couple of days through you. I must finish now, as the post is going. Sorry about all this, but you'll get this on Sunday; send everything on Monday.

Ch.[30]

Another object of his nervous state was the Pleyel piano which had been shipped to Nohant to coincide with his arrival. It turned out to have a poor tone, and Chopin kept bashing it furiously while trying to work on his music. After a couple of weeks he insisted that Pleyel have it taken away and a new one sent down. Next, Chopin turned his attention to his servant, whom he fired and sent away in July. But there was something else which was irritating him more seriously. Marie de Rozières, a pupil whom he had introduced to George Sand as a piano teacher for her daughter Solange, was its principal cause. She had somehow managed to ingratiate herself with George Sand, and this nettled Chopin. She had also recently become the mistress of the feckless Antoni Wodzinski, who was back in Paris. The extent to which she had insinuated herself into his life made Chopin apprehensive, as he explained to Fontana:

> Between ourselves, she's an unbearable old sow who has somehow managed to tunnel into my garden, and is rooting around looking for truffles among the roses. She is a person to avoid, for she only has to touch something to make a great indiscretion. In a word, she's an old maid. We bachelors are far better.[31]

During that spring she committed some sort of indiscretion which infuriated him. Marie de Rozières and Wodzinski were to have come down to Nohant, but in view of Chopin's attitude George Sand wrote to her telling her not to come down yet and certainly not with Wodzinski, whom she wrongly assumed to be the object of Chopin's irritation. When Chopin heard this, he became frantic. "I thought he would go mad," George Sand wrote. "He wanted to leave, he told me I was making him out to be mad, jealous, ridiculous, that I was creating bad blood between him and his friends."[32] The reason for these histrionics lay in the fact that, coming hard on the news of Maria Wodzinska's marriage in Poland at the end of July, a sudden show of hostility toward Antoni would make Chopin look spiteful and foolish. To make things worse, Chopin knew that Antoni Wodzinski cared little for his mistress and was preparing to jilt her and return to Poland, unknown to George Sand, who seems to have thought that it was the passion of the century.

George Sand challenged Chopin on the subject, and a "bitter discussion" ensued,[33] but either he avoided giving an explanation or she failed to grasp his meaning. The situation continued tense, as she explained to Marie de Rozières:

> You will ask me why he is piqued and why indisposed toward you? If I knew that I should know where the sickness lay, and would be able to cure it; but with his exasperating nature, one can never know anything. He went through the whole of the day before yesterday without uttering a syllable to anyone. Was he ill? Had someone annoyed him? Had I said something to upset him? I searched and searched, I know his sensitive spots as well as anyone can, but I was unable to discover anything, and I shall never know, any more than I know about a million other little things, which he may not even know himself.[34]

It is clear that the original harmony between them had broken down. Chopin was growing defensive, and a rather juvenile tendency to withdraw into dignified silence becomes more and more noticeable in his relations with George Sand at this point. His almost hysterical reactions to minor vexations suggest a chronic and fundamental frustration. Those determined to pin down the date at which George Sand began to deny him her bed would do well to look at the spring of 1841; both his tense condition and their apparent alienation would appear to point in that direction. This is borne out by the tone of irony and impatience in which she now described his behavior; there is something of the schoolmistress recounting the antics of a spoiled child in her letters on the subject. Her feelings toward him altered perceptibly, and she began to humor him like a child rather than to challenge him like a lover. She clearly failed to understand the cause of his neuroses, and saw them as symptoms of a "malady." This was a dangerous explanation, as it allowed her to put down every quirk and every fit of temper, whether it was understandable or not, to the "malady." She thereby absolved herself of any part in provoking his behavior or inadvertently encouraging his humors.

The arrival of the new Pleyel at the beginning of August and a short visit by Witwicki did much to restore Chopin's nerves.[35] The Viardots also came to stay, which helped to ease the tension. Louis Viardot sat about with George Sand and her dingy philosopher-friend Pierre Leroux, discussing their project for a new independent paper. Chopin and Pauline went for long walks or played billiards with the perpetually drunk Hippolyte Chatiron, George Sand's half-brother. Things went so much better that, toward the end of September, George Sand suggested that Chopin, who had been looking for a new Paris apartment with more sun than that in the Rue Tronchet (which suggests that he was thinking of spending more time there), give up the idea and come and live with her in the Rue Pigalle. (This seems to belie her later statements about how she wanted to loosen the bonds between them gradually.) Chopin liked the idea and agreed to take over a room in the pavilion occupied until now by Maurice, for which he paid her some rent. He would share her drawing room and give his lessons there.

Some of his pupils balked at the distance they now had to travel for their lessons, the Rue Pigalle being a long way further out than the Rue Tronchet. Chopin, prompted by George Sand, politely explained that he gave better lessons in his own room at twenty francs, but that if they preferred to send their carriages and thirty francs, he was prepared to do his best at their houses. He could afford to play the *grand seigneur*, for people were queuing up for the favor of taking lessons from him, and pianists from other countries traveled all the way to Paris to do so. The most notable of these was the twelve-year-old Hungarian Karl Filtsch, who had arrived while Chopin was at Nohant and had taken a few lessons from Liszt while he waited for Chopin. "When that boy starts to travel, I shall shut up shop!" Liszt exclaimed after hearing him.[36] Chopin was equally delighted, calling him "my little urchin who knows everything," and took him around everywhere to show him off, introducing him with the words: "That, ladies, is what is called talent!"[37] The boy had a remarkable touch and could play Chopin's music perfectly. "No one in the world will ever play it like him . . . except myself," Chopin once declared after listening to Filtsch playing one of the nocturnes of opus 48, written that summer, and on one occasion he burst into tears while listening to the boy playing his music.

Not long after his return to Paris, on December 2, Chopin was again asked to play to the Royal Family at the Tuileries, and was rewarded for his pains with a sumptuous present. The previous year's success and the financial gains had whetted his appetite, and in the new year he once more decided to give a concert of his own. The event took place on February 21, 1842. Once again the whole of Paris fought for the expensive tickets, and once again it was "a charming soirée, a feast peopled with delicious smiles, delicate and pretty faces, small, shapely white hands; a magnificent occasion where simplicity was married to grace and elegance, and where good taste served as a pedestal to riches."[38] Chopin played a ballade, various nocturnes, preludes, études, mazurkas, and an impromptu, punctuated by Pauline Viardot's singing of a song by Dessauer, some pieces by Handel, and a song of her own composition, in which she was accompanied on the piano by Chopin. In the middle, Franchomme played one of his own pieces for the cello.

The reviews were ecstatic, going on for column after column of superlatives; as George Sand wrote to her half-brother:

> The great Chopin's concert has been as beautiful, as brilliant, as lucrative as last year's (more than 5000 francs' profit, a unique result in Paris, which merely proves how eager people are to hear the most perfect and the most exquisite of musicians). Pauline was admirable . . . Chopin is relaxing by giving his lessons.[39]

Such relaxation could not quickly repair the strain of the concert, however, and a visiting compatriot who saw Chopin at the Marlianis' a few days after the concert wrote: "He looks even worse than last year, there's only skin and bones left."[40] A few days later he had an attack of what George Sand called rheumatism, and was bedridden for nearly two weeks. "I have to lie in bed all day long," he wrote to Grzymala, "my mouth and tonsils are aching so much."[41]

Hardly had he recovered from this when disaster struck. Jan Matuszynski, who was in the terminal stages of tuberculosis, had been taken in by Chopin, so they could keep each other company during their illness. Toward the end of April, after "a slow and cruel agony," he died in Chopin's arms. Chopin seemed to be going through this agony with his friend, and showed himself "strong, courageous and devoted, more so than one could expect from such a frail being, but afterwards he was broken."[42] As usual on such occasions, Chopin's health and general condition deteriorated, and as a result George Sand took him down to Nohant at the first opportunity, on May 6.

On his arrival there, Chopin was thoroughly examined by Dr. Papet, who found his chest and larynx intact and sound, and explained that the choking and the coughing resulted from the fact that both throat and larynx were awash with "mucus." It seems extraordinary that a competent doctor could have ascribed Chopin's steady decline to a mysterious quantity of mucus, but it was probably just as well that the existence of tuberculosis was consistently denied, for Chopin might have gone to pieces completely had he known that he had the disease. As it was, he muddled along and was soon feeling much better, well enough to start working again. Only three weeks after their arrival, George Sand wrote to Delacroix that "Chopin has written two adorable mazurkas which are worth more than forty novels and say more than the whole literature of this century."[43]

What cheered everyone at Nohant was the news that Delacroix was coming down for a stay. "My Chopinet is very happy and agitated as he awaits you," George Sand wrote to him. "He keeps wondering what we can do to amuse you, where we can go for walks, what we can give you to eat, what he can play you on his piano."[44] Even Maurice, a surly character "not generous with his affection" in his mother's own words,[45] was happy, as he worshiped the painter. Delacroix was delighted with Nohant, as he explained to a friend:

> The place is very agreeable and the hosts could not be more pleasing. When one is not gathered together for dinner, lunch, billiards or walks, one is left in one's room to read or laze around on a sofa. From time to time the window opening onto the garden admits gusts of music from Chopin, who is working in his room; it mingles with the songs of the nightingales and the scent of roses . . .[46]

In the tranquillity of Nohant, Chopin paid more attention to Delacroix and his conversations and began to feel respect for the artist as well as liking for the man. "I have never-ending conversations with Chopin, whom I love and who is a man of rare distinction; he is the most real artist I have ever met," wrote Delacroix. "He is one of the very small number whom one can both admire and esteem."[47] It was during this stay at Nohant that he finally worked out his project for the ceiling of the library in the Palais du Luxembourg, a problem which had been worrying him ever since he had been given the commission. He now saw it clearly; Virgil presenting Dante to Homer, surrounded by all the greatest poets of antiquity. The head of Dante was to be a portrait of Chopin.

Toward the end of July, Witwicki came for a few days, but Balzac, who had been expected, did not turn up, to the great relief of Delacroix, for "he is a chatterbox who would have broken the spell of nonchalance in which I am indulging with great pleasure."[48] The weeks passed far too quickly for Chopin, and when Delacroix had gone, he was once again a little bored. "Chopin always wanted Nohant but could never bear Nohant," George Sand later wrote, which was not altogether surprising, as the tedium there could be intense. Even Delacroix had remarked that "one could fossilize very quickly here."[49] But Chopin was as well as could be expected, and his relations with George Sand remained outwardly unchanged. When the subject of moving from the Rue Pigalle came up that summer, there was no question of their not living together in Paris, and when they started looking for new accommodation, she wrote to Charlotte Marliani that "Chopin could not decide on the apartment without me nor I without him."[50]

For once the search was not being carried out by Fontana, nor indeed was any other part of Chopin's business, which had been transferred to Grzymala's shoulders. There are no extant letters from Chopin to his former factotum from this summer, and at some stage during the next year Fontana left Paris for America. What *has* survived is a letter from Fontana to his sister in Poland, written in Paris that May just as Chopin was setting off for Nohant, in which he tells her that he is at the end of his tether financially and psychologically and which contains the following lines:

> I always relied on one friend, who was to open up my career
> for me, but who has been consistently dishonest and false
> . . . I even left Paris for a time to get away from his

influence, and that did me a lot of harm. I only started composing again after my return . . .[51]

It is difficult to see how the friend who was going to open up Fontana's musical career could have been anyone but Chopin, and this seems corroborated by the fact that Fontana was in dire poverty at a time when the proverbially generous Chopin had just raked in thousands of francs as a result of his concert. How far Chopin could have helped a musical mediocrity like Fontana is debatable, but he certainly did not try very hard, in contrast to the effort he made for his equally mediocre pupil Gutmann. How Chopin repaid Fontana for his copying, his secretarial work, and his total devotion is not known, but at least the latter lived free at the Rue Tronchet apartment until that was gotten rid of in the autumn of 1841. It does look as though the unfortunate Fontana had let himself be used without getting much out of it, and however one chooses to look at it, Chopin's part in the affair does not redound to his credit.

It was Charlotte Marliani who searched for new accommodation, and at the end of July, Chopin and George Sand traveled up to Paris to see what she had found. Having decided which apartment to take, they returned to Nohant for the rest of the summer. The extreme heat of that August made Chopin suffer, and he could not compose. George Sand, too, suffered from the heat and had persistent migraines. "It is then that one has to see Chopin exercising his function of zealous, ingenious, devoted nurse," wrote Marie de Rozières, who had come down to look after Solange and recover from having been finally jilted by Antoni Wodzinski. "He calls her his angel," she added, "but the angel has very large wings which sometimes hit you."[52]

The Viardots came to Nohant for a couple of weeks, after which the whole party returned to Paris in the last days of September, Chopin and George Sand preparing to settle into their new home. This was situated in a large private courtyard off the street, the Square d'Orléans. George Sand had taken a medium-sized apartment on the first floor of No. 9, which consisted of a large drawing room with a billiard table, a smaller salon with a piano, and accommodation for herself and Maurice, who had managed to rent a studio in one of the other houses on the square. Across the graveled courtyard, at No. 5, Chopin had taken two rooms on the ground floor, with a view onto the courtyard on one side and gardens at the back. The Marlianis had an elegant apartment in one of the other houses in the square, and it was there that the two usually met for dinner, George Sand lending her cook and Chopin contributing financially to the communal meals. The square was nicknamed "*La petite Athènes*," as it had long been a favorite place for artists and writers. When Chopin moved in, other apartments in the square were occupied by Kalkbrenner and his family, the pianist Zimmermann, and his friend the young composer Alkan.

For Chopin it was an ideal arrangement. For one thing, the rent was low, since he needed only two rooms and a little attic for his new servant, Jan, whom Witwicki had unearthed for him. In these two rooms he was as independent of George Sand and her family as he could wish, while at the same time surrounded by her and other friends, whom he could call on whenever the need arose.

It was a busy winter for Chopin: he was working harder than usual at his lessons, which did not end before six o'clock now. He was also going out a good deal more than in the last few years. Liszt was in Paris for the season, and Chopin had to keep up the semblance of cordiality, although he disliked him more than ever. What irritated him particularly was the way in which Liszt was turning himself into a public figure with his politics, his decorations, and his Beethoven memorial. As he wrote to Fontana, "Liszt is bound to become a deputy—or maybe even a King in Abyssinia or the Congo—

but as for the themes of his compositions, they will lie forgotten."[53]

For Chopin, there were receptions at the Czartortskis' and at the Rothschilds', where he and Karl Filtsch played his E minor concerto on two pianos before five hundred guests, after which Pauline Viardot, Mario, Grisi, and Lablache sang. A good deal less brilliant was the unfortunate Fontana's matinee concert on March 17, 1843, to which Chopin went with Thalberg, for, as one witness put it, the event "did not rise above mediocrity at any point."[54]

As had become usual, Chopin again fell ill in February, but this time a new doctor was called in, a homeopathic specialist called Molin, who brought a radical change into the treatment Chopin had been undergoing. Whether Molin thought that his patient had tuberculosis or not is not known, but he only prescribed the gentlest treatment designed mainly to ease his respiration. As a Polish friend noted in his diary:

> Every second day [Chopin] spends five minutes sniffing a little bottle of something. The result of this is that he breathes more freely, he can walk upstairs without becoming exhausted, and he no longer coughs. He has developed a rash from ear to ear which, according to some, augurs well.[55]

In mid-May, Chopin and George Sand went down to Nohant, this time taking the newly built railway as far as Blois, and spent the next two months entirely alone, except for Pauline Viardot's baby daughter, whom George Sand had taken in while her mother went on tour to Vienna. There was an element of sadness and resignation in their relations, George Sand working hard on her writing, Chopin trying to work but spending most of the days playing with Pauline Viardot's daughter instead. "She says *petit Chopin* in a way that would disarm all the Chopins on earth, and Chopin loves her and spends his days kissing her little hands."[56] One cannot help feeling that it was now that Chopin had the idea of writing the Berceuse (opus 57), a work full of intense, though restrained, happiness. It illustrates more clearly than most of the pieces written at this time how far Chopin had gone in the last few years. It is brimming over with sentiment and tenderness, and yet there is no trace of sentimentality in it, for the expression is reduced to the indispensable.

They both felt well and relaxed and made the most of the good weather:

> Chopin and I go on long excursions, he on a donkey and I on my own legs. The donkey is a fine creature. It will only walk with its nose in my pocket, which is full of crusts of bread. The day before yesterday we were pursued by an enterprising ass who wanted to make an attempt on her virtue. She defended herself like a real Lucrèce, with hefty kicks. Chopin shouted and laughed, while I attempted to fend off the Sextius with my umbrella.[57]

In July the monotony of their days was broken by the arrival of Delacroix, who again spent whole days with Chopin "strolling along the avenues, talking of music, and the evenings on a sofa listening to it, when God descends upon his divine fingers."[58] When Delacroix left, Chopin went up to Paris to collect Solange for the holidays, and they were soon followed down to Nohant by the Viardots, who joined them on the numerous excursions into the surrounding countryside which George Sand had grown so keen on. Chopin always went on his donkey, but he slept on the straw in a stable along with the others, and seemed to be thriving on the exercise.

But he was clearly beginning to find the atmosphere of Nohant stifling when it was not diluted by the presence of other guests. As his relationship with George Sand grew less satisfactory, he longed more for Paris and for the comforting presence of his friends. As a result, when he realized that she was planning to stay on in the country until the winter, Chopin decided to go back to Paris independently at the end of October.

11

Breakdown of an Affair

When at the end of October 1843 Chopin set off from Nohant with Maurice, he was followed by a torrent of letters from George Sand to various friends in Paris, urging them to look after him as though he had been a helpless invalid. Grzymala was begged to see him and take him out in the evenings, Marie de Rozières was told to spy on his health and mood, Maurice was to report on his everyday condition, and Charlotte Marliani also received her instructions:

> Here is my little Chopin, I entrust him to you, look after him in spite of himself. He doesn't look after himself when I am not there, and his servant is good but stupid. I am not worried about his dinners, for he will be invited on all sides, and it is no bad thing for him to have to wake up a little at that time of day. But in the morning, in the rush of his lessons, I am afraid that he will forget to swallow a cup of chocolate or stock which I usually force down his throat when I am there . . . Nothing could be easier than for his Pole to make him a little broth or a cutlet, but he will not order it and may even forbid it. You must therefore lecture and threaten . . .[1]

Her apprehensions were not misplaced, for Chopin did have a severe illness about halfway through November, during a spell of extreme cold and damp. "He is all right during the daytime, but at night he coughs, chokes and spits," Maurice informed his mother. Dr. Molin was not seriously worried, only confining Chopin to his room for a couple of weeks and giving him some homeopathic potions.[2] His appetite remained good, and after a few days he felt quite well again, but George Sand wrote to Grzymala:

> I know very well that he suffers without me, I know that he would be happy to see me; but I also know that he would be saddened and almost humiliated in the delicacy of his heart if he saw me abandon my important work in favor of being his sick-nurse, as he puts it, the poor child! although I am his sick-nurse so willingly. He writes that I should stay here, he begs me. He does not want me to know that he is ill, he thinks I don't know it . . . I miss him as much as he misses me, I need to look after him as much as he needs my care. I miss his face, his voice, his piano, his slight sadness, and I even miss the heartrending sound of his cough. Poor Angel! I shall never abandon him, you can be sure of that; my life is consecrated to him forever.[3]

A couple of days later she wrote to another friend:

> Chopin's love for me is of an exclusive and jealous character. It is a little fantastic and sickly, like him, the poor angel. If he were strong enough to bear the suffering it creates in him, I should combat it with mockery and I should laugh it off. But it hurts him so much that I find myself forced at the age of forty to put up with the ridicule of having a jealous lover at my side.[4]

These passages reveal the extraordinary emotional acrobatics which she was beginning to perform vis-à-vis Chopin. While reasserting her deep attachment to him, she spoke of him as though he were her child or invalid father, and laughed off the idea that he still loved her as a woman, pleading her great age of forty. In this she was being dishonest, for she was about to be unfaithful to Chopin, and after their separation she would have a stream of lovers well into her fifties.

George Sand had always shown protective and motherly instincts toward her friends. In the early 1830s she had steered Liszt through a period of crisis and dejection. Within days of meeting Grzymala, she was mending his shirts for him. A couple of years later she took up the young Pauline Garcia, engineered her marriage to Louis Viardot, and arranged her career. She invariably referred to Pauline as her "daughter" and bestowed similar epithets on other favorites, such as the young Louis Blanc. By the mid-1840s these tendencies had grown into a real need to play the mother (not, incidentally, to her real children) and by the end of the decade into something of an obsession.

She had looked after and pampered Chopin from the start, and unconsciously pushed him into the role of her child. She had often referred to him as her "little one" or her "child," but it was only now that she began to call him her "son"—a more categorical word that cannot be dismissed as a term of endearment.

Having cast him as one of her children, she tried to laugh off his continuing love for her as a sort of absurd joke, and branded it as "sickly." This fitted perfectly into her concept of his "malady":

> No soul could be nobler, more delicate, more disinterested; no friendship more faithful and loyal, no wit more brilliant in its gaiety, no intelligence more complete and more serious in its own domain; but on the other hand, alas! no temper was more unequal, no imagination more umbrageous and more delirious, no susceptibility more difficult not to irritate, no demand of the heart more impossible to satisfy. And none of this was his fault. It was the fault of his malady . . .[5]

She consistently refused to acknowledge the possibility that her own treatment of him might be the cause of this "malady." Instead of examining her own behavior or reassessing the state of the relationship, she merely indulged her instincts more and more, as she explained to Charlotte Marliani:

> The net result of my total devotion is to render his life at best bearable! But that is something at least, and I shall not grow tired of it because he deserves it and because all devotion carries its own reward. It has almost become a necessity for me to assist and nurse him.[6]

While this all sounds most commendable, it was dictated not by altruism but rather by her urge to dominate and mother. When she did at length get sick of playing the mother and her sexual urges reasserted themselves, no other consideration carried much weight. Her devotion and saintliness were double-edged, for while it made Chopin more and more dependent on her, it also made him more insecure, as it became more obvious that she acted not out of love but out of what seemed to be kindness. Her refusal to acknowledge his love made him jealous and suspicious, and his neurotic tendencies flourished in this climate.

Chopin was only thirty-three years old, yet his behavior was sometimes that of a middle-aged psychopath. Nowhere can this be seen as well as in the pages of the meticulously kept diary of Zofia Rozengardt, the nineteen-year-old daughter of a Warsaw restaurateur who had come all the way to Paris to take lessons from him. The diary is of course that of an exalted girl, who, having nurtured visions of garrets and dedication to art, was put out to find Chopin so worldly, and who took all his moods very personally. It is nevertheless a priceless document, for it gives an outside view of the man just at the moment when his emotional life was beginning to grow impossible.

Miss Rozengardt took lessons from him throughout November, December, and January, at irregular intervals, and Chopin's mood was different every time. One day he would be cold and distant, another charming, another angry and frightening. On January 2, for instance, she arrived at the wrong time, owing to a mixup by his incompetent servant Jan, and found Chopin in a blind rage. He shouted and stamped his feet "like a spoiled child," and she was sorely tempted to "administer a sound rap across those divine fingers."[7] Having vented his rage for a while, he started the lesson and she sat down at the piano, but then it turned out that she had not brought the score of the nocturne she was studying, meaning to play it from memory. He was furious and upbraided her at length, telling her that she did not know how to take lessons and that he had no time for people to waste. When he had calmed down again, she started playing the nocturne, but it was not to Chopin's liking, and he walked up and down the room nervously. His manner was so peremptory and hostile that she finally burst into tears, at which point he suddenly melted and became charming. At the end of the lesson, he gave her the score of one of his works. "What shall I write on it for you?" he asked, to which she replied: "Write that I am a very poor pupil and that you scold me too much." He picked up a pencil and wrote: "To Miss Zofia Rozengardt, because she is a great baby, F. Chopin." When she saw this, she thought to herself: "The scoundrel, he knows the world—he knows how to make it up when he has hurt someone!"[8]

After taking numerous lessons from him, she described his character in a letter to her brothers:

> . . . strange, incomprehensible man! You cannot imagine a person who can be colder and more indifferent to everything around him. There is a strange mixture in his character: vain and proud, loving luxury and yet disinterested and incapable of sacrificing the smallest part of his own will or caprice for all the luxury in the world. He is polite to excess, and yet there is so much irony, so much spite hidden inside it! Woe to the person who allows himself to be taken in. He has an

extraordinarily keen eye, he will catch the smallest absurdity and mock it wonderfully. He is heavily endowed with wit and common sense, but then he often has wild, unpleasant moments when he is evil and angry, when he breaks chairs and stamps his feet. He can be as petulant as a spoiled child, bullying his pupils and being very cold with his friends. Those are usually days of suffering, physical exhaustion or quarrels with Madame Sand . . .[9]

All such portraits are perforce subjective, but this one is corroborated by other accounts. Two separate sources tell of an occasion on which Meyerbeer dropped in on Chopin during a lesson, and pointed out that one of the pieces being played was in a different time to that printed on the score. Chopin icily replied that he was wrong, but Meyerbeer stuck to his point, and repeated his opinion. Upon this Chopin played the piece through, beating time as he went, but Meyerbeer did not give in. Chopin grew angry, and after another attempt at convincing his visitor, rushed out of the room slamming the door.[10] There are plenty of other accounts testifying to his petulance, and one pupil said that he always felt he had to treat Chopin like a lady he was eager to please.[11] What is interesting is that all these incidents or opinions come from those pupils who were professional musicians, even when they happened to be women, while the recollections of his society pupils bristle with references to his charm, good manners, kindness, and consideration. With them he would never tire of explaining every note, he would gently coax and encourage, for he knew that a breach of good manners there would cost him dearly.[12]

Much has been written about Chopin's snobbishness and love of the aristocracy, and both George Sand and Mickiewicz slightly despised him for it, but it was by no means exclusive. Like many classless people standing astride different artistic and social circles, he was fascinated by the rich and the exalted, at the same time often preferring the company of the simplest and most humble. He did not think twice about inviting the communist Louis Blanc to the same musical evening as the Czartoryskis, and as far as he was concerned, the houses of bankers like Mallet, Leo, or Rothschild were as good a venue for such an evening as the drawing room of the Comte de Perthuis or the Marquis de Custine. He was just as happy to spend the evening with Franchomme or Thomas Albrecht and their families, whose social origins were no grander than his own.

Although he complained to Zofia Rozengardt that he was more easily tired than in previous years, and permanently short of breath, Chopin went out often. The Czartoryskis, who had just moved into the magnificent Hôtel Lambert on the Ile St. Louis, received on a grand scale. There were also musical soirées like that given by the Baron de Rothschild in December, and there was the opera, where Donizetti was in vogue that season. Liszt turned up toward the end of the season and gave the usual couple of concerts to which Chopin had to go in order to maintain the façade of good relations, and in March there was the concert of his own pupil, Gutmann, to be attended and supported. One cannot help feeling that it was out of a sense of duty too that Chopin went, along with George Sand, Victor Hugo, and Lamartine, to hear Mendelssohn's new music for the *Antigone* to be staged that year in Paris.

In February, Chopin had caught the influenza which brought down half of Paris, but to him the slight deterioration in his condition was less noticeable and less aggravating than to healthy people like George Sand, whom he helped to nurse when she too caught it. Nor did it stop him from having himself driven on a freezing day to the cemetery of Père Lachaise for the burial of Camille Pleyel's mother.

It was two months later, on May 12, 1844, that he received news from Warsaw that his own father had died there on the third. He immediately shut himself up in his room and re-

fused to speak to anyone, neither George Sand, nor Franchomme, nor Dr. Molin, whom she had called over to help
her break in on his grief. It was not so much a question of the
loss he had sustained, for he had not seen his father for some
nine years, and had in any case not been particularly close to
him either temperamentally or intellectually, but it was another link with home and family that had broken, and above
all, it was another death to be taken personally. Although he
soon came out of his isolation (a severe toothache forced him
to admit Dr. Molin), he would not stop brooding and, typically, wrote off to one of his brothers-in-law begging for a detailed description of the last hours of his father's life.

George Sand looked after him admirably, wrote to his
mother, and tried to reason with him, but soon realized that
the best cure would be movement. At the end of May, therefore, she took him down to Nohant, where she dragooned
him into long walks and rides through the countryside and
managed at length to break down his melancholy through
sheer exhaustion. But while her perfect care and attention
helped to consolidate the motherly position she had adopted
toward him, and while it made him obviously more dependent on her, he began to long with ever greater intensity for
some kind of ideal of his lost family and home. It is a wide-
spread phenomenon among exiles that they long more for
their own country the longer they live in an adopted one, in
spite of or partly because of the fact that their memory of
their original home becomes more disembodied, unreal, and
confused. This was true of Chopin, and news like that of his
father's death tended to alienate him from his actual surroundings by bringing to mind the lost environment.

In the circumstances, nothing could be more welcome than
the news that Chopin's favorite sister, Ludwika, was coming
to Paris for the summer with her husband. George Sand hastened to write to Ludwika explaining Chopin's state of
health, for she anticipated the shock she would feel on seeing

how much her brother had changed in fifteen years. She assured her that, although there had been illness, there had been no marked deterioration in the last six years (i.e., since she had become his mistress), and that Chopin was now set on a steady course and would "last as long as any other, given a regular way of life and some care."[13]

On July 15, Chopin traveled to Paris to meet his sister and her husband, Jozef Kalasanty Jedrzejewicz, a professor of law and now a judge in Warsaw, a practical and dull man of forty-one. They put up at George Sand's apartment in the Square d'Orléans, and Chopin spent the next ten days exclusively with them, showing them the sights, taking them to the opera, and introducing them to other Poles. He managed to exhaust himself completely with this activity and, on July 25, went back to Nohant, whither they were to follow him in a couple of days, after they had finished their sightseeing. But Kalasanty, who was interested in technology and viewed his stay in Paris as a golden opportunity to see things of which he could only dream in the backwater that Warsaw had become, was not eager to go to Nohant and made Chopin wait another two weeks before coming with his wife.

"We've gone mad with happiness," Chopin wrote to Marie de Rozières when, on August 9, the Jedrzejewiczes did finally arrive at Nohant.[14] George Sand had feared that Ludwika would turn out to be a more provincial version of her brother, whom she regarded as backward and bigoted in everything except music, but to her delight, she found in her "a woman totally superior to her age and her country, and with an angelic character."[15] She spent most of her free time with them, going for walks or sitting around talking, and later remembered that summer as "one of the happiest periods in our life."

On August 27, the Jedrzejewiczes left Nohant, accompanied by Chopin and Maurice, who were to bring Pauline Viardot back on their return journey. Chopin spent a couple of days with them in Paris, took them to the opera again, and on their last evening played to them with Franchomme. It was with a heavy heart that he saw them leave for Warsaw, and his mood was not improved by the fact that, instead of returning with him, Maurice followed Pauline Viardot down to her country house, where he proceeded to have an affair with her.

On September 4, Chopin was back at Nohant, where the mood of happiness persisted throughout the rest of the stay. "Without irony and without exaggeration, Chopin is all that is purest and best on earth," George Sand wrote to Pauline Viardot, for once harmony had been re-established the old affection returned.[16] They both worked hard, she at her novels, he on the B minor Sonata (opus 58) and on teaching a Beethoven sonata to the sixteen-year-old Solange, who had now finished her boarding school. Apart from a flying visit to Paris toward the end of September—since the disappearance of Fontana, Chopin had to see to his own business—during which he went to call on Grzymala, who had nearly broken his back by falling down the stairs, he spent the next three months at Nohant. He was working on "quite a little baggage of new compositions, saying as usual that he cannot seem to write anything that isn't detestable and miserable," George Sand informed Delacroix, adding that "the funniest thing is that he says this in perfectly good faith!"[17]

Once again he returned to Paris ahead of George Sand, on November 28, but he kept his return quiet so as to have a few days of peace before would-be pupils started laying siege to his apartment. He called on old friends like Franchomme and Thomas Albrecht, and was delighted to find Grzymala not only recovered but "dancing like a twenty-year-old." This was in marked contrast to his own health, which began to make him feel "mummifically old"[18] and rather helpless, for he now often had to be carried upstairs or in and out of his carriage by his devoted Jan. It was a bitterly cold December and he found himself sitting in front of the Franchommes' fire with three layers of flannel underclothes, nevertheless feeling "yellow, wilted and frozen" while their little baby son, "pink, fresh, warm and barefoot," played at his feet.[19] He fought his weakness for all he was worth and adhered to a rigid discipline which prevented him from giving up. Lindsay Sloper, an English musician who had begun taking lessons from him, recorded that when he came for his lessons, at eight o'clock in the morning, he would invariably find Chopin perfectly dressed and ready to start, even though he was sometimes so weak that he had to conduct the whole lesson reclining on a sofa and sniffing his bottles. Music, whether he was listening to it or playing it, always eased his suffering. Charles Hallé accompanied Franchomme to Chopin's rooms one day, and they found him "hardly able to move, bent like a half-opened penknife and evidently in great pain." They begged him to postpone the performance he had promised them, "but he would not hear of it; soon he sat down at the piano, and as he warmed to his work, his body gradually resumed its normal position, the spirit having mastered the flesh."[20]

Among the new pupils he acquired during this winter, two were to play an important part in the last years of his life. One was Jane Stirling, a forty-year-old Scottish spinster, an undistinguished pianist but an ardent admirer of him and his music, who was to be a great help but also a great nuisance to him in the future; the other was Princess Marcelina Czartoryska. She was born Princess Radziwill and had married Prince Adam Czartoryski's nephew, Aleksander, who lived in Vienna and was himself an amateur musician of note. Princess Marcelina had studied under Czerny and was, according to Berlioz, who heard her in Vienna, "a musician of wide knowledge and exemplary taste, and a distinguished pianist."[21] She was to become one of Chopin's best pupils and, by general consensus, the most faithful to his style. She was also a striking young woman of twenty-three and, although not beautiful in the accepted sense, she was, according to

Delacroix, the sort of woman with whom one could fall hopelessly in love. Chopin of course appreciated the *grande dame* in her as well as the fine musician, and an affinity sprang up between them, tinged on her part with solicitude for the wilting artist.

This was all the more welcome to him, for not only was the harsh winter preventing him from recovering his strength, but his relations with George Sand were becoming very difficult during the first months of 1845. She was beginning to face with trepidation the prospect of being lumbered for the rest of her days with somebody who was beginning to decline seriously and was turning into an emotional invalid—she was still convinced that it was not his health but his "malady" that lay at the root of his condition. She consoled herself as best she could by having a short affair with the young Louis Blanc, and at the same time heaped more "devotion" on Chopin, who, for his part, sought consolation in music and in his closest friends. The lack of sympathy he sometimes met at George Sand's apartment in the Square d'Orléans was made up for by that which he found at the Hôtel Lambert, which had grown into a sort of court in exile. The various members of the Czartoryski family and some of their relations had apartments in different parts of the huge building. There was also an institute for Polish young ladies being run by the Princess, and the house served as an almost daily rallying point for people like Grzymala and other friends of Chopin. During the spring of 1845 he celebrated Easter there and often went there for soirées and musical evenings, at some of which he played.[22]

He was not, however, to be tempted to play outside the homes of friends, except for one occasion, in April, when the dying republican Cavaignac expressed a wish to hear music before his end. Louis Blanc, to whom the request was made, immediately went to beg Chopin for the favor, which the latter readily granted, knowing and liking the young man and being ignorant of the affair he was having with George Sand. He played for hours to the dying man, who listened with tears running down his face.[23]

Nor did the musical attractions of the season inspire him, for, apart from his pupil Gutmann's concert in March, he only went to two during the first six months of the year. Their nature is eloquent: Mozart's *Requiem* and Haydn's *Creation*. Chopin and Delacroix set off to the Conservatoire Hall like a couple of pilgrims to listen in ecstasy to this music they knew well from the scores, but which they had never heard, and returned feeling that there was no comparable music being written in their time.

However independent their behavior may have seemed during the winter and spring, there was still no hint of Chopin and George Sand separating, and on June 12 they drove to Nohant together in Chopin's new calèche. Not only were they going to spend the summer together as usual, but George Sand had made up her mind to scrape together as much money as possible in order to go to Italy or the South of France with him for the winter, feeling that a full eighteen months without cold weather would put them both right.

After heavy rains which brought serious flooding to the countryside, the summer turned into a hot one, and Chopin sat around "cooking in the sun" with Pauline Viardot, who had accompanied them.[24] They did not make much music together, on account of the good weather, but Pauline did sing him her own arrangements of Spanish songs, which he found beautiful and curiously moving. On July 3 she left for Paris, and Grzymala, who had been expected, announced that he was unable to come down. Chopin felt bored, listless, and isolated. The notoriously lazy letter writer, who preferred to drive across Paris rather than pen a note of three lines, who often kept his parents waiting up to six months for a letter from him, now spent hours writing long, rambling epistles to

Ludwika in Warsaw, to whom he confided: "I am not made for the country."[25] The letters are spread over several days and clearly reveal that they were written in order to kill time:

> I'm not playing much, as my piano has got out of tune, and I'm writing even less. I feel strange here this year; I often look into the room next door [where they had stayed in the previous year], but there's nobody there. It is sometimes taken over by some guest who comes down for a couple of days—And I don't drink my chocolate in the morning—and I've moved the piano to a different place; by the wall, where the sofa and the little table used to be, where Ludwika used to sit and embroider my slippers while the lady of the house worked at something else. In the middle of the room stands my desk, on which I write, to the left are some of my musical papers, Mr. Thiers and poetry; on the right, Cherubini; in front of me the repeater you sent me, in its case (4 o'clock). Roses and carnations, pens, and a little piece of sealing wax Kalasanty left behind. I have always one foot in your world— the other in the room next door, where the lady of the house is working—but I am not at all with myself at the moment, only, as usual, in some strange vacuum . . .[26]

During the first month at Nohant, he had managed to write three new mazurkas (opus 59), but by the beginning of July he was incapable of putting his mind to anything. He would spend hours doing nothing, pacing his room or staring idly out of the window, or else he would play the piano for a moment with Solange. She was the only person who seemed to have time to go for drives with him, and they would set off aimlessly, accompanied by the huge dog Jacques, whose head stuck out of one side of the cabriolet, while his rump and tail hung out on the other. Chopin would then come back to his room and sit down once more to his letter to Ludwika, adding the latest gossip about Victor Hugo's amorous adventures, jumbled up with information he had read in the papers of the opening of the telegraph between Washington and Baltimore and of Liszt's antics at the unveiling of the Beethoven memorial.[27]

Chopin's listlessness was not entirely the product of boredom and had much to do with the tension which was beginning to invade the atmosphere of Nohant. While George Sand kept to her room and her work most of the time, her twenty-two-year-old son, Maurice, began, imperceptibly at first, to assume the role of the master of the house. He had always been a rather shy, surly, and characterless boy, but his mother was convinced that he had great talent and loved him as her favorite. He had come a long way in self-assurance, for that summer George Sand wrote to Marie de Rozières that "Maurice paints, teases, twirls his moustaches, sniggers, swaggers, wears his boots outside his trousers, and smells of the stable."[28] He also kept his jealousy and dislike of Chopin ill-concealed, and he began to question, at first only by his manner, the latter's position and rights in the Sand household.

Solange, who was an illegitimate daughter, had never been George Sand's favorite. While her mother had not been able to cope and had sent her to boarding-school, she had also spoiled her. Presumably this was out of a desire to make up for her neglect, but as Solange later put it: "It was not dresses and a horse that I needed, but love."[29] What little she had gotten had come from Chopin, who had from the start taken a liking to her and had been a substitute father. Now that Chopin himself began to feel that he was being excluded from George Sand's affection in favor of Maurice, their sympathy for each other grew. They spent much of that summer together, for she was as bored as he was at Nohant: "Solange gets dressed, then undresses, climbs on to her horse and then gets off it, scratches, yawns, opens a book and then closes it, combs her hair . . ." as George Sand wrote to Marie de Rozières.[30]

What often happens in this kind of situation occurred here

too, for while Maurice grew more aggressive and protective of his mother, and she began to treat Chopin with a certain tolerance that suggested a weakening of his position, Solange began to court Chopin and, since he was not her father, did not fail to use all the appeal that a blossoming seventeen-year-old girl holds for a depressed, insecure, and prematurely aging man of thirty-five.

Already having a daughter who felt unloved and wronged, George Sand proceeded to do the most rash thing she could have done: she "adopted" another. This was Augustine Brault, the twenty-one-year-old daughter of a cousin of George Sand's, a wretched and loutish character who, not being able to pay for his daughter's education, could think of no better solution than to make her a courtesan. George Sand had already helped the Braults on Augustine's behalf, and now decided to take her into her own family, for she loved her and knew that Maurice was also extremely partial to her. Augustine was pretty and intelligent, and George Sand thought her endowed with all the virtues, but both Chopin and Solange thought the worst of her. Solange's resentment is self-explanatory, particularly as Augustine was prettier than she, but Chopin's dislike is less easy to explain.

The result of this new addition to the family was that two distinct camps were formed. Maurice and Augustine were inseparable, and flirted together most of the time, George Sand looked on benignly and thought them both charming, while Solange deeply resented her cousin and her brother's behavior, and Chopin found companionship only with her. The only serious rumblings of war that summer, however, took place over Chopin's servant. Jan was not popular in the kitchen, as he vented his antipathy toward the cook in the crude but direct French he had picked up; the more mentionable examples of which were "ugly like pig" and "mouth like asshole."[31] He was not popular with George Sand, either, for he had an irritating habit of ringing the dinner bell for fifteen minutes on end when three rings would have done, and this in spite of threats that she would empty a bucket of water over him if he persisted. Chopin had for some time been thinking of the possibility of getting rid of Jan, but was loath to do so, for he had "gotten used to him" and needed to have someone around with whom he could speak Polish.[32] But Jan soon fell foul of Maurice, and then the matter was settled.

On the face of it, however, nothing had changed, and when, in the middle of September, Chopin had to go to Paris briefly to settle some business, he and George Sand wrote to each other every day, as usual when they were apart. Hardly any of her letters to him survive, but one of those that do dates from this trip and ends with the words: "Love me, my dearest angel, my dearest happiness, I love you."[33]

Chopin returned to Nohant at the end of the month and spent the whole of October and November there. His health was quite good, but he was, according to George Sand, "worrying, like all sickly people, and burying himself in advance all the time, with a certain relish."[34] This view was echoed by Dr. Papet, who again made a full examination and found no signs of illness or damage, but thought him "inclined to hypochondria and destined to be perpetually alarmed until he reaches the age of forty and his nerves lose some of their excessive sensitivity."[35] One cannot help wondering at Papet's opinions, for the thirty-five-year-old composer by now looked moribund to most people, and there was clearly something other than "excessive sensitivity" at the bottom of his condition. But Papet's invocation of the magic age of forty found favor with George Sand, who soldiered on in the belief that all the neuroses would suddenly vanish when this was reached.

It is of course true that Chopin's condition was aggravated by anxiety, particularly on account of his work:

Oh, how time does fly! I don't know why, but I just do not seem to be able to do anything good, and it's not that I'm being lazy; I don't spend my time wandering about like I did with you [Ludwika], but stay in my room for whole days and evenings. I must finish some manuscripts before I leave here, because I cannot compose anything in winter.[36]

His anxiety was to some extent well founded, for although in terms of quality he was at his peak (he had just started work on the Barcarolle, which many consider to be his greatest achievement), there was a marked falling-off in the facility with which he could work and, as a result, in the quantity produced. The last and greatest stage of his output had begun in 1841, when he had produced a dozen important works, including some of his best. The next two years saw a progressive drop in the quantity being produced, with a half-dozen substantial pieces in 1842 and the same number of shorter ones in 1843, while in the whole year of 1844 he could finish only one work, the B minor Sonata (opus 58). In the following year he wrote three mazurkas and started on the Barcarolle. It is of course true that he was putting more and more thought into these later works, and that their composition represented weeks of agonized reworking and frustration. Nevertheless it is obvious that his powers of concentration were failing and that his inspiration was beset by anguish, both emotional and intellectual.

On the other hand, he was being more adventurous in his composition. The Barcarolle, of which he wrote most after his return to Paris at the end of November, was a new departure, both in form and content. Another adventurous undertaking was the Sonata for Piano and Cello, which he had clearly been thinking of for some time, with Franchomme in mind, but which he only began to put together now. The last time he had written anything for another instrument had been over ten years before, and then he had made Franchomme write most of the cello part, but he had spent hours over the last years playing pieces with him and had developed a familiarity with the instrument. At the same time he was embarking on "something else which I don't know what I'll call," as he described it to Ludwika.[37] This was the Polonaise-Fantaisie (opus 61), the final and logical step in Chopin's development of the polonaise form; from the salon piece of the 1820s through the great polonaises of the late 1830s and early 1840s, which were both evocative of past grandeur and declamatory in their rebelliousness, to the pure musical fantasy couched in the language of the polonaise.

His attempts at working in Paris were thwarted by the constant flow of visitors to his rooms. Liszt was back in Paris, Meyerbeer was on a visit from Berlin, August Klengel, a musician Chopin had known in Dresden, had turned up, and they all came to see Chopin, to talk, and to play. Such friends as Custine and Delacroix were equally anxious to greet the composer, for of late he was spending most of the year at Nohant. The only thing that put a stop to this was the influenza epidemic which brought down everyone, including Chopin himself. But to Chopin influenza made little difference in his way of life, while some perfectly healthy people died of it. As he wrote to Ludwika at Christmas, "I've outlived so many people who were younger and stronger than I that I'm beginning to think I'm eternal."[38] Even his favorite pupil, Karl Filtsch, who had spent an exhausting year giving concerts all over Europe, had died in Venice at the age of fifteen.

Christmas was lugubrious in Paris that year, with half of society ill, and even the Poles did not celebrate in the usual way. The first months of 1846 were hardly more lively. Apart from a grand ball at the Hôtel Lambert, to which he went with George Sand, Solange, and Delacroix, Chopin did not go out much, for he felt fragile and tired easily. His evenings were most often spent with Delacroix, Grzymala, the poet Zaleski, and Franchomme, with whom he kept trying out pieces of the sonata he was writing. In April he went to stay with Franchomme's family near Tours, but was back toward the end of the month in order to prepare for his journey to Nohant. Before leaving Paris he had a musical evening at his own apartment, to which he invited the Czartoryskis, Princess Sapieha, Delacroix, Louis Blanc, and the Viardots. It was a typically Chopinesque evening: the rooms were filled with flowers and beautifully lit, ices and savories were served, and Chopin played for hours.

On May 27, Chopin arrived at Nohant, whither George Sand had preceded him a couple of weeks before. He came with presents for her and an ingenious new ice-making machine so that they could have cold drinks when the hot weather started. Concessions had been made on both sides. Chopin had acquired a French servant who was quiet and polite; George Sand had invited a friend of Chopin, Laura Czosnowska, whom she did not particularly like but who would keep him happy for a time. But the spirit of conciliation was not to last.

For the last couple of months George Sand had been engaged in writing a new novel, *Lucrezia Floriani*. It is the story of a famous actress who, disillusioned with love and fame, retires to the seclusion of a lakeside villa hidden away in the depths of the countryside, where she avoids any contact with the world and concentrates on bringing up her illegitimate children. Chance brings two travelers into her seclusion; one an erstwhile friend and would-be lover, the other a delicate, virginal, and melancholy prince, Karol. The Prince falls ill and cannot be moved in the morning, and by the time Lucrezia has nursed him back to life, they are in love. There follows a period of bliss, but gradually the Prince's restless mind, his jealousy, and, yes, his "malady" begin to torment him and drive her mad. One day she simply "dies" of sorrow and exasperation.

Lucrezia is of course sagacious, understanding, strong yet supremely feminine, unaffected, and noble. She is a "real person," reasonable and competent in dealing with all the problems of life, from medicine to religion, and she suffers from the same astonishing lack of self-criticism as George Sand herself. Her guiding principle in life has been love, and she has been misunderstood and reviled on account of this. Disappointed by her various lovers, she has abjured sexual love and has concentrated all her affection on her children, to whom she intends to devote the rest of her life. Although some stress is laid on the fact that Lucrezia is still highly attractive, she does not want to have any more affairs with men, and the fact that Prince Karol is an intruder into her ordered life, albeit a reluctant and passive one, is represented as a violence done to her. The novel clearly depicts her as a victim.

Prince Karol is a somewhat disembodied figure exuding refinement and nervousness, an exquisite work of art hopelessly unsuited to normal human life. His motivation is by no means obvious, and as a character he is insipid and deeply unconvincing. At times he is little more than a stage prop used to create the conditions for the author's turgid descriptions of Lucrezia's emotional martyrdom. But there are occasional passages, describing particular traits in his character, which have the ring of truth:

> As he was polite and reserved in the extreme, nobody could even suspect what was going on inside him. The more exasperated he was, the cooler he grew, and one could only judge the degree of his fury by his icy contempt. It was then that he was truly unbearable, as he wanted to reason and to subject real life, of which he had never understood a thing, to principles he could not define. Then he would find wit, a false and brilliant wit, in order to torture those he loved. He would become supercilious, stiff, precious, and aloof. He seemed to nibble playfully, yet inflicting wounds which penetrated to the depths of one's soul. Or else, if he lacked the courage to contradict and mock, he would wrap himself in disdainful silence, in a distressing sulk.[39]

The book is of course about George Sand and Chopin (Prince Karol's traveling companion is a portrait of Grzymala). After the first installments began to appear in the press in June, Paris was buzzing with gossip, and even in faraway St. Petersburg, Turgenev was in no doubt as to whom it referred.[40] Everyone was particularly excited by the book, for while George Sand was known to enjoy carrying out vicious autopsies on her dismissed lovers, this was the only instance of her going in for vivisection.

"One should never put those one loves or those one hates into a novel," George Sand later wrote,[41] and although she rarely put anything else into her novels, one must assume that she did so only semi-consciously. In the introduction to a later edition of *Lucrezia Floriani*, she explained that in literature it is not possible to portray a character, only a "sentiment." "One therefore has to create the characters to suit the sentiment one wishes to describe, and not the sentiment for the characters."[42] By "sentiment" it seems she meant the reactions of a character to a situation, for that is indeed what the book is about. George Sand wrote so much, so quickly and so subjectively, and the line separating personal experience from fantasy in her novels is so thin, that it is possible she was not aware that she was describing her own relationship with Chopin. She certainly denied it vehemently when accused of it. This enhances the value of the book as a document, for it provides a detailed picture of how she saw the relationship at this stage.

The central theme of the novel is the gradual transformation of Prince Karol's gentle character by his "malady," which in turn kills Lucrezia. The various neuroses which one can recognize as Chopin's are presented as symptoms of some spiritual evil, and not as the result of any human emotional tangle. George Sand's pragmatism comes out in the fact that Prince Karol is always shown to be wrong, whether on matters of principle or on more down-to-earth subjects. When he stands by his judgments or opinions, he is merely being "sickly." The combination of his physical, emotional, and spiritual incompetence not only makes the character of Prince Karol hard to swallow; it also shows that George Sand was making no effort to understand Chopin as a person.

Lucrezia's reactions to Prince Karol's neuroses reveal the main reason for the disintegration of the Chopin-Sand ménage. Lucrezia feels smothered by the situation, and her continual allusions to being "murdered with pinpricks" are echoed in George Sand's contemporary correspondence with reference to Chopin. The same is true of the almost pathological way in which Lucrezia uses her children as a pretext, laboring the idea that they have a sacred priority in her life to which everything else must be sacrificed. George Sand was suddenly becoming very conscious of her duty toward her own children, a concept that had been curiously absent until her son reached the age of twenty-three and her daughter that of seventeen.

Although the message of the book does seem to be: "If you go on being nasty to Mummy, she'll die, and then you'll be sorry!" it is unlikely that it was written as a warning to Chopin not to take too much for granted. If it was, it failed gloriously to get through. George Sand read out some of the installments before Chopin and other houseguests that summer, one of whom, Delacroix, recalled: "I was in agony during the reading . . . the victim and the executioner amazed me equally. Madame Sand seemed to be completely at ease, and Chopin did not stop making admiring comments about the story."[43]

It seems more likely that the plot of the book crystallized by itself, without any intentional direction from her, largely under the influence of her growing paranoia, and that the central question, for Lucrezia, of children versus lover was one that was emerging in her own consciousness and demanded discussion. Whatever the intention behind it, the book shows the stage she had reached and how she viewed the future of the affair with Chopin. She was convinced that he was in some way stifling and tormenting her, and in this she was not alone, for even Adam Mickiewicz believed that Chopin was her "moral vampire" and that he would kill her in the end.[44] What is also obvious from a reading of the book is that she had seized on her children as a shield, and that she was going to make use of them in order to escape from Chopin's influence.

The first step in this was a hardly perceptible transference to Maurice of the rights which Chopin, as the man in the family, had come to consider as his. Soon after his arrival, Chopin was dismayed to find that the old gardener, who had been at Nohant for twenty years, had been sacked, and two more old retainers were dismissed during the course of the summer. Chopin felt that this was Maurice's doing, but above all resented the change, for, as George Sand explained: "He was a man of imperious habits, and every change, however small, was a terrible event in his life."[45] Even without being a man of imperious habits, he was bound to feel worried as he watched the old cobwebs being swept away around him, for he was beginning to feel like one of them.

Halfway through June, Chopin apparently had a difference of opinion with Maurice on some domestic matter and was mortified when George Sand took her son's side. "I lost my temper, which gave me the courage to tell him a few home truths, and to threaten to get sick of him," she wrote to Marie de Rozières, adding that "since then, he has been sensible, and you know how sweet, excellent, admirable he is when he is not mad."[46] But this was only an apparent truce; the various conflicts within the household gathered in strength.

Augustine and Maurice were having an affair, though it is impossible to tell at what level. Solange was bored and was becoming jealous of Augustine, who seemed to be attracting more attention than she was, and she therefore began to flirt with Chopin, whose frustrated feelings toward George Sand were gradually transferring themselves to the daughter. In these circumstances, the arrival of Grzymala and Laura Czosnowska, a twenty-six-year-old and very coquettish friend of Ludwika's from Warsaw, did little to ease the tension. Everybody liked Grzymala, but neither George Sand nor Augustine nor Maurice could stand Laura. Snide comments were made and there was sniggering behind her back, which Chopin noticed and attributed to Augustine's influence. Solange agreed with him and provided the sympathy he was not getting from the rest of the family.

That summer there was a terrible heat wave which enervated everyone, most of all Chopin, for, as George Sand explained to Marie de Rozières:

> Chopin is amazed to find himself sweating. He's quite upset by it and claims that, however much he washes, he still *stinks!* We laugh to the point of tears to see such an *ethereal* creature refusing to sweat like everyone else, but don't ever mention it—he would be furious. If the world or even just you were to know that he *sweats*, he could not go on living. He only reeks of Eau de Cologne, but we keep telling him he stinks like Pierre Bonnin the carpenter, and he goes scuttling back to his room, as though he were being pursued by his own *smell.*[47]

After the heat came swarms of little bugs which bit everyone, gradually working their way up the legs. Soon everyone was sitting around scratching unashamedly, particularly Delacroix, who had come down for the last two weeks of August. His visit brought relief to Chopin, and they spent "some delightful moments" together, talking of Mozart's operas and Beethoven's sonatas, some of which Chopin played to his friend.[48] Chopin was so glad to be with Delacroix that he now, for the first time, uttered a phrase of recognition of his talent, calling him, in a letter to Franchomme, "an artist worthy of the highest admiration."[49]

Chopin was desolate to see Delacroix go, and felt like returning to Paris with him, but his usual inertia kept him at Nohant. As he and George Sand saw him aboard the mail coach at Châteauroux on August 30, carrying Chopin's entire work for the summer, three mazurkas (opus 63), they met her friend Emmanuel Arago and a young friend of Maurice's off the incoming coach. As they drove back to Nohant, Chopin felt more isolated than ever.

He was not, however, one to let his feelings show, and he put on as brave a face as possible. When Matthew Arnold dropped in to visit George Sand, he found Chopin very much in evidence, and whenever the house party needed entertaining, Chopin could still be counted on. He did not bore them by playing only highbrow music, but varied his program continually. A typical evening was recorded by another visitor, who describes how Chopin started with a takeoff of a Bellini opera, which produced general mirth, "such was the finesse of the observation and the witty mockery of Bellini's musical style and habits." He then played a "prayer for Poles in distress," followed by an étude and a funeral march, after which he woke everyone up with a lusty rendition of a bourrée, a local peasant dance of which he had made some transcriptions. He finished off the evening with another joke: an imitation of a defective musical box:

> If we had not been in the same room we could not have believed that it was a piano tinkling under his fingers. All the rippling finesse and rapidity of the little steel struts which cause the invisible cylinder to vibrate were rendered with matchless delicacy, and then, suddenly, a faint, barely audible cadence made itself heard, only to be interrupted by the machine, which had something wrong with it. He played us one of those airs, a Tyrolese one I think, in which one note was missing from the cylinder, which got stuck each time the moment for this note came around.[50]

At other times Chopin would invent musical mimes; he

would act out an argument between two people, or a drunkard walking down the street. As George Sand explained, the
later famous Nohant puppet theater had:

> all started with pantomime, and this had been invented by
> Chopin . . . He would be at the piano improvising, while the
> young ones would mime and dance comic scenes and ballets
> . . . He would lead them as he wanted, and would, according
> to his whim, make them pass from the pleasant to the severe,
> from the burlesque to the solemn, from the graceful to the
> passionate. Costumes were improvised in order to play the
> successive roles, and as soon as the artist saw them appear, he
> would vary his theme and his accent wonderfully to suit their
> character.[51]

In spite of this Chopin could not help feeling left out
much of the time, and when in September the whole house
party went away on excursions, he remained at Nohant, writing letters to Ludwika and trying to work, with only one of
the dogs for company. The work did not come easily, however, and he complained to Franchomme that "I do everything I can in order to work but it's no good. If this goes on,
my new compositions will not resemble the chirruping of
warblers or even the sound of smashing china."[52] He was
probably referring to the Sonata for Piano and Cello, which
had already taken him longer than any other work and was
still not finished. He had also managed to finish the Polonaise-Fantaisie, a couple of nocturnes and the three mazurkas
of opus 63, but he was not happy about them either. "I don't
think they'll be as good as some of the others," he wrote
about the mazurkas, "but one needs time to judge properly.
When you write something it seems good—otherwise one
would never write anything. Later on, reflection comes, and
either accepts or rejects. Time is the best censor and patience
the best teacher."[53] But time was the greatest problem, and
he felt it was running out; he could no longer concentrate and

was beginning to feel that he was drying up. This was to be his last spurt of composition.

"His mood is good, calm and gentle," George Sand wrote to Charlotte Marliani, but this was only the result of boredom and resignation. Even now, when he was mostly alone at Nohant, he was told he could not invite a friend who had arrived in Paris from Warsaw. Maurice on the other hand was allowed to invite several friends. As he watched the way of life he had grown used to gradually slipping away from him, Chopin was haunted by the old fear of being alone. "Now I don't have a single one of my school friends left alive in Paris," he complained to Ludwika.[54] This fear of solitude was no passing thought. In the whole extant correspondence of Chopin, the subject of dreams crops up only three or four times; yet two of the dreams related, almost twenty years apart, center on the theme of dying away from home, family, and friends. In the last couple of years of his life the image of dying in a poorhouse is conjured up several times in his letters, principally to Grzymala. He had never been an independent or self-sufficient person, but eight years of George Sand's tenderness had made it impossible for him to envisage life on his own.

There was little he could do, except wait, as the plan of spending the winter in a warmer place had been shelved on Maurice's instance, and the latter had also decided that it would be best if the whole family, including his mother, remained at Nohant throughout the winter months. The only ray of hope for Chopin was that Solange had met a young man who wanted to marry her, and that Maurice seemed to be thinking of espousing Augustine, a match that George Sand was encouraging. Chopin thought that when the children were married off and settled the mother would return to him, and so, thinking it best to be out of the way, he left for Paris alone, on November 11. George Sand was taken in by his apparent serenity and felt that he was finally going to "round the cape" and settle down to a quiet middle age.

While they were both deceiving themselves, Parisian society had already jumped to various conclusions. Coming not long after the publication of *Lucrezia Floriani*, Chopin's return to Paris alone set tongues wagging. Liszt wrote to Marie d'Agoult from the depths of the Ukraine: "Is the break between Chopin and Madame Sand definite? And for what reasons?"[55] Although there had been no dramatic break, he was not wrong to make such surmises, for the affair had well and truly come to an end.

12

A Sad Year

Chopin's relief at finding himself back in his own world is evident. Those of his letters to George Sand that survive make him sound a little distant, although full of good wishes and tenderness. He felt well, in spite of the bad weather, and the treatment he had just started to take from a Swedish masseur was doing him good—it seems likely that apart from anything else he suffered from poor circulation. He did not lack attention and care, as Charlotte Marliani was still living in the Square d'Orléans, and he could drop in for dinner whenever he felt too lazy to go out. Marie de Rozières was in almost daily attendance, as were Grzymala and Franchomme, while friends like Delacroix and Delfina Potocka, who was back in Paris, tried to distract him as much as possible.

He resumed his lessons and tried to write, but, as he complained to Ludwika, "I write a little and cross out a lot." He was still wrestling with the Sonata for Piano and Cello. "I'm sometimes happy with it, sometimes not," he wrote. "I throw it into a corner and then take it up again."[1] This hesitant progress can to a certain extent be felt in the finished piece. As Moscheles put it, having studied the score, "I often find passages which sound to me like someone preluding on the piano, the player knocking at the door of every key and clef, to find if any melodious sounds were at home."[2] But he was still capable of bursts of activity, and in November he apparently wrote a *Veni Creator*, presumably for choir and organ, on the occasion of the wedding of his friend Zaleski to his former pupil Zofia Rozengardt. The manuscript has unfortunately been lost, which is a great pity, since it is the only religious work Chopin is known to have composed.

Although he did see such French friends as Legouvé and Franchomme, or other expatriates, like Thomas Albrecht, he now clung more than ever to his ties with Poland. He saw a good deal of his fellow-musician Nowakowski, who had come from Warsaw, even though the man had gone a little senile; Chopin "often knocked at his soul, but there was nobody there."[3] Grzymala's soul, however, could be depended on, and Delfina Potocka was as affectionate as ever, while the Hôtel Lambert in itself represented a small kingdom of Poland. On December 24, Prince Adam's name day, Chopin went to a reception there, during which the venerable Soliva conducted a choir of girls from the Princess's institution, which must have brought back poignant memories. It was there, too, that Chopin saw in the new year of 1847, wearing every overcoat he could find and wishing, no doubt, that he could have been in Italy with George Sand instead of a snowbound Paris.

George Sand arrived in Paris on February 5 accompanied by Solange and Augustine, in order to settle the legal aspects of her daughter's marriage to the young Fernand de Preaulx. She was busy with all the arrangements, and behind in her work, so Chopin did not see much of her. She was of course present, along with Grzymala, Delacroix, and her friend Emmanuel Arago, when, on February 17, Chopin and Franchomme played through the final version of the sonata, and three days later she accompanied Chopin and Delacroix to Franchomme's concert at the Conservatoire.

A few days before, she had been introduced to a sculptor by the name of Clesinger at the Marlianis'. She took Solange to visit him in his studio and was impressed by his work. After the visit he showered mother and daughter with compliments, presents, and flowers, and begged to be allowed to carve busts of them both. This of course involved more visits, during which he seduced them by his temperament, with the result that before the end of February, Solange told Preaulx that she had had to reconsider her decision to marry him. "She's changed her mind," Chopin wrote to Ludwika. "I regret it and I'm sorry for the boy, who is decent and loving, but I suppose it's better it happened before than after the wedding."[4] The thirty-three-year-old Clesinger was a drunkard, a gambler, and had a bad reputation, but George Sand was overwhelmed by his exuberance and saw in him a sort of Delacroix in marble. Delacroix himself summed up the sculptor's talents as "daguerrotype in sculpture" and disliked his manner.[5] The Marlianis disapproved of him, and the man who had introduced him to George Sand wrote to her warning that he had a bad character and was not to be trusted. Chopin thought him odious. He wondered at all the admiration heaped on him by George Sand and Solange, but assumed that the infatuation would pass and did not interfere.

On April 1, Delacroix took George Sand and Chopin to see the ceiling he had finished in the library of the Palais du Luxembourg, in which Chopin could recognize his portrait in the figure of Dante. A few days later George Sand left Paris with Solange, hoping that a stay in the country might help her daughter compose her thoughts. Chopin was supposed to join them at Nohant at the beginning of June, with Delacroix, but he was not sure himself whether he would go. He was of half a mind to try to meet some of his family or Tytus in Germany, and, as he explained:

> I honestly don't feel like it [Nohant], as, apart from the lady of the house, the son and the daughter, the other people will be new faces I shall have to get used to, and I can't be

bothered anymore. Of all those Ludwika saw there, not a single one is left. Five new servants.[6]

To George Sand he wrote: "Be happy, well-disposed, look
after yourself and write a few words when you have the
time."[7] He was making a conscious effort to distract himself,
as his suddenly rather detailed letters to Ludwika reveal. On
April 13 he gave several lessons and went to a soirée at
Auguste Leo's; on the fourteenth he gave five lessons and
then went to Ary Scheffer's studio to pose for a portrait; he
did the same on the following day, and on his way home
dropped in on Delacroix for a chat. When he got home, he
"did not feel like dressing for dinner, so I spent the evening
playing to myself; I played it away with melodies from the
banks of the Vistula."[8] The following day he gave seven lessons, after which he went to a vaudeville with the composer
Alkan, who lived next door. Next morning he received a letter
from George Sand announcing that she would be coming to
Paris for a few days at the end of the month, so he ordered
her rooms to be prepared. He gave four lessons and spent the
evening at the Count de Perthuis's soirée.

Instead of arriving in Paris, George Sand sent Chopin a letter in which she informed him that Solange was to be married
to Clesinger. She professed herself happy with her prospective
son-in-law, whom she described as "bold, well-read, active and
ambitious." "I suppose she thinks those are virtues!" Chopin
wrote to Ludwika.[9] He was deeply upset by the news, for he
had perhaps too good an opinion of Solange and a poor one
of Clesinger:

> All her friends—Marliani, Arago, Delacroix and myself—have
> had the worst reports concerning the person: that he's in
> debt; that he's a brute who beats his mistress, whom he has
> abandoned in pregnancy now that he's getting married, etc.,
> etc.; that he drinks (we all knew that, but of course it's put
> down to genius) . . . I don't give them a year after their first
> child—and the mother will have to pay the debts.[10]

But Chopin kept his opinion to himself, for he was ostentatiously not being encouraged to give it. George Sand had written to Grzymala that:

> I think Chopin, standing apart from all this, must have suffered from not knowing the persons and factors involved, and from not being able to advise. But his advice in the real business of life cannot possibly be considered. He has never looked straight at realities, never understood human nature on any point; his soul is pure poetry and music and he cannot tolerate anything that is different from himself. Moreover, his interference in the affairs of my family would mean total loss of all my dignity and love both from and toward my children.[11]

Having made her decision, George Sand was now doing all she could to hurry along her seventeen-year-old daughter's marriage to the thirty-three-year-old sculptor. To Delacroix she wrote: "It is impossible not to like him." Delacroix found it not only possible but extremely easy to dislike the man intensely. She refused to take any notice of the warnings people gave her, and waxed lyrical on the subject of Clesinger's genius and honesty. As Chopin wrote to his sister: "Madame Sand is a dear, but she hasn't a penny's worth of common sense."[12] "A pity really," he added meditatively, "or perhaps not at all, looking at it from the point of view that Madame Sand always acts in remarkable ways, and that everything always works out well for her—even things that look impossible at first sight."[13]

On May 2, Winterhalter came to Chopin's rooms to make a pencil portrait, but found him suffering from an attack of asthma, which lasted about four days. Chopin begged Gutmann and Marie de Rozières, who were looking after him, to keep his illness secret from George Sand so as not to worry her needlessly, but Princess Czartoryska wrote to Nohant. George Sand was "sick with worry" and would have come up to Paris but for the fact that she could not leave her daughter unchaperoned with her fiancé in the country. Though Chopin wrote telling her that he was well and happy, she remained anxious, more for her own sake than for his. "For the last seven years I have been living with the certainty that I shall see him aging at my side, but one never gets used to these horrible certainties, and one goes on suffering," she wrote to her publisher. "He has done me so much harm with his sickness that for a long time I hoped to die before him."[14]

On the same day she wrote to Grzymala, saying:

> It is all very difficult and delicate, and I can see no way of helping a sick mind which is irritated by the very efforts one makes to cure it. For a long time now the disease which gnaws at the body and soul of this poor creature has been killing me, and I see him fading away, without ever having been able to do him any good, since it is this anxious, jealous and touching affection he bears for me which is the main cause of his misery. For the last seven years I have lived like a virgin with him and with other men. I have made myself old before my time, even without any effort or sacrifice, for I was weary of passion and disillusioned beyond hope. If there is a woman on this earth who should inspire him with confidence it is I. He has never understood that. I know that people accuse me, some of having killed him by the violence of my passion, others of having exasperated him with my temperance. I think you know the real state of affairs! He complains that I have killed him by denying him, while I was certain that I would kill him if I acted otherwise. Look at my position in this fatal friendship, in which I have made myself his slave in every situation I could without actually showing a wrongful and impossible preference for him over my children, and in which the dignity I have had to maintain before my children and my friends has been so delicate and difficult to preserve! On that score I have achieved miracles of patience of which I did not believe myself capable, I who am not endowed with the nature of a saint like the Princess! [Czartoryska] I have achieved martyrdom, but the heavens are implacable toward me, as though I had great crimes to ex-

piate; for in the middle of all these efforts and all these sacrifices, the man I love with an absolutely chaste and maternal love is dying, the victim of the ridiculous love he bears me![15]

One cannot help feeling that she was making rather heavy weather of it all, for at that moment she was far more obsessed with him than he with her. On May 15, in answer to her letter containing the details of Solange's impending wedding, he wrote to her, thanking her and sending his best wishes to Solange. He signed off: "God support you always in your strength and your deeds. Be happy and serene. Your completely devoted Ch."[16]

Solange was married quietly to Clesinger a few days later, while Chopin went off to Ville d'Avray near Paris to spend a week with his friend Thomas Albrecht. When he returned, he found that the young couple were back in Paris, so he called on them to pay his respects and gave Solange a bouquet of roses and carnations. "Sol was polite to me, as always, he was also as polite as he could be, I was my usual self—but I felt sad inside," he wrote to Ludwika.[17] He rarely saw the Clesingers after that. George Sand herself arrived in Paris on June 1 to arrange the marriage between Augustine and the young painter Rosseau, but he did not see much of her, either. Two weeks later, she returned to Nohant, looking forward to a long, restful summer, and to the arrival of Chopin and Delacroix, who were to come down together. From Nohant she wrote to a friend who naïvely wondered whether *Lucrezia Floriani* was about her and Chopin:

I am neither as crazy, nor as good, nor as great [as Lucrezia], for if I were united to Prince Karol, I must admit that I would not let myself be killed, but would politely dump him there and then. However, I am feeling very well, and would never dream of separating myself from a friend who has become invaluable to me through eight years of mutual devotion.[18]

Chopin was in good spirits, in spite of the news of Witwicki's death in Italy, which reached him in June. He was beginning to get used to the way in which death seemed to be encroaching on his life, and merely acquiesced with sadness, as he had done when he had heard of Antoni Wodzinski's demise a couple of months earlier. He must have realized that others thought he would be dying soon, for he was now posing for the fourth portrait of himself specially commissioned by a friend—in this case Auguste Leo—during the last two months.

By the beginning of July he had stopped most of his lessons and was busy copying and correcting the Piano and Cello Sonata for the printers, having at long last decided that it was ready. He had decided he would go to Nohant after all, since Delacroix was prepared to go with him, and he aimed to set off halfway through July.

Meanwhile, the Clesingers, who had gone down to stay at Nohant, began to behave in a hateful way. The sculptor had of course married mainly for what he believed to be George Sand's riches, and, having been told that she could not give him more, suspected everyone, particularly Maurice and Augustine, of foul plots. Solange seconded him ably and did all she could to spite the rest of the family. After a few days, Clesinger had a row with Maurice, threatened to kill him with a hammer, hit George Sand, who interposed herself, and nearly had his head blown off by Maurice, who had fetched his gun. George Sand threw them out of Nohant, saying she never wanted to see either of them again, whereupon they moved into the neighboring town of La Châtre and began spreading the foulest slander against all the inhabitants of Nohant.

From La Châtre, Solange wrote to Chopin:

> My dear Chopin! I am ill and the journey by the Blois mail coach would tire me out. Will you lend me your carriage for my return journey to Paris? Please answer immediately. I

await your answer at La Châtre, where life is difficult for me.
I have left Nohant forever, after the most horrible scenes by
my mother. *Wait for me, I beg you, before leaving Paris.* I
need to see you urgently. I was positively refused your carriage, so if you wish me to use it, send me a note with your
permission, which I can send on to Nohant. Good-bye, until
soon, I hope. Solange.[19]

Chopin received this note on July 13, and immediately
wrote a letter to George Sand, which has unfortunately not
survived, but which seems to have been a general inquiry and
clearly presumed that some of the right might be on Solange's
side. It also stated that she could use his carriage if she
wanted. Next day he wrote Solange a fairly curt note, telling
her the carriage was at her disposal. On receipt of Chopin's
letter, George Sand wrote back. This missive is also unfortunately lost, which is a great pity, for it seems to have been cru-
cial, but some of its contents can be deduced with certainty.
She described the scene at Nohant only in the vaguest terms
and while she wrote in great detail on the subject to Marie de
Rozières and Delacroix, she enjoined them to keep silent:
"Don't tell him how far things went, we shall try to hide as
much as possible from him."[20] On the other hand, the letter
to Chopin went on at some length about himself and his
place in her life. She announced to him that Clesinger was a
bounder, and even seems to have reproached Chopin for not
having warned her. Finally, she ordered him to keep his doors
closed to Solange when the latter turned up in Paris, and not
to mention her name at all when he and Delacroix came
down to Nohant in the following week.[21]

Chopin immediately told Delacroix of the letter and, a few
days later, on July 20, showed it to him. The painter noted in
his diary:

One has to admit that it [the letter] is atrocious. Cruel passions and long pent-up impatience erupt in it, and by a contrast which would be amusing if it did not touch on such a

tragic subject, the author from time to time takes over from
the woman, and launches into tirades which look as though
they were borrowed from a novel or a philosophical homily.[22]

Chopin did not answer this letter for some ten days; perhaps he was waiting for another, calmer letter, or perhaps he
simply did not know what to write. Meanwhile the Clesingers
had turned up in Paris. Solange had clearly wasted no time in
calling on Chopin and telling him about the events at Nohant, and her version was by now becoming increasingly lurid.
Whether he believed it or not, it was the only full version he
had been afforded, since George Sand was determined to keep
the truth from him.

George Sand had been expecting Chopin and Delacroix
daily, but time passed and there was no sign of either. She
grew anxious about Chopin's health, thinking that perhaps he
had had another attack, and considered rushing to Paris to
see him. Then, two weeks after she had written, she received
his reply:

> I have nothing to say to you about M. Cl[esinger]. I had not
> heard the name of M. Cl until the day you decided to give
> him your daughter. As for her, she cannot be indifferent to
> me. You will remember that I interceded with you on behalf
> of your children, without preference, whenever the opportu-
> nity presented itself, in the certitude that you were destined
> to love them *always*—for those are the only affections that do
> not change. Misfortune can cloud them but never change
> their nature. The misfortune must be very great at this mo-
> ment if it forbids your heart to hear the name of your daugh-
> ter, at the beginning of her mature life, at the moment when
> her physical condition requires more than ever the care of a
> mother.
>
> In the face of such a serious matter, which concerns your
> most sacred affections, I shall not go into the matters con-
> cerning myself. Time will act. I shall wait—*always the same.*
> Your wholly devoted. Ch.[23]

George Sand was at the end of her tether in more ways than one when this letter arrived. Exhausted by work, which she had stepped up in order to cover the expenses of Solange's wedding, she had endured the most terrifying scenes at Nohant, and watched the marriage she had arranged turn into a fiasco. Her efforts to marry off Augustine had also come to nothing, the young painter having heard rumors spread by Solange and her husband and backed out. Maurice was not only useless as a support, he was going through a personal crisis and needed her help. In the circumstances, she was longing for the arrival of a calm Chopin and an affable Delacroix, and overreacted when she perceived treason in that quarter too.

Chopin's reply found her in the middle of a letter to Emmanuel Arago, and turned it into one of the longest letters ever written, for she began setting down her reactions as they crystallized. The astonishing seventy-one-page document is therefore of immense value.[24] What had stung her to the quick in Chopin's letter was its cool, collected, and slightly pompous tone. It was the letter of someone who felt in this particular case that he had a right to express an opinion, and discreetly pointed to the fact that the match with Clesinger was her doing, at the same time turning squarely against her own hobbyhorse of the sanctity of maternal instincts. From the "impractical" Chopin who "has never understood a thing about human life," she found such level-headed observations downright insulting, and she immediately scotched any discussion of their wisdom by declaring that he had been disloyal in making them. As she later pointed out to Louis Viardot:

> If I had committed faults, even crimes, Chopin should not have believed them, should not have *seen them*. There is a certain degree of respect and gratitude past which we no longer have the right to examine the behavior of those beings who have become sacred for us.[25]

He had clearly never succeeded in becoming sacred to her himself, and he was now branded as disloyal and having joined "the enemy camp." In her search for an explanation of this perfidy, she hit on the great "revelation" that Chopin had been in love not with her but with Solange all along. Of course, Chopin's attack of asthma the day after he heard of Solange's engagement to Clesinger was eloquent proof of his jealousy (the fact that there had been no similar fit after her engagement to Preaulx, a union which he had warmly encouraged, was conveniently forgotten). Her novelist's mind found no difficulty in unearthing evidence to substantiate this theory; Chopin and Solange had always got on well, and during the last couple of years they had enjoyed an intimacy which excluded herself and Maurice. Chopin's dislike for Augustine, too, was seen as emanating from Solange's influence (in spite of the fact that Chopin's dislike predated Solange's). Now George Sand saw clearly that Chopin's jealousy of other men who approached her, which had irritated her so much over the years, was in fact not jealousy over her, but Solange. Clear as daylight, too, was the fact that Chopin's great passion for her had in fact been not love but hatred all along!

It is clear that there had been some warmth of feeling between Chopin and Solange; Arago, on whom Solange had tried her charms as well, wrote in his reply to George Sand's interminable letter:

> For several years, he has been fascinated by her and accepted from her with pleasure behavior that would have exasperated him coming from another. I could see, did see, and saw often that he had for her a deep feeling which at first resembled paternal affection, and which changed, probably under her influence, when she turned from a child into a young girl and from a young girl into a woman.[26]

There was, however, a great difference between the bored and aging Chopin's no doubt prurient appreciation of the golden-haired Solange's coquetry and the lurid sexual passion which George Sand now "discovered." She could not resist making crude observations on his possible sexual performance with her daughter, for she was deeply wounded by what she immediately saw as his desertion of her, and was mortified to find that a man she had taken for granted and considered an importunate lover could show such independence. Her answer to his letter, dated July 28, was no less icy and pompous than his own had been:

I had ordered post-horses for yesterday and was about to leave by cabriolet in this awful weather, although very ill myself; I was proposing to spend a day in Paris in order to find out how you were. Your silence had worried me on the score of your health. Meanwhile you were reflecting calmly, and your answer is very composed. That is fine, my friend, do what your heart dictates, and take its instinct for the language of your conscience. I understand perfectly.

As for my daughter, her illness is no more worrying than last year's [There are in fact two letters from her to other people from the same period expressing deep concern over her daughter's health], and neither my zeal nor my care, nor my entreaties have ever been able to dissuade her from defying her constitution and behaving like someone who wants to make herself ill. She can hardly be saying that she needs the love of a mother whom she slanders and loathes, whose most sacred actions and whose house she sullies with her hideous insinuations. You are happy to listen to all that and perhaps to believe it. I shall not enter into a battle of that nature, it repels me. I prefer to see you go over to the enemy rather than to defend myself against an enemy born from my womb and nourished with my milk.

Look after her, since it is to her that you think you should devote yourself. I shall not hold it against you, but you will understand that I am cast in the role of outraged mother, and that nothing from now on can make me abandon the authority and the dignity of this role. It is enough to be fooled and

made a victim. I forgive you and will not address any re-
proaches to you, since your confession is sincere. It surprised
me a little, but since you feel more at ease and freer now, I
shall not suffer from this extraordinary volte-face.

Good-bye, my friend, may you be rapidly cured of your
malady, as I believe you will (I have my reasons for that),
and I shall thank God for this strange denouement to nine
years of exclusive friendship—Give me news of yourself sometimes. It is pointless to ever come back on the rest.[27]

Chopin was predictably dumfounded by this letter, with its
talk of his "going over to the enemy" and of his "confession."
He was informed that he was being forgiven, though it was
not at all obvious why forgiveness was called for. It was a dismissal as clear as could be, leaving no door ajar for him to
creep back through. It was the last letter that passed between
them.

Chopin thought that George Sand had gone a little mad,
and felt that the attack of hysteria would subside. He saw his
own position as being perfectly correct throughout, and the
tone of his letters to his family shows that he felt no guilt.
Sooner or later George Sand would recognize this and their
friendship would resume. Pauline Viardot had been in Germany, whither George Sand had written, explaining events.
On her return to Paris, she went to see Chopin, and although
she had always been primarily a friend of George Sand, she
felt obliged to take Chopin's part in a letter she wrote to Nohant:

There is in your good letter one passage that I cannot allow
to pass over in silence. It is that in which you state that
Chopin is a member of a Solange faction, representing her as
a victim and denigrating you. This is absolutely false, I swear
to you, at least as far as he is concerned. On the contrary, this
dear and excellent friend is afflicted by one thought only: the
harm that this whole unfortunate business has done you and
is still doing you. I have not found the slightest change in

Chopin, painted by Eugène Delacroix in the summer of 1838. This canvas was subsequently cut out of what had been a double portrait of Chopin and George Sand.

George Sand. An early photograph. Courtesy Radio Times Hulton Picture Library.

Eugène Delacroix. A self-portrait painted in the late 1830s.

Pauline Viardot. Self-portrait.

Left, Maurice Dudevant-Sand. Painted by Josephine Calamatta in 1845. Right, Solange Dudevant-Sand. A bust carved by Auguste Clesinger in the spring of 1847.

Jane Stirling.

Marie de Rozières.

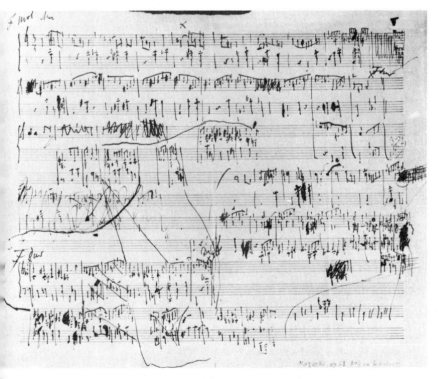

he first version of the Mazurka in F Minor (Opus 68, No. 4). An example of the sort of scrawl
hopin would send to Fontana for copying.

Above,
Princess Anna Czartoryska.
A photograph taken
in the early 1840s.

Left,
Prince Adam Czartoryski.
Painted by Henry Scheffer
c. 1840.

Above,
Princess Marcelina Czartoryska.

Left,
Countess Maria Kalergis.
A drawing by the poet
Cyprian Norwid, c. 1849.

Chopin. A photograph taken during the last months of his life.

him—he is as kind, as devoted as ever—adoring you as always, rejoicing only in your joy, afflicted only by your sufferings.

Her husband's postscript was even more definite:

> To be quite frank, I may sum up what Chopin said as follows: Solange's marriage is a great misfortune for herself, her family and her friends. Daughter and mother were both deceived and realized their mistake too late. But since they both shared in the mistake, why should only one bear the blame? The daughter wanted, insisted on, an ill-assorted match; but had the mother, who consented, no share in the fault? With her great gifts and experience, could she not have enlightened a girl who was led more by mortification than love? . . . one should not be pitiless toward a mistake to which one has contributed. I, pitying both from the bottom of my heart, try to console the only one I am allowed to see.
>
> That is all, dear Madame Sand, not a word more; without reproaches or bitterness, only with deep sorrow.[28]

Of course, this rubbing in of her own rash behavior, of the way she had let herself be taken in by Clesinger in spite of many sensible warnings, was only calculated to make George Sand feel more wounded in her pride. She almost included the Viardots in "the enemy camp," which was already impressively crowded: Delacroix, who had written to say that he was not coming down to Nohant after all, the "silly goose" Marie de Rozières, the "weak and frivolous" Grzymala, the Marlianis, and even the "Saintly" Princess Anna Czartoryska were all ruthlessly relegated to it.[29]

The realization that Chopin had not been disloyal or motivated by preference for Solange did finally percolate through to George Sand, but it made no difference to her behavior, for she was not going to admit that she had acted with anything but wisdom. To reinforce her reasons for the break with Chopin, she now began to dredge up every piece of unfavorable evidence concerning his behavior over the last nine years, and discovered that she had been in a sort of prison. Chopin had apparently prevented her from thinking or speaking freely, and of course she had been the victim of his "coterie," who had made her responsible for his health and happiness. As she concluded, in her letter to Arago, she would now be able to "Work, Run, Sleep!"[30] To Marie de Rozières, who had tried to suggest a reconciliation, she replied that she had "no cause to regret the loss of his affection."[31]

She certainly acted accordingly. In her later writings on the subject, she depicted Chopin as a hopeless neurotic with whom she had had a chaste relationship, based only on her admiration for the artist and her feeling of maternal duty toward a lost and unhappy soul. With the help of her son, she destroyed all the letters between herself and the composer on which she could lay her hands. This was in marked contrast to Chopin's behavior; he kept all her letters religiously among his most valued possessions and carried the first note he had received from her everywhere until his death.

George Sand's behavior ensured that the affair and its end were widely discussed. While some believed her version, many more saw Chopin as a greater victim than in fact he was, and her as a sort of man-eating harpy. Before ten years were out, Liszt, in the first biography of Chopin to appear, summed up the relationship as "a prison in which he found himself being garroted by bonds saturated with venom; their corrosive suppuration could not touch his genius, but they consumed his life and took him off too soon from the earth, from his motherland, from Art!"[32]

This was, of course, largely rubbish. The relationship had had its good side as well as its bad, and Chopin and George Sand owed many years of great happiness to it. Her subsequent distortion of her own feelings was probably the worst aspect of it, and turned it into a happy hunting ground for scandalmongers of every sort.

Chopin did not realize what was going on in George Sand's head, and assumed that everything would straighten itself out. To his great relief, the Clesingers, who were enjoying the sensational aspects of the whole fracas, left Paris to go and stay with Solange's father. Chopin had lent them money and tried to help Clesinger with his work, for the latter's debts had now overtaken him. Chopin was convinced that there would soon be a reconciliation between Solange and her mother, and pressed her to bring it about, not realizing quite how badly she had behaved. As for himself, he waited in vain. Neither Grzymala nor Delacroix, Marie de Rozières nor the Marlianis had any news from Nohant. But Chopin remained confident that when George Sand calmed down he would be vindicated. "Madame Sand cannot but find a good memory of me in her soul when one day she looks back," he wrote to Ludwika.[33]

It was not a happy period for Chopin. He spent some time with his friend Thomas Albrecht at Ville d'Avray, went for a weekend to the great Rothschild mansion at Ferrières, but otherwise spent the summer and autumn in Paris. Grzymala had crashed financially, the Marlianis were getting divorced, and Delacroix was in a doleful mood. Other friends tried to keep Chopin busy, and the void left in his life by the absence of George Sand was quickly filled by a whole gaggle of women eager to mother him. The Czartoryski ladies were joined by Delfina Potocka, Marie de Rozières, his pupil Elise Gavard, Princess Obreskoff, mother of another pupil, and above all by Jane Stirling, who vied with the others in her zeal. She was a generous and motherly Scottish spinster, six years older than Chopin, with musical and intellectual pretensions which were not warranted by her talent or her intelligence. She was not one of Chopin's favorite pupils, and his joy was all the greater when he acquired a new one whose talent and personality were more to his taste. This was a six-foot beauty, the Countess Maria Kalergis. She had been born in Warsaw, to a Russian father and a Polish mother, and had married a Russian diplomat of Greek descent, whom she had soon deserted. Her father, Count Nesselrode, was the Chief of Police in Warsaw, and her uncle was Chancellor of the Russian Empire. Countess Maria enjoyed embarrassing them by her unorthodox behavior and manifestations of pro-Polish feeling. She was only twenty-five years old, but had already managed to have affairs with Liszt, Musset, the future Napoleon III and Théophile Gautier, who wrote a poem for her entitled *Symphonie en Blanc Majeur* (she always dressed in white). Heine, who disliked her cordially, retaliated with another poem called *L'Éléphant Blanc* and described her as "a Pantheon in which so many great men lie buried."[34] She was a very good pianist and just the sort of person Chopin enjoyed teaching, and she helped to distract him as he sat in his limbo, waiting to see what happened next.

Nothing did happen. George Sand made no overtures, even though some measure of reconciliation had taken place with her daughter. By December she had taken on a young lover, who was duly installed in Chopin's old room at Nohant. "I am like an old cobweb, and the walls are beginning to fall away," Chopin moaned to one Polish friend.[35] Mendelssohn's death in November reinforced the feeling that something was coming to an end, for they had been the same age. The cold winter and influenza epidemic intensified the lugubrious mood of that season. "I have my own habitual splutterings to think about, so I don't fear the grippe," he wrote to his family. "I occasionally sniff at my homeopathic bottles, I give a lot of lessons at home, and somehow I'm managing not too badly."[36] But to Solange he wrote: "This horrible year must end," a sentiment echoed in a note from Princess Czartoryska, which ended: "What sadness everywhere!"[37]

13

London and Scotland

One day toward the end of January 1848, Thomas Albrecht, Pleyel, Auguste Leo, and the Count de Perthuis came to Chopin and suggested that he give a concert. It seems likely that they were prompted not only by the desire to hear him, but also by the consideration that, as his health deteriorated, he had to cut down on lessons, and his income dwindled as a result. A concert or two would provide him with some capital to store up.

Chopin raised every conceivable objection, but they dismissed these and promised to take all the arrangements on themselves. A small announcement appeared in the press to the effect that the public might expect a concert by Chopin in the near future, and Pleyel's offices were flooded with letters and callers applying to reserve tickets. By the time a date had been fixed, some two weeks before the night, the three hundred tickets had all been sold, and there was a waiting list of six hundred people trying to obtain seats for a possible second concert. Pleyel was keen that Chopin should take advantage of this, but Chopin had not the slightest intention of complying, declaring that one concert was "quite enough of a bore."[1] "I am amazed by this enthusiasm," he wrote to Ludwika, "and now I shall have to play, if only out of gratitude, although I feel that I play worse than ever."[2]

At the beginning of February he was ill for a few days, but came to life once more as the event approached. A few days before the date set, February 16, he held a small rehearsal at Delfina Potocka's before the Czartoryskis, Maria Kalergis, Delfina's sister the Princess de Beauveau, and the Zaleskis. His usual nervousness was allayed by the fact that the whole business was being prepared exactly as he wished. There were no posters, no printed programs, and the tickets were in fact stiff cards printed like invitations: Monsieur Frédéric Chopin requests the presence of whoever it was at a musical evening at Monsieur Pleyel's salons. Pleyel filled the hall with flowers, while Jane Stirling flapped about ensuring that it would be warm enough yet not too stuffy. "I shall be completely at home and see only familiar faces," Chopin wrote to Ludwika, and it was true, for on the night he was surrounded by friends, and on the dais itself sat Grzymala, Custine, the Czartoryskis, Delacroix, and Zaleski. This has given rise to the impression that it was not a public concert at all, and that the whole audience had been carefully selected by Chopin.[3] This was not the case. It was simply that his friends, who knew of the impending event sooner, put their names down first, while he did also reserve some seats for friends who applied late.

Chopin played a Mozart trio with Franchomme and the violinist Alard, and the last three movements of his Sonata for Piano and Cello with Franchomme. Apart from that he filled out the program alone, playing the Berceuse, the Barcarolle, and the D flat major Waltz (opus 64).

In spite of Chopin's fears the audience was in raptures, and his frailty did not interfere with the quality of his playing. He had been weakening so gradually over the years that he had had time to substitute technique for force. Already in 1842

one of his pupils had commented that "his pianissimo is so
delicate that he can produce the greatest effects of crescendo
without requiring the strength of the muscular virtuosi of the
modern school."[4] An English pianist who was present at the
concert was astonished to find the emaciated Chopin capable
of playing with regularity and force.[5]

The *Revue et Gazette Musicale* stated that one would need
Shakespeare's pen to describe Chopin's playing, and the other
papers echoed its paean of praise,[6] but perhaps the most
fitting comments on the concert and on Chopin's position in
general were made by Custine, who sent him a little note afterward:

> You have gained in suffering and poetry; the melancholy of
> your compositions penetrate still deeper into the heart; one
> feels alone with you in the midst of a crowd; it is no longer a
> piano, but a soul, and what a soul! Preserve yourself for the
> sake of your friends; it is a consolation to be able to hear you
> sometimes; in the hard times that threaten, only art as you
> feel it will be able to unite men divided by the realities of
> life; people love each other, people understand each other, in
> Chopin. You have turned a public into a circle of friends; you
> are equal to your own genius; that says it all.[7]

Chopin must have been persuaded to change his mind
about giving a second concert, as Pleyel announced one for
March 10. But on February 22 revolution broke out in Paris,
and with the barricades up in the streets there could be no
question of such an event taking place. Chopin was feeling ill
and spent the week of the fighting idly in bed, but by the
time it had subsided, his life had resumed its normal course.
It was difficult getting about, since the cobbles had been torn
up and some of the barricades were not cleared for weeks, but
many of his pupils were not affected by the events and continued to come for their lessons.

The regime of Louis Philippe had been satisfactory to few
people, and had governed under incessant attack from left

and right. As a result, a relatively high proportion of Parisian society felt neither worried nor threatened by its fall. The court that had patronized Chopin was gone, and friends like the Count de Perthuis with it, but on the whole there was little for Chopin's pupils and friends to fear, particularly as most of them were either foreigners or musicians. The Poles, even exalted ones like the Czartoryskis, continued to enjoy wide popularity. Nevertheless, outbreaks of street violence were a hazard, and it was impossible to tell what course events would take. Whatever happened, the next few months would be difficult for Chopin, and the prospect of spending another summer in Paris was not one to which he looked forward. He again considered the possibility of meeting some of his family in Germany, while Jane Stirling hotly advocated the idea of his visiting England and taking in the London season.

In the first days of March he had a letter from Solange, announcing that she had had a baby. The news delighted Chopin, who felt it might provide a bridge for complete reconciliation between Solange and her mother. A vague hope lingered in his mind that George Sand might get over the "kind of madness" which he saw as the explanation for her behavior, and relent in her attitude toward him also. But to Ludwika he wrote that he had no regrets for the eight years he had spent with her, and concluded:

> Perhaps these are the necessary conditions for her life, for her life as an author, for her happiness? But do not worry about it, it's all past. Time is a great doctor. Though I am still feeling unhappy about it.[8]

Chopin could not understand how George Sand could forget him so completely, whatever her idea of his villainy might have been. As Grzymala noted, Chopin was one of those people "who stand aloof from the crowd, and do not make their affections dependent upon their judgment of the caprices of fortune and the quirks of fate."[9] He himself found it impossible to eradicate her from his mind so easily. He was soon to see her again.

The fall of the July Monarchy, which she had so heartily despised, brought George Sand to Paris, for many of her friends were in the provisional government, and she herself wanted to play an active part in the revolution. Chopin did not know this, for she had taken rooms elsewhere, having given up the Square d'Orléans apartment, and on March 4 he went to dinner, as he still often did, at Charlotte Marliani's. As he was leaving with the French traveler Edmond Combes, he came face to face with George Sand in the vestibule. She was just on her way in, accompanied by a young friend of Maurice's. They greeted each other politely, and then Chopin asked her whether she had heard from her daughter recently.

"More than a week ago," she replied. "You did not get a letter yesterday, or the day before?" asked Chopin. "No." "In that case I must inform you that you are a grandmother; Solange has a daughter, and I am happy to be the one to tell you of it." With these words, he went on down the stairs, but, reaching the bottom, realized that he had not mentioned Solange's condition. As he could not climb the stairs himself, he begged Combes to run up and tell her that Solange was well. George Sand came down the stairs with Combes and eagerly asked for details, after which she asked after his own health. He said it was good and, bowing, called to the concierge to open the door.[10] As she later described the scene:

> I pressed his trembling and icy hand, I wanted to speak to him; he fled. It was my turn to say that he no longer loved me. I spared him that suffering . . .[11]

Combes accompanied Chopin back to the Square d'Orléans on foot, and noted that he was "very sad, very depressed."[12] The ice which had formed between them could only have been broken by a concerted effort, but the emotion was still there, on his side at least. Four days later he heard from Solange that she had lost her baby, and in his comforting reply he urged her to make contact with George Sand, because, he continued, "she is worthy of the deepest sympathy, it is a heavy blow for her too, of that I am sure . . ."[13] He was never to see her again.

Paris was not the only place which experienced a revolution that year; there was a series of eruptions throughout Europe, and even the Prussian-occupied piece of Poland, the Duchy of Posen, became the scene of skirmishes and a movement toward secession. Many of the Parisian exiles, including Prince Adam Czartoryski, set off for the duchy. Some of the poorer ones borrowed from Chopin for the journey, but to Fontana, who had suddenly written from America, saying he wanted to go and fight in Poland, Chopin replied urging him to await further developments. He found it difficult to share the sanguine hopes of some of his compatriots and was appalled at the prospect of more violence. At the same time he clutched at any straw, as he sat in Paris watching his old way of life collapse around him. "It won't come without horrors," he wrote to Fontana, "but at the end of it all, there *must* be a great, magnificent Poland; a real Poland."[14] To Kozmian, the friend who had shown him around London ten years before and whom he was now seeing off at the station, he said:

> My public career is over. In your village you have a little church; you can give me a little bread for the rest of my life, and I shall play hymns to Our Lady on the organ.[15]

Whether he seriously thought in these terms is difficult to tell. But as he watched his friends caught up in the events, he began to feel unwanted and lost. In the end he gave in to Jane Stirling's blandishments and decided to follow her to London.

He left on April 19 and, without being "particularly sick"

on his sea passage, arrived in London the next day, which was Maundy Thursday. He found the city "quiet and dreary," but the coal smoke made an immediate impression on his lungs.[16] Jane Stirling and her sister, Mrs. Erskine, had provided him with an apartment on Bentinck Street, off Cavendish Square, and had thought of everything to make him comfortable, including his favorite drinking chocolate and notepaper with his monogram on it. But the rooms were expensive and did not suit him, and he immediately mobilized Major Szulczewski, the London agent of the Hôtel Lambert, who acted as his factotum, to look for more suitable ones.

Having nothing else to do over the Easter weekend, he drove down to Kingston to see the exiled French Royal Family and their entourage, which included his friend the Count de Perthuis. Otherwise, he kept to himself during the first ten days, as he did not feel well and could not face starting his calls. At the end of April he moved into new rooms on Dover Street, off Piccadilly. "At last I have a room—fine and large— in which I shall be able to breathe and play—and today the sun has visited it for the first time," he wrote to Franchomme on May 1.[17] His Pleyel piano was unpacked, and since Érard and Broadwood both insisted on lending him instruments of their make, he had three in his large drawing room, but, as he wrote to Gutmann, "What use are they, since I have no time to play them?"[18] The moment he had found his bearings, he found himself paying and returning calls and his days passed "like lightning."

Chopin had an enormous number of acquaintances in London, for he had met and sometimes taught many society ladies when they had come to Paris to visit their relatives at the embassy or simply to do the Paris season. They included useful people like Lady Cadogan, who was lady-in-waiting to the Duchess of Cambridge, and the Duchess of Somerset. Through them, and through the letters that Paris friends had given him, he soon met all the more interesting people in

London. He visited the Chevalier d'Orsay at Kensington Gore; went to Cheyne Row several times to see Carlyle, whose wife, Jane Welsh, noted that "I never heard the piano played before—could not have believed the capabilities that be in it";[19] dined with Ralph Waldo Emerson, met Charles Dickens, the once-famous singer Adelaide Sartoris, and Lady Byron, "with whom, apparently, I have great affinity—we talk like a goose to a pig, she in English, I in French." "I'm not surprised she bored Byron," he added.[20] At the opera he was impressed by the figure of the young Queen, more so still by "Wellington in the box below the Queen's, like an old monarchist watchdog sitting in a kennel under his crowned lady."[21]

One thing that Chopin had not expected to find in London was the swarm of Continental musicians, who had done exactly what he had. One of them was Berlioz, who at that moment was penning the introduction to his *Memoirs*, in a somewhat apocalyptic mood:

> Time is short. As I write, the Juggernaut of Republicanism rolls across Europe. The art of music, long since dying, is now quite dead. They are about to bury it, or, rather, throw it on the dung-heap . . . But now, with the first tremors from the continent, flocks of frightened artists come hurrying from all points to seek refuge, as sea birds fly landwards before great storms. Will the British capital be able to maintain so many exiles?[22]

Among the exiles were Pauline Viardot, Jenny Lind, Thalberg, and various less exalted artists, while Kalkbrenner had just left, having failed to achieve anything. Meeting Pauline Viardot slightly shook Chopin, for it brought back memories, particularly as she told him that George Sand had asked for news of him in her last letter. Meeting Jenny Lind, on the other hand, was a pleasant surprise; he found her voice astonishing and the character of her singing fascinating. He wrote to Grzymala on May 13:

Yesterday I went to dinner at Jenny Lind's, who then sang
Swedish things for me until midnight. They have a very special spirit, just as our music has. We have something Slavonic, they something Scandinavian, and they are completely
different, but we're closer to each other than an Italian is to
a Spaniard.[23]

Pleasant as it was meeting people and going to the opera,
Chopin had to think of promoting his own success in London, and the presence of so much competition, combined with
the fact that he found what he considered a deplorable love
of Mendelssohn and Moscheles prevalent in the musical
world, made him more than ever circumspect. He started off
with what might have been an extremely unwise move. He was
done the great honor of being asked to play one of his concertos with the Philharmonic Society, an honor recently denied to Charles Hallé and Kalkbrenner. He refused this offer,
explaining to Grzymala that "their orchestra is like their roast
beef or their turtle soup—strong, pungent and nothing
more."[24] What in fact put him off was that there was no possibility of a rehearsal with the orchestra before the public performance, and he was growing fussier than ever over getting
things right. Another consideration was that he would not be
able to muster enough strength to play one of his concertos.
With solo works, he could lower the volume, thereby making
it possible to produce powerful crescendos at the appropriate
moments, but if he lowered the volume of the piano part in
the rendering of one of his concertos, it would be completely
drowned by the orchestra. There had been a tendency for this
to happen even in his youth, and it was for this reason that
he had not played one of his concertos with full orchestra for
well over a dozen years.

Chopin was determined to make his mark in his own way;
as he explained to Gutmann: "When I have played before
the Queen, I shall have to give a *matinée musicale* in a private house for a limited number of listeners!"[25] One point

that he had overlooked was that the director of the Philharmonic Society was the man responsible for arranging concerts
at court, and he was not pleased at the high-handed manner
in which Chopin had turned down his offer of a concert. He
did, however, get an opportunity to play before Victoria,
though not at court. It was on the occasion of the christening
of the Duchess of Sutherland's baby, to which the Queen
stood as godmother, at Stafford House (now Lancaster
House) on May 15. The party consisted of some eighty people, including the Queen and her Consort, the future Wilhelm I of Prussia, the Duke of Wellington, and "everything
that is most Garter," as Chopin put it to Grzymala. He could
not find words to describe the magnificent picture made by
the Queen, standing on the great staircase surrounded by her
entourage, and found himself wishing some latter-day Vero-
nese could have captured it.[26]

Chopin played some short pieces of his own, and then
some Mozart for two pianos with the English pianist Bene-
dict. The Parisian singers Mario, Lablache, and Tamburini
also performed, but Chopin felt that he had made an impression on Her Majesty, who "addressed a few gracious words"
to him afterward. Unfortunately, he seems to have been
taken in by the regal good manners, because the entry in
Queen Victoria's diary for that evening reads: "There was
some pretty music, good Lablache, Mario and Tamburini
singing, and some pianists playing."[27]

Although his hopes were dashed on that score, Chopin had
a great following in certain circles in England, particularly
among the aristocracy. He earned a respectable sum of money
from playing at soirées at the Marquess of Douglas's, the
Duchess of Somerset's, the Duchess of Cambridge's, Lady
Gainsborough's and "many other Ladies, whose names go in
one ear and come out the other."[28] He felt his reception in
these circles good, for, as he wrote to Grzymala:

They don't talk while I play, and apparently they all speak well of my music, but it is above all the hopelessness of my local colleagues, who are in the habit of being pushed around, which is the reason why they consider me a sort of amateur. I shall soon become a grand seigneur, because I have clean shoes and don't carry about cards saying: "Will give lessons at home, available for evening parties, etc."[29]

The English were apparently less squeamish of talking about money than their French counterparts, and were a little baffled by Chopin's style on this point. After his return to Paris, he enacted a scene for Grzymala's amusement. A lady who had asked him to play at her party then assumed a wary expression and asked:

"Oh, Mr. Chopin, how much do you cost?"
"Madame, I take twenty-five guineas."
"Oh, but I only want a tiny little piece!" she exclaimed, clasping her hands.
"It is always the same price."
"Oh, so you could play a *lot!*"
"Even for two hours, if you like."
"Well, that's agreed then. Do I have to pay the twenty-five guineas in advance?"
"No, Madame, afterward."
"Oh, that's very fair!"[30]

On another occasion, old Lady Rothschild approached him and, on hearing how much he asked for playing, said that, to be sure, he played "very prettily" but that the price was wanting in "moderation."[31] Another lady, whose daughter took two lessons a week at half a guinea each from another pianist, wanted to give her daughter the pleasure of lessons from Chopin, but on hearing that he charged a whole guinea per lesson decided that one per week would do just as well in his case.

Expensive as he was for the English market, he did not lack pupils. Some of them admittedly took only a few lessons, merely wishing to let it be known that they had been taught by him. By the middle of the season he was giving up to five lessons a day, and since there was no shortage of demand for him to play at soirées, he was doing well financially. In a letter to Grzymala, he claimed that he would be able to save a considerable sum if the season lasted long enough. But the season was short and hectic, and he did not have the energy to fall in with its pace. He complained that he could not get up before eight in the morning, and that much of his time and energy were being taken up by paying calls. Jane Stirling and her sister were particularly irritating, for they would insist on dragging him from one house to another, obviously enjoying the opportunity to show off their catch. Judging by the number of unused letters of introduction left among his papers, he never had time to take up all his connections.

On June 23, Chopin gave the first of his concerts, at the house of the singer Adelaide Sartoris in Eaton Place. The audience was restricted to 150 people. One of them was Thackeray, who urged a friend to accompany him to "Mrs. Sartoris' swoary" to hear the "very pretty music." (A long way from Balzac's gushings about "a soul expressing itself in lyricism."[32]) From Chopin's point of view, the main consideration was the financial gain, which, at 150 guineas, was considerable. Two weeks later, on July 7, he followed it up with a second appearance. This was a matinée concert given in St. James's Square, in the house of Lord Falmouth, an amateur violinist of eccentric ways. "In the street you'd give him threepence, but his house is full of servants—dressed better than he," Chopin explained.[33]

While Broadwood was arranging the concert, Pauline Viardot heard of it and offered to sing. Chopin could not refuse, although he was wary of her, believing her to be in too close touch with George Sand (it is possible he may have thought her one of the people responsible for perpetuating the break). She sang some of her own arrangements of his mazurkas, which she had already sung at Covent Garden, and Chopin played mostly short pieces, with the exception of the B flat minor Scherzo. The audience was again small, but the takings large, and this time the event was extensively reviewed in the press. The *Daily News*, for instance, carried the following fragment:

> In these various pieces he showed very strikingly his original genius as a composer and his transcendental power as a performer. His music is as strongly marked with individual character as that of any master who has ever lived. It is highly finished, new in its harmonies, full of contrapuntal skill and ingenious contrivance; and yet we have never heard music which has so much the air of unpremeditated effusion. The performer seems to abandon himself to the impulses of his fancy and feeling, to indulge in a reverie, and to pour out, unconsciously as it were, the thoughts and emotions that pass through his mind . . .[34]

Only his old enemy Davison (the one who had written the extraordinarily vituperative review of some mazurkas in 1841), reviewed his playing unfavorably in the "*Teims*," as Chopin insisted on spelling it.

All this success led Chopin to wonder about the possibility of staying on in England and perhaps settling here. There were several arguments against this. "These English are so different from the French, whom I have grown to accept as my own people," he explained to his family. "They are so pound-conscious in everything, liking the arts above all because they represent luxury; they are kind people, but so weird . . ."[35]

More to the point was what Chopin saw as their attitude to music. To Grzymala he explained that the middle classes only wanted things fantastic or mechanically exciting, while the aristocrats, although discerning and cultivated, and genuinely loving music, were so bored and stunted by conventionality and the hectic pace of their lives that they rarely had time to listen. There was music at every social function, whether it was a flower show or a dinner, and the musicians producing it had never tried to rebel against this tradition of background noise. Chopin felt that he could not survive for long in such conditions. He also realized that the English did not begin to understand his music. He was always being asked to play the pretty little waltzes with their pearly passages, and then being told that "it sounds just like water." Even his English pupils astonished him. "They all look at their hands and play the wrong notes with feeling."[36] According to him, these evils stemmed from a retarded attitude to music in general, for, as he explained to Grzymala:

> If you say you're an artist, the Englishman will think you're a painter, a sculptor or an architect . . . no musician will be called an artist in word or print, because in their view it is not an art but a profession.[37]

Although he rather overstates the case, he is right, for in England the eighteenth-century attitudes had largely survived the great Romantic revolution which had placed music at the apex of the expressive arts. There had been no Liszt living with a member of the English aristocracy, no Chopin sitting at dinner next to the highest in the land and then being discreetly begged to deign to play something. London was full of "Czechs and Savoyards," according to Chopin, and they would sit down and play whatever was expected of them, without demanding anything in exchange except their fee.

Nevertheless, Chopin was sorely tempted to stay on, for he saw that his way of practicing his art was meeting with a certain recognition. "If I could still spend my days calling on this one and that one, if I had not been spitting blood for the last few days, if I were younger, if I did not have my head full of attachments, as I have, then I would perhaps start life all over again," he wrote to Grzymala.[38] To his family, he put it more earthily: "If London were not quite so black, the people not quite so heavy, and if there were no smell of coal and no fog, I would probably start learning English."[39] But while he was tempted in principle, it was in the end the more down-to-earth considerations which counted.

The English climate did not suit him. "Often in the morning I think I'm going to cough up my very soul," he wrote at the beginning of June, and although Mrs. Grote, the eccentric wife of a Whig MP, who had introduced Chopin to Jenny Lind and helped him in various ways, thought that "the climate rather suits him, because it is cool and fresh this season," he was almost perpetually ill.[40]

As usual with Chopin, dejection followed in the wake of his physical collapses. He was often in "a fit of spleen" and felt lonely in London, brooding endlessly over the events which had washed him up here with nobody close to talk to. Major Szulczewski provided a useful and comforting presence, as did Chopin's former pupil Tellefsen, now working in London, and Broadwood, "the most wonderful and genuine friend."[41] Broadwood was full of delicate attentions. When he heard that Chopin had slept badly, he had good pillows and a mattress sent to his lodgings; when, later, he was arranging Chopin's journey to Scotland, he booked the seat opposite, so that the composer could stretch his legs out. But this could not make up for the absence of friends like Grzymala, Franchomme, and Delacroix.

Another minor, but for Chopin powerful, irritant was that the Italian servant he had taken on after his arrival was inefficient, lazy, and dishonest. Chopin needed everything done for him by this stage, and he had grown used to servants with whom he could have some kind of a relationship. This one was unsympathetic and threw Chopin's money around, which, combined with the composer's own profligacy and the expense of life in London during the season, meant that his sizable earnings were whittled down to some two hundred guineas after all the bills had been paid.

By the end of the season, which came all too quickly for Chopin, he was exhausted and at loose ends. "I am suffering from some sort of stupid yearning," he wrote to Grzymala. "In spite of all my resignation, I just don't know what to do next, and I worry about it."[42] Paris had gone through a bloodier round of fighting since he had left, and there seemed no promise of its settling down quickly. The news from Poland and other countries was equally ominous, and England seemed the obvious place for him to stay, but, as he himself observed, "20 years in Poland, 17 in Paris—it's not surprising I don't feel happy here."[43] Just as in Vienna seventeen years before, he was surrounded by kindness and good-will but felt sorry for himself. Although his mood varied markedly, when it was low it was very low:

> I no longer know how to be sad or happy about anything anymore—I have exhausted all my feeling completely—I'm just vegetating and waiting for it all to end soon.[44]

The end of the season left him undecided. He had accepted a booking to give a concert in Manchester at the end of August, but had no idea of how he would fill up his time before and after that. He had plenty of invitations to stay in the country, but could not muster enough enthusiasm to take up any of them. It was only as a result of the relentless persuasion of Jane Stirling that he left London at all.

In the first days of August, therefore, he left for Edinburgh, where he spent a day sightseeing, and thence for Calder House in Midlothian, to stay with Jane Stirling's brother-in-law, Lord Torpichen. "The park here is beautiful, the host very excellent—and I am as well as I can be," he wrote to Franchomme, but this was not very well; after a week or so he was again coughing badly and spitting up particles of blood. He found the Scots ugly but charming, and was greatly impressed by the beauty of the cows, whose produce he lapped up with delight. Had he been able to rest at Calder for some

time, he might well have improved in health, but soon he was
on the move again.[45]

He arrived in Manchester toward the end of August, and
was put up at the house of a German Jew called Salis
Schwabe, who had settled in England thirty years before and
amassed great wealth. The Schwabes were widely traveled
and cultivated, and their fine mansion just outside Manchester, Crumpsall House, was often used by visiting artists.
One of their local friends, Hermann Leo, was the brother of
Chopin's Paris friend and was one of the people most instrumental in attracting Charles Hallé to Manchester.

Chopin was a little astonished to find that "in this smoky
place there is the most charming music room imaginable,"
and although he found himself face to face with one of the
largest audiences he had ever played to, twelve hundred people, he was delighted with the concert, which took place on
August 28.[46] The pianist Osborne, who had returned to settle
in England a few years before, was accompanying one of the
singers taking part in the concert. Chopin begged him not to
listen to his, Chopin's, playing:

> You, my dear Osborne, who have heard me so often in Paris,
> will you not remain with those impressions? I know that my
> playing will be lost in such a large room, and my composi-
> tions will be ineffective. Your presence will be painful to both
> you and me.[47]

As the critic of the *Manchester Guardian* noted, Chopin
ascended the platform with "an almost painful air of feeble-
ness in his appearance and gait," but once he was seated at
the piano, this vanished.[48] Osborne felt that his prediction
had been right, for "his playing was too delicate to create enthusiasm, and I felt truly sorry for him."[49] Charles Hallé, who
was also present, felt that Chopin had been "little understood," and this would appear to have been borne out by one
of the critics, who found him inferior to Thalberg and Herz.[50]

Chopin himself was delighted with the event and with the money he had earned, and did not dwell on whether he had been understood or not.

A couple of days after the concert, Chopin left Manchester for Edinburgh, where, instead of staying at a hotel, he put up with Dr. Lyszczynski, a Pole who had settled in the city in 1831. "I don't know what I shall do next—I shall choke and I shall cough, that is certain, and I shall love you as much as ever," he wrote to Thomas Albrecht.[51] His indecision was once again curtailed by the appearance of Jane Stirling, who took him off to stay with one of her sisters, Mrs. Houston, of Johnstone Castle. There was a large houseparty at the castle, but this did little to cheer up Chopin, who found himself stuck indoors all day with the old and infirm, while the younger guests were out shooting grouse. Needless to say, this company began to bore Chopin prodigiously, as he complained to Grzymala:

> Here you are best with cousins of Great Families that nobody has ever heard of on the continent. The conversation is invariably genealogical; it sounds a little like the Bible—this one begot that, that one begot another, the other begot a third, and before you know where you are you've arrived at Jesus Christ.[52]

In the first week of September, while staying at Johnstone, he went for a drive, the horses bolted and the carriage eventually smashed into a tree. While Chopin was lucky to emerge alive, let alone unscathed, the accident shook him seriously. He realized how helpless he would have been had he broken a leg or been seriously injured, for while he loved attention and needed it, he resented too much of it and hated being made to feel like an invalid. "I'm angry and sad, and people irritate me with their exaggerated care," he wrote. "I cannot rest and I cannot work. I feel alone, alone, alone, although I am surrounded by people."[53]

This feeling of being a useless vegetable was partly the result of his being unable to work. He had not written a single piece for over six months, and could not get into the mood for it. "Not one musical thought," he complained to Franchomme. "I am out of my rut, I feel like a donkey at a masked ball, or a violin bow trying to play a double-bass."[54] Although the following passage from a letter to Fontana is tinged with a sort of conciliatory self-pity, it is nevertheless eloquent of how he felt:

> We are like two old harpsichords on which time and circumstance have played out their wretched trills . . . the belly is excellent, only the strings have snapped and some of the pegs have fallen out. The trouble is that we were built by some famous old craftsman, some Stradivarius *sui generis*, who is no longer about to repair us. We cannot give out new sounds under poor hands, and we stifle inside us everything that, for lack of a good craftsman, nobody will ever manage to draw out of us. I'm hardly breathing, *je suis tout prêt à crever* . . . I don't know why I suddenly find myself thinking of poor dead Jasio and Antek, and Witwicki, and Sobanski! Those with whom I was in the closest harmony have died; even Ennike, our best tuner, has drowned himself. So I can never again have a piano tuned just as I want it. Moos has died, so nobody will ever make me a comfortable pair of boots again. If another four or five go to St. Peter's gates, then my whole life would really become more comfortable in heaven . . .[55]

Another concert had been organized for Chopin in Glasgow on September 27, but instead of awaiting it at nearby Johnstone Castle, Chopin dashed off to Edinburgh, pausing only at Strachur to see Lady Murray, a former pupil. The reason was that he had received a letter from Princess Marcelina Czartoryska, who had arrived in Edinburgh with her husband. The haste with which he joined the Czartoryskis is symptomatic of his feelings. They were hardly old friends, but, as he wrote to Grzymala, "I breathed again in their Polish spirit, and it gave me enough strength to play in Glasgow."[56]

The Glasgow concert was a matinee and was held under the highest patronage, including the Duchess of Argyll and half of the local aristocracy. As a result it was very well attended. A Glaswegian records his impressions of that day:

> On entering the hall I found it about one-third full. The audience was aristocratic . . . and I fancied that many of the ladies might have had finishing lessons in music from the great and fashionable pianist in France.
>
> It was obvious indeed that a number of the audience were personal friends of Mr Chopin. No portrait of that gentleman had I seen; no description of him had I ever read or heard; but my attention was soon attracted to a little fragile-looking man, in a pale grey suit including frock-coat of identical tint and texture, moving about among the company, conversing with different groups, and occasionally consulting his watch, which seemed to be 'in shape no bigger than an agate stone on the forefinger of an alderman'. In this small grey individual I did not hesitate to recognize the musical genius we had all come to see. Whiskerless, beardless, fair of hair, and pale and thin of face, his appearance was interesting and conspicuous; and when, after a final glance at his miniature *horloge*, he ascended the platform and placed himself at the instrument, of which he was so renowned a master, he at once commanded attention. I had frequently seen Thalberg sitting with serene countenance banging out some air with clear articulation and power, in the midst of perpetual coruscations of the most magnificent *fioriture*. Liszt too I had often beheld, tossing his fair hair excitedly, and tearing the wild soul of music from the ecstatic keys—but the manner of Chopin was different. No man has composed pianoforte music of more technical difficulty. Yet with what consummate sweetness and ease did he unravel the wonderful varieties and complexities of sound! It was a drawing-room entertainment, more piano than forte, though not without

occasional episodes of both strength and grandeur. He took the audience as it were into his confidence, and whispered to them of zephyrs and moonlight rather than of cataracts and thunder. Of the whirl of liquid notes he wove garlands of pearls. The movements and combinations were calculated to excite and bewilder.[57]

On this occasion, Chopin played a selection of études, nocturnes, mazurkas, and the ever popular waltzes of opus 64. The longest works he played were a ballade and the Berceuse. It is significant that he did not, by this time, feel strong enough even to play a polonaise, which would require greater power. But while some of the listeners were a little baffled, like the one quoted above, the musical amateurs and those already acquainted with his music were delighted, and all the reviews were very favorable.

After the concert the Czartoryskis accompanied Chopin back to Johnstone Castle for dinner, during which Chopin seemed to be happier than he had been for a long time. But when they left for Edinburgh he relapsed into his former mood of boredom and languor. He had plenty of invitations to stay at places like Inverary, but felt little enthusiasm, and had it not been for Jane Stirling's insistence, he would have gone nowhere at all. She took him off to Keir House and later to Stirling Castle, both inhabited by members of her family. "Everywhere received with the most cordial kindness and boundless hospitality, I find excellent pianos, beautiful pictures and choice libraries; there are also shoots, dogs, dinners that never end and cellars, of which I take less advantage," he wrote to Gutmann from Calder, where he once more arrived in mid-October. "It is hard to describe the refined luxury and the comfort one finds in English [*sic*] country houses," he added.[58] He was certainly taking in a good many of them, for Jane Stirling and Mrs. Erskine were shunting him around from one to another in a desperate attempt to distract him.

This was beginning to tell on his health, which he described in a letter to Grzymala:

> The whole morning, until about two o'clock, I am now completely useless—later, when I've got dressed, everything makes me uncomfortable, and I sit there panting until dinnertime—after which one has to sit for two hours with the men at the table and look at them speaking and listen to them drinking. Bored to tears (thinking of other things, in spite of their attentions and the attempts at conversation in French at the table), I then go to the drawing room, where I need all my strength of mind to come to life a little—because then they usually want to hear me play—after that my kind Daniel [his new Irish servant who was devoted to him] carries me up the stairs to my bedroom, undresses me, puts me to bed, lights a candle, and leaves me to pant and dream until morning, when it all starts over again. As soon as I get a little more used to somewhere, I have to move to somewhere else, because my Scottish ladies won't leave me in peace, and keep coming to fetch me in order to drive me around their family.[59]

By the beginning of October, when he returned to Edinburgh once again to give the concert that had been arranged by Jane Stirling, he was in poor fettle. He again stayed at Dr. Lyszczynski's, where he was put up in a tiny nursery and spent most of the day sitting with his feet almost in the fire, shivering. The unfortunate Mrs. Lyszczynska found him extraordinarily difficult, always complaining that his laundry was not white enough and his boots not clean enough, but he did occasionally atone for everything by sitting down to their little piano.[60]

On October 4 he managed to pull himself together enough to give his recital in the Hopetoun Rooms, where he played alone for two hours. The reviews were satisfactory, but Chopin cared more for the fee he had earned, as he was now desperately trying to accumulate a small reserve of cash against

the moment when he would be taken seriously ill and inca-
pacitated. He was not allowed to rest for long after it was
over, as Jane Stirling came and dragged him off to stay with
Lady Bellhaven at Wishaw, and then at Calder once again.
On his own initiative he spent a few days at Hamilton Palace,
but caught a chill and rushed back to Edinburgh into the
comforting arms of Dr. Lyszczynski.

He was by now desperate to leave Scotland, and not just on
account of the cold weather. His "Scottish ladies," as he
called them, were beginning to be a serious problem. Mrs.
Erskine had decided to convert him to the Church of Scotland, and drove him mad with Bible readings and talk of
the next world, while her sister, Jane Stirling, revealed more
mundane intentions. She was in love with Chopin. He was
used to being pampered by women, and had therefore allowed her to insinuate herself into his life, although he found
her naïve and tedious. Now she began to presume certain
rights on his affections, and he was at last forced to tell her
plainly that: "Friendship is friendship, but it does not give
anyone a right to anything else." This does not seem to have
put off Jane Stirling, who continued to pursue him. "My
Scottish ladies are kind, but such bores, God help me!" he
wrote. "Every day I get letters from them, I don't reply to a
single one, and the moment I go anywhere they come running along after me if they possibly can." Jane Stirling had to
drag her sister about with her as a chaperone, but even so
tongues wagged and rumors reached Paris, whence an
alarmed Grzymala wrote to inquire the truth. Chopin answered that he was "closer to the grave than the nuptial
bed."[61]

The ridiculous notion of starting a new life only served to
underline more poignantly his actual condition. He was convinced that he was spent, that his life was over, and that it
was only his body which needed time to expire. "Where has
my art gone?" he wrote to Grzymala. "And where did I lose

my heart? I can hardly remember how they sing back in Poland. This world seems to be leaving me behind; I'm losing myself; I have no strength left . . ." The physical suffering and the artistical barrenness of his life during this period made him long for a release. "Why does God not kill me straight away, only bit by bit," he complained, and in his despair he could not prevent his thoughts from drifting back to George Sand. "I have never cursed anyone, but life is so unbearable now that I am beginning to think that I might feel better if I could curse Lucrezia. But she must be suffering too . . ."[62]

At the end of October he managed to rouse himself to return to London, where he promptly fell ill. He did not leave the rooms Szulczewski had found him in St. James's Place for the next three weeks. He spent them sitting in front of the fire in his overcoat, because he had to keep the windows wide open so he could breathe in the small room. Princess Marcelina, who was installed in Chopin's old rooms in Dover Street two hundred yards away, took charge of him. She called in Dr. Mallan, the leading homeopath in London, and the Royal Physician, Sir James Clark, who was an authority on tuberculosis and had treated Keats in Italy. There was little they could do except suggest that he leave London as soon as he was strong enough.

Chopin did leave his rooms once during this period, in spite of Dr. Mallan's entreaties. The occasion was the "Annual Grand Dress and Fancy Ball and Concert in aid of the Funds of the Literary Association of the Friends of Poland," held at the Guildhall on November 16. Chopin was particularly keen to make his small contribution to the national cause, since Princess Marcelina, who was acting as an agent of the Hôtel Lambert, was herself involved in organizing the event. It was being greeted with opposition, particularly from *The Times*, which felt that in this year of 1848 Polish aspirations constituted a serious threat to peace in Europe.

The evening began with a concert; Chopin played and his former pupil Lindsay Sloper conducted a small orchestra. This was followed by the ball, for which Chopin did not stay. The event was deemed a great success, but Chopin's playing was somewhat wasted. As Princess Marcelina reported to her uncle the next day: "The concert went off very well, Chopin played like an angel, much too well for the inhabitants of the City, whose artistic education is a little problematic."[63] Chopin was delighted with the occasion, and his appearance caused the predictable sensation among the Poles present, but on his return home he could not sleep all night and felt weak for the next few days.

The second half of November brought fog and cold weather, and Chopin suddenly broke into a panic at the prospect of spending the winter in London. His desire to leave was reinforced by the arrival in London of Jane Stirling and her pious sister. "One day longer here and I won't just die— I'll go mad," he wrote to Grzymala. "My Scottish ladies are such bores that God save me—they've latched on so hard that I cannot get away. Only Princess Marcelina is keeping me alive, and her family, and good Szulczewski." At the same time he asked Grzymala to prepare his rooms at the Square d'Orléans, and also to place a bouquet of violets, his favorite flowers, in the drawing room. "At least I can have a breath of poetry when I return, as I pass through on the way to my bedroom, where I shall probably lie down for a very long time."[64]

On November 23, Chopin and his traveling companion, Leonard Niedzwiedzki (another Hôtel Lambert agent) were driven to the station by Broadwood, who was full of attentions. He brought last-minute gifts, settled Chopin into the compartment he had booked, and recommended him to the conductor of the train. Princess Marcelina, her husband, and her son were at the station to see them off.

As the train pulled out, Chopin suddenly had a seizure; a sort of cramp on the right side below his ribs. As the terrified

Niedzwiedzki looked on helplessly, Chopin unbuttoned his coat, waistcoat, and trousers and started massaging himself, explaining that this often happened. The cramp passed, and they continued their journey uneventfully as far as Folkestone, where they had a lunch of soup, roast beef, and wine. This was subsequently "taken away" by the sea during the crossing, Chopin being copiously sick into a bowl held by Niedzwiedzki. After a bad night at Boulogne, the two travelers took a train to Paris, where they arrived the next day.[65]

No sooner had the cab rolled into the Square d'Orléans than Grzymala, Franchomme, and Marie de Rozières appeared to greet him. He was home at last.

14

Death

Getting back to Paris was a great relief to Chopin, but his health did not improve for some time. Dr. Molin, the homeopathic specialist who had the secret of improving his condition, had died. He was replaced by a whole succession of doctors in whom Chopin had little faith. "They poke about but do not bring me any relief," he wrote to Solange in January 1849. "They all agree on the need for a good climate, calm and rest. I shall have the rest one day without their help."[1] They irritated him by putting him on a diet and ordering him to drink no coffee, only cocoa, which he claimed made him sleepy and "stupid." Nevertheless, he felt confident that he would revive, and wrote to Solange that "the spring sun will be my best doctor."[2]

Much had changed in Paris while he had been away. The only friend left in the Square d'Orléans was Alkan; the Marlianis had left Paris altogether, many of his aristocratic French friends were still lying low, and even Grzymala was being kept out of Paris by a combination of financial and political problems. Many of his French pupils had left and he was now limited in his lessons to those who were very ad-

vanced and therefore not too demanding on him, and to
those who were prepared to put up with last-minute cancel-
lations on account of his health. These included Princess
Soutzo, Maria Kalergis, Delfina Potocka, the Baroness de
Rothschild, and, from March, Princess Marcelina.

Although he could rarely go out that winter, he did not
suffer too much from his great enemy, loneliness, for a small
group of old friends, including Franchomme, Legouvé, Princess Obreskoff (Princess Soutzo's mother), Baron Stockhausen, Thomas Albrecht, Charles Gavard, and Marie de Rozières, conspired to keep it at bay. Now that Grzymala was
only rarely in Paris, Chopin's favorite companion became
Delacroix, who used to call on "my poor great dying man," as
he called him, whenever he had a spare moment. He would
drop in late in the day, when he knew Chopin would have
finished giving his lessons, and the two would talk for hours,
about life, art, and George Sand. Delacroix's mood was not
very different from Chopin's at this time, and they felt a great
affinity with each other. He would often come to the informal
little evenings at the Square d'Orléans, where "the en-
chantress Madame Potocka" and Maria Kalergis sang and
Chopin played; or else come in the afternoon and accompany
Chopin on the drives he began to take with the arrival of
spring. On a typical afternoon, at the beginning of April, the
two friends climbed into the cabriolet and set off along the
Champs-Élysées, chatting about art and music. Delacroix
questioned Chopin at length on the theory of music, and
asked him to explain what constituted logic in musical
thought. "He enlightened me on the meaning of harmony and
counterpoint," the painter noted in his diary, "explaining that
the fugue is what one might call the pure logic of music, and
that therefore to be a master of the fugue is to be familiar
with the elements of all reason and all development in
music."[3] They went on to talk of Mozart, Chopin explaining why he thought him technically superior to Beethoven,

and, after stopping at the Étoile for a drink, they trotted back to the Square d'Orléans.

On other days Delacroix would find Chopin "hardly breathing" and unable to move, for, as Pauline Viardot pointed out, his condition fluctuated greatly during that spring:

> His health is declining gradually, with passable days when he can drive out and others when he has fits of coughing that choke him and he spits out blood. He no longer goes out in the evenings, but he still manages to give some lessons, and on his better days he can be quite merry.[4]

He did in fact occasionally go out. In mid-April he dragged himself to the first night of Meyerbeer's *Le Prophète*. He had been looking forward to hearing Pauline Viardot in the leading role and to seeing the elaborate sets, the electrical sun rising and the full-scale fire contrived with gas on stage, all much-publicized. But the music horrified him, and the great production failed to fill him with the same enthusiasm as had that of *Robert le Diable* almost eighteen years before.

When his thoughts were not obliterated by suffering, he was often tormented by boredom. He tried to combat this by working, but he was not up to the effort, and he found it difficult to concentrate. The fruits of these attempts bear this out; the Mazurkas No. 2 of opus 67 and No. 4 of opus 68 are clearly works of a certain maturity, but this cannot hide their lack of inspiration. Another product of these efforts to fight boredom were the notes for a theoretical method for the piano that he had decided to write, probably at the instigation of Delacroix. But this did not come to him easily either, and his own rather "instinctive" instruction now took its revenge, making it difficult for him to formulate methodical thoughts on the subject. The notes he left behind are of little value.

One thing that all the doctors who had treated him agreed

on was that it would be madness for him to remain in Paris during the summer months, when the heat and the dust would make it difficult for him to breathe. Other considerations were that there was a cholera epidemic gaining ground in the city, and that the forthcoming elections were expected to be accompanied by violence. As a result, it was decided that Chopin should move out of Paris, and his friends duly found him an apartment in Chaillot, a quiet place more or less where the Trocadero now stands. The apartment was expensive, but half the rent was secretly paid by Princess Obreskoff, with the result that Chopin wondered at the cheapness of it.

He moved toward the end of May and was delighted by the spacious main room and the magnificent "Roman view" afforded by the five windows of the apartment, from which he could see the Tuileries, the Chamber of Deputies, the tower of St. Germain l'Auxerrois, Notre Dame, the Panthéon, St. Sulpice, and the Invalides. The fresh air and the fact that he had stopped taking medicine altogether improved his appetite, and after a few weeks he felt much better, although he could still not work or indeed play.

June passed pleasantly enough, and he was not as isolated as he had feared. The cholera epidemic, which had just carried away Kalkbrenner and the old singer Angelica Catalani, whom Chopin had first met in Warsaw, was chasing everyone from the capital, and Delfina Potocka moved to Versailles while Princess Obreskoff and the "Scottish ladies," who had appeared on the scene, took lodgings at St. Germain. The result was that they were bored and therefore visited him more than if they had remained in Paris. In the case of Jane Stirling and her sister, it was clearly too often. "They will drive me into my grave," Chopin could not help complaining to Grzymala.[5] Delacroix, on the other hand, had left Paris for the summer, wondering sadly whether he would ever see Chopin again.

Franchomme and Gutmann often visited him at Chaillot, as did various members of the Czartoryski family, who supplied him with one of their nannies as a night nurse, and one day early in June he had a pleasant surprise when Jenny Lind came to see him. Although she was only in Paris for a few days, she came back for a small musical evening he arranged. The Princess de Beauveau and the Baroness de Rothschild were among those who listened as Jenny Lind and Delfina Potocka took turns to sing, to Chopin's great delight.

In the last week of June he started hemorrhaging seriously and his legs began to swell up. The night nurse alerted Princess Sapieha, who called in Dr. Cruveilher, the greatest authority on tuberculosis in France, who had treated Talleyrand and Chateaubriand. The doctor was in no doubt, for the disease was now entering its terminal stage, with the attendant symptoms of persistent diarrhea and swelling of the legs. Chopin deduced, from the drugs Cruveilher prescribed, that he had diagnosed tuberculosis. He must have realized that the end was near, for while he made brave noises about going to Poland the following spring, he began to make desperate appeals for Ludwika to come to Paris. "I am very weak, and no doctor can help me as much as you can," he wrote, telling her to bring her needle and thimble, for there would be much sitting at his bedside.[6]

Ludwika received letters from her brother and from Princess Obreskoff simultaneously, and after persuading her husband, who did not want to stir, she managed to borrow money from her mother and started the struggle to obtain a passport. In fact, both Princess Marcelina and Delfina Potocka had been using their influence and connections to obtain a passport for Ludwika for some two months, so there must have been a secret plan afoot earlier to bring her to Paris.[7]

The month of July passed slowly and wretchedly; Chopin was lonely and bored and had given up all attempts at keeping himself occupied with work. He still gave a few lessons, but could only play with the greatest difficulty. A niece of Prince Adam's and former pupil of his moved into the apartment above his with her husband and children, which meant that she could play to him to dispel his boredom. It also meant that the old Prince and his mother-in-law, Princess Sapieha, called more often, but apart from them, the faithful Franchomme, and Charles Gavard, who would occasionally read to him in the afternoons, he rarely saw anyone. In the afternoons, if he felt well enough, he would go for a drive in the Bois de Boulogne, and once even drove as far as Passy to have tea with the Zaleskis.

At the end of July his existence was suddenly disturbed once more by the intrusion of his "Scottish ladies." One day he had apparently complained to Franchomme that he had little money left, and the latter told Jane Stirling, whom he knew to be wealthy and devoted to Chopin. Hearing this, she made a great show of surprise and announced that she had sent him the staggering sum of twenty-five thousand francs only in March. Quizzed on this point, Chopin stated that he had never received any such sum and would have sent it back if he had. Jane Stirling then got hold of the man who had allegedly delivered the packet to Chopin's concierge, and sent him to see a famous clairvoyant by the name of Alexis. The latter promised to solve the mystery, but said he needed something belonging to the concierge to help him think. Chopin was forced to persuade poor Madame Etienne to come all the way from the Square d'Orléans, and to invent a stratagem to get her to give him a lock of her hair. This was duly delivered to Alexis, who then announced that the packet had been handed to Madame Etienne and placed by her behind the clock on her mantelpiece in a moment of distraction. There it was found, to the astonishment of Madame Etienne, who could remember no such packet being delivered.

Chopin trusted Madame Etienne implicitly and was convinced that the whole farce had been arranged by Jane Stirling three days before out of a desire to cover up some self-imputed neglect of his needs. "There's a good heart behind it, but also a lot of ostentation," he wrote to Grzymala. The whole business worried and irritated him so much that he could not sleep at night and got migraine trying to straighten out the facts. He refused the gift, but eventually accepted fifteen thousand francs as a loan.[8]

By the beginning of August, he was feeling very weak and was beginning to despair of Ludwika. "I pant and cough and feel sleepy; I don't do anything, I don't want to do anything," he wrote to Grzymala, who only visited him fleetingly in Chaillot, since the police were trying to round up and expel from France members of the Polish Democratic Club, of which he was one.[9]

On August 9, however, Ludwika arrived with her husband, Kalasanty, and daughter. Chopin was as happy as he could be; at last he had someone to talk to, and not just during the day, for he suffered from insomnia and grew anxious on his own. "He liked to talk at night," Ludwika later wrote, "to tell me his sorrows and to pour into my loving and understanding heart all his most personal thoughts . . . I swallowed my tears so he should not know that his suffering was hurting me too."[10] Kalasanty soon got tired of sightseeing and wanted to return to Warsaw and leave the man to die alone. Ludwika, however, was determined to see her brother through the illness, and still deluded herself that he might survive the crisis. In the end, Kalasanty left his wife and little daughter and returned to Poland.

In spite of his condition, Chopin was still giving lessons to Princess Soutzo and perhaps others until the end of August. He was still, apparently, unconscious of the severity of the illness, and pathetically deluded himself that he might go and meet Tytus, who was traveling across Germany toward Belgium. He also hoped to take up Delfina Potocka's invitation to spend the winter at her villa in Nice, whither she had gone herself. But on August 30, Cruveilher, who had been in attendance every couple of days, called in two other eminent doctors and held a consultation the outcome of which was that travel was out of the question, and that, if Chopin were to survive the winter at all, he must be found a warm and sunny apartment in Paris.

While his friends set to work looking for the right place, the news began to spread that Chopin was dying. George Sand, encouraged by a friend of hers who had been prompted by Marie de Rozières, wrote to Ludwika asking for news, but the tone of the letter was not calculated to placate. The phrase "one can be deserted and forgotten by one's children without ceasing to love them" was not only pompous but also insulting, since it was for voicing a very similar sentiment that Chopin had been expelled from her life two years before.[11] The letter went unanswered.

Others came to pay their last respects, like the poet Norwid, who described his visit:

> I found him lying on his bed fully dressed, his swollen legs encased in stockings and pumps. The artist's sister, whose profile was strangely similar to his, was sitting next to him . . . He looked remarkably beautiful, propped up against the cushions in the shadows of the deep curtained bed, wrapped in a shawl. He had, as always, something in even the most commonplace of his movements that was so accomplished, so monumental . . . something the Athenian aristocracy might have made into a cult at the height of the Hellenic civilization . . . In a voice interrupted by coughing and choking, he began to berate me for not having called on him recently. Then he teased me in the most childlike way for my mystical tendencies, to which, as it evidently gave him pleasure, I readily lent myself. After that I talked with his sister. There were more fits of coughing. Finally the moment came to leave him in peace, so I started taking my leave. Pressing my hand, he

threw the hair back from his forehead and said: "I'm leaving
this . . ." and was interrupted by coughing. Hearing this, and
feeling that it was good for him to be contradicted, I assumed
the usual false tone, and, embracing him, said, as one does to
a healthy man: "Every year you say you're leaving this world,
and yet, thank God, you're still alive!" But Chopin, finishing
the sentence interrupted by his coughing, said: "I'm leaving this apartment and moving to another in the Place
Vendôme."[12]

By the middle of September an apartment had been found
for him. It consisted of five rooms on the *entresol* of No. 12
Place Vendôme, the house in which Thomas Albrecht had
his office. The rooms were warm and sunny, as the windows
faced south onto a small courtyard, rather than onto the
beautiful square. The rooms in the Square d'Orléans were
relet and the furniture and effects brought to the Place Vendôme, where, along with the things from Chaillot, including
the mahogany grand piano still on loan from Pleyel, they
filled the five rooms of the new apartment.[13] Chopin moved
in at the end of September, and although he was once or
twice well enough to wander about the rooms, he never left
them again. He soon took to his bed, and by October 12, Dr.
Cruveilher was so certain of impending death that he
suggested that the Last Sacrament be administered.

Chopin's preparation for death had been worrying many
of his Polish friends for some time, as he had not practiced
his religion actively for years, and was what one might call a
lapsed Catholic. People like Princess Sapieha, Norwid, and
Zaleski tried, ineffectively, to make him ponder the subject
and prepare for death; he would simply ask them to pray for
him and listened with devotion when they once or twice did
so at his bedside.[14] At this point Chopin's old acquaintance,
Aleksander Jelowicki, who had since taken holy orders, turned
up in Paris and made a more determined onslaught. He came
on October 12 and begged Chopin to make a full confession

and accept the Last Sacrament, but Chopin replied that, while he would gladly confess to him as a man whom he respected, he found it impossible to believe in the act as a sacrament. Jelowicki returned the next day and found Chopin in an altered mood. The dying man confessed to him and received the Last Sacrament, after which he gave the sacristan an enormous sum of money instead of the usual token gift. When Jelowicki protested at this, Chopin answered: "It is not too much, because what I have received is above all price!" He then added: "Without you, my friend, I would have died like a pig."[15]

That day his condition continued to deteriorate, but he hung on with extraordinary courage, which astonished even the doctors. "I have never seen such tenacious vitality," Grzymala wrote to a friend.[16] It must have been exhausting for Chopin, as friends and pupils from all over Paris came to pay their last respects, and, as Jules Janin put it: "He had in his anteroom I know not how many princesses, countesses, marchionesses, and even a few bourgeoises, who, on their knees, awaited the hour of his last agony."[17] Pauline Viardot, who was not one of them, wrote to George Sand, with a note of sourness, that "all the grandes dames of Paris felt obliged to come and faint in his room, which was cluttered with artists making hasty sketches and a daguerrotyper, who wanted the bed moved to the window so that the dying man could be in the sun."[18] Grzymala talks of Chopin's "worshipers in ermine and in rags who during four consecutive days and nights recited prayers on their knees."[19] The poet Krasinski commented that "it all smelled of the theater and the Paris trottoir."[20]

Such accounts are all based on information culled at second hand and give the wrong impression of the scene. Chopin was in fact permanently surrounded by a small group of people; his sister Ludwika, who had moved into the apartment with him; Solange, who had come up to Paris specially; Princess Marcelina, who had taken rooms in the same square;

and one or two others, including Thomas Albrecht and Gutmann. They looked after Chopin and kept him company, talking to him, reading to him, and praying with him. At the same time, a great number of people called to pay their last respects or simply to inquire about his condition, but they remained in one of the outside rooms, which did, clearly, become a little crowded at times. When he was not suffering too much, Chopin was entirely lucid and would admit people to his bedside in order to talk to them, "with a goodness and an indulgence which are not of this world."[21] He took his leave of them bravely, thanking some, encouraging others, and giving instructions about his affairs. He asked that all unfinished musical manuscripts in his portfolio be destroyed, and that only complete pieces be published at any time. He bequeathed his notes on the proposed piano method to his friend Alkan, as a mark of respect for the latter's revolutionary piano technique. He even remembered to leave Madame Etienne, the concierge at the Square d'Orléans, the princely sum of one thousand francs. At a more personal level, he asked that his body be cut open and his heart sent to Warsaw, and that Mozart's *Requiem* be sung at his funeral.

On October 15, Delfina Potocka arrived from Nice, a gesture of loyalty that must have moved Chopin deeply. He begged her to sing for him one last time, and, the piano being duly rolled up to the bedroom door, she obliged.

Next day he was in great agony and kept asking for music. The piano was again wheeled up to the door, and Princess Marcelina and Franchomme played him some Mozart. He then asked to hear his own Sonata for Piano and Cello, but after a few bars of this he began to suffocate, and they stopped. By this time it had become obvious that the end was close. Most of the callers had gone, leaving only the more intimate friends. As Charles Gavard records:

> The whole evening of 16th was spent reciting litanies; we gave the responses, but Chopin remained silent. Only by his strained breathing could one tell that he was still alive. That

evening two doctors examined him. One of them, Dr. Cruveillher, took a candle and, holding it before Chopin's face, which had become quite dark with suffocation, remarked to us that his senses had ceased to act. But when he asked Chopin whether he was suffering, we quite distinctly heard the answer: "No longer!" These were the last words I heard from his lips.[22]

As the night wore on, more people went home, leaving only Ludwika, Princess Marcelina, Gutmann, Solange, and Thomas Albrecht.[23] The end came at about two o'clock in the morning of October 17. Chopin was awake and Solange sat beside him, holding his hand. Suddenly, he appeared to have a seizure. The terrified Solange called Gutmann, who took Chopin in his arms. "We wanted to give him a drink, but death prevented us," wrote Solange. "He passed away with his gaze fixed on me, he was hideous, I could see the tarnishing eyes in the darkness. Oh, the soul had died too!"[24]

Epilogue

Next morning, Clesinger turned up to make a death mask, having already started work on a project for the monument. The painter Kwiatkowski spent the whole day drawing the composer's face, which had resumed all its beauty and an expression of youthful serenity. When the heart had been removed, the body was taken to the crypt of the Madeleine, and the apartment sealed up. Ludwika had removed Chopin's private papers in fear of potential prying on the part of the Russian Consul, and set about sorting them out. She found all George Sand's letters to Chopin neatly wrapped in a little casket which contained all his money and most treasured possessions. There was more money than anyone had expected, and she was able to settle immediately most of the outstanding debts, as well as his various legacies.[1]

The funeral proved difficult to arrange. If Mozart's *Requiem* were to be performed, a special dispensation had to be obtained from the Archbishop of Paris to allow women to sing in the Madeleine. As it was bound to be a well-attended ceremony, invitation cards had to be issued in order to control the numbers.

The ceremony took place on October 30, 1849, almost two weeks after Chopin's death. The front of the Madeleine was draped with black velvet, the initials F.C. embroidered in silver on it. Some three thousand people entered the church with their invitations, while a huge crowd gathered outside. "At noon, the somber servants of death appeared at the entrance to the temple bearing the coffin of the great artist. At the same moment a funeral march well known to all admirers of Chopin burst from the recesses of the choir. A shiver of death ran through the congregation," wrote Théophile Gautier. "As for me, I felt I could see the sun grow pale and the gilding of the domes take on greenish and alarming tints . . ."[2]

Mozart's *Requiem* was heard, in one of the most distinguished performances it could ever have had. Pauline Viardot was one of the soloists, the others including Lablache, singing the *Tuba Mirum* as he had done at Beethoven's funeral more than twenty years before. Habeneck conducted the orchestra and chorus of the Conservatoire, still the best in Europe. During the offertory the organist of the Madeleine played two of Chopin's preludes.

After the service the coffin was borne from the Madeleine to the cemetery of Père Lachaise. The chief mourner was Prince Adam Czartoryski, the four pallbearers were Meyerbeer, Delacroix, Franchomme, and either Pleyel, Gutmann, or Prince Aleksander Czartoryski (the accounts differ). They were followed by "the whole general staff of the virtuosos of Paris" and literally thousands of the dead man's friends and admirers, some of the ladies walking on foot, with their escutcheoned carriages following in an immense procession.[3] At the cemetery the coffin was lowered into the grave without any sermon or speech, and the crowd slowly dispersed. A year later a small ceremony was held during which Clesinger's monument was unveiled and a casket of Polish earth placed inside.

News of the composer's death spread, and lengthy obituaries appeared, from the pens of people like Hector Berlioz and Théophile Gautier. Few were as moving as that by the poet Norwid, which ended with the words:

> He knew how to divine the greatest mysteries of art with astonishing ease—he could gather the flowers of the field without disturbing the dew or the lightest pollen. And he knew how to fashion them into stars, meteors, as it were comets, lighting up the sky of Europe, through the ideal of art. In the crystal of his own harmony he gathered the tears of the Polish people strewn over the fields, and placed them as the diamond of beauty in the diadem of humanity.[4]

One of Charles Hallé's Manchester pupils, who was very fond of Chopin's music, exclaimed, on hearing of the composer's death: "Capital! Now I can have his complete works bound!"[5] Some people were more personally affected. George Sand felt crushed by the news. Jane Stirling never recovered from it and started a semi-religious cult of his memory. But perhaps the one who missed both man and artist most was Delacroix, who kept a little drawing of Chopin as Dante in his bedroom, and until his death remembered "the incomparable genius for whom heaven was jealous of the earth, and of whom I think so often, no longer being able to see him in this world, nor to hear his divine harmonies."[6]

List of Works in Chronological Order

This list does not pretend to place the pieces in order of composition, and merely sets them in the year which saw the essential work done on them.

Dedications given in brackets denote those written into people's albums or presented to them in manuscript form. Those outside brackets are the official dedications printed in the first editions. It is worth noting the degree of social and professional design implicit in the dedications of this category; apart from a few obviously gratuitous dedications to close friends, such as Tytus Woyciechowski or Stefan Witwicki, there are few to friends of the composer (the most shocking absences are those of Grzymala, Delacroix, Princess Marcelina Czartoryska, and indeed George Sand). It has been suggested that Chopin used this as an additional source of income, and that many of the official dedications were paid for. It is unlikely that this was a policy of the composer's, since many important works were printed without dedications at all. The answer is probably that he attached little significance to the question, merely using the dedication as an instrument of showing gratitude, respect, or good-will at moments when this was in some way expected of him.

Date	Title	Opus No.	Dedicated to	First Published
1817	Polonaise G minor		Countess Wiktoria Skarbek	Privately 1817
	Polonaise B flat major			Posthumous
	Military March		[Empress Maria Fydorovna]	Lost
1818	Two polonaises			Lost
1820	Mazurka D major			Posthumous
1821	Polonaise A flat major		[Adalbert Zywny]	Posthumous
1822	Polonaise G sharp minor		[Madame Du Pont]	Posthumous
1824	Variations for Flute and Piano on Rossini's "Cenerentola"			Posthumous
	Waltz C major			Lost
	Mazurka B major			Warsaw 1826
	Variations E major on German air: "Schweizerbube"		[Katarzyna Sowinska]	Posthumous
1825	Rondo C minor	1	Madame Linde	Brzezina 1825
	Mazurka A minor	17/4	Madame Lina Freppa	Schlesinger 1834
	Mazurka G major			Posthumous
	Waltz C major			Posthumous
1826	Polonaise in B flat minor on Rossini's "Gazza Ladra"		[Wilhelm Kolberg]	Posthumous
	Songs to words by Adam Mickiewicz			
	Variations D major for two pianos		[Emilia Elsner]	
1827	Rondeau à la Mazur	5	Countess Alexandrine de Moriolles	Warsaw 1828
	Andante Dolente B minor			Lost
	Ecossaise B major			Lost
	Waltz A sharp major			Lost
	Variations F major for four hands		[Tytus Woyciechowski]	Lost
	Polonaise D minor	71/1		Posthumous
	Funeral March C minor	72/1		Posthumous
	Nocturne E minor	72/2		Posthumous

Year	Work	Opus	Dedication	Publication
1828	Waltz A sharp major		[Emilia Elsner]	Posthumous
	Waltz E sharp major		[Emilia Elsner]	Posthumous
	Mazurka A minor	68/2		Posthumous
	Sonata C minor	4	Jozef Elsner	Posthumous
	Variations for Piano and Orchestra on *La ci darem*, from Mozart's *Don Giovanni*	2	Tytus Woyciechowski	Haslinger 1830
	Trio for Piano, Violin, and Cello in G minor	8	Prince Antoni Radziwill	Schlesinger 1833
	Fantasia on Polish Airs for Piano and Orchestra	13	Johann Peter Pixis	Schlesinger 1834
	Rondo on Cracovian Themes	14	Princess Anna Czartoryska, née Sapieha	Schlesinger 1834
	Mazurka D major	71/2		Posthumous
	Polonaise B major	71/3		Posthumous
	Polonaise F minor	73		Posthumous
	Rondo C major for two pianos			Posthumous
	Waltz D minor			Lost
	Waltz E sharp major			Lost
	Waltz A major			Lost
1829	Three nocturnes	9	Madame Marie Pleyel, née Mocke	Schlesinger 1833
	Polonaise for Cello and Piano	3	Joseph Merk	Mechetti 1831
	Concerto for Piano and Orchestra F minor	21	Countess Delfina Potocka	Schlesinger 1836
	Études in F major, F minor, A flat major, E flat major	10/8, 9, 10, 11	Franz Liszt	Schlesinger 1833
	Waltz C major	68/1	[Wilhelm Kolberg]	Posthumous
	Waltz B minor	69/2		Posthumous
	Waltz D flat major	70/3		Posthumous
	Polonaise G sharp major			Posthumous
	Mazurka G major		[Vaclav Hanka]	Posthumous

Date	Title	Opus No.	Dedicated to	First Published
1830	Variations A major: *Souvenir de Paganini*			Posthumous
	Two songs to poems by Stefan Witwicki: *"Gdzie Lubi"* and *"Życzenie"*	74/1, 5		Posthumous
	Waltz E major			Posthumous
	Four mazurkas	6	Countess Paulina Plater	Schlesinger 1833
	Five mazurkas	7	Paul Emile Johns	Schlesinger 1833
	Etudes C major, A minor, G flat major, E flat minor	10/1, 2, 5, 6	Franz Liszt	Schlesinger 1833
	Concerto for Piano and Orchestra E minor	11	Friedrich Wilhelm Kalkbrenner	Schlesinger 1833
	Three nocturnes	15	Ferdinand Hiller	Schlesinger 1834
	Waltz E sharp major	18	Emma Horsford	Schlesinger 1834
	Scherzo B minor	20	Thomas Albrecht	Schlesinger 1835
	Introduction to Polonaise for Cello and Piano	3	Joseph Merk	Mechetti 1831
	Grande Polonaise for Piano and Orchestra E flat major	22	Baroness d'Est	Schlesinger 1836
	Ballade G minor	23	Baron Stockhausen	Schlesinger 1836
	Mazurka F major	68/3		Posthumous
	Three ecossaises	72		Posthumous
	Four songs to poems by Stefan Witwicki: *"Wojak," "Hulanka," "Poseł,"* and Adam Mickiewicz: *"Precz z moich oczu"*	74		Posthumous
	Song to Witwicki's poem *"Czary"*			Posthumous
	Waltz E minor			Posthumous
	Nocturne C sharp minor, *"Lento con gran espressione"*			Posthumous
1831	Etude C minor, "Revolutionary"	10/12	Franz Liszt	Schlesinger 1833

Year	Work	Opus	Dedicatee	Publisher
	Waltz A minor	34/2	Baroness d'Ivry	Schlesinger 1838
	First of the 24 preludes	28	Camille Pleyel	Pleyel 1840
	Allegro of proposed Concerto for Piano and Orchestra (rewritten as piano solo in 1841)	46	Friederike Müller	Schlesinger 1841
	Two songs to poems by Stefan Witwicki: "Smutna Rzeka," "Narzeczony"	74		Posthumous
	Song to poem by Ludwik Osinski: "Piosnka Litewska"	74		Posthumous
1832	Etudes E major, C sharp minor, C major	10/3, 4, 7	Franz Liszt	Schlesinger 1833
	Rondo E flat major	16	Caroline Hartmann	Schlesinger 1834
	Three mazurkas	17/1, 2, 3	Madame Lina Freppa	Schlesinger 1834
	Grand Duo Concertante on themes from Meyerbeer's Robert le Diable, written in collaboration with Auguste Franchomme		Adele Forest	Schlesinger 1833
1833	Mazurka B flat major		[Aleksandra Wolowska]	Posthumous
	Mazurka D flat major			Posthumous
	Bolero	19	Countess Emilie de Flahault	Prillip 1834
	Variations B minor	12	Emma Horsford	Paris 1833
	Études: A minor, E minor, G sharp minor, D flat major, G flat major, B minor	25/4, 5, 6, 8, 9, 10	Countess Marie d'Agoult	Schlesinger 1837
1834	Mazurka C major			Posthumous
	Mazurkas G minor, C and B flat minor	24/1, 2, 4	Count de Perthuis	Schlesinger 1836
	Etude A minor	25/11	Countess Marie d'Agoult	Schlesinger 1837
	Andante Spianato	22	Baroness d'Est	Schlesinger 1836
	Two polonaises	26	Joseph Dessauer	Schlesinger 1836
	Mazurka A sharp major		[Celina Szymanowska]	Posthumous

Date	Title	Opus No.	Dedicated to	First Published
1835	Largo E sharp major			Posthumous
	Cantabile B major			Posthumous
	Prelude A major		[Pierre Wolff]	Posthumous
	Fantaisie-Impromptu	66	[Baroness d'Est]	Posthumous
	Mazurka A flat	24/3	Count de Perthuis	Schlesinger 1836
	Two nocturnes	27	Countess Apponyi	Schlesinger 1836
	Waltz A flat	34/1	Countess Josephine Thun-Hohenstein	Schlesinger 1838
	Mazurka G major	67/1	[Anna Mlokosiewicz]	Posthumous
	Mazurka C major	67/3	[Mrs. Hoffmann]	Posthumous
	Waltz G flat major	70/1		Posthumous
	Waltz A flat major	69/1	[Maria Wodzinska]	Posthumous
1836	Etudes A flat major, F minor, F major, C sharp minor, C minor	25/1, 2, 3, 7, 12	Countess Marie d'Agoult	Schlesinger 1836
	Four mazurkas	30	Princess Maria Wurttemberg, née Czartoryska	Schlesinger 1838
	Two nocturnes	32	Baroness de Billing, née de Courbonne	Schlesinger 1837
	Song to poem by Witwicki: "Pierscien"	74		Posthumous
	Song to poem by Wincenty Pol: "Leca Liscie z drzewa"	74	[Maria Wodzinska]	Posthumous
	Impromptu A flat major	29	Countess Caroline de Lobau	Schlesinger 1837
	Scherzo B flat minor	31	Countess Furstenstein	Schlesinger 1837
1837	Funeral March	35		Troupenas 1840
	Four mazurkas	33	Countess Roza Mostowska	Schlesinger 1838
	Variation in E major: "Hexameron"			Paris 1837
	Song to poem by Adam Mickiewicz: "Moja Pieszczotka"			Posthumous
	Nocturne C minor	74		Posthumous

Year	Opus	Work	Dedication	Publisher
1838	28	Remainder of 24 preludes	Camille Pleyel	Pleyel 1840
	34/3	Waltz F major	Baroness d'Eichthal	Schlesinger 1838
	41/1	Mazurka C sharp minor	Stefan Witwicki	Troupenas 1840
	74	Song to poem by Witwicki: "Wiosna"		Posthumous
1839	35	First movement, Scherzo and Finale of B minor Sonata		Troupenas 1840
	36	F sharp major impromptu		Troupenas 1840
	37	Two nocturnes		Troupenas 1840
	38	Ballade F major	Robert Schumann	Troupenas 1840
	39	Scherzo C sharp minor	Adolf Gutmann	Troupenas 1840
	40	Two polonaises	Julian Fontana	Troupenas 1840
	41/2, 3, 4	Three mazurkas	Stefan Witwicki	Troupenas 1840
		Three études		Paris 1840
1840		Canon in F minor		Posthumous
	42	Waltz A flat major		Pacini 1840
	70/2	Waltz F minor		Posthumous
		Waltz E major, "Sostenuto"		Posthumous
		Song to poem by J. B. Zaleski: "Dumka"		Posthumous
1841	44	Polonaise F sharp minor	Princess Ludmila de Beauveau, née Komar	Schlesinger
	43	Tarantella		Troupenas 1841
	45	Prelude C sharp minor	Princess Elisabeth Chernishev	Schlesinger 1841
	47	Ballade A flat major	Princesse Pauline de Noailles	Schlesinger 1841
	48	Two nocturnes	Laure Duperre	Schlesinger 1841
	49	Fantasie F minor	Princess Catherine Souzzo	Schlesinger 1841
	50	Three mazurkas	Leon Szmitkowski	Schlesinger 1842
		Mazurka A minor	Émile Gaillard	Chabal 1841
	74	Song to poem by J. B. Zaleski: "Sliczny Chlopiec"		Posthumous

Date	Title	Opus No.	Dedicated to	First Published
1842	Impromptu G flat major	51	Countess Jeanne Esterhazy, née Bathiany	Schlesinger 1843
	Ballade F minor	52	Madame Nathaniel de Rothschild	Schlesinger 1843
	Polonaise A flat major	53	Auguste Leo	Schlesinger 1843
	Scherzo E major	54	Countess Jeanne de Caraman	Schlesinger 1843
	Nocturne F minor	55/1	Jane Wilhelmina Stirling	Schlesinger 1844
	Three mazurkas	56	Catherine Maberly	Schlesinger 1844
1843	Berceuse D flat major	57	Elise Gavard	Meissonier 1845
	Moderato E major		[Countess Sheremetieff]	Posthumous
	Nocturne E flat major	55/2	Jane Wilhelmina Stirling	Schlesinger 1844
1844	Sonata B minor	58	Countess de Perthuis	Meissonier 1845
1845	Three mazurkas	59		Brandus 1845
	Barcarolle F sharp major	60		Brandus 1846
	Songs to poems by J. B. Zaleski: "Dwojaki Koniec," "Niema Czego Trzeba"	74	Baroness Stockhausen	Posthumous
1846	Sonata for Piano and Cello begun	65	Auguste Franchomme	Brandus 1847
	Polonaise-Fantaisie	61	Madame A. Veyret, née Kreisler	Brandus 1846
	Two nocturnes	62	R. de Konnerlitz	Brandus 1846
	Three mazurkas	63	Laura Czosnowksa	Brandus 1847
	Waltz D flat major	64/1	Countess Delfina Potocka	Brandus 1847
	Waltz C sharp minor	64/2	Baroness de Rothschild	Brandus 1847
	Waltz A flat major	64/3	Countess Katarzyna Branicka	Brandus 1847
	Sonata for Piano and Cello finished	65	Auguste Franchomme	Brandus 1847
	Mazurka A major	67/4		Posthumous
	Veni Creator			Lost
1847	Song to poem by Zygmunt Krasinski: Melodia	74	[Countess Delfina Potocka]	Posthumous

Year	Composition	Opus	Dedication	Status
1848	Waltz B major			Lost
1849	Mazurka G minor	67/2		Posthumous
	Mazurka F minor	68/4	[Mrs. Erskine]	Posthumous

The Case of the
Chopin-Potocka "Letters"

Chopin's early biographers, some of whom, like Liszt, knew him personally, relied not on documents but on their own reminiscences, those of others, and a certain amount of hearsay and gossip. The world of the 1840s was a small one, in which artists, aristocrats, and professional people met each other across frontiers and all knew a great deal about each other. It is therefore significant that not one of his early biographers dropped the slightest hint about the existence of any intimate link between Chopin and Delfina Potocka. Her other affairs were known throughout Europe, as was his with George Sand, but as far as his contemporaries were concerned, she was just another of the great ladies who, like Marcelina Czartoryska and Maria Kalergis, held a special position in his life because they were among the most gifted of his pupils, because they were *grandes dames*, and because they were Polish. The published and unpublished correspondence of the period, including those of such renowned gossips as Balzac and Dumas, those of the vindictive Countess d'Agoult and of others who prided themselves on knowing everything that went on in Paris (and no regular affair could go on for long without everyone knowing about it), make no allusion, suppose nothing.

But in the last quarter of the nineteenth century a new kind of biography became popular: that which looked at the lives of artists in particular through the prism of their emotional lives. This worked well with a Liszt but made Chopin's biography virtually impossible to write. It was at this moment that certain writers began to look for evidence to fill in the emotional lacunae in his life. An indeterminate affair was "discovered" to fill his adolescence, a young Czech girl was dredged up to enliven the Bad Reinerz holiday, and then, one of the most famous of all Polish historical gossips, Ferdynand Hoesick, hit on Delfina Potocka to enliven the first few years in Paris. He hinted and suggested, found people who had been alive at the same time as Chopin, interviewed them and promoted them, and finally hinted that he knew of the existence of a batch of letters from the composer to the Countess, allegedly kept under lock and key by puritanical "descendants." Others took up his hints, and soon a tradition had been created. The Countess herself began to come to life with the publication during the 1920s and '30s of much contemporary correspondence, particularly that of her great lover, the poet Krasinski.

In 1939, a woman called Paulina Czernicka approached Radio Wilno, saying that she had several unpublished letters of Chopin's to Delfina Potocka, around which she could build a program. With the outbreak of war the plan came to nothing, and nothing more was heard until 1945, when the same lady, now resettled in Western Poland, approached Radio Poznan and successfully broadcast extracts from alleged letters written by Chopin. This of course aroused enthusiastic interest, heightened by the fact that archives and collections throughout Poland had been methodically destroyed by the Germans. But the enthusiasm was tempered, as more extracts were published by Czernicka, by the occasional erotic passages which were exposed. A debate started up as to whether Chopin could have or would have written such stuff, and whether he had or had not had a sexual relationship with Delfina Potocka.

The newly founded Chopin Institute asked Czernicka to supply the originals, so that they could verify them and publish this valuable find. She signed an agreement with them, promising to supply transcripts and originals. A few months later, however, she stated that the originals were "temporarily lost," but that she would produce photographs of them. She then explained that she had given some of the originals to a French officer in Wilno in 1939, and that these were now in France, but that others were hidden in Poland and would be produced shortly. On the day she was supposed to bring them to Warsaw, the Frédéric Chopin Society received a telegram from her saying that, as she was waiting for the train, the briefcase containing the originals had been grabbed by a thief employed by her Komar relatives, who did not wish to see the compromising letters published. She fed the Society with various other stories, claiming on one occasion that the originals were in Australia, on another that her aunt had them in America, and on a third that they were in France, but nobody has to this day seen any such originals. Paulina Czernicka committed suicide in 1949.

The provenance of the letters was no more probable than were their mystifying peregrinations. Czernicka claimed that she had gotten them from a relative who was a member of the Komar family, but although the name was the same, this particular Komar family had no traceable relationship in the last three hundred years with that into which Delfina was born, and lived in a completely different area of the country. Moreover, Delfina's Komars had died out completely, and her heirs were a Countess Tyszkiewicz and a Countess Raczynska, neither of whom had the faintest recollection of any such correspondence existing. Furthermore, none of Czernicka's relatives had ever heard a word about any such letters.

Much has been written on Paulina Czernicka herself, and all the evidence from people who knew her well points to the fact that she was a psychopath with a miserable emotional life and a strong vein of madness in the family (both her brothers and her mother also committed suicide). Moreover, she had from early life nurtured a cult of Chopin, avidly collecting every publication on the subject.

It was not until many years later that her papers were found and a full compilation made of the texts, which had hitherto been broadcast or printed only fragmentarily. It then became possible to look at the basic issue; whether or not these texts were or could be genuine transcripts from letters written by Chopin.

A cursory reading of the texts, which include two full letters, one of them dated, and a hundred or so fragments, varying in length, will strike anyone who knows the authentic correspondence of Chopin in two ways. One reaction is that the style is indeed very "Chopinesque," so much so that one begins to wonder after a while at the abundance of turns of phrase, neologisms, puns, and jokes which seem familiar. They are of course familiar because they all occur in different forms or contexts in the authentic correspondence, though far less frequently. If this is indeed the real Chopin writing, he is trying to show off. The second thing that strikes one is that this collection of texts provides, already made up into perfectly quotable passages, everything that the biographer and the historian vainly struggled to find in Chopin's real correspondence. The authentic correspondence betrays little about Chopin's emotional life, let alone his sexual habits; here they are described in staggering detail. The authentic correspondence makes no

judgments on other musicians or composers, and gives no clue as to
how Chopin considered his music or how he felt about creating it.
Czernicka's texts talk of nothing else; one is overwhelmed by the judgments on Liszt, Schumann, Berlioz, Mozart, Beethoven, Bach; by
Chopin's statements about certain pieces of his own; his observations
on playing the piano; on the theory of music and just about anything
related to it. The authentic correspondence also leaves one guessing at
his relationship to the Polish Romantic movement in general and the
poets Slowacki, Mickiewicz, and Norwid in particular. Czernicka's
texts are full of vignettes and conversations which fill this gap too. In
fact, were these texts to be genuine, they would make the biographer's
task much easier.

All the evidence points in the other direction: To begin with, a historical examination of the texts reveals certain serious faults. The only
dated letter is written from Chopin in Paris to the Countess in Paris,
regarding a tryst for that evening. Now it is known that Delfina spent
the whole of that year in Naples, having a torrid affair with Krasinski.
Some have argued that Czernicka could have written down the wrong
year when transcribing the original, but research has shown that in no
year in which this letter could have been written were they both in
Paris in the month, which, written out in full, is unlikely to have been
copied wrong. There are several meetings described which could never
have taken place, and small mistakes, such as the fragments in which
Chopin sends her books by Mickiewicz, Witwitcki, and Krasinski, in
spite of the fact that during Chopin's lifetime Krasinski only published one book, and that so anonymously that nobody in Paris knew
who the author was.

There are various other features which are highly dubious. For instance, in the texts, Chopin talks much of the young poet Norwid and
refers to him in the same way as and with greater respect than he
does of Mickiewicz. Now Mickiewicz was an old friend of Chopin and
was generally regarded in Paris, by Frenchmen as well as Poles, as
being the spiritual cousin of Byron and Goethe. Norwid was an unknown young man in his early twenties, who had published pieces
here and there in periodicals, and was not discovered in Poland until
the beginning of this century, and not fashionable until the 1930s,
when there was a veritable fad for him in Poland. Another curious
point is that the erotic passages reveal a distinctly post-Freudian association of sexual libido and artistic creativity which does not fit in
with either the atmosphere or the psychological make-up of the society in which Chopin lived in the 1830s and '40s.

Finally, there is the evidence provided by a linguistic examination
of the texts. Apart from the fact that the person writing one of the
erotic passages gets his or her own gender mixed up at one stage, there

are many examples of words which did not appear in Polish until this century, or else changed their meaning, and are here used in the twentieth-century and not the nineteenth-century meaning. The texts are also full of word endings and usages common to Galicia and Volhynia in Eastern Poland, wholly different from those used in Warsaw and Mazovia, as in Chopin's authentic correspondence. Some of Chopin's own neologisms are here repeated with a different gender from the one they have in the authentic correspondence. There is also an avalanche of words such as "art," "artistic creativity," "work of art," "inspiration," which are totally absent from the authentic correspondence and which, moreover, did not acquire their present meaning in the Polish language until after Chopin's death.

It is worth noting that among Paulina Czernicka's papers there are books on Chopin with underlined passages which can be recognized, only slightly amended, in her texts, and there are whole lines in her texts which are taken directly from statements by Chopin's pupils, published later, and from his own notes for a piano method. Her own manuscript texts are full of crossings-out, of phrases added in different inks with a different pen, which suggests confection rather than copying.

There can be no doubt that these texts are in fact forgeries, probably made during the 1930s, and that the forger was almost certainly Paulina Czernicka. One or two Chopin enthusiasts, however, have carried on championing the cause of their authenticity, and they had a field day in 1964, when a few photocopies, purporting to be of the originals, mysteriously appeared among the papers of the deceased composer Szeligowski. They came into the possession of his brother-in-law, living in England, Adam Harasowski, who, for reasons which are not altogether clear, did not publish them until 1973, in *Music and Musicians*, to support his view that some of the "letters" to Delfina Potocka were genuine, while others were forgeries. The Warsaw Chopin Institute showed the photocopies to an expert graphologist, who declared them to be of forgeries. A fierce champion of the authenticity of the letters, M. Glinski, showed them to another expert, who declared them to be copies of original letters written by Chopin. The Institute then handed them to the forensic department of the Polish Police, who carried out extensive and well-documented photographic tests which revealed that the photocopies were made by juxtaposing photographs of lines, words, and expressions from facsimiles or photographs of authentic letters, and even traced from which publications certain words were photographed. Who concocted these photocopies is not known, but they must be regarded as irrelevant to the issue. The entire body of "letters" must be treated as forgeries, and the happy compromise that "some of them are genuine" and Czernicka embroidered around these cannot be accepted by anyone pretending to write history. Nothing short of the discovery of original letters in Chopin's handwriting can alter the balance of the facts, which *all* testify to the whole story being an enormous and squalid hoax.

Notes

CHAPTER 1

1 For documents relating to Nicolas Chopin's origins and move to Poland, see Introduction in vol. I of *Correspondance de Frédéric Chopin*, B. E. Sydow, S. Chainaye, and D. Chainaye.

2 Letter to Polish Lit. Assoc., January 16, 1833, and to Fetis, March 27, 1836, in *Korespondencja Fryderyka Chopina*, Ed. B. E. Sydow, vol. I, pp. 224 and 277 respectively. Also letter from Ludwika Jedrzejewicz to her brother, March 21, 1842, ibid., vol. II, p. 57.

3 Article in *Gazeta Korespondenta Warszawskiego i Zagranicznego*, p. 1733. See also Julian Fontana's introduction to Chopin's complete works, Paris 1853.

4 Eugeniusz Skrodski (pseud. G. Wielislaw) quoted in: *Fryderyk Chopin*, A. Czartkowski and Zofia Jezewska, p. 7.

5 Eugeniusz Skrodski, quoted in Czartkowski and Jezewska, op. cit., p. 12, also K. W. Wojcicki, *Cmentarz Powazkowski*, vol. I, p. 202, and Eustachy Marylski on pp. 55 and 56 of Ms. 7125 in Biblioteka Narodowa, Warsaw.

6 Eugeniusz Skrodski, quoted Czartkowski and Jezewska, op. cit., p. 12.

7 Nicolas Chopin to his son, November 27, 1831, *Korespondencja Fryderyka Chopina*, vol. I, p. 188.

8 *Pamietnik Warszawski*, 4th Year, vol. X, January 1818.

9 Aleksandra z Tanskich Tarczewska, *Historia Mego Zycia*, Warsaw 1967, p. 243.

10 A. E. Kozmian, *Wspomnienia*, vol. I, pp. 73 and 170.

11 J. U. Niemcewicz, *Nasze Przebiegi* in *Przeglad Polski*, zeszyt 10, 1873, pp. 72–81.

12 Wojcicki, op. cit., vol. II, p. 18, see also Hoesick, F.: *Chopin*, vol. I, p. 61.

13 *Korespondencja Fryderyka Chopina*, vol. I, p. 36.

Notes

CHAPTER 2

1 *Kurier dla Plci Pieknej,* year I, vol. I, Warsaw 1823.
2 Letter to Wilhelm Kolberg, August 19, 1824. *Korespondencja Fryderyka Chopina,* vol. I, p. 40.
3 Kuner Szafarski, ibid., p. 39.
4 Ibid., p. 43.
5 Ibid., p. 42.
6 Ibid., p. 45.
7 Krystyna Kobylanska, *Nieznane Utwory Chopina w Zapomnianym Albumie,* in *Ruch Muzyczny,* no. 20, October 1972, pp. 7–8.
8 Franciszek German, *Chopin i Literaci Warsawscy,* p. 228.
9 Quoted in Niecks, Frederick, *Chopin as Man and Musician,* vol. I, p. 51.
10 Letter to Jan Bialoblocki, July 8, 1825, *Korespondencja Fryderyka Chopina,* vol. I p. 48.
11 Letter to Jan Matuszynski, August 1825, ibid., vol. I, p. 52.
12 Letter to parents, August 26, 1825, ibid., p. 53.
13 A. E. Odyniec, *Wspomnienia z Przeszlosci Opowiadane Deotymie,* pp. 325–26. (Although Odyniec places this evening in late 1826 or early 1827, he notes that Chopin was wearing the Lyceum uniform, which would seem to place it prior to July 1826.)
14 K. W. Wojcicki, *Cmentarz Powazkowski,* vol. I, p. 18. The evening probably took place in the house of Colonel Gutkowski, who died at the beginning of May 1826. The St. Catherine's Day in question would probably have been November 25, 1825.
15 Letter to Elsner, August 29, 1826, *Korespondencja Fryderyka Chopina,* vol. I, p. 72.
16 Wanda Tomaszewska, *Chopin w Dusznikach,* in *Muzyka,* 1961, vol. 4, p. 88.

CHAPTER 3

1 Elsner to Chopin, November 27, 1831. *Korespondencja Fryderyka Chopina,* vol. I, p. 197.
2 Letter to Elsner, August 29, 1826, ibid., p. 72.
3 *Chopin i Literaci Warszawscy,* F. German, pp. 56 ff.
4 Letter to family, wrongly dated in *Korespondencja Fryderyka Chopina,* vol. I, p. 50; see K. Kobylanska: *Korespondencja Chopina z Rodzina,* p. 257.
5 Related by Friederike Müller, quoted by F. Niecks; *Chopin as Man and Musician,* vol. II, p. 340.
6 Eugène Delacroix; *Journal,* vol. I, p. 270.
7 *Gazette Musicale de Paris,* September 21, 1834.
8 Letter to family, August 12, 1829, *Korespondencja Fryderyka Chopina,* vol. I, p. 93.
9 Letter to family, September 20, 1828, ibid., p. 83.
10 Mendelssohn to Fanny Hensel, ibid., p. 263.
11 *Gazette Musicale de Paris,* May 15, 1834.
12 Letter to Tytus, December 27, 1828, *Korespondencja Fryderyka Chopina,* vol. I, p. 87.
13 Quoted, ibid., p. 88.
14 See note ibid., p. 487.

15 Entry in register of the Warsaw Conservatoire, reproduced; K. Kobylanska, *Chopin w Kreju*, p. 125.
16 J. Reiss: *Slazak Jozef Elsner*, p. 39.
17 Letter to parents, August 8, 1829, *Korespondencja Fryderyka Chopina*, vol. I, p. 90.
18 Ibid., p. 91.
19 Letter to parents, August 12, 1829, ibid., p. 92.
20 Letter to Tytus, September 12, 1829, ibid., p. 104.
21 Letter to parents, August 12, 1829, ibid., p. 93.
22 Letter to family, August 19, 1829, ibid., p. 96.
23 Letter to parents, August 12, 1829, ibid., p. 93.
24 Letter to family, August 19, 1829, ibid., p. 96.
25 Ibid.
26 Ibid.
27 Letter to family, August 12, 1829, ibid., p. 94.
28 Ibid.
29 Quoted in F. Niecks, op. cit., vol. II, pp. 99–102.
30 Ibid.
31 Ibid.
32 Letter to family, August 26, 1829, *Korespondencja Fryderyka Chopina*, vol. I, p. 101.

CHAPTER 4
1 *Kurier Warszawski*, No. 230 (August 29, 1829); *Gazeta Polska*, No. 230 (August 30, 1829 and No. 247 (September 16, 1829); *Dziennik Powszechny Krajowy*, August 30, 1829, and September 15, 1829.
2 Oskar Kolberg's reminiscences, quoted in Czartkowski and Jezewska, op. cit., p. 41.
3 Letter to Tytus, October 20, 1829, *Korespondencja Fryderyka Chopina*, vol. I, p. 109.
4 Letter to Tytus, November 14, 1829, *Korespondencja Fryderyka Chopina*, vol. I, p. 112.
5 Liszt, Franz: *Chopin*, p. 215.
6 Letter to Tytus, November 14, 1829, *Korespondencja Fryderyka Chopina*, vol. I, p. 112.
7 Ibid.
8 *Kurier Warszawski*, December 23, 1829.
9 *Kurier Warszawski*, March 5, 1829, p. 309.
10 *Powszechny Dziennik Krajowy*, no. 62, 1830.
11 Karol Kurpinski's diary, quoted in Hoesick, op. cit., vol. I, p. 219.
12 Letter to Tytus, March 27, 1830, *Korespondencja Fryderyka Chopina*, vol. I, p. 115.
13 *Powszechny Dziennik Krajowy*, no. 77, March 19, 1830.
14 *Kurier Polski*, no. 107, March 22, 1830.
15 *Kurier Polski*, no. 110, March 26, 1830.
16 *Kurier Polski*, no. 107, March 22, 1830.
17 Letter to Tytus, March 27, 1830, *Korespondencja Fryderyka Chopina*, vol. I, p. 116.
18 Letter to Tytus, April 10, 1830, *Korespondencja Fryderyka Chopina*, vol. I, p. 118.
19 Letter to Tytus, April 17, 1830, ibid., p. 121.

20 Letter to Tytus, March 27, 1830, ibid., p. 116.
21 Letter to Tytus, April 10, 1830, ibid., p. 120.
22 Ibid.
23 Letter to Tytus, October 3, 1829, ibid., p. 108.
24 Letter to Tytus, May 15, 1830, ibid., p. 125.
25 Jozef Elsner to Chopin, November 13, 1832, ibid., p. 221.
26 Letter to Tytus, June 5, 1830, ibid., pp. 128–29.
27 Ibid., pp. 126–27.
28 Letter to Tytus, August 21, 1830, ibid., p. 130.
29 A. Rajchman, *Kolebka Chopina*, in *Echo Muzyczne, Teatralne i Artystuczne*, no. 424.
30 Letter to Tytus, August 31, 1830, *Korespondencja Fryderyka Chopina*, vol. I, p. 132.
31 Letter to Tytus, September 4, 1830, ibid., p. 135.
32 Letter to Tytus, September 18, 1830, ibid., p. 138.
33 Letter to Tytus, January 14, 1830, ibid., p. 113.
34 Letter to Tytus, October 5, 1830, ibid., p. 146.
35 K. Wojcicki, *Pamietniki Dziecka Warszawy*, vol. II, p. 545.
36 Letter to Tytus, October 5, 1830, *Korespondencja Fryderyka Chopina*, vol. I, p. 145.
37 Letter to Tytus, October 12, 1830, ibid., p. 147.
38 Chopin's album diary, p. 12. Quoted in *Correspondance de Frédéric Chopin*, ed. B. E. Sydow, S. Chainaye, and D. Chainaye, vol. II, p. 210.

CHAPTER 5

1 Letter to family, November 14, 1830, *Korespondencja Fryderyka Chopina*, vol. I, p. 152.
2 Letter to Jan Matuszynski, November 22, 1830, ibid., p. 153.
3 Letter to family, December 1, 1830, ibid., p. 158.
4 Ibid., p. 155.
5 Letter to family, December 22, 1830, ibid., p. 160.
6 Letter to family, December 1, 1830, ibid., p. 157.
7 Ibid., p. 156.
8 Ibid., p. 156.
9 Ibid., p. 156.
10 Letter to Tytus, December 12, 1831, ibid., p. 199.
11 Letter to Jan Matuszynski, December 26, 1830, ibid., p. 162.
12 Ibid., p. 165.
13 Romuald Hube's memoirs. Jagiellonian Library, Cracow, Ms. 6687/II, p. 63.
14 Letter to family, December 22, 1830, *Korespondencja Fryderyka Chopina*, vol. I, p. 161.
15 Letter to Matuszynski, December 26, 1830, ibid., p. 166.
16 Ibid.
17 Ibid., p. 163.
18 Ibid., p. 162.
19 Ibid., p. 163.
20 Letter to Matuszynski, January 1, 1831, ibid., p. 170.
21 Fragment of Chopin's diary, ibid., p. 167.
22 Letter to Elsner, January 29, 1831, ibid., p. 171.
23 Letter to family, December 22, 1830, ibid., p. 161.

24 Letter to Jan Matuszynski, December 26, 1830, ibid., p. 165.
25 *Allgemeine Musikalische Zeitung*, no. 30, September 21, 1831.
26 Fragment of Chopin's diary, quoted in *Korespondencja Fryderyka Chopina*, vol. I, p. 167.
27 Letter to family, December 22, 1830, ibid., p. 160.
28 Letter to Matuszynski, December 26, 1830, ibid., p. 164.
29 Letter to Matuszynski, December 26, 1831, ibid., p. 161.
30 Letter to Matuszynski, January 1, 1831, ibid., p. 168.
31 Ibid., p. 162.
32 Stefan Witwicki to Chopin, July 6, 1831, ibid., p. 179.
33 Letter to parents, July 16, 1831, ibid., p. 182.
34 Letter to family, May 14, 1831, ibid., p. 173.
35 Letter to family, July 16, 1831, ibid., p. 181.
36 Fragment of Chopin's diary, ibid., p. 167.
37 *Flora*, no. 87, August 30, 1831.
38 Fragments of Chopin's diary in *Korespondencja Fryderyka Chopina*, vol. I, pp. 183–84.
39 See letter to Kumelski, November 18, 1831, ibid., p. 187.
40 Fragments of Chopin's diary, ibid., pp. 185–86.

CHAPTER 6
1 Letter to Kumelski, November 18, 1831, *Korespondencja Fryderyka Chopina*, vol. I, p. 187.
2 Ibid.
3 Ibid.
4 Ibid., p. 186.
5 Letter to Tytus, December 12, 1831, ibid., p. 202.
6 Ibid., p. 201.
7 Ibid., pp. 199–200.
8 Letter to Kumelski, November 18, 1831, ibid., p. 187.
9 Elsner to Chopin, November 27, 1831, ibid., p. 197.
10 Letter to Tytus, December 12, 1831, ibid., p. 199.
11 Letter to Tytus, December 12, 1831, ibid., p. 203.
12 Letter to Tytus, December 25, 1831, ibid., p. 209.
13 Franz Liszt, *Chopin*, p. 174.
14 Ibid., p. 21.
15 Ferdinand Hiller; open letter to Franz Liszt, reproduced in M. Mirska and W. Hordynski: *Chopin na Obczyznie*, p. 69.
16 Letter to Tytus, December 12, 1831, *Korespondencja Fryderyka Chopina*, vol. I, p. 201.
17 Quoted in Hoesick, F.: *Chopin*, vol. II, p. 91.
18 G. A. Osborne: *Reminiscences of Frederick Chopin*, p. 19. There are several errors of detail in his account, which was written fifty years after the event.
19 A. Orlowski to family, December 9, 1832, quoted in F. Hoesick, op. cit., vol. II, p. 47.
20 *Revue Musicale*, March 3, 1832.
21 Letter to Nowakowski, April 15, 1832, *Korespondencja Fryderyka Chopina*, vol. I, p. 213.

22 Franz Liszt, op. cit., p. 119.
23 F. Niecks; *Chopin as Man and Musician*, vol. I, p. 247. Interviews with Liszt, Hiller, and Franchomme.
24 Zofia Lissa; *Chopin w Swietle Korespondencji Wydawcow*, Muzyka 1961, no. 1, p. 3 ff.
25 Hector Berlioz; in *Feuilleton, Journal des Débats*, October 27, 1849.
26 Slowacki, J., *Dziela*, Wroclaw 1949, vol. XI, pp. 48, 63.
27 Ferdinand Hiller, open letter to Franz Liszt, quoted Mirska, M.; *Chopin na Obczyznie*, p. 69.
28 Juliusz Slowacki to mother, September 3, 1832. *Korespondencja Fryderyka Chopina*, vol. I, p. 216.
29 Franz Liszt, op. cit., p. 146.
30 Hector Berlioz, *Les Années Romantiques*, p. 399.
31 Liszt's letter to Pictet in Thérèse Marix-Spire: *Les Romantiques et la Musique*, p. 552.
32 Eugène Delacroix; *Journal*, vol. I, p. 365.
33 Quoted in Niecks, op. cit., vol. II, p. 110.
34 Gutmann, quoted in Niecks, op. cit., vol. I, p. 265.
35 Delacroix; *Journal*, vol. I, p. 365.
36 Ferdinand Hiller, quoted in M. Mirska and W. Hordynski, op. cit., p. 69.
37 *Gazette Musicale de Paris*, January 5, 1834.
38 Ernest Legouvé: *Soixante ans de souvenirs*, vol. I, p. 307.
39 Nicolas Chopin to his son, April 13, 1833, in *Korespondencja Fryderyka Chopina z Rodzina*, ed. K. Kobylanska, p. 87.
40 *Korespondencja Fryderyka Chopina*, vol. I, p. 223.
41 Charles Hallé: *Life & Letters*, p. 31.
42 Jozef Filtsch to parents, in A. Hedley: *Selected Correspondence of Fryderyk Chopin*, p. 216.
43 Jozef Filtsch, quoted in A. Hedley: *Selected Correspondence of Fryderyk Chopin*, p. 216. See also F. Niecks, op. cit., vol. II, p. 101.
44 Quoted in M. Mirska, op. cit., p. 69.
45 Wilhelm von Lenz, quoted in Czartkowski and Jezewska: *Chopin*, p. 392.
46 George Sand, *Histoire de ma vie*, vol. XX, p. 152.
47 H. de La Joudre to George Sand, July 31, 1844, G. Lubin, op. cit., vol. VI, p. 594.
48 Franz Liszt, op. cit., p. 177.
49 Ernest Legouvé, op. cit., vol. I, p. 307.
50 Legouvé to Chopin, *Korespondencja Fryderyka Chopina*, vol. I, p. 421.
51 Custine to Chopin, n.d., *Korespondencja Fryderyka Chopina*, vol. I, p. 207; see also Thérèse Marix-Spire, op. cit., p. 601, Appendix II.
52 Zofia Lissa; *Chopin w Swietle Korespondencji Wydawcow*, in *Muzyka*, 1960, no. 1, p. 10.
53 Ibid., p. 8.
54 Ibid., p. 10.
55 Inside cover of Chopin's 1834 diary, Frederick Chopin Society, Warsaw. Some of those on the list, such as Chopin's lodger Hoffmann, obviously owed him money.
56 Antoni Orlowski to family, November 29, 1832, quoted Hoesick, op. cit., vol. II, p. 67.

57 J. Mycielski to wife, September 26, 1852, in J. M. Smoter: *Spor v Listy Chopina do Delfing Potockiej*, p. 33.
58 Ibid., pp. 31–32.
59 Letter to Tytus, December 12, 1831, *Korespondencja Fryderyka Chopina*, vol. I, p. 204.
60 See George Sand to Grzymala, June 1838, ibid., vol. I, p. 438.
61 Franz Liszt, op. cit., p. 210.
62 Letter to Auguste Franchomme, September 18, 1833, *Korespondencja Fryderyka Chopina*, vol. I, p. 228.
63 Liszt, Chopin, and Franchomme to Hiller, June 20, 1833, ibid., pp. 226–28.
64 Hector Berlioz, *Les Années Romantiques*, p. 263. See also H. Berlioz, *Selected Letters*, ed. Searle, p. 56.
65 Quoted Maria Mirska, op. cit., p. 69.
66 Ibid.
67 Jan Matuszynski to family, in *Selected Correspondence of Fryderyk Chopin*, p. 123.
68 M. Mirska, op. cit., p. 69.
69 *Revue Musicale*, December 21, 1833.
70 *Gazette Musicale*, May 15, 1834.
71 Rellstab, quoted in Hoesick, op. cit., vol. II, p. 93.
72 Felix Mendelssohn, quoted Niecks, op. cit., vol. I, p. 273.
73 M. Mirska, op. cit., p. 133.
74 Letter to Regina Hiller, May 1834, *Korespondencja Fryderyka Chopina*, vol. I, p. 393.

CHAPTER 7
1. Liszt to Marie d'Agoult, September 13, 1834, in *Correspondance de Liszt avec la Comtesse d'Agoult*, p. 113.
2 Quoted Czartkowski and Jezewska, op. cit., p. 420.
3 Jozef Filtsch to parents, August 19, 1842, in *Selected Correspondence of Fryderyk Chopin*, ed. Hedley, p. 221.
4 On teaching in general, see Eigeldinger, J. J.: *Chopin vu pas ses éleves*, pp. 34–59, and Niecks, op. cit., vol. II, pp. 174 ff.
5 Matthias, quoted in Czartkowski and Jezewska, op. cit., p. 393.
6 Hector Berlioz, in *Feuilleuton, Journal des Débats*, October 27, 1849.
7 Legouvé, op. cit., vol. I, p. 307.
8 Charles Hallé to parents, December 2, 1836, Charles Hallé, *Life & Letters*, p. 225.
9 Jules Janin; *Journal des Débats*, April 6, 1835.
10 *Gazette Musicale de Paris*, April 12, 1835.
11 Minute books of the *Association of Polish Ladies in Paris*, vol. III, pp. 40–43, in Bibliothèque Polonaise, Paris, uncatalogued Mss.
12 Letter to Kalasanty Jedrzejewicz, August 16, 1835, *Korespondencja Fryderyka Chopina*, vol. I, p. 260.
13 See *Tygodnik Emigracji Polskiej*, September 7, 1835.
14 Ludwika Jedrzejewicz to Chopin, December 15, 1835, *Korespondencja Fryderyka Chopina*, vol. I, p. 269.
15 Maria Wodzinska to Chopin, September 1835, ibid., p. 261.
16 F. Wieck, quoted M. Mirska, op. cit., p. 138.

17 Mendelssohn to Fanny Hensel, October 6, 1835, *Korespondencja Fryderyka Chopina*, vol. I, pp. 406–7.
18 Mendelssohn, *Letters to Moscheles*, p. 125.
19 Ibid., p. 138.
20 Maria Wodzinska to Chopin, September 1835, *Korespondencja Fryderyka Chopina*, vol. I, p. 262.
21 See A. Jelowicki, *Listy do Ksaweryny Chodkiewiczowej*, p. 208; also Hoesick, op. cit., vol. II, p. 124; and Julian Ursyn Niemcewicz's diary, Bibliothèque Polonaise, Paris, Ms. P.E. 501, p. 70.
22 *Kronika Emigracji Polskiej*, vol. IV, February 22, 1836, pp. 109–10.
23 See minute books of the *Association of Polish Ladies in Paris*, vol. II, p. 150, and vol. III, p. 38.
24 *Kurier Warszawski*, January 8, 1836.
25 Jozef Browski's diary, quoted Czartkowski and Jezewska, op. cit., p. 225.
26 Madame Émile de Girardin, *Le Vicomte de Launay*, vol. I, p. 169.
27 Quoted Marquis de Luppé: *Astolphe de Custine*, pp. 200–1.
28 Ibid., p. 248.
29 Custine to Chopin, June 6, 1836, *Korespondencja Fryderyka Chopina*, vol. I, p. 419.
30 Niemcewicz's diary, Bibliothèque Polonaise, Paris, Ms. P.E. 501, p. 188.
31 Liszt to Marie d'Agoult, May 1836, *Correspondance de Liszt avec la Comtesse d'Agoult*, p. 170.
32 Marquis de Luppé, op. cit., p. 186.
33 Teresa Wodzinska to Chopin, September 14, 1836, *Korespondencja Fryderyka Chopina*, vol. I, p. 286.
34 Schumann to Heinrich Dorn, September 14, 1836, ibid., p. 420.
35 Quoted Niecks, op. cit., vol. I, p. 310.
36 Ibid.
37 From Henriette Voigt's diary, quoted Niecks, op. cit., vol. I, p. 311.
38 *Neue Zeitschrift für Musik*, no. 33, 1836.
39 Liszt to Marie d'Agoult, December 1839, *Correspondance de Liszt avec la Comtesse d'Agoult*, p. 313.
40 Thérèse Marix-Spire, op. cit., p. 530.
41 Sainte-Beuve, *Mes Poisons*, p. 106.
42 Berlioz to Liszt in *Gazette Musicale*, August 11, 1839.
43 Ferdinand Denis, *Journal*, ed. P. Moreau, p. 60.
44 Czartkowski and Jezewska, op. cit., p. 212.
45 Ibid., p. 213.
46 Ibid., p. 214.
47 Ibid., p. 215.
48 Ferdinand Hiller, *Open Letter to Franz Liszt*, quoted in Niecks, op. cit., vol. II, p. 8.
49 Karasowski, *Fryderyk Chopin*, vol. II, p. 75.
50 Heinrich Heine, *Lutèce*, pp. 48–49.
51 Marie d'Agoult, *Mémoires*, p. 208.
52 Quoted in Markiewicz, *Spotkania Polsko-Francuskie*, p. 75.
53 Wladyslaw Mickiewicz: *Zywot Adama Mickiewicza*, vol. II, p. 375.
54 Letter to Teresa Wodzinska, November 1, 1836, *Korespondencja Fryderyka Chopina*, vol. I, p. 291.
55 Maria Wodzinska to Chopin, ibid., p. 289.
56 Maria Wodzinska to Chopin, January 25, 1837, ibid., p. 295.

57 Maria Wodzinska to Chopin, spring 1837, ibid., p. 297.
58 Malvezzi, A., *La Principessa Christina di Belgiojoso*, vol. II, p. 209.
59 Czartkowski and Jezewska, op. cit., p. 219.
60 George Sand to Marie d'Agoult, April 6, 1837, G. Lubin, ed. *Correspondance de George Sand*, vol. III, p. 769.
61 Marie d'Agoult to George Sand, April 8, 1837, ibid., p. 807.
62 Custine to Chopin, spring 1837, *Korespondencja Fryderyka Chopina*, ed. B. D. Sydow, vol. I, pp. 424–25.
63 Czartkowski and Jezewska, op. cit., pp. 223–33.
64 Ibid., p. 232.
65 Ibid., pp. 234–35.
66 Chopin to Fontana, July 1837, *Korespondencja Fryderyka Chopina*, vol. I, p. 306.
67 Stanislaw Egbert Kozmian to brother, July 1837, quoted Hoesick, op. cit., vol. II, p. 145.
68 See Z. Jablonski, *Chopin w Anglii*, in *Ruch Muzyczny*, 1960, no. 7.
69 Chopin to Teresa Wodzinska, August 14, 1837, *Korespondencja Fryderyka Chopina*, vol. I, p. 307.
70 George Sand, *Journal Intime*, p. 86.
71 Letter to Marie de Rozières, November 2, 1848, *Korespondencja Fryderyka Chopina*, vol. II, p. 279.
72 See J. Slowacki to mother, February 1845, *Korespondencja Fryderyka Chopina*, vol. II, p. 126, and Wladyslaw Mickiewicz: *Zywot Adama Mickiewicza*, vol. IV, p. 255.
73 Quoted in Niecks, op. cit., vol. II, p. 16.
74 Heinrich Heine: *Lettres Confidentielles*, in *Revue et Gazette Musicale de Paris*, February 4, 1838.

CHAPTER 8
1 Thérèse Marix-Spire, op. cit., p. 619.
2 Marquis de Luppé, op. cit., p. 199.
3 George Sand to Grzymala, May 1838, G. Lubin, *Correspondance de G. Sand*, vol. IV, pp. 428–39.
4 Balzac, *Lettres à Madame Hanska*, vol. I, pp. 584–85.
5 Letter to Grzymala, n.d., *Korespondencja Fryderyka Chopina*, vol. I, p. 325.
6 George Sand to Grzymala, May 1838, G. Lubin, op. cit., vol. IV, pp. 428–39.
7 Ibid., p. 438.
8 George Sand to Grzymala, June 1838, ibid., p. 445.
9 Letter to Grzymala, n.d., *Korespondencja Fryderyka Chopina*, vol. I, p. 325.
10 Félicien Mallefille to Chopin, ibid., p. 441.
11 George Sand to Eugène Delacroix, September 7, 1838, in G. Lubin, op. cit., vol. IV, pp. 480 ff.
12 Ibid.
13 See Curtis Cate: *George Sand*, p. 457.
14 Custine to Sophie Gay, October 22, 1838, quoted; *Correspondance de Frédéric Chopin*, ed. B. E. Sydow, D. Chainaye, and S. Chainaye, vol. II, p. 279.
15 George Sand to Charlotte Marliani, G. Lubin, op. cit., vol. IV, p. 512.

16 Quoted in Marcel Godeau, *Le Voyage à Majorque de George Sand et Frédéric Chopin*, p. 54.
17 Letter to Fontana, November 15, 1838, *Korespondencja Fryderyka Chopina*, vol. I, p. 327.
18 George Sand, *Un Hiver à Majorque*, p. 10.
19 George Sand to Christine Buloz, November 14, 1838, G. Lubin, op. cit., vol. IV, p. 515.
20 Letter to Fontana, December 3, 1838, *Korespondencja Fryderyka Chopina*, vol. I, p. 330.
21 George Sand to Grzymala, December 3, 1838, G. Lubin, op. cit., vol. IV, p. 528.
22 Letter to Pleyel, November 21, 1838, *Korespondencja Fryderyka Chopina*, vol. I, p. 443.
23 Letter to Fontana, December 14, 1838, ibid., p. 332.
24 George Sand to Gautthier d'Arc, November 14, 1838, G. Lubin, op. cit., vol. IV, p. 521.
25 Letter to Fontana, December 28, 1838, *Korespondencja Fryderyka Chopina*, vol. I, p. 333.
26 George Sand, *Un Hiver à Majorque*, p. 107.
27 Letter to Fontana, December 28, 1838, *Korespondencja Fryderyka Chopina*, vol. I, p. 332.
28 George Sand to Charlotte Marliani, G. Lubin, op. cit., vol. IV, p. 569.
29 George Sand, *Un Hiver à Majorque*, p. 161.
30 George Sand, *Histoire de ma vie*, vol. XX, p. 146.
31 George Sand to Charlotte Marliani, January 22, 1839, G. Lubin, op. cit., vol. IV, p. 569.
32 Letter to Fontana, December 14, 1838, *Korespondencja Fryderyka Chopina*, vol. I, p. 332.
33 Letter to Fontana, December 28, 1838, ibid., p. 333.
34 Letter to Grzymala, March 12, 1839, ibid., p. 341.
35 George Sand, *Histoire de ma vie*, vol. XX, p. 161, where she says she would gladly have stayed on another two or three years; also George Sand to Charlotte Marliani, January 22, 1839, in G. Lubin, op. cit., vol. IV, p. 560, where she has no intention of leaving.
36 For evidence discrediting the alleged excursion to Arenys de Mar by Chopin and George Sand, see "Por qui escribí *Chopin en Arenys de Mar*; un dietario apócrifo," in *Destino*, Barcelona, February 18, 1950.
37 Curtis Cate, *George Sand*, p. 476.
38 George Sand to Charlotte Marliani, February 15, 1839, G. Lubin, op. cit., vol. IV, p. 569.
39 George Sand to Charlotte Marliani, February 26, 1839, ibid., p. 577.
40 *Un Hiver à Majorque*, written autumn 1840, and *Histoire de ma vie*, vol. XX, written in 1850.
41 George Sand to Charlotte Marliani, March 8, 1839, G. Lubin, op. cit., vol. IV, p. 588.
42 Letter to Grzymala, March 12, 1839, *Korespondencja Fryderyka Chopina*, vol. I, p. 341.
43 Letter to Fontana, end of March 1839, ibid., p. 342.
44 Letter to Fontana, December 28, 1838, ibid., p. 333.
45 Letter to Fontana, March 12, 1839, ibid., pp. 339–40.
46 Ibid., p. 340.

47 Letter to Fontana, n.d., ibid., p. 338.
48 Letter to Grzymala, April 12, 1839, ibid., p. 345.
49 George Sand to Charlotte Marliani, April 26, 1839, G. Lubin, op. cit., vol. IV, p. 646.
50 Letter to Fontana, March 7, 1839, *Korespondencja Fryderyka Chopina*, vol. I, p. 337.
51 George Sand to Charlotte Marliani, April 1839, G. Lubin, op. cit., vol. IV, p. 625.
52 George Sand to Charlotte Marliani, April 26, 1839, ibid., p. 645.
53 Letter to Grzymala, June 2, 1839, *Korespondencja Fryderyka Chopina*, vol. I, p. 349.
54 George Sand to Charlotte Marliani, June 3, 1839, G. Lubin, op. cit., vol. IV, p. 663.

CHAPTER 9
1 George Sand to Charlotte Marliani, June 15, 1839, G. Lubin, op. cit., vol. IV, p. 684.
2 George Sand to Charlotte Marliani, June 20, 1839, ibid., p. 688.
3 Audrey Bone: *Jane Wilhelmina Stirling*, p. 52.
4 The accounts of the Majorcan trip, of various anecdotes in Chopin's life as related in *Histoire de ma vie*, are often either embellished or tendentious, or both, while the letter to Grzymala referred to (May 12, 1847) contains one or two inaccuracies and a rather significant untruth: her protestation of total faithfulness to Chopin can be definitely faulted on one count at least.
5 George Sand to Charlotte Marliani, June 20, 1839, G. Lubin, op. cit., vol. IV, p. 688.
6 Letter to Fontana, August 8, 1839, *Korespondencja Fryderyka Chopina*, vol. I, p. 353.
7 Ibid., pp. 353–54.
8 George Sand to Grzymala, July 8, 1839, G. Lubin, op. cit., vol. IV, p. 716.
9 George Sand to Charlotte Marliani, July 24, 1839, ibid., p. 726.
10 George Sand to Charlotte Marliani, September 18, 1839, ibid., p. 750.
11 Letter to Fontana, September 25, 1839, *Korespondencja Fryderyka Chopina*, vol. I, pp. 357–58.
12 Letter to Grzymala, September 29, 1839, ibid., p. 358.
13 Letter to Fontana, October 8, 1839, ibid., p. 366.
14 Berlioz to Liszt, January 22, 1839, *Les Années Romantiques*, p. 399.
15 Letter to Fontana, August 8, 1839, *Korespondencja Fryderyka Chopina*, vol. I, p. 354.
16 Marie d'Agoult to Liszt, January 19, 1840, *Correspondance de Liszt avec la Comtesse d'Agoult*, p. 360.
17 George Sand to Lamennais, July 21, 1839, G. Lubin, op. cit., vol. IV, pp. 720–21.
18 Marie d'Agoult to George Sand, August 20, 1839, ibid., p. 758.
19 George Sand to Charlotte Marliani, September 28, 1839, G. Lubin, op. cit., vol. IV, p. 757.
20 Marie d'Agoult to George Sand, ibid., p. 798.
21 Marie d'Agoult to Liszt, November 30, 1839, *Correspondance de Liszt avec la Comtesse d'Agoult*, p. 321.
22 Liszt to Marie d'Agoult, December 29, 1839, ibid., p. 346.

23 Marie d'Agoult to Liszt, March 1840, ibid., p. 412.
24 Stephen Heller to Robert Schumann, April 4, 1840, quoted L. Bronarski in *Chopin*, in *Ruch Muzyczny*, no. 20, pp. 1–3.
25 Friederike Müller's diary, quoted Niecks, op. cit., vol. II, p. 340.
26 Quoted in Hoesick, op. cit., vol. II, p. 85.
27 Charlotte Moscheles; *The Life of Moscheles*, vol. I, p. 295.
28 Mendelssohn to Moscheles, *Letters of Felix Mendelssohn to Ignaz and Charlotte Moscheles*, ed. Felix Moscheles, p. 97.
29 E. Perenyi, *Liszt*, pp. 206–9.
30 Quoted in Niecks, op. cit., vol. II, p. 71.
31 Ibid., vol. II, p. 73.
32 Balzac to Hanska, May 28, 1843, Balzac: *Lettres à Madame Hanska*, vol. II, p. 226.
33 Friederike Müller's diary, quoted Niecks, op. cit., vol. II, p. 340.
34 George Sand to Hippolyte Chatiron, February 2, 1846, G. Lubin, op. cit., vol. IV, p. 861.
35 George Sand to Hippolyte Chatiron, July 1, 1840, G. Lubin, op. cit., vol. V, p. 88.
36 Ibid., p. 98.
37 Chopin to Grzymala, July 13, 1842, quoted Aleksander Janta, *Losy i Ludzie*, London 1961, pp. 243–44.
38 George Sand to Maurice, September 20, 1840, G. Lubin, op. cit., vol. V, pp. 132–33.
39 Thérèse Marix-Spire, op. cit., pp. 579–80.
40 Ibid.

CHAPTER 10
1 George Sand to Pauline Viardot, April 18, 1841, Bibliothèque Nationale, Paris, Ms. Nouvelles Aquisitions Françaises, 16273, f. 36.
2 Marie d'Agoult to Lehmann, April 21, 1841, quoted Hedley: *Selected Correspondence of Fryderyk Chopin*, p. 193.
3 Pupil's evidence, quoted Niecks, op. cit., vol. II, p. 78.
4 George Sand to Pauline Viardot, April 18, 1841, Bibliothèque Nationale, N.A.Fr. 16273, f. 36.
5 *Gazette Musicale de Paris*, May 2, 1841.
6 Quoted in Niecks, op. cit., vol. II, p. 78.
7 *La France Musicale*, May 2, 1841.
8 Heinrich Heine, *Lutèce*, p. 187.
9 *Gazette Musicale de Paris*, May 2, 1841.
10 Quoted in Niecks, op. cit., vol. II, p. 279.
11 Quoted in Arthur Hedley, *Chopin*, p. 131.
12 Schumann, *Neue Zeitschrift für Musik*, 1841, no. 10.
13 *Robert Schumann a Fryderyku Chopinie*, Pasntwowa Szkoda Muzyczna, Katowice, p. 37.
14 Jozef Elsner to Chopin, September 14, 1834, *Korespondencja Fryderyka Chopina*, vol. I, p. 246.
15 Franz Liszt; *Chopin*, p. 10.
16 *Gazette Musicale de Paris*, May 2, 1841.
17 Schumann, *Neue Zeitschrift für Musik*, 1841, no. 10.
18 Quoted in Bronarski, L.: *Chopin et l'Italie*, p. 16.
19 Quoted by Arthur Hedley: *Chopin*, p. 54.

20 Honoré de Balzac, *Lettres à Madame Hanska*, April 6, 1843, vol. II, p. 189.

21 Balzac; *Ursule Mirouët*, quoted; *Correspondance de H. de Balzac*, Paris 1966, vol. IV, p. 408.

22 Astolphe de Custine to Chopin, *Korespondencja Fryderyka Chopina*, vol. I, p. 422.

23 Eugène Delacroix, *Correspondance Générale*, vol. II, p. 286.

24 Quoted in Niecks, op. cit., vol. II, p. 100.

25 George Sand to Hippolyte Chatiron, April 26, 1841, G. Lubin, op. cit., vol. V, p. 290.

26 Witwicki to Zaleski, May 2, 1841, Stefan Witwicki, *Listy do J. B. Zaleskiego*, p. 69.

27 Josef Filtsch to parents, March 8, 1842, *Selected Correspondence of Fryderyk Chopin*, A. Hedley, ed., p. 217.

28 Letter to Fontana, August 20, 1841, *Korespondencja Fryderyka Chopina*, vol. II, p. 31.

29 George Sand to Dr. Gaulert, August 1, 1841, G. Lubin, op. cit., vol. V, p. 391.

30 Letter to Fontana, early June 1841, *Korespondencja Fryderyka Chopina*, vol. II, p. 20.

31 Letter to Fontana, August 24, 1841, *Korespondencja Fryderyka Chopina*, vol. II, p. 33.

32 George Sand to Marie de Rozières, July 11, 1841, G. Lubin, op. cit., vol. V, p. 361.

33 George Sand to Marie de Rozières, August 29, 1841, ibid., p. 407.

34 George Sand to Marie de Rozières, July 11, 1841, ibid., p. 362–63.

35 Witwicki to Mickiewicz, July 29, 1841, Bibliothèque Polonaise, Paris, Ms. P.E. 696/13.

36 Related by Wilhelm Lenz, quoted in Czartkowski and Jezewska, op. cit., p. 410.

37 Josef Filtsch to parents, March 8, 1842, *Selected Correspondence of Fryderyk Chopin*, ed. A. Hedley, p. 216.

38 *La France Musicale*, February 27, 1842.

39 George Sand to Hippolyte Chatiron, March 4, 1842, G. Lubin, op. cit., vol. V, p. 607.

40 Kornel Krzeczunowicz to Teofil Ostaszewski, February 26, 1842, Jagiellonian Library, Cracow, Ms. Przyb. 51/64.

41 Letter to Grzymala, n.d., *Korespondencja Fryderyka Chopina*, vol. II, p. 59.

42 George Sand to Pauline Viardot, April 29, 1842, G. Lubin, op. cit., vol. V, p. 647.

43 George Sand to Delacroix, May 28, 1842, ibid., p. 682.

44 Ibid.

45 Ibid.

46 Delacroix to Pierret, June 7, 1842, Delacroix, *Correspondance Générale*, vol. II, p. 108.

47 Delacroix to Pierret, June 22, 1842, ibid., p. 114.

48 Ibid.

49 Ibid., p. 111.

50 George Sand to Charlotte Marliani, July 25, 1842, G. Lubin, op. cit., vol. V, p. 733.

51 Fontana to sister, early May 1842, Biblioteka Narodowa, Warsaw, Ms. 7133, f. 10.
52 Marie de Rozières to A. Wodzinski, wrongly dated in *Correspondance de Frédéric Chopin*, ed. B. E. Sydow and S. and C. Chainaye, vol. III, p. 81.
53 Letter to Fontana, September 11, 1841, *Korespondencja Fryderyka Chopina*, vol. II, p. 34.
54 Leonard Niedzwiedzki's Diary, Biblioteka Polskiej Akademii Nauk, Kornik, Ms. B.K. 2416, f. 133.
55 Ibid., f. 138.
56 George Sand to Pauline Viardot, June 8, 1843, G. Lubin, op. cit., vol. VI, p. 163.
57 George Sand to Maurice, June 6, 1843, ibid., p. 156.
58 Delacroix to George Sand, May 30, 1842, *Correspondance générale*, vol. II, pp. 104–5.

CHAPTER 11

1 George Sand to Charlotte Marliani, October 28, 1843, G. Lubin, op. cit., vol. VI, p. 253.
2 Maurice to George Sand, November 18, 1843, ibid., p. 287.
3 George Sand to Grzymala, November 18, 1843, ibid., p. 284.
4 George Sand to Ferdinand François, November 1843, ibid., p. 915.
5 George Sand, *Histoire de ma vie*, vol. XX, p. 160.
6 George Sand to Charlotte Marliani, June 1844, Lubin, op. cit., vol. VI, p. 565.
7 Zofia Rozengardt's diary, Jagiellonian Library, Cracow, Ms. 9261, f. 23 verso, entry for January 2, 1844.
8 Ibid., f. 24.
9 Zofia Rozengardt to brothers, December 24, 1843, Jagiellonian Library, Cracow, Ms. 9292.
10 Charles Hallé, *Life & Letters*, p. 34, and Wilhelm Lenz, quoted in Czartkowski and Jezewska, op. cit., pp. 416–17.
11 Wilhelm Lenz, quoted in Czartkowski and Jezewska, op. cit., p. 412.
12 Arthur Hedley, *Nieznana Uczenica Chopina*, in *Ruch Muzyczny*, 1970, no. 4, and also T. Niesmieyanova and S. Semienovsky, *Dnievnik Uchenmitsy Shopena*, in *Muzikalnaya Zhizn*, Moscow 1960, n. 4.
13 George Sand to Ludwika Jedrzejewicz, July 1844, G. Lubin, op. cit., vol. VI, p. 574.
14 Letter to Marie de Rozières, August 11, 1844, *Korespondencja Fryderyka Chopina*, vol. II, p. 104.
15 George Sand to Charlotte Marliani, September 8, 1844, G. Lubin, op. cit., vol. VI, p. 621.
16 George Sand to Pauline Viardot, August 22, 1844, ibid., p. 605.
17 George Sand to Delacroix, November 12, 1844, ibid., p. 691.
18 Letter to George Sand, December 5, 1844, *Korespondencja Fryderyka Chopina*, vol. II, p. 383.
19 Ibid.
20 Charles Hallé, *Life & Letters*, p. 36.
21 Hector Berlioz, *Mémoirs*, pp. 465–66.
22 Leonard Niedzwiedzki's diary, Library of the Polish Academy of Sciences, Kornik, Ms. B.K. 2416, pp. 131, 221, 234, etc.

23 Louis Blanc, *Histoire de la Révolution de 1848*, p. 210.
24 Solange Dudevant-Sand to Marie de Rozières, July 3, 1845, G. Lubin, op. cit., vol. VII, p. 9.
25 Letters to family, July 13, 1845, *Korespondencja Fryderyka Chopina*, vol. II, p. 136.
26 Ibid., pp. 136–37.
27 Ibid., pp. 138–42.
28 George Sand to Marie de Rozières, July 19, 1845, G. Lubin, op. cit., vol. VII, p. 63.
29 Quoted by Charlotte Marliani in letter to George Sand, October 20, 1849, ibid., vol. IX, p. 298.
30 George Sand to Marie de Rozières, August 19, 1845, G. Lubin, op. cit., vol. VII, p. 63.
31 Letter to family, July 13, 1845, *Korespondencja Fryderyka Chopina*, vol. II, p. 141.
32 Ibid.
33 George Sand to Chopin, late September 1845, G. Lubin, op. cit., vol. VII, p. 97.
34 George Sand to Charlotte Marliani, November 7, 1845, ibid., p. 159.
35 Ibid.
36 Letter to family, August 1845, *Korespondencja Fryderyka Chopina*, vol. II, p. 146.
37 Letter to family, December 12–26, 1845, ibid., p. 155.
38 Ibid., p. 157.
39 George Sand, *Lucrezia Floriani*, p. 249.
40 Turgenev to Pauline Viardot, November 1846, *Lettres à Mme. Viardot*, ed. É. Halperine-Kaminsky, Paris 1907, p. 4.
41 George Sand, *Histoire de ma vie*, vol. I, p. 267.
42 George Sand, *Lucrezia Floriani*, p. 4.
43 Caroline Jaubert, *Souvenirs*, p. 43.
44 Quoted in Z. Markiewicz, *Spotkania Polsko-Francuskie*, p. 71.
45 George Sand: *Histoire de ma vie*, vol. 20, p. 140.
46 George Sand to Marie de Rozières, July 24, 1846, G. Lubin, op. cit., vol. VII, p. 430.
47 George Sand to Marie de Rozières, June 18, 1846, ibid., p. 378.
48 Delacroix to Villot, August 16, 1846, *Delacroix, Correspondance Générale*, vol. II, p. 283 and Chopin to Franchomme, August 30, 1846, *Korespondencja Fryderyka Chopina*, vol. II, p. 165.
49 Letter to Franchomme, August 26, 1846, *Korespondencja Fryderyka Chopina*, vol. II, p. 398.
50 Quoted in *George Sand en Berry*, by Georges Lubin, pp. 28–29.
51 Quoted in S. and D. Chainaye; *De quoi vivait Chopin*, p. 100.
52 Letter to Franchomme, July 8, 1846, *Korespondencja Fryderyka Chopina*, vol. II, p. 396.
53 Letter to family, October 11, 1846, ibid., vol. II, p. 175.
54 Ibid., p. 170.
55 Liszt to Marie d'Agoult, February 10, 1847. *Correspondance de Liszt avec la Comtesse d'Agoult*, vol. II, p. 374.

CHAPTER 12

1 Letter to family, October 11, 1846, *Korespondencja Fryderyka Chopina*, vol. II, p. 175.
2 *The Life of Moscheles with Selections from His Diaries and Correspondence*, vol. II, p. 172.
3 Letter to family, March 28, 1847, *Korespondencja Fryderyka Chopina*, vol. II, p. 193.
4 Ibid., p. 191.
5 Delacroix, *Journal*, vol. I, p. 309.
6 Letter to family, June 8, 1847, *Korespondencja Fryderyka Chopina*, vol. II, p. 204.
7 Letter to George Sand, April 10, 1847, ibid., pp. 190–91.
8 Letter to family, March 28, to April 19, 1847, ibid., p. 194.
9 Letter to family, June 8, 1847, ibid., p. 204.
10 Ibid., p. 203.
11 George Sand to Grzymala, May 12, 1847, G. Lubin, op. cit., vol. VII, p. 700.
12 Letter to family, June 8, 1847, *Korespondencja Fryderyka Chopina*, vol. II, p. 202. •
13 Ibid., p. 205.
14 George Sand to P. J. Hetzel, May 12, 1847, G. Lubin, op. cit., vol. VII, p. 703.
15 George Sand to Grzymala, May 12, 1847, ibid., pp. 700–1.
16 Letter to George Sand, May 15, 1847, *Korespondencja Fryderyka Chopina*, vol. II, p. 200.
17 Letter to family, June 8, 1847, ibid., p. 204.
18 George Sand to Hortense Allart, June 22, 1847, G. Lubin, op. cit., vol. VII, p. 756.
19 Solange Clesinger to Chopin, June 12, 1847, wrongly dated in *Korespondencja Fryderyka Chopina*, vol. II, pp. 210, 415.
20 George Sand to Marie de Rozières, July 16?, 1847, G. Lubin, op. cit., vol. VIII, p.12.
21 Cf. Delacroix, *Journal*, vol. I, p. 322, also Chopin to George Sand, July 24, 1847, in *Korespondencja Fryderyka Chopina*, vol. II, pp. 417–18, also Chopin to Ludwika Jedrzejewicz, December 26, 1847, ibid., p. 224: "*w swoim slawnym liscie mi pisala ze ziec niezly.*" See also Franchomme's account, in Niecks, op. cit., vol. II, p. 200.
22 Delacroix, *Journal*, vol. I, p. 322.
23 Letter to George Sand, July 24, 1847, *Korespondencja Fryderyka Chopina*, vol. II, pp. 417–18.
24 George Sand to Emmanuel Arago, July 18–26, 1847, G. Lubin, op. cit., vol. VIII, pp. 18–49.
25 George Sand to Louis Viardot, December 1, 1847, Bibliothèque Nationale, Paris, N.A.Fr., 16273, f. 69–72.
26 Quoted G. Lubin, op. cit., vol. VIII, p. 49 note.
27 George Sand to Chopin, July 28, 1847, ibid., pp. 54–55.
28 Pauline Viardot to George Sand, November 19, 1847, *Lettres Inédites de George Sand et de Pauline Viardot*, ed., Thérèse Marix-Spire, pp. 235–36. And Louis Viardot to George Sand, November 19, 1847, postscript, quoted in *Selected Correspondence of Fryderyk Chopin*, ed. A. Hedley, p. 298.

29 George Sand to Pauline Viardot, December 1, 1847, Bibliothèque Nationale, N.A.Fr. 16273, f. 70.
30 See George Sand to Emmanuel Arago, July 18–26, 1847, G. Lubin, op. cit., vol. VIII, p. 48.
31 George Sand to Marie de Rozières, August 14, 1847, ibid., p. 72.
32 Franz Liszt, *Chopin*, p. 247.
33 Letter to Ludwika Jedrzejewicz, December 26, 1847, *Korespondencja Fryderyka Chopina*, vol. II, p. 225.
34 Quoted in S. Szenic, *Maria Kalergis*, p. 183.
35 Quoted by Kozmian in *Przeglad Poznanski*, p. 690, vol. IX, 1849.
36 Letter to Ludwika Jedrzejewicz, December 26, 1847–January 6, 1848, *Korespondencja Fryderyka Chopina*, vol. II, p. 225.
37 Letter to Solange Clesinger, November 24, 1847, ibid., p. 424; and Princess Czartoryska to Chopin, end of December 1847, ibid., p. 223.

CHAPTER 13
1   Letter to family, February 11, 1848, *Korespondencja Fryderyka Chopina*, vol. II, p. 229.
2   Letter to Ludwika Jedrzejewicz, February 10, 1848, ibid., p. 228.
3   Otto Goldschmidt, in *Proceedings of the Musical Association*, G. Osborne: pp. 102–3.
4   Josef Filtsch, quoted by Arthur Hedley; *Selected Correspondence of Fryderyka Chopin*, p. 216.
5   Otto Goldschmidt, in *Proceedings of the Musical Association*, G. Osborne, p. 102.
6   *Revue et Gazette Musicale*, February 28, 1848.
7   Astolphe de Custine to Chopin, wrongly dated in *Korespondencja Fryderyka Chopina*, vol. I, p. 422.
8   Letter to Ludwika Jedrzejewicz, December 26, 1847, to January 6, 1848, ibid., p. 225.
9   Albert Grzymala's private notebooks, Bibliothèque Polonaise, Paris, uncatalogued mss. of the Société Historique et Littéraire Polonaise; quotation appears on verso of p. 76 of what appears to be the earliest of the three notebooks.
10 Letter to Solange Clesinger, March 5, 1848, *Korespondencja Fryderyka Chopina*, vol. II, p. 431.
11 George Sand, *Histoire de ma vie*, vol. XX, p. 254.
12 *Selected Correspondence of Fryderyk Chopin*, ed. Arthur Hedley, p. 309.
13 Letter to Solange Clesinger, March 11, 1848, *Korespondencja Fryderyka Chopina*, vol. II, p. 433.
14 Letter to Fontana, April 4, 1848, ibid., p. 239.
15 Kozmian in *Przeglad Poznanzki*, vol. IX, 1849, p. 687.
16 Letter to Marie de Rozières, private collection, Vienna.
17 Letter to Franchomme, May 1, 1848, *Korespondencja Fryderyka Chopina*, vol. II, pp. 434–35.
18 Letter to Gutmann, May 6, 1848, ibid., p. 436.
19 Jane Welsh Carlyle, quoted in A. Bone, *Jane Wilhelmina Stirling*, p. 66.
20 Letter to family, August 19, 1848, *Korespondencja Fryderyka Chopina*, vol. II, p. 266.
21 Letter to Grzymala, May 4, 1848, ibid., p. 244.
22 Berlioz, *Mémoirs*, pp. 33–34.

23 Letter to Grzymala, May 13, 1848, *Korespondencja Fryderyka Chopina*, vol. II, p. 245.
24 Ibid.
25 Letter to Gutmann, May 6, 1848, ibid., p. 436.
26 Letter to family, August 19, 1848, ibid., p. 264.
27 Queen Victoria's diary, entry for May 15, 1848, Royal Library, Windsor Castle.
28 Letter to unknown correspondent, June 1, 1848, *Korespondencja Fryderyka Chopina*, vol. II, p. 246.
29 Letter to Grzymala, June 2, 1848, ibid., p. 249.
30 Quoted by Hoesick, *Chopin*, vol. III, p. 183.
31 Letter to Grzymala, June 2, 1848, *Korespondencja Fryderyka Chopina*, vol. II, p. 249.
32 Thackeray, *Letters and Private Papers*, ed. G. N. Ray, vol. II, p. 390.
33 Letter to family, August 19, 1848, *Korespondencja Fryderyka Chopina*, vol. II, p. 263.
34 *Daily News*, July 10, 1848.
35 Letter to family, August 19, 1848, *Korespondencja Fryderyka Chopina*, vol. II, p. 272.
36 Letter to Grzymala, October 21, 1848, ibid., p. 283.
37 Letter to Grzymala, October 21, 1848, ibid., p. 282.
38 Letter to Grzymala, June 2, 1848, ibid., p. 248.
39 Letter to family, August 19, 1848, ibid., p. 272.
40 Mrs. Grote to Alexandrine Faucher (Wolowska), July 3, 1848, Bibliothèque de l'Institut de France, Paris, Ms. 6028, no. 72.
41 Letter to family, August 19, 1848, *Korespondencja Fryderyka Chopina*, vol. II, p. 269.
42 Letter to Grzymala, July 8–17, 1848, ibid., p. 253.
43 Letter to Grzymala, June 2, 1848, ibid., p. 249.
44 Letter to Grzymala, July 18, 1848, ibid., p. 255.
45 Letter to Franchomme, August 11, 1848, ibid., p. 257.
46 Letter to Thomas Albrecht, Manchester, September 1, 1848. Fryderyk Chopin Society, Warsaw, Ms.
47 G. A. Osborne: *Reminiscences of Frederick Chopin*, in *Proceedings of the Musical Association*, p. 101.
48 *Manchester Guardian*, August 30, 1848.
49 G. A. Osborne, op. cit., p. 101.
50 See Charles Hallé, op. cit., p. 111; also, S. Brookshaw: *Concerning Chopin in Manchester*, p. 22 for other reviews.
51 Letter to Thomas Albrecht, Manchester, September 1, 1848. Fryderyk Chopin Society, Warsaw, Ms.
52 Letter to Grzymala, September 9, 1848, *Korespondencja Fryderyka Chopina*, vol. II, p. 274.
53 Letter to Grzymala, September 9, 1848, ibid., p. 274.
54 Letter to Franchomme, August 11, 1848, ibid., p. 257.
55 Letter to Fontana, August 18, 1848, ibid., pp. 259–60.
56 Letter to Grzymala, October 1, 1848, ibid., p. 276.
57 Sir James Hedderwick, quoted in A. Bone, *Jane Wilhelmina Stirling*, pp. 73–74.
58 Letter to Gutmann, October 16, 1848, *Korespondencja Fryderyka Chopina*, vol. II, p. 281.

358 *Notes*

59 Letter to Grzymala, October 10, 1848, ibid., p. 278.
60 Niecks, op. cit., vol. II, p. 292.
61 Letter to Grzymala, October 30, 1848, *Korespondencja Fryderyka Chopina*, vol. II, p. 285.
62 Letters to Grzymala, November 17–18, 1848, October 30, 1848, November 17–18, 1848, respectively, ibid., pp. 285 and 287 respectively.
63 Princess Marcelina Czartoryska to Prince Adam Czartoryski, November 17, 1848, Czartoryski Library, Cracow, Ms. Ew. XVII/841, k. 541–44.
64 Letter to Grzymala, November 21, 1848, *Korespondencja Fryderyka Chopina*, vol. II, p. 289.
65 Leonard Niedzwiedzki, private diary, in Library of the Polish Academy of Sciences, Kornik, Ms. 2416, p. 278.

CHAPTER 14
1 Letter to Solange Clesinger, January 30, 1849, *Korespondencja Fryderyka Chopina*, vol. II, p. 292.
2 Letter to Solange Clesinger, April 13, 1849, ibid., p. 294.
3 Delacroix; *Journal*, vol. I, p. 364.
4 Pauline Viardot to George Sand, *Korespondencja Fryderyka Chopina*, vol. II, p. 450.
5 Letter to Grzymala, June 18, 1849, ibid., p. 299.
6 Letter to Ludwika Jedrzejewicz, June 1849, ibid., p. 301.
7 Princess Marcelina Czartoryska to Prince Wladyslaw Czartoryski, May 16, 1849, Czartoryski Library, Cracow, Ms. Ew. XVII, 951, k. 107.
8 Letters to Grzymala, July 28, 1849, *Korespondencja Fryderyka Chopina*, vol. II, pp. 309–11 and August 3, 1849, ibid., p. 312.
9 Ibid., p. 312.
10 Ludwika Jedrzejewicz to Kalasanty Jedrzejewicz. Fryderyk Chopin Society, Warsaw, Ms.
11 George Sand to Ludwika Jedrzejewicz, September 1, 1849, *Korespondencja Fryderyka Chopina*, vol. II, p. 458.
12 Cyprian Norwid; *Czarne Kwiaty*, in *Pisma Wybrane*, ed. J. W. Gomulicki, vol. V, pp. 37–39.
13 For details of Chopin's last apartment and its furnishings, see Henri Musielak; *Dokumenty Dotyczace Spadku po Chopinie*, in *Ruch Muzyczny*, no. 14 (July 2), no. 15 (July 17), no. 16 (July 30), 1978.
14 Zaleski to J. Kozmian, in *Korespondencja Jozefa Bogdana Zaleskiego*, vol. II, p. 128.
15 Aleksander Jelowicki to Ksawera Grocholska, October 21, 1849, *Korespondencja Fryderyka Chopina*, vol. II, pp. 318–21.
16 Grzymala to Auguste Leo, ibid., p. 462.
17 Jules Janin; *Lettres à sa femme*, ed. Mergier, vol. I, p. 476.
18 Pauline Viardot to George Sand, *Korespondencja Fryderyka Chopina*, vol. II, p. 464.
19 Grzymala to Auguste Leo, *Korespondencja Fryderyka Chopina*, vol. II, p. 462.
20 Krasinski; *Listy do Jerzego Lubomirskiego*, p. 525.
21 Grzymala to Auguste Leo, *Korespondencja Fryderyka Chopina*, vol. II, p. 462.
22 Quoted in Niecks, op. cit., vol. II, p. 321.
23 Ludwika Cichomska's account in Czartkowski and Jezewska, op. cit., p.

544 (originally printed in *Kurier Warszawski*, August 7, 1882), which claims, among other things, that Gutmann was not in Paris at the time, must be treated with caution. Gutmann's presence is confirmed in Grzymala's, Solange's, and Niedzwiedzki's accounts.

24 Bibliothèque Nationale, *George Sand, Visages du Romantisme*, 1977, no. 349, p. 83.

EPILOGUE

1 Ludwika Jedrzejewicz to Kalasanty Jedrzejewicz, Fryderyk Chopin Society, Warsaw, and also Henri Musielak, *Dokumenty Dotyczace Spadku po Chopinie*.

2 *La Presse*, November 5, 1849.

3 On the funeral see: *The Musical World*, November 10, 1849; Niecks, op. cit., vol. II, p. 324; Liszt, *Chopin*, p. 307; Théophile Gautier in *La Presse*, November 5, 1849; *Revue et Gazette Musicale de Paris*, November 4, 1849.

4 Cyprian Norwid, in *Dziennik Polski*, Poznan, October 25, 1849, nr. 117.

5 Charles Hallé, *Life & Letters*, p. 120.

6 Delacroix to Grzymala, January 7, 1861, *Korespondencja Fryderyka Chopina*, vol. II, p. 467.

Sources

A: MANUSCRIPT

CZARTORYSKI LIBRARY, CRACOW; Letters from Chopin to Grzymala (Ew. XVII/1173, 651–53), from Princess Marcelina Czartoryska to Prince Adam Czartoryski (Ew. XVII/841) and to Prince Wladyslaw Czartoryski (Ew. XVII/951). File on Charity Concert, April 4, 1835 (IV/5664).

JAGIELLONIAN UNIVERSITY LIBRARY, CRACOW; Romuald Hube's Memoirs (Ms. 6687, II), Letter from Kornel Krzeczunowicz to Teofil Ostaszewski (Przyb. 51/64), Diary, Papers and Correspondence of Zofia Rozengardt-Zaleska (9261, III), Diaries of Jozef Bogdan Zaleski (9158, I).

NATIONAL LIBRARY, WARSAW; Eustachy Marylski's Memoirs (copy) (7125), Julian Fontana's letters to sister (7133), Chopin's letters to Fontana (copy) (7125).

BIBLIOTHÈQUE NATIONALE, PARIS; Correspondence of Pauline Garcia-Viardot (N.A.Fr. 16272 and 16273), Correspondence of Comtesse Marie d'Agoult (N.A.Fr. 25175 and 25187).

BIBLIOTHÈQUE POLONAISE, PARIS; Zofia Rozengardt-Zaleska diary (fragment; copy) (P.E. 543/30), Julian Ursyn Niemcewicz diary (P.E. 500–4), Marie d'Agoult, letters to Mickiewicz (M.A.M. 480), Albert Grzymala's personal notebooks (uncatalogued Mss.), minute books of the Benevolent Association of Polish Ladies in Paris (vols. 1–3), Stefan Witwicki, letters to Adam Mickiewicz (M.A.M. 696), Albert Grzymala, letter to A. Kozuchowski (P.E. 466/II), Princess Marcelina Czartoryska, letter to Dr. Seweryn Galezowski (P.E.).

INSTITUT DE FRANCE, PARIS; Correspondence of Alexandrine Wolowska-Faucher (6028), Chopin letter to Alkan (1988).

LIBRARY OF THE POLISH ACADEMY OF SCIENCES, KORNIK; Leon Niedzwiedzki's diary (2416).

BIBLIOTHÈQUE HISTORIQUE DE LA VILLE DE PARIS; Fonds Sand, M. 237, G. 3880, G. 5532. Letters from the Marquis de Custine, Henri de Latouche, and Stefan Witwicki.

ROYAL LIBRARY, WINDSOR; Queen Victoria's personal diary, by kind permission of Her Majesty Queen Elizabeth.
FRYDERYK CHOPIN INSTITUTE, WARSAW; Letters to Grzymala, Albrecht, etc., Ludwika Jedrzejewicz to Kalasanty Jedrzejewicz, Chopin's private diaries for 1834, 1848, 1849.

B: PRINTED

AGOULT, MARIE DE FLAVIGNY, COUNTESS D'; *Mémoires*, Paris 1927.
APPONYI, RODOLPHE; *Vingt-cinq ans à Paris*, Paris 1913, vol. II.
BALZAC, HONORÉ DE; *Lettres à Madame Hanska*, Paris 1968, vols. I and II. *Correspondence*, Paris 1966, vol. IV.
BERLIOZ, HECTOR; *Correspondance Inédité*, Paris 1879. *Les Années Romantiques, correspondance 1819–42*, Paris, n.d. *Mémoirs*, transl. David Cairns, Panther Books, London, 1974. *Selected Letters*, ed. Searle, London 1966.
BIBLIOTHÈQUE NATIONALE; *George Sand: Visages du Romantisme, Catalogue*, Paris 1977.
BLANC, LOUIS; *Histoire de la Révolution de 1848*, Paris 1880.
BONE, AUDREY; *Jane Wilhelmina Stirling*, 1960.
BRAULT; *Une Contemporaine*, Paris 1848.
BRONARSKI, L.; *Stephen Heller*; *Chopin*, in Ruch Muzyczny, no. 20, 1960.
BRONARSKI, LUDWIK; *Chopin et l'Italie*, 1948.
BROOKSHAW, SUSANNA; *Concerning Chopin in Manchester*, 1951.
CATE, CURTIS; *George Sand*, London 1975.
CHAINAYE, S. AND CHAINAYE, D.; *De Quoi vivait Chopin*, Paris 1951.
CHOPIN, FRÉDÉRIC; *Correspondance*, ed. B. E. Sydow, S. and D. Chainaye, 3 vols., Paris 1953.
CHOPIN, FRYDERYK; *Korespondencja*, ed. B. E. Sydow, 2 vols., Warsaw 1955.
CHOPIN, FRYDERYK; *Korespondencja Chopina z Rodzina*, ed. Krystyna Kobylanska, Warsaw 1972.
CHOPIN, FRYDERYK; *Selected Correspondence*, transl. and ed. by Arthur Hedley, London 1963.
CZARTKOWSKI, ADAM AND JEZEWSKA, ZOFIA; *Fryderyk Chopin*, Warsaw 1970.
DELACROIX, EUGÈNE; *Journal*, Paris 1893, vol. I. *Correspondance générale*, ed., Joubin, Paris 1936, vols. I and II.
DENIS, FERDINAND; *Journal*, ed. P. Moreau, Fribourg 1932.
EIGELDINGER, J. J.; *Chopin vu par ses élèves*, Neuchatel, 1970.
EMERSON, R. W.; *The Letters of Ralph Waldo Emerson*, ed. by Ralph A. Rusk, Columbia University Press, 1939, vol. IV.
FERRA I PERELLO; *Chopin and George Sand in the Cartuja de Valldemosa*, Palma 1932.
GERMAN, FRANCISZEK; *Chopin i Literaci Warszawscy*, Warsaw 1960. *Chopin i Mickiewicz* in Rocznik Chopinowski I, Warsaw 1955. *Chopin i Witwicki* in Annales Chopin, no. 5, Warsaw 1960.
GIRARDIN, MME. EMILE DE; *Le Vicomte de Launay*, IV vols., Paris 1857.
GLINSKI, M.; *Chopin; Listy do Delfiny*, New York 1970.
GODEAU, MARCEL; *Le Voyage à Majorque de George Sand et Frédéric Chopin*, Paris 1959.
GRABOWSKI, AMBROZY; *Wspomnienia*, Cracow 1909, vol. II.
HALLÉ, SIR CHARLES; *Life & Letters*, London 1896.
HEDLEY, ARTHUR; *Chopin*, London 1947.

HEDLEY, ARTHUR; *Nieznana Uczenica Chopina* in Ruch Muzyczny, no. 4, 1970.

HEINE, HEINRICH; *Lutèce*, Paris 1855.

HOESICK, FERDYNAND; *Chopiniana*, Warsaw 1912. *Chopin*, 3 vols., Cracow 1967.

HOFFMANOWA, KLEMENTYNA Z TANSKICH; *Pamietniki*, Berlin 1849.

JABLONSKI, Z.; *Chopin w Anglii*, in Ruch Muzyczny, no. 7, 1960.

JANIN, JULES; *Lettres à sa femme*, ed. Mergier, Paris 1973, vol. I.

JANTA, A.; *Losy i Ludzie*, London 1961.

JAUBERT, CAROLINE; *Souvenirs*, Paris 1881.

JELOWICKI, ALEKSANDER; *Listy do Ksaweryny Chodkiewiczowej*, ed. Franciszek German, Warsaw 1964.

KANSKI, J.; *Niedokonczony Fetywal i Czeskie Chopiniana*, in Ruch Muzyczny, no. 20, 1968.

KARASOWSKI, M.; *Fryderyk Chopin*, Warsaw 1882, 3 vols.

KARLOWICZ, MIECZYSLAW; *Niewydane Dotychczas Pamiatki po Chopinie*, Warsaw 1904.

KOBYLANSKA, KRYSTYNA; *Rekopisy Utworow Chopina—Katalog*, Cracow 1977, 2 vols. *Nieznane Utwory Chopina w Zapomnianym Albumie*, in Ruch Muzuczny, no. 20, 1972. *Chopin w Kraju*, Cracow 1955.

KOZMIAN, A. E.; *Listy*, Lwow, 1894. *Wspomnienia*, Poznan 1867, 3 vols.

KOZMIAN, JAN; *Przeglad Poznanski*, vol. IX, 1849.

KRASINSKI, ZYGMUNT; *Listy do Delfiny Potockiej*, ed., Z. Sudolski, Warsaw 1975–76 (3 vols.). *Listy do Jerzego Lubomirskiego*, ed. Z. Sudolski, Warsaw 1965.

KRZYWON, ERNST; *Heinrich Heine und Polen*, Vienna 1972.

LEGOUVÉ, E.; *Soixante ans de souvenirs*, vol. I, Paris 1886.

LETOWSKI, LUDWIK; *Wieczor u Pana Chopina w Paryzu*, in Miscellanea, vol. I, Cracow 1860.

LISSA, ZOFIA, ED.; *The Book of the First International Musicological Congress Devoted to the Works of F. Chopin*, Warsaw 1963. *Chopin w Swietle Korespondencji Wydawcow*, in Muzyka, 1960, no. 1.

LISZT, FRANZ; *Chopin*, Leipsig 1879. *Correspondance de Liszt avec la Comtesse d'Agoult*, vols. I and II, Paris 1933.

LONG, ESMOND R.; *A History of the Therapy of Tuberculosis and the Case of Frederic Chopin*, 1956.

LUBIN, GEORGES; *George Sand en Berry*, Hachette, Paris 1967.

LUPPÉ, MARQUIS DE; *Astolphe de Custine*, Monaco 1957.

MALVEZZI, A.; *La Principessa Christina di Belgiojoso*, Milan 1936, vol. II.

MARIX-SPIRE, THÉRÈSE; *Les Romantiques et la Musique. Le cas George Sand*, Paris 1954.

MARKIEWICZ, Z.; *Spotkania Polsko-Francuskie*, Cracow 1975.

MENDELSSOHN, FELIX; *Letters of Felix Mendelssohn to Ignaz and Charlotte Moscheles*, London 1888.

MICKIEWICZ, WLADYSLAW; *Zywot Adama Mickiewicza*, Poznan 1892, 3 vols.

MIRSKA, MARIA; *Szlakiem Chopina*, Warsaw 1949.

MIRSKA, MARIA, AND HORDYNSKI, WLADYSLAW; *Chopin na Obczyznie*, Cracow 1965.

MOSCHELES, CHARLOTTE; *The Life of Moscheles with Selections from His Diaries and Correspondence*, London 2873, 2 vols.

MUSIELAK, HENRI; *Dokumenty dotyczace Spadku po Chopinie*, in Ruch Muzyczny, nos. 14, 15, 16; 1978.

Sources

363

NIECKS, FREDERICK; *Frederick Chopin as Man and Musician*, London 1890, 2 vols.

NIEMCEWICZ, J. U.; *Nasze Przebiegi*, in *Przeglad Polski*, zeszyt 10, 1873.

NIESMIEYANOVA, T. AND SEMIENOVSKY, S.; *Dnievnik Uchenmitsy Shopena*, in *Muzikalnaya Zhizn*, Moscow 1960, no. 4.

NORWID, CYPRIAN KAMIL; *Pisma Wybrane*, ed. J. W. Gomulicki, Warsaw 1968, vol. V. *Listy*, Warsaw 1937.

ODYNIEC, A. E.; *Wspomnienia z Przeszlosci Opowiadane Deotymie*, Warsaw 1884.

OSBORNE, G. A.; *Reminiscences of Frederick Chopin*, in *Proceedings of the Musical Association*, Sixth Session, London, April 5, 1880.

PERENYI, E.; *Liszt*, London 1975.

PRZYBYLSKI, T.; *Fragmenty Dziennika Karola Kurpinskiego* in *Muzyka*, no. 4, 1975.

RADCLIFFE, PHILIP; *Mendelssohn*, London 1967.

RAJCHMAN, A.; *Kolebka Chopina*, in *Echo Muzyczne, Teatralne i Artystuczne*, no. 424, Warsaw, November 2, 1891.

REISS, JOZEF; *Slazak Jozef Elsner*, Katowice 1936.

RZEWUSKA, COUNTESS ROZALIA; *Mémoires*, Rome 1939.

SAINTE-BEUVE; *Mes Poisons*, Paris 1926. *Correspondance générale*, ed. Bonnerot, Paris 1958.

SAND, GEORGE; *Lettres Inédités de George Sand et de Pauline Viardot*, ed. Thérèse Marix-Spire, Paris 1959. *Correspondence*, ed. Georges Lubin, Paris 1967–72, vols. 3–9. *Histoire de ma vie*, Paris 1854–56, vols. 1–20. *Lucrezia Floriani*, Paris 1853. *Un Hiver à Majorque*, Paris 1869. *Journal intime*, Paris 1926.

SCHUMANN, ROBERT; *O Fryderyku Chopinie*, Karowice 1963.

SIKORSKI, JOZEF; *Wspomnienia Szopena, Bibliotaka Warszawska*, December 1849.

SKARBEK, FRYDERYK COUNT; *Pamietniki*, Poznan 1878.

SLOWACKI, JULIUSZ; *Dziela*, Wroclaw 1949, vol. II.

SMOTER, J. M.; *Spor v Listy Chopina do Delfing Potockiej*, Cracow 1976.

STARZYNSKI, J.; *Delacroix et Chopin*, Paris 1962.

SZENIC, S.; *Maria Kalergis*, Warsaw 1963.

TARCZEWSKA, ALEKSANDRA Z TANSKICH; *Historia Mego Zycia*, Warsaw 1967.

THACKERAY, WILLIAM MAKEPEACE; *Letters and Private Papers*, ed. G. N. Ray, Cambridge 1945, vol. II.

TOMASZEWSKA, WANDA; *Chopin w Dusznikach*, in *Muzyka*, 1961, no. 4, p. 88.

TURGENEV, I. S.; *Lettres à Mme. Viardot*, Paris 1907.

WITWICKI, STEFAN; *Listy do Jozefa Bohdana Zaleskiego*, Lwow 1901.

WODZINSKI, A.; *Les Trois romans de Frédéric Chopin*, 1886.

WOJCICKI, K. W.; *Cmentarz Powazkowski*, Warsaw 1855–58, 3 vols. *Pamietniki Dziecka Warszawy*, Warsaw 1974, 2 vols.

ZALESKI, JOZEF BOHDAN; *Korespondencja, Jozefa Bogdana Zaleskiego*, Lwow 1901, 2 vols.

C: CONTEMPORARY NEWSPAPERS AND PERIODICALS

Gazeta Korespondents Warszawskiego i Zagranicznego, Warsaw 1818.
Pamietnik Warszawski, Warsaw 1818.

Kurier dla Plci Pieknej, Warsaw 1823.
Kurier Warszawski, Warsaw, 1820–30.
Gazeta Polska, Warsaw 1829.
Dziennik Powszechny Krajowy, Warsaw, 1829–30.
Kurier Polski, Warsaw, 1829–30.
Gazeta Warszawska, Warsaw, 1818, 1849.
Dziennik Polski, Poznan, 1849.
Tygodnik Literacki, Poznan 1840.
Tygodnik Emigracji Polskiej, Paris 1835.
Kronika Emigracji Polskiej, Paris 1836.
Trzeci Maj, Paris 1842.
Dziennik Narodowy, Paris 1841–42.
La France Musicale, Paris 1841.
Revue Musicale, Paris 1832, 1833.
Gazette Musicale de Paris, Paris 1834, 1835, 1839, 1841.
Journal des Débats, Paris 1835, 1849.
Revue et Gazette Musicale de Paris, 1838, 1848, 1849.
La Presse, 1849.
Le Ménestrel, Paris 1841.
Daily News, London 1848.
The Musical World, London 1849.
Manchester Guardian, 1848.
Allgemeine Musikalische Zeitung, Leipzig 1831.
Neue Zeitschrift für Musik, Leipzig 1834–41.

Index

Ivry, Baroness d', 329

Jan, Chopin's Polish servant, 233, 236, 252
Janin, Jules (1804–74), journalist, 128, 166, 318
Jarocki, Feliks Pawel (1790–1865), zoologist, 36–7
Jedrzejewicz, Jozef Kalasanty (1803–53), university professor, husband of Ludwika Chopin, 244, 249, 315
Jelowicki, Aleksander (1804–78), writer and publisher, later priest, 148, 317
Johns, Paul Emile, American musician, 328

Kalergis, Countess Maria, née Nesselrode (1822–74), pupil of Chopin, 281, 284, 310, 334
Kalkbrenner, Friedrich Wilhelm (1785–1849), pianist and composer, 27, 82, 93, 94, 99, 103, 107, 108, 233, 290, 291, 312, 328
Kastner, J. G., 224
Keats, John (1795–1821), poet, 306
Kessler, Jozef (1800–72), pianist, 49
Kicka, Teresa (d. 1865), literary hostess, 14, 28
Kissielev, Countess, née Zofia Potocka (1800–75), 91–2
Klengel, August (1783–1852), organist, 254
Kolberg, Wilhelm (1807–91), school friend of Chopin, 88n, 326, 327
Komar family, 91, 96, 102, 114, 336, *see also* Potocka, Delfina
Könnerlitz, R. de, pupil of Chopin, 332
Kozmian, Stanislaw Egbert (1811–85), Polish patriot, 158, 288
Krasinski, Count Zygmunt (1812–59), poet, 318, 332, 335, 337
Krasinski family, 11
Kreutzer, Konradin (1780–1849), musician, 44
Kumelski, Norbert Alfons (1801–53), naturalist, 84, 86, 87, 90–2
Kurpinski, Karol (1785–1857), Polish composer, 23, 52–3, 56, 65
Kwiatkowski, Teofil (1809–91), painter, 321

Lablache, Louis (1794–1858), singer, 234, 292, 322
Lachner, Franz (1803–90), composer, 45

Laczynska, Maria, later Walewska (1786–1817), 3
Laczynski family, 3
Lamartine, Alphonse de (1790–1869), poet and statesman, 106, 136, 144, 166, 242
Lamennais, Félicité, Abbé de (1782–1854), philosopher, 144, 201
Lanner, Joseph (1801–43), composer, 77
Lannes, Jean, Duke de Montebello (1769–1809), Marshal of France, 101
La Touche, Henri de (1785–1851), poet and friend of George Sand, 110
Legouvé, Ernest (1807–1903), playwright, 111, 128, 161, 163, 266, 310
Leiser, General, 47
Leo, Auguste, banker, close friend of Chopin and Moscheles, 102, 161, 185, 186, 205, 242, 268, 272, 283, 299, 332
Leo, Hermann, brother of Auguste, Manchester industrialist, 299
Leroux, Pierre (1797–1871), Socialist philosopher, 143, 227
Lesueur, Jean François (1760–1839), composer, 92–3
Lichnowsky, Prince Moritz, patron and friend of Beethoven, 44, 73
Lind, Jenny (1820–87), singer, 290, 297, 313
Linde, Mrs., née Nusbaum, 326
Linde, Samuel Bogumil (1771–1847), Rector of the Warsaw Lyceum, 5
Lipinski, Karol (1790–1861), violinist, 40, 134
Liszt, Franz (1811–86), composer, 19, 39, 44, 51, 78, 82, 92, 93, 97–100, 103–7, 110, 111, 115, 117–20, 124, 125, 126, 127, 129, 134, 135, 138, 141–52, 159, 161, 163–6, 193, 201–8, 211, 212, 216, 217, 220–2, 228, 233, 238, 242, 250, 254, 264, 280, 282, 296, 302, 328, 329, 335, 337
Lobau, Caroline de, pupil of Chopin, 330
Louis XVIII (1755–1824), King of France, 101
Louis Philippe (1773–1850), King of the French, 90, 163, 285
Lyszczynski, Dr., 300, 304–5

Maberly, Catherine, pupil of Chopin, 332